D1599141

Investigated Reporting

THE HISTORY OF COMMUNICATION

Robert W. McChesney and John C. Nerone, editors

A list of books in the series appears at the end of this book.

Investigated Reporting

Muckrakers, Regulators, and the Struggle over Television Documentary

CHAD RAPHAEL

University of Illinois Press
Urbana and Chicago

Library of Congress Cataloging-in-Publication Data

Raphael, Chad, 1966–
Investigated reporting : muckrakers, regulators, and the struggle
over television documentary / Chad Raphael.
p.   cm. — (The history of communication)
Includes bibliographical references and index.
ISBN 0-252-03010-9 (cloth : alk. paper)
1. Documentary television programs—United States—History and criticism.
2. Television broadcasting of news—United States.
3. Television broadcasting policy—United States—History.
I. Title.
II. Series.
PN1992.8.D6R36   2005
070.4'3'0973—dc22   2005002625

CONTENTS

ACKNOWLEDGMENTS

I am beholden to Chuck Kleinhans, Manjunath Pendakur, Robert Entman, Michael Curtin, and especially Rick Maxwell, for their comments on drafts of this work and encouragement of my research. I am also indebted for their valuable advice to Nick Lawrence, Benjamin I. Page, and David Hesmondhalgh. I am grateful as well to those who offered research assistance and advice, including Charles Puckette and Emilio Castilla.

Many librarians and archivists helped me to navigate their troves, including the staffs at the State Historical Society of Wisconsin (Madison, Wisconsin); the Special Collections Division of the University of Maryland (College Park, Maryland) and Washington University in St. Louis (St. Louis, Missouri); the Broadcast Pioneers Library (College Park, Maryland); the Montgomery County Community College Library (Rockville, Maryland); the National Archives and Records Administration (Washington, D.C., and College Park, Maryland); the Library of Congress (Washington, D.C.); the Billy Rose Theater Collection at Lincoln Center Archives (New York, New York); the Museum of Television and Radio (New York, New York); the Columbia University Oral History Collection (New York, New York); the Special Collections Division of the Rutgers University Libraries (New Brunswick, New Jersey); the California State University–Sacramento Archives (Sacramento, California); the UCLA Film and Television Study Center (Los Angeles, California); and the Stanford University Libraries (Palo Alto, California.)

Grants from Northwestern University and Santa Clara University helped to support my work. I am grateful to Stanford University, where an enlightened policy offering domestic partner benefits allowed me to use the library. I would not have been able to write this work otherwise. My colleagues in the Department of Communication at Santa Clara University encouraged my work and offered a congenial professional home. Students in my 2001 senior thesis class on investigative reporting helped advance my thinking about media response to muckraking on television.

Friends and family hosted me on research trips and sustained me when I lagged. My thanks to Ann Wiener, Gregg Houston, Monique Houston, Jenifer Getz, Tim Raphael, Erin and Heather Findlay, Alice Hill, Sharon Achinstein, Merle Ann Siegelman, Ellen Noonan, Sam Sifton, Linda Singer and Joe Stern-lieb, and the staff and board of the Jessie Smith Noyes Foundation. Others enriched my intellectual and social life in Menlo Park, California, where I wrote this work, including Amy Gerstein and Richard Heintze, Richard Leider and Katherine Murphy, Laura Stokes and Ciara Cox, Kelly and Gideon Clark, Bill Rowe, Ben Trautman and Sarah Kuehl, Brad Stam and Jack Millam.

I thank Kerry Callahan at the University of Illinois Press for shepherding this project, John Nerone and Robert McChesney for including it in this book series, and the anonymous reviewers of the manuscript for their insights into how it could be improved. Thanks also to Ann Youmans for copyediting the book and to Katherine Jensen for indexing it.

I am most grateful to my wife, Betty Achinstein, for supporting me through the writing process, and to my son Adin for diverting me from it. This book is for them.

ABBREVIATIONS

CD Contested documents
CSUS California State University–Sacramento Archives, Sacramento, Calif.
LOC Library of Congress, Washington, D.C.
NARA National Archives and Records Administration, Washington, D.C., and College Park, Md.
NPM Nixon presidential materials housed at the NARA
POF President's office files
RG Record Group
ROSA Records of the office of the secretary of agriculture, Record Group 16, NARA
SF Subject files
SHSW State Historical Society of Wisconsin, Madison, Wis.
SMOF Staff member office files
UMCP University of Maryland at College Park Libraries, College Park, Md.
WHCF White House central files
WHSF White House special files

Investigated Reporting

INTRODUCTION

Classical liberal theorists of the media's role in democracy, from John Locke to Thomas Paine, saw journalism's primary mission as serving as a watchdog on government, by checking abuses of power, exposing corruption, and giving citizens the information they need to manage public affairs. The inheritors of this vision often hold up investigative reporting as the best example of the media's ability to maintain government's accountability to the public. In this view, investigative journalism is also the main reason to free the media from regulation, which inevitably threatens to mute journalistic criticism of government.[1] This book examines the spread of investigative reporting on American television in the 1960s and early 1970s and the government backlash it attracted. At this time, officials turned the tables on journalists by investigating the fairness and accuracy of muckraking reports more often and more extensively than at any time in television's history. I find that the roles of journalists and officials were more complicated, and interesting, than liberal theory leads us to expect. Investigative reports were largely shaped by official forces rather than simply acting as a check on government, and regulation in many ways served the cause of investigative journalism rather than hampering it.

The very existence of investigative reporting on television from 1960 onward owed a debt to government regulators. Television muckraking appeared stillborn at the end of the 1950s when CBS canceled Edward R. Murrow and Fred Friendly's *See It Now*. The program's extensively researched and critical coverage of contemporary issues, especially its trenchant reports on Senator Joseph McCarthy, offered the first experiments in investigative journalism on the small screen.[2] They were the only such efforts in the 1950s, when fifteen-minute network evening news programs offered little time for more than "hopscotching the world for headlines," as NBC news anchor John Cameron Swayze promised viewers each night. As for documentaries, they were dominated by historical retrospectives on the victories of World War II—CBS's *Air Power* and NBC's *Victory at Sea*. Both series featured uncritical compilations of archival film, much of it shot by the American military. However, muckraking reemerged in the new, prime-time documentary series each network developed in the early 1960s, largely in response to regulatory pressure.

Many observers attributed the growth of documentaries to the industry's need to appease regulators in the wake of the quiz-show scandals, when producers were found to be rigging the outcomes of popular game shows.[3] Some have argued that pressure from Federal Communications Commission (FCC) chairman Newton Minow was the driving force behind the rise of documentary at the time.[4] Others claim that the networks also hoped to stave off antitrust investigations by pleasing congressional overseers.[5] Michael Curtin, who has treated the question most comprehensively, shows how the documentary's rise also expressed a broad elite consensus over revitalizing television, democracy, and America's role in the world.[6] Network executives and Kennedy administration figures hoped that documentaries would teach isolationist Americans about the dangers of communism, the virtues of America's leadership in the world, and the need for an activist New Frontier foreign policy. Looking abroad, the networks and the United States Information Agency aimed to use documentary to extend American economic and cultural influence, winning the hearts, minds, and eyeballs of the world's citizens. Thus network executives also saw the format as having economic potential, both for stifling government investigations of television's commercialism and for putting the networks' best face forward at a time when they began to expand into international video markets. The FCC and television's liberal critics liked the public-service connotations of documentary, hoping that the genre would lift the medium's cultural standards and offer a fair payback for its financial success. For them, the documentary would help provide for more enlightened public participation in politics, giving citizens greater analysis of the pressing social issues of the day. Television journalists, for their part, were attracted to the longer format because it offered a chance to raise their prestige to the level of print journalists, conferring upon them the status of expert mediators between the political realm and citizens.

By the late 1960s, this "documentary coalition" had shattered, and the genre became the most troubled of television news offerings. As documentarians began to engage in investigative reporting, they sparked widespread private objections, government probes, and media criticism. Muckraking's opponents raised numerous complaints about the fairness and accuracy of programs before the FCC. House committees held four lengthy inquiries into documentaries in the years 1968 to 1971 alone, and Kennedy, Johnson, and Nixon administration officials conducted their own probes into several programs. Documentaries sparked repeated threats to regulate news more stringently and a close call for one network president, who narrowly escaped being cited for contempt of Congress and potentially jailed. Ironically, an initiative created in part to dispel charges of commercialism and staging game shows became the object of similar accusations. In 1970, the same House subcommittee that had helped to expose the quiz-show scandals prefaced one of its many probes into documentaries by arguing, "Fraud and deception in the presentation of purportedly bona fide news events is no more protected by the First Amendment than is the presentation of fraud and deception in the context of commercial advertising or quiz programs."[7]

This book examines network investigative reports that were most extensively investigated by government between 1960, when muckraking began to be institutionalized in the prime-time documentary, and 1975, when regulators began to pull back from scrutinizing television news content. The reports discussed here were chosen not because they were representative of all documentaries but because they provoked the lengthiest probes by government forces in the White House, FCC, or Congress.[8] Because these investigations were widely reported in the print media, they were public controversies that likely helped to influence politicians' and the public's views of exposé reporting. By examining these controversial reports and the government scrutiny they provoked, this book not only illuminates a formative period for television news and regulation. It also contributes to our larger understanding of media-state relations, including the persistent and vexing question of whether the media have become more adversarial to government since the 1960s. And the book informs current debates about the influences that shape investigative reporting and this journalism's impact on political reform.

Television Muckraking and Regulation

Histories of investigative reporting have not accounted sufficiently for why muckraking gained a lasting foothold in television at this time. Accounts of the resurgence of investigative reporting in the 1960s, many by print journalists, pay little or no attention to television.[9] One recent casebook of investigative reports in American history draws just two of its 122 examples from television, while another ignores television entirely.[10] Yet, at the high point of the documentary boom in 1962, ABC, NBC, and CBS produced 447 reports, over twice as many as they had aired four years earlier.[11] Not all were investigative in nature, but television's contribution to the mainstream media's first sustained period of muckraking since the Progressive era compares more favorably to print than is usually thought. The expansion of network documentary units in the early 1960s predated the first permanent investigative teams at metropolitan newspapers by several years.[12] If investigative documentaries were a rarity, they were probably no fewer per network than the handful of exposés published annually in each paper. Despite documentaries' low ratings relative to other prime-time programming, they reached far more American homes than any newspaper's investigative series. In the early 1960s, about 90 percent of American households saw at least one documentary per month.[13] In the early 1970s, when even the largest city papers reached under a million readers, the average prime-time CBS documentary drew 7 to 12 million viewers.[14]

Nor have histories of television or documentary fully accounted for the growth of muckraking and the controversies it engendered in this period.[15] Greater attention has been paid to Murrow and Friendly's isolated efforts in the 1950s and to how television newsmagazines, especially *60 Minutes,* replaced the longer documentary format from the 1970s onward with a collection of briefer stories.[16] Some scholars of television documentary have focused on its formal development, tracing its emergence from radio, newsreel, and film traditions and identifying television's innovative reporting techniques.[17] Others have attempted to explain why the format arose and declined, mentioning political controversy generated by the documentary only briefly as one factor in the genre's demise.[18] A handful of sources examine controversies created by individual reports, but do not locate them within any larger historical explanation or theory of how investigative reporters framed stories or why they were attacked.[19] These studies generally lack the perspective provided by archival materials and political histories written since the 1970s. Much of this work cited above is media centered, failing to examine how investigative reporting is shaped by political and regulatory forces. As a result, this work too often presents reporters as developing stories in a historical vacuum and misses regulators' multiple motives for scrutinizing controversial reporting.

Histories of television regulation also have not dealt well with the state's relationship to muckraking. Almost all the major works that treat in any depth the subject of regulation's impact on the media's role as watchdog portray television journalism as struggling to throw off the heavy yoke of government oversight.[20] This work, which draws its sharpest examples of government abuses of power from the Nixon administration's campaign against the media, presents regulation as exclusively coercive and restrictive of journalism. There is little understanding here of the ways in which government has enabled television journalism to speak powerfully by licensing the spectrum and restricting competition (thereby making each speaker more powerful). Nor does this work appreciate the role of government in strengthening professional standards by setting expectations for public-service programming that foster substantive journalism and protect it from being choked out by more lucrative entertainment and infotainment.

Media-State Relations

The controversial reports discussed in this book were produced in a period often characterized as one of great conflict between the American media and state.[21] Reporters and officials clashed over coverage of the Vietnam War and of protests against it, over news of the civil rights movement and urban uprisings in black neighborhoods, over the release of the Pentagon Papers, over the Nixon administration's attempts to manage the media, and over coverage of the Watergate scandals. Combined, these incidents brought forth a remarkable rise of criticism and scrutiny of the media by state forces. Executive branch officials, the Pentagon, presidential commissions, congressional committees, and the FCC investigated television news programming more regularly and more closely than government had before and has since. Private groups increasingly petitioned government to regulate television news. Liberal forces, including churches, civil rights groups, and public-interest law centers, organized on behalf of greater citizen access to the airwaves and a broader diversity of views expressed in the news. Conservatives founded watchdog groups such as Accuracy in Media (AIM) to demand fairer treatment of their views. All appealed to the FCC, Congress, and the courts to accomplish their ends. In short, television news became an object of public struggle with a greater frequency and intensity than at any other time in the medium's history.

Political conservatives offer one explanation for the heightened controversy that swirled around the media in these years. Public figures such as Vice President Spiro Agnew and Senator Daniel Patrick Moynihan argued that an adversarial culture permeated newsrooms in the 1960s, turning reporters against traditional voices of authority and fostering a "culture of disparagement" towards American government and ideals.[22] Moynihan blamed the rising power and incomes of television journalists, which he claimed emboldened them to criticize mainstream American institutions. Agnew took a more partisan tone, attacking the denizens of the eastern establishment media, and television journalists in particular, for being more liberal and critical than the rest of America and for forcing their views on the public. This "closed fraternity," in Agnew's words, was unelected and unaccountable to the public and therefore properly subject to government regulation.[23] The conservative complaint found support from a number of political scientists, who blamed a newly oppositional media for the decline of public confidence in political institutions and plunging respect for American leaders, as expressed in polling data.[24] In addition, theorists of postindustrial society identified journalists, along with academics, professionals, and philanthropists, with a "new class" of knowledge workers who purportedly staked a claim to political and economic leadership.[25] The growing status of the new class made them a potent and dangerous force in the eyes of some who subscribed to postindustrial theory. In this view, journalists and their ilk were lukewarm capitalists at best, self-serving advocates of government regulation of the economy, and jealous and skeptical of uncredentialed power holders.[26]

Corporate critics also alleged media liberalism and adversarialism. Facing a precipitous decline in public trust in industry, business attributed its poor image in part to a newly aggressive journalism.[27] W. Lee Burge, chairman and president of Equifax, spoke for many executives when he protested that "it often seems that the media purposefully set out to undermine the economic system of which they are a part and on which they prosper."[28] The corporate critique of the media focused not only on the perceived leftward thrust of reporters but also on their alleged economic illiteracy and irresponsibility. "Reporters plunge into issues that mean life or death for management, employees, customers—even a community—without the slightest sense of business perspective," complained Louis Banks, a magazine editor turned Harvard Business School professor. "Some of them are like kids with loaded pistols, prowling through the forests of corporate complexity to play games of cowboys and indians, or good guys and bad guys. Their only interest in business is to find a negative story that will get them promoted out of business into Woodward and Bernstein."[29]

Although most journalists did not see themselves as part of a liberal elite or new class, many embraced an image of themselves as nonpartisan yet inherently adversarial to government and corporate abuses of power.[30] Journalists such as Tom Wicker of the *New York Times* encouraged "the developing tendency of the press to take on an adversary position toward the most powerful institutions of American life."[31] Daniel Schorr, a CBS reporter at the time, said, "My keenest enjoyments, I must confess, came from finding out something that people in power didn't want known and telling people not in power something they should know."[32] This self-image became widely held by investigative reporters, who, in a 1991 survey, identified the primary motive for their work as satisfying the reformer in them.[33]

The conservative critique of the news that sprang up in the 1960s is still very much with us. Cries of media leftism can be heard regularly from talk radio programs and think tanks that have helped rationalize cuts to public broadcasting budgets and fueled best-selling books on the news.[34] Allegations of adversarialism echo in the seemingly endless debate over whether the media "lost" Vietnam by turning Americans against the war and whether reporters should have been granted wider access to cover subsequent wars. These charges also influence current disputes over the media's treatment of political candidates and coverage of the private lives of public figures.[35] Even President Clinton attacked the "knee-jerk liberal press," demonstrating the enduring nature of the epithet (and revealing as much about the uncertain state of contemporary liberalism).[36]

However, an impressive body of scholarship casts doubt on claims of mainstream media liberalism. The strongest empirical support for these claims are surveys purporting to reveal that journalists' views fall to the left of most Americans. But the most sophisticated of these studies found that only a small majority of journalists described themselves as "liberal," and the survey focused entirely on elite, Washington reporters.[37] These journalists expressed more liberal views than other Americans on social issues but not on economic issues.[38] More important, surveys of journalists' beliefs fail to show how their views shape news content. Sociological studies of news work suggest that reporters' allegiance to the professional ideal of objectivity and the organizational dictates they work within militate against their injecting personal beliefs in the news; that journalists' political opinions change often and are not deeply held; that news organizations screen reporters to weed out "activists"; and that journalists depend mainly on official sources to shape the tenor of routine reporting.[39]

As for antipathy to business, many commentators have pointed to powerful structural constraints against news criticism of corporations. Broadcasters depend on advertising for almost all of their revenues. If news organizations sometimes undermine the interests of specific advertisers, they are less likely to challenge the prerogatives of their patrons as a whole. Broadcasting companies are also constrained by their ties to the larger corporate community through interlocking boards of directors, financing arrangements, and increased diversification by the networks into other businesses. Purported media hostility to business, some have noted, does not translate into sympathetic coverage of labor.[40] Others argue that when broadcast journalists criticize business they attack instances of corruption rather than the free market system itself, and that this criticism often reflects government censure of business.[41]

The strongest case against claims of an adversarial media emphasizes journalism's tendency to restrict the field of criticism to the kinds of opposition expressed in official circles. Along these lines, Daniel Hallin offers a useful model for thinking about critical reporting during times of elite dissensus, one that is employed throughout this book.[42] Media coverage, he argues, generally falls within one of three concentric spheres. The sphere of consensus forms the core of this model, encompassing "noncontroversial" values such as anti-communism or patriotism in wartime. In this sphere, reporters advocate or celebrate what they take to be widely supported beliefs, actors, or institutions, validating them to the larger public. Beyond this sphere lies the sphere of legitimate controversy, the region of electoral contests and legislative debates between the two major parties. In covering legitimate controversy, journalists generally attempt to observe the dictates of objectivity and balance. Beyond this sphere lies the sphere of deviance, where actors, views, and institutions deemed outside mainstream politics are exposed, condemned, or excluded from the public agenda. Hallin notes that political actors and viewpoints may shift from one circle to another over time. He also sees internal gradations in each sphere, particularly between the kind of objectivity practiced within the sphere of legitimate controversy. When issues in this realm are closer to the sphere of consensus, journalists are more likely to offer a stenographic record of official statements, whereas issues closer to the sphere of deviance may inspire more critical commentary from opposing sources and independent investigations of the kind associated with muckraking. This model is supported by a growing body of work, initiated by Lance Bennett, that demonstrates how the range of views and sources in the news is calibrated, or indexed, to the scope of mainstream government debate.[43]

The controversial reports examined in this book offer especially appropriate tests of the claims of increased media adversarialism. For several reasons, these disputed reports are limit cases where we would most expect to see evidence of an oppositional media. First, the controversies emerged in an era generally considered as one of increasing conflict between the media, on the one hand, and government and business, on the other. Second, most of these reports involved overt criticism of economic practices or government programs and policies. Third, all of the reports were attacked intensely by government and business forces and came to serve as examples in larger indictments of the news media as hostile. Fourth, investigative reporting offered greater license for journalists to express dissent than other forms of news less concerned with taking strong moral-political stances on public issues.[44] Documentary units enjoyed some organizational insulation from the routines and constraints of daily news production. Unlike their colleagues at the nightly news programs, documentarians were not saddled with restrictive beats, enjoyed more resources, were given longer airtime to tell their stories, and worked on lengthier deadlines. Documentarians valued filming what they took to be the direct experiences of their subjects. For example, Reuven Frank, an NBC producer who later ran the network's news division, favored documentaries because they sent him and his reporters "out of the building to where real people dealt with real problems, giving the world in which news occurs a tangibility it does not have in dispatches or film."[45] Each of these factors allowed muckrakers to seek out nonofficial views. In short, if the adversarialism theory cannot explain how these reports covered politics and sparked controversy, it has a lot of explaining to do.

These cases also offer important tests for the nascent research suggesting that the news media index debate to official voices. The indexing rule is still unsettled law in the literature. Some of these studies have found that journalists turn to other sources as well to help shape coverage, such as interest groups and leaders of other governments whose interests are implicated in foreign policy crises.[46] Thus the news may also be tailored by, and amplify, the views of those who journalists perceive as having some power to affect policy outcomes—what John Zaller and Dennis Chiu call "power indexing."[47] The reports studied here can shed light on how and when interest groups can help influence muckraking news because many of these reports covered issues of concern to some of the major social movements of the time—including the civil rights, antipoverty, labor, and consumer movements. Another limit to indexing studies is that they have focused entirely on coverage of foreign policy, where journalists and the public may be most dependent on government sources to frame policy choices because of a lack of direct experience or knowledge of international affairs. This book not only extends the theory to the genre of investigative reporting, but tests it on coverage of domestic policy as well. In doing so, this analysis offers perhaps the toughest test for the indexing approach, because muckraking appears to be the kind of news least dependent on government sources. If indexing theory can explain how these reports framed policy disputes, it can explain a lot.

This book also helps to overcome a methodological and conceptual difficulty of prior indexing work. Typically, these studies show correlations between the sources and level of policy support in news and in independent measures of elite opinion, such as congressional votes or debate (as captured in the *Congressional Record*). Government opinion is assumed, but not demonstrated, to be the independent variable. Although less likely, it may be that the range of views expressed by political leaders is in fact influenced by the range of views they see in the media. Or it may be that policy elites' opinions are shaped by powerful interest groups associated with business or social movements. By using a historical case-study approach, this book can offer more fine-grained analyses of the play of influence between interest groups, government, and the media than prior work in this vein. This allows for greater confidence in conclusions about the factors that shaped the reports' framing of policy debates and officials' reactions to them. I compare each report's sources and framing of issues to the sources and frames in concurrent congressional hearings and the *Congressional Record,* executive branch policy reports, and archival materials. Because these cases are thirty to forty years old, there is a substantial secondary literature about them that also helps to explain the range of views on these issues at the time of the reports and journalists' and politicians' choices.

Investigative Reporting: Influences and Impacts

Investigative reporting is often conceived of by its practitioners through what has been called the "mobilization model" of muckraking.[48] Independent media exposés of wrongdoing and injustice are said to activate the public to defend their rights and interests.[49] Outraged citizens demand corrective action and politicians enact reforms. However, this book, like the most thoroughgoing studies of investigative reporting, suggests otherwise. Prior work has shown that the public is not always mobilized to take action. When reports do spur reforms, interest groups and political leaders are often the main sources of pressure on the policy community. The importance of investigative reporting, then, may lie in its ability to influence the thinking of elites more than the public. Watergate reporting, for example, seems to have stirred only faint public cries for the resignation of Richard Nixon, and the public played little role in generating political support for his impeachment.[50]

In addition, muckraking often has less independent impact on policy changes than the traditional model assumes. The authors of *The Journalism of Outrage* have offered the strongest evidence of this. They conducted a number of case studies of investigative reports based on participant observation of journalists and officials during each stage of the news-making process. The authors also surveyed public opinion before and after the stories were released. They found that some investigative stories had no effect on public opinion, and that others changed attitudes toward the topic without moving the public to action. Some policy changes occurred *regardless* of public reaction, often because of negotiations between journalists and political actors before the reports were released, or because policy makers seized on the reports to promote changes they already supported. I find similarly close alliances between reporters and officials in producing disputed investigative reports, confirming that these reports are often the product of enterprising politicians and bureaucrats advancing their agendas through the media. The image of independent muckrakers is undermined by this "coalitional journalism," which requires government partnership in revealing wrongdoing.[51] Examples of this kind of journalism are better thought of as intragovernmental jousting within the sphere of legitimate controversy. As opposed to the journalism of outrage, this is the journalism of *in*rage among political elites themselves.

This book shows that investigative reporting's impact can also be checked by political backlashes, which are not anticipated by the mobilization model. The dynamics of these hostile responses have not been studied systematically in the past. Since the 1960s, muckraking has increasingly drawn return fire, including attacks on specific reports or on the muckraking genre as a whole through regulatory complaints and threats, public relations campaigns, lawsuits, and the activities of media watchdog groups. In the 1960s, network critics developed many of these techniques for countering investigative reports. I show how critics' attempts to discredit stories often blocked political allies from using these reports to support their policy positions by rallying public and elite opinion. I also offer the first systematic study of media response to controversial investigative reports, finding substantial disagreement with their findings and methods in the media, and showing the power of critics to distract subsequent coverage from muckrakers' charges and focus it on media ethics issues.

The Dimensions of Conflict

Why, then, did investigative reporting on television spark so many controversies between 1960 and 1975, and how did the reactions to these disputes shape subsequent muckraking and regulation? To answer these questions requires considering the political, representational, and regulatory dimensions of these controversies. We need to pay attention to these three aspects of the conflicts not only to explain the full range of reasons for them but also to appreciate the scope of conflicts *within* government and media over investigative reporting.

Part one of the book examines the controversies as political disputes arising from elite struggles to frame the issues presented in the reports. Not surprisingly, most contentious documentaries focused on issues that increasingly split political elites at the time of their airing. Chapter 1 examines reports on poverty and welfare against the background of a changing rural economy, the Johnson administration's War on Poverty, and the civil rights movement. Chapter 2 discusses reports on America's Cold War foreign policy in Berlin, the Caribbean, and Vietnam. Chapter 3 delves into documentaries on the rising consumer politics of the time, focusing on exposés about banking and pensions. Each chapter excavates the origins and historical context of the reports, showing their debts to government and interest group sources and their framing of controversial issues. Each chapter also recounts the complaints and investigations into the reports. History is always messier than our accounts of it, and a handful of highly investigated reports were about subjects other than these three. Their significance for regulation is discussed in subsequent chapters.

In this first part of the book, I discuss both the reports' policy frames and broader ideological frames. Both notions of framing have been used to account for how journalists perceive and select what constitutes news and what sense they make of it for audiences. Robert Entman offers the clearest application of the concept: "To frame is to select some aspects of a perceived reality and make them more salient in a communicating text, in such a way as to promote a particular problem definition, causal interpretation, moral evaluation, and/or treatment recommendation for the item described."[52] Entman's definition can be used to identify how a report frames policy issues such as welfare by diagnosing its problems, defining their causes, and posing remedies. It can also be used to locate how a report partakes of a wider ideological frame through its moral-political treatment of key actors and institutions, such as presenting public-aid recipients as victims of a market economy or as the eternally lazy and undeserving poor.

Part 2 assesses these conflicts over investigative reporting as struggles over the particular means of representing reality on television news. Chapter 4 examines response to the controversies in the print media and by network affiliate stations. It shows that there was no uniformly liberal or adversarial reaction among the media, and that even journalistic commentators who expressed support for these investigative reports tended to defend them on First Amendment or ethical grounds, deflecting attention from the reports' specific charges. Chapter 5 looks more deeply at how politicians and journalists reacted, revealing their growing concerns over television's representational techniques, which created fault lines within both the media and government. These cracks in both institutions opened largely because of stresses between national and local interests, between the culture of print and of television, and between the ideals of journalistic objectivity and the allure of muckraking. Readers looking for a definition of investigative reporting, which has been a matter of much dispute in itself, will find a somewhat different one here. Drawing on film and literary theory, I suggest that this kind of reporting is best defined not by the methods used to produce it or by its effects on the public, but as a *genre* that creates particular expectations in its producers and audiences.

Part 3 evaluates the regulatory dimension of these controversies, which were also clashes over the proper role of government oversight and media accountability. Chapter 6 demonstrates that just as television muckrakers were not monolithically opposed to government, regulators were not all hostile to the media. As the investigative documentary became a significant battleground over regulating television news content, the FCC repeatedly shielded muckrakers by refusing to enforce its fairness and distortion rules against reports. Elements within Congress and the judiciary also helped the media stave off stricter regulation. The fearsome threats to journalistic independence described by many critics of FCC and congressional scrutiny were in fact a brand of symbolic politics that exerted less oversight of television news than advertised. However, the Nixon administration began to dilute the power of network news by reining in adventurous reporting on public television while offering commercial broadcasters a Faustian bargain: greater license security in exchange for increased competition from cable and satellite television. The administration also solved the contradictions of conservatives' approach to the media, which demanded less government regulation of business but greater oversight of the commercial news media to manage the news.

Chapter 7 traces the legacy of these clashes for news regulation, concluding that the mission of investigative reporting and its ability to serve the public interest were better served under the regime of the 1960s than they are today. Deregulation has not set muckrakers free, but it has increased the role of the judiciary in overseeing news and lashed investigative reporting more tightly to the wheel of market pressures, which are themselves a form of regulation. Indeed, the new, "deregulatory" regime is better understood as one of privatized regulation, in which news disputes are fought out between private plaintiffs in tort suits, and between muckrakers fending off the demands of advertisers and conglomerate media owners to shape coverage to their interests rather than the public's.

The final chapter steps back from these cases to draw several conclusions for theories of news. It summarizes the evidence against claims of media adversarialism toward government. It offers a model for understanding how muckraking is assembled and how its critics attempt to subvert its legitimacy. And it locates these struggles over investigative reporting within a larger account of the media's role in democracy. This role has more to do with muckraking and its discontents' ironic ability to foster public consent to government than dissent from it.

PART I

POLITICS

Investigating Poverty and Welfare

Some of the most controversial documentaries of the 1960s peered behind the image of America's postwar affluence to gaze at the lives of the poor. Three reports on poverty were most extensively investigated by government forces: *Harvest of Shame* (CBS, 1960), *The Battle of Newburgh* (NBC, 1962), and *Hunger in America* (CBS, 1968). Journalists and television critics often cite these documentaries as milestones of network muckraking.[1] Yet all three documentaries, and the conflicts they engendered, emerged primarily from intragovernmental struggles over antipoverty policy. To be sure, citizen groups, particularly those associated with the labor and civil rights movements, influenced public discussion on the subject matter of these reports. But the documentaries themselves drew heavily on government sources and their framings of the plight of migrant laborers and public-aid recipients. As such, these reports were as much collaborations between government sources and journalists as they were muckraking investigations of government failures.

The discussion of each documentary sets it within the evolving historical and political context of poverty in the 1960s. Each report can be shown to have grown out of prior action by officials and movements, and these actors shaped the stories' origins and the major sources relied on by journalists. After this analysis, we turn to political critics' attacks on the documentaries and the networks' response, considering the impact on poverty policy of each report and the controversy it generated. All three reports shared common features in the ways in which they framed poverty and welfare, frames located within the range of official policy debate and ideologies about poverty at the time.

Migrant Farm Workers and the *Harvest of Shame*

After World War II, the corporatization of farm ownership and increased crop specialization drove small farmers off their land at an alarming rate.[2]

Many displaced tenant farmers and sharecroppers became migrant laborers, as federal policy makers urged them to travel from farm to farm during wartime labor shortages. During the war and afterwards, corporate and other farmers accelerated the mechanization of American agriculture, further reducing the need for full-time, year-round farm labor. On many large farms, technologies such as mechanical planting and spraying limited demand for workers to the harvest season. The number of hired farm workers fell from 3.89 million to 1.89 million in the decade before 1960. Planters and their political allies kept farm workers' wages low through racial oppression and the neo-feudal sharecropping system in the South, through the importation of Mexican and Caribbean labor, and by lobbying against federal regulation of working conditions and a minimum wage for agricultural workers. Eventually, some displaced farmers and migrant workers settled in the cities of the North, Midwest, and California. There they became a constituency of the urban liberal politicians who would support the Johnson administration's War on Poverty.

Itinerant farm labor was the subject of CBS's *Harvest of Shame,* the documentary often cited as the first great example of television muckraking in the 1960s.[3] Produced by David Lowe, narrated by Edward R. Murrow, and reported by both men, the documentary condemned the poor living and working conditions endured by migrants on the eastern seaboard and in California.[4] It aired as part of the network's flagship documentary series, *CBS Reports,* on November 25, 1960, the day after Thanksgiving. Although *Harvest of Shame* criticized growers' exploitation of farm labor, it did so primarily by emphasizing the migrants' impoverished living conditions, setting it squarely within antipoverty debates of the era. Therefore, it is discussed here rather than in the chapter on business, labor, and consumers.

The documentary's introductory sequence began with a montage of hawkers calling out wages to recruit African American laborers for day work at a morning "shape up." In a voice-over, Murrow told viewers that what they were seeing did not occur in Africa but in Florida, and that "these are citizens of the United States, 1960." "This is the way the humans who harvest the food for the best-fed people in the world get hired," he continued over shots of migrants cramming into the backs of open trucks to be hauled to the fields. "One farmer looked at this and said, 'We used to own our slaves, now we just rent them.'" Murrow then introduced the major opposing points of view on the issue. Secretary of Labor James Mitchell deplored the migrants' plight as "the shame of America." Charles Schuman, president of the American Farm Bureau Federation, the largest organization representing farmers' interests, maintained that growers provided work to people who were "practically unemployable." Over images of African American and Mexican laborers, Murrow declared, "This is an American story that begins in Florida and ends in New Jersey and New York state with the harvest. It is a 1960s *Grapes of Wrath* that begins at the Mexican border in California and ends in Oregon and Washington." The documentary then mainly followed farm workers from Florida up the East Coast in their annual migration to harvest crops while Murrow introduced the afflictions of migrant life along the way.

Harvest of Shame detailed the miseries of farm laborers' working conditions largely by focusing on the poverty that resulted. Murrow and the workers interviewed spoke of the small pay and job insecurity that were their reward, concluding with a long sequence of shots from a Florida bread line that fed migrants thrown out of work after a freeze killed crops. The report especially documented farm workers' poor housing conditions. The Farm Bureau president maintained that farming was the only industry that furnished housing to its workers and that "we do not condone substandard housing." But Lowe repeatedly interviewed migrants in dilapidated labor camps that farmers provided for their workers, noting the inadequate water supplies and outhouses. Murrow contrasted the images of crowded, tumbledown shacks at a New Jersey camp with a $500,000 horse stable just a few miles away. He showed rural slums in Long Island, aptly named "The Bottoms," where migrants had settled. A Florida police chief told of workers sleeping in parks and packing houses as they waited for crew leaders to arrive with jobs. Harrison Williams Jr. (D-N.J.), chairman of the Senate Subcommittee on Migratory Labor, demanded federal legislation to set minimum wages and to fund housing for migrants.

Harvest of Shame also focused on the hazards of migrants' travel. Accompanied by images of exhausted and grim-looking workers and their children packed in crew leaders' buses and trucks for the long trip north, farm laborers spoke of how they wished they could settle in one place but were forced to range thousands of miles for work. Murrow described the migrants' long, cramped bus rides with few rest stops. By contrast, he noted, "the vegetables the migrants picked yesterday move north swiftly on rails" or in refrigerated trucks "carefully packed to prevent bruising." Federal law, he added, required that cattle must be fed and rested frequently in transport while the migrants "often ride ten hours without stop for food or facilities." A farmer interviewed in his fields claimed that his black workers "got a little gypsy in their blood" and were in fact "the happiest race of people on earth." Murrow countered with footage of a highway accident that had killed twenty-one migrants a few years prior. Secretary of Labor Mitchell decried the lack of national safety standards for transporting the laborers.

The report paid much attention to migrancy's toll on children, including

the use of child labor and the children's lack of day care and educational opportunity. Murrow maintained, "Everyone who knows anything about this
situation agrees that the best hope for the future of the migrants lies in the
education of their children." But in interviews, families discussed how their
children were forced to accompany them to the fields, either because parents
could not afford to pay for child care or needed the extra money children
could earn by picking. Other children were shown left to care for each other
as their parents worked in the fields. In a migrant classroom in New Jersey,
one of the few states to fund schools for farm workers' children, youngsters
spoke of their hopes of becoming teachers and doctors. Their teacher said she
doubted they would be able to finish high school given their parents' poverty
and need to move for work. Murrow noted that state laws restricting the use
of child labor exempted agriculture. He pointed out that although the federal
government spent $6.5 million per year to protect migratory wildlife, it failed
to approve a proposed $3.5 million to educate migrant children.

   Harvest of Shame suggested two solutions to the problems of the migrants:
unionization and federal legislation. Murrow explained the lack of unions
for farm workers by telling viewers that agriculture was excluded from laws
protecting workers' right to organize. Secretary Mitchell observed that the
AFL-CIO was now attempting to unionize farm labor in earnest for the first
time. A farmer maintained that industrial unions had no place in his sector,
and Farm Bureau president Schuman said that "the right to strike at the time
of the harvest ought to be regulated in some manner." But the documentary
then showed a long sequence of an organizing meeting in California, in which
an AFL-CIO organizer reported on negotiations with cherry pickers, and
several workers stood and spoke passionately about their low pay, job insecurity, and need to unionize, receiving enthusiastic applause. In his conclusion,
Murrow addressed viewers from the studio, endorsing recommendations for
federal action made by the Presidential Committee on Migratory Labor that
addressed the issues discussed in the broadcast. "The migrants have no lobby,"
Murrow said. "Only an enlightened and perhaps angered public opinion can
do anything about the migrants. The people you have seen have the strength
to harvest your fruits and vegetables. They do not have the strength to influence legislation. Maybe we do."

Context and Sources: Efforts to Assist Migrants

Harvest of Shame emerged from major efforts to address the issue of itinerant farm labor by federal policy makers and a coalition of labor and other
organizations. The documentary's appearance and the political conflict that

ensued stemmed from a national struggle over farm policy at the time, one that divided the Eisenhower administration and Congress. The treatment of farm workers had become a legitimate controversy among political leaders well before CBS arrived on the scene. It was also a public struggle before the documentary aired. All the major California papers had covered the onset of the AFL-CIO organizing drive there.[5] National print media coverage of the migrants' problems was also widespread in the years before *Harvest of Shame*. Howard Van Smith, a *Miami News* reporter, touched off the media attention with his Pulitzer Prize–winning 1958 series on Florida farm workers.[6] He appeared at the end of *Harvest of Shame*, vowing to continue his efforts on behalf of migrants.

The Eisenhower administration's policy reflected a larger split in the Republican Party over farm labor.[7] Secretary of Labor Mitchell, identified with the moderate wing of the party led by New York's governor Nelson Rockefeller and Senator Jacob Javits, championed migrant reform as cochair of the administration's Committee on Migratory Labor. Before *Harvest of Shame* aired, Mitchell's labor department took several steps to push for reform. The department held public hearings on migrant issues, conditioned farmers' ability to advertise for labor through the U.S. Employment Service on their providing sanitary facilities for workers and not using immigrant labor, and closed some of worst labor camps for failing to meet housing standards. However, agriculture secretary Ezra Taft Benson, who also cochaired the presidential Committee on Migratory Labor, represented farmers' interests in staving off efforts that would increase the cost of labor. Similarly, the Department of Health, Education, and Welfare opposed legislation in 1960 that would have extended federal funding to migrant education.

In the Senate, the Subcommittee on Migratory Labor, chaired by Harrison Williams Jr. and stocked with liberal northern senators, led efforts to enact reform. After holding hearings in several states, Williams proposed seven migrant-related bills in the summer of 1960. This package of legislation was more specific and far-reaching than the presidential committee's recommendations for state and federal action, which were diluted by the dissensus within the cabinet. The presidential committee's report, released shortly before *Harvest of Shame* aired, called for applying workers' compensation, transportation safety, and child labor laws to farm laborers; requiring crew leaders to register with the government and follow minimum labor standards; nationwide extension of the housing programs for migrants then offered by only a few states; and increased education, health, and job training programs for agricultural workers' families.[8] Williams' proposed legislation addressed each of these issues in more specific and stringent terms, and went further in setting a minimum wage for agricultural work and curbing the importation of Mexican labor through the bracero program.[9]

Harvest of Shame relied heavily on these official sources. Senator Williams appeared in the report to argue that federal action was needed to raise wages because states were unlikely to act if it meant making their farmers less competitive. Secretary Mitchell was given the longest airtime of any speaker in the documentary besides Murrow. Mitchell legitimated the report's claims both as a source of official expertise and as a moral voice. As an official source, Mitchell testified to the dangers of migrants' transportation and frequency of highway deaths they suffered. He was called on to refute at length a farmer's claim that chain supermarkets set the prices of agricultural goods, limiting growers' abilities to raise wages. Murrow built on Mitchell's characterization of the farm workers as having "no voice" in Congress and his statement that there were "no greater pressure lobbies" in Washington than the farmers' to support the documentary's famous conclusion that the migrants had no strength to push legislation, but "maybe we do." Mitchell's participation allowed Murrow to present official demands for reform as bipartisan—no mention of the fierce congressional and administration resistance to them was made. At the end of the broadcast, Murrow read from and endorsed the milder reforms proposed by the presidential committee rather than the more sweeping legislation offered by Senator Williams. As a moral voice, Mitchell called the migrant's situation "the shame of America," inspiring the report's title. He derided farmers' hypocrisy in resisting federal intervention on behalf of migrants while "participat[ing] in government largesse" by receiving federal price supports for their crops. Mitchell called it "morally wrong . . . for any man, for any employer, to exploit his workers," and vowed, "as a citizen, in or out of this office . . . to continue to raise my voice until the country recognizes that it has an obligation to do something for them." Murrow paired the secretary's pledge with Miami reporter Van Smith's to create a sense of official and journalistic consensus for reform.

A coalition of labor, religious, civil rights, civil liberties, and other organizations that comprised the National Advisory Committee on Farm Labor and the National Council on Agricultural Life and Labor had also raised their voices for reform.[10] After *Harvest of Shame* aired, several of these groups sponsored a showing of the documentary for Congress as part of their lobbying efforts. As Mitchell noted in the CBS report, the AFL-CIO was mounting its first serious project to organize in the fields. In 1959, it formed the Agricultural Workers Organizing Committee (AWOC), which garnered $1 million in labor support over the next six years, one of the largest investments in unionizing efforts at the time.[11] Secretary Mitchell introduced and offered crucial legitimation for the AFL-CIO's organizing drive in the documentary when he argued that farmers could emulate the garment industry's improvements in wages and working conditions, which he credited to the efforts of clothing workers' unions. The secretary's recognition that unions might be part of the answer opened the segment covering the AFL-CIO's organizing meeting in California. *Harvest of Shame* also reflected religious organizations' participation in the farm workers' movement by drawing on a minister's and a chaplain's moral denunciations of exploitation and poverty in the fields and citing a National Council of Churches survey of migrants that listed the hardships of labor camps.

Reaction and Impact: Farm Interests Counterattack

The American Farm Bureau Federation and congressional representatives from agricultural states quickly probed and attacked the report. First, the Farm Bureau enlisted the program's sponsor, Philip Morris, to renounce the program and apologize to farmers for portraying them unfavorably.[12] Critics of *Harvest of Shame* denounced it from the floor of the House and Senate and in the pages of the *Congressional Record.* Florida congressman Paul G. Rogers entered into the *Record* a sixteen-part *Palm Beach Post* series dedicated to showing, in the paper's words, "another side of the story, a side not presented in the *Harvest of Shame.*"[13] Senator Spessard Holland (D-Fla.) denounced CBS in the Senate for abandoning fairness and objectivity, implying the need for further regulation. Holland claimed that CBS had violated the dictates of fairness, "which the American public has a right to expect from those who hold and use a valuable franchise given by all the American people." Echoing almost identical language as the Farm Bureau's complaint against *Harvest of Shame,* Holland argued that "slanted documentary films are fully as unethical as rigged quiz shows. Perhaps they are more dangerous to a free society, since they present a false picture as a basis for shaping public opinion and the laws resulting therefrom."[14]

The Farm Bureau and sympathetic congressmen made several specific allegations against the documentary. They faulted CBS for overstating the number of migrants and exaggerating their poverty and lack of educational opportunities by focusing on worst-case examples. The opponents claimed that the report misrepresented the Florida bread line as having occurred in 1960, saying that it had happened several years earlier. The critics maintained that the report erred in claiming that imported labor drove down migrants' wages and ignored that federal law already provided safety mandates for migrant transportation. The report's foes said it unfairly blamed farmers for occasional abuses committed by work crew leaders with whom the farmers contracted

Farm state critics accused *Harvest of Shame* of inaccuracy, including its portrayal of a Florida bread line. CBS News.

for labor and that it failed to show improvements in migrants' working and living conditions.[15]

CBS's reply addressed most complaints by pointing to official sources of information their journalists had relied on to make the disputed claims. Many points of controversy, such as whether imported labor drove down wages for all workers or whether substantial progress had been made to better migrants' lives, were matters of dispute among policy makers at the time. Three claims of factual errors were not addressed or disproved by the network's response. Holland countered Murrow's claim that no migrant child had graduated from college with a handful of examples of graduates from his state. In one interview, the report left the impression that a migrant woman had fourteen children to support. Holland said that she had seven children (the others had died) and a husband who earned considerably higher wages at a sugar mill. And when Murrow said that housing in the migrants' winter home of Belle Glade, Florida, was beyond their means at fifteen dollars per room per week, he overstated local housing costs twofold according to Holland. CBS refused the Farm Bureau's request for equal time to respond on the air but said it would broadcast another program with a variety of views on migrant labor. When the FCC declined to rule on complaints of unfairness, the conflict appeared to be dead.[16]

However, when President Kennedy invited Murrow to run the United States Information Agency (USIA), the controversy took on a Cold War hue. Murrow faced angry questioning from farm state legislators again at his Senate confirmation hearings in March 1961. At the same time, the British Broadcasting Corporation (BBC) aired the documentary in the United Kingdom. The Farm Bureau, the Kennedy administration, and some members of Congress expressed fears that Murrow's role in the program would suggest to viewers abroad that the U.S. government endorsed the film's unflattering portrait of exploitation on the farm. Senator Holland was livid, telling the Senate that CBS, "for a few 'pieces of silver,' permit[ted] this malicious and false slander against our nation to be presented abroad."[17] In response, Murrow asked the BBC to cancel its plans to show the documentary on the day he would be sworn in as USIA director. Murrow appears to have been pushed by Senator Holland to stop the broadcast, perhaps in exchange for a unanimous confirmation vote.[18] The old broadcaster would later regret attempting to suppress his own work, especially because Holland promptly revealed this on the Senate floor, spurring anti-Murrow editorials and a protest by the American Civil Liberties Union.[19] After Holland convinced the State Department to intervene, CBS agreed to add a notice at the start and end of the film indicating that Murrow made it before joining the U.S. government and that the network would not actively promote it for sale in other countries.

Holland was unappeased, issuing a final barrage against CBS on the Senate floor that not only linked the defense of farming interests to America's Cold War struggle but also to the growing challenges of the civil rights movement, which would increasingly influence poverty discourse in the decade to come. He brandished British press clippings that he said confirmed his fears that *Harvest of Shame* would tarnish America's image abroad and warned that "Russia has seized upon this broadcast" to embarrass the United States further.[20] Attacking CBS's patriotism, he said, "[I]t seems incomprehensible to me that anyone claiming to be an American could have been a party to this monstrous outrage."[21] Holland expressed special concern about how sources in the documentary likened migrants to slaves "in conjunction with the showing of members of the Negro race who were among these migratory workers . . . I was sure that that factor would be among the troubles and misunderstandings which this film would create."[22]

Some have claimed that *Harvest of Shame* played a significant role in enacting corrective legislation on the migrant issue, but the measures passed in 1961 were neither dramatic nor easily traceable to the film's impact.[23] In August, the Senate passed three of Senator Williams's seven proposed bills, providing funding for educating migrant children, requiring farm crew chiefs to keep full financial records and meet some minimal labor standards, and providing modest funding for local governments to offer health services for migrants. That the presidential commission had already endorsed these reforms prior to *Harvest of Shame* suggests that they reflected a preexisting consensus. In the same year, Congress did not act on issues that still provoked disagreement, rejecting a minimum wage for farm workers and reauthorizing the importation of Mexican labor. This set the tone for the migrant legislation that followed in the 1960s as Congress opted to provide services to farm workers rather than significantly restructure the farm labor market by boosting wages or facilitating unionization.[24] Although legislators eventually repealed the bracero program in 1964, four years after *Harvest of Shame*, it is the AFL-CIO that is generally credited with removing this major obstacle to unionization, which helped Cesar Chavez's United Farm Workers to establish its footing in the fields.[25] In short, the social-service reforms passed after *Harvest of Shame* were already agreed upon by a Republican cabinet and Democrat Senate leader on the issue, and the labor reforms were minimal and probably more closely tied to a multiyear, million-dollar organizing effort than to the documentary.

Farm state conservatives' attacks against *Harvest of Shame* likely helped to diminish its use as political currency by reform-minded politicians. Senator William Proxmire, the first to mention the report in the Senate, hailed it for sparking "a sudden and overwhelming wave of compassion for migratory workers" in his home state of Wisconsin.[26] However, once Holland began to criticize the documentary in the Senate, no other senators defended it. In a long colloquy between Holland and Williams on the Senate floor, Holland repeatedly attempted to force Williams into renouncing the report as inaccurate and sensational. Williams tried again and again to return to the subject of his legislation but finally conceded that although he felt the film usefully publicized the issue, "I believe unfortunately it has gotten us into too much tension too, through its lack of objectivity, and has gotten us away from the substance of the problem of dealing with health, education and welfare."[27] Similarly, Holland succeeded in isolating Murrow from his supporters in the news media by pressuring him to block the BBC broadcast, further damaging the report's credibility and diverting attention from farmers' ethics to Murrow's.

The Battle of Newburgh and the Battle over Welfare

During the summer of 1961, the city manager of Newburgh, New York, Joseph M. Mitchell, led a racially charged campaign to clamp down on public aid in a city that had experienced significant black in-migration. Thanks in part to a burst of intense and often uncritical media coverage, Mitchell touched off what one poverty historian has called "postwar America's first national debate about welfare."[28] Mitchell's thirteen-point plan for reforming public assistance both crystallized and aimed to implement the stringent restrictions on aid advocated by the right wing of the Republican Party, sparking controversy even within his own party. NBC entered the fray with an hour documentary, *The Battle of Newburgh,* an edition of its *NBC White Paper* documentary series that aired January 28, 1962, raising the ire of congressional conservatives and leading to the decade's first FCC probe of a documentary.

The report began with shots of Newburgh's dilapidated downtown housing. A white resident, later revealed to be a welfare recipient, said in an interview that he had lived in the city all his life, that "it deteriorated over the years and nobody seemed to notice." "And then Mr. Mitchell came along," he added, "and Newburgh was just ripe for something like him." City Manager Joseph M. Mitchell then appeared, giving a public address in which he blamed public aid and the "moral chiselers and loafers" who received it for fostering slums, crime, and broken families and destroying the town's business and residential districts, "emptying the city of responsible taxpaying citizens." Several white men in business suits were shown in a bar debating whether undeserving people were taking advantage of welfare in Newburgh, a device that threaded throughout the program. They agreed that after hearing about Mitchell, people would "think twice before they come to Newburgh . . . and sign up for welfare." Narrator Chet Huntley introduced Mitchell as a "national figure carrying his war against welfare far beyond the tiny boundaries of his city" over footage of Mitchell walking through an airport and appearing on a television program. Huntley promised that the program would examine the city manager's portrayal of welfare and his efforts to curb it.

The next section of the report traced the history of the Hudson River city's decline, casting doubt on public-aid recipients' culpability for it. Accompanied by shots of Newburgh's run-down black neighborhoods, Mitchell maintained in voice-over that the promise of welfare checks had attracted the city's poor, who had created slums out of its downtown. Two white merchants gave a different view, blaming city government for allowing the downtown to decline and absentee landlords who overcrowded their apartments to make more money from renters. Huntley explained that city retailers were losing business to suburban shopping malls as viewers saw images of empty streets and boarded-up storefronts. He pointed to Newburgh's loss of industrial jobs, especially the low-skilled and semi-skilled positions that welfare recipients might have held in the past. After Mitchell was shown claiming that "anyone who really wants work can find it," Huntley countered that because of the city's high unemployment, the U.S. Department of Labor classified it as a surplus labor area.

Battle of Newburgh then countered Mitchell's image of public assistance as a magnet for migrants from the South. After the bar patrons debated who was moving to the city and why, Huntley explained that middle-class families had abandoned the city and that blacks had arrived in search of cheaper housing and low-skilled work in the 1950s, most of them coming from elsewhere in New York State rather than directly from the South. As viewers were shown images of black children playing and a mother rocking her baby, Huntley noted that 90 percent of the town's blacks were not on public aid and that blacks comprised less than half of the city's welfare caseload. At a press conference, a journalist challenged Mitchell's plan to require welfare recipients show evidence of having moved to the city with a job offer in hand rather than for relief, arguing that this would restrict American's freedom of movement and simply shift the problems of poverty and unemployment to another community.

The city's board of education provided an alternative approach to addressing the needs of the poor, Huntley noted. School district officials explained in. interviews that because low-income children needed to work or watch their siblings after school, they could not take part in sports programs and faced difficulties in studying in overcrowded and poorly lit homes. Given equal facilities and opportunities, the officials said, these children could succeed in school. Images of black youths delivering packages and working at a store gave way to extensive footage from a school Christmas pageant starring black and white children, enthusiastically applauded by a large crowd of parents and hugged by their white teacher. These images of racial cooperation and Christian observance clashed with Mitchell's characterization of public-aid recipients as "moral chiselers" and breeders of "social diseases" (a euphemism for venereal disease), reclaiming the moral high ground for the city's poor.

Next the report countered Mitchell's vision of widespread welfare cheats and his claim that public assistance was the cause of unemployment and social problems. Huntley conceded that the town had made "a modest start" in solving its social and economic problems but said that Mitchell still single-mindedly cited welfare as the city's scourge. Implying a parallel with Senator Joseph McCarthy's anticommunist hunts of the 1950s, Huntley found that "Mitchell seems to find welfare guilty by association." The newscaster read a long excerpt from a report by a state welfare official that concluded that social problems "are not caused by welfare, they are the reasons for welfare. The public welfare structure exists to provide the means in a free society to help the victims of these social forces." Mitchell appeared facing a hostile audience, decrying as failures Franklin D. Roosevelt's welfare programs as New York governor and president. He dismissed welfare bureaucrats as adhering to the "Freudian philosophy of the irresponsibility and godlessness of man" to jeers from the audience. A Newburgh minister stood and countered that Mitchell had not found any examples of welfare cheats. Mitchell maintained there were "technically qualified" recipients on the rolls who were not truly needy. Huntley introduced a series of interviews aimed at humanizing aid recipients by saying it was one thing to talk about them "in the abstract" but another to meet them. A white woman mourned the lack of compassion in the city, saying she did not mind being taxed to support welfare when she was working. She revealed her frustration at not being able to afford birthday presents and Boy Scouts for her children. An elderly white male spoke of losing his business after he became ill and his embarrassment at having to rely on public aid. A black mother told of budgeting her monthly check carefully to support her kids.

The report's longest segment examined where Newburgh spent its welfare money. Mitchell claimed the town spent almost $1 million a year on welfare. Huntley noted that over half of that was reimbursed by the state and federal governments, and that only 11 percent of Newburgh's share went to the kinds of support Mitchell campaigned against: general assistance for the able-bodied poor and Aid to Families with Dependent Children (then called ADC). The rest paid for the city's home for infirm elders, foster care for children, and the disabled. Representatives of each group were interviewed. The tavern debaters returned, one accusing welfare families of having illegitimate children and another (the bartender) saying that children should be removed from neglectful parents who were "drinking in the bars." A Newburgh family court judge rejected Mitchell's proposal to limit ADC to three months of support, deny assistance to women who bore a second child out of wedlock, and remove the children to a foster home. A minister dismissed the possibility of finding enough foster homes as impractical and expensive.

The documentary's final segment emphasized the harm to the city's poor caused by the welfare reform plan. Huntley said that the Kennedy administration advocated more job training and other programs aimed at helping recipients become self-sufficient, but Newburgh had no such programs. He reported that state courts had blocked implementation of Mitchell's thirteen-point plan for remaking public assistance but that the city manager declared victory anyway. Mitchell spoke at a press conference of screening welfare department employees "for those who would be loyal to our policy" and mounting a "propaganda or psychological warfare campaign" to reduce the rolls. A welfare caseworker interviewed said that her department had been "demoralized almost completely." The family court judge recounted seeing a long line of seniors forced to report to police headquarters to be interrogated before picking up their checks. "Most of them were white," he added, "and there was an atmosphere of fear." The minister returned to denounce the "un-American assumption" that the poor were "guilty until they prove themselves innocent," again recalling McCarthy's tactics. Elderly recipients spoke of feeling like criminals. In an extended, emotional interview, a tearful white couple with their children on their laps told of struggling to eat and pay rent after being unjustly denied public aid. The barroom debate concluded with one of the group's welfare critics conceding that he would not want to hurt children by cutting off aid. The family court judge, perched on a park bench, delivered a kind of moral to the story, saying that there were "no simple solutions to complicated problems." "But humanity and decency and morality are in the long run the only solutions to these problems or any other kind of problems," he said. "And if we have that, we can solve them." The children from the Christmas pageant could be heard singing "We Three Kings From Orient Are" as a lone black figure, his back to the camera, walked away down a wintry city street.

Context and Sources: Welfare Controversy

By the time NBC arrived on the scene, Mitchell's campaign had driven a wedge into the Republican Party and welfare politics. In New York, several counties and towns voted to adopt or support Mitchell's plan, but Republicans Governor Nelson Rockefeller and Senator Jacob Javits both rejected it, as did several local Democratic Party officials. William F. Buckley and others attempting to organize a Conservative Party in hopes of pushing the Republicans to the right were trying to draft Mitchell to run against Javits. The New York State Board of Welfare and the State Supreme Court had blocked Newburgh from implementing the plan, finding that it violated federal and state welfare laws. Nationally, Kennedy administration Secretary of Health, Education, and Welfare Abraham Ribicoff had attacked Newburgh's proposals as unsound, while Senator Barry Goldwater and other Republican conservatives lined up behind Mitchell's reforms and numerous state and local governments expressed interest in adopting them.[29]

Although *Battle of Newburgh* focused on the voices of the poor, it often drew on official opposition to discredit Mitchell's arguments. Huntley's evidence of high unemployment in the town, that most blacks had not migrated directly from the South, that blacks made up a small percentage of Newburgh's welfare rolls, and his breakdown of the city's welfare spending all came from statistics marshaled by the New York State Board of Welfare that were published in prior media reports.[30] So did the long passage from the report he read that rejected Mitchell's claim that welfare was the cause, rather than the solution, of social problems. Huntley offered Newburgh's board of education and the Kennedy administration's plans as more attractive models for reducing the welfare rolls. The family court judge who denounced Mitchell's treatment of poor elders and delivered the documentary's conclusion was not simply a wise observer of the brouhaha; he had provided legal representation to Mitchell's opponents before the state supreme court.[31]

Although social movement actors had intervened in the controversy, they were not directly represented in *Battle of Newburgh*. The conservative student group Young Americans for Freedom had marched in the city to show support for Mitchell, and the John Birch Society had organized a letter-writing campaign to him to boost his efforts, which may help explain why he was able to claim that 90 percent of the almost fifteen thousand letters he received were supportive.[32] The Urban League and National Association for the Advancement of Colored People (NAACP) petitioned the federal government to oppose Newburgh's plan, noting that the town's crackdown on welfare recipients followed closely on the heels of a successful black voter registration drive and black resistance to an urban renewal program that aimed to evict residents from downtown waterfront neighborhoods. Instead of turning to movement sources, the documentarians briefly featured opposition to Mitchell's policies from a white Protestant minister and a social worker. Indeed, almost all of the city's Catholic, Protestant, and Jewish leaders and charitable organizations spoke out against Mitchell, and Catholic Charities assisted NBC in identifying needy families interviewed in the film.[33] The National Association of Social Workers organized an informational campaign against Newburgh's welfare plan and a letter-writing campaign to NBC in support of *Battle of Newburgh*.[34]

Histories of poverty in the 1960s routinely cite the Newburgh debate as a major public policy controversy, one that was not discovered by any one reporter or news organization. Prior media coverage had been intense before NBC's report aired. National media greeted the announcement of Newburgh's plan in late May 1961 with an initial round of widespread and uncritical publicity. Out-of-town reporters did not investigate Mitchell's claims about welfare recipients until the New York welfare board debunked them several months later. Mitchell's policies garnered editorial support from five of the seven New York City daily papers, with only the *New York Times* and *New York Post* in opposition. "For a time in the early sixties," wrote one local reporter, "it appeared as though the newsmen in Newburgh outnumbered the welfare recipients."[35]

Reaction and Impact: Finessing Welfare Reform

In response to *Battle of Newburgh,* Mitchell demanded an FCC probe into
whether the documentary violated the fairness doctrine. Of the eighteen objections Mitchell raised to the report, most had to do with matters of balance.[36]
He accused NBC of having "rigged" the documentary by choosing unrepre-
sentative examples of welfare recipients, by portraying all of Newburgh as
a slum, by omitting evidence of his reforms' success and public support for
them, and by permitting Huntley to editorialize against Mitchell while feign-
ing objectivity.

Mitchell also charged NBC with staging scenes by urging interviewees on
public aid to dress in their shabbiest clothes, by rehearsing scenes to increase
their pathos, and by paying a public-aid recipient to lie about why he had
been denied welfare. Finally, Mitchell alleged inaccuracy, claiming that NBC
overstated the portion of Newburgh's welfare budget spent on the aged and
understated southern migration to the city. Congressman Thomas B. Curtis

City manager Joseph Mitchell attacked *Battle of Newburgh,* alleging that reporters
coached public-aid recipients to lie about their plight. Reprinted with permission
from A. William Bluem, *Documentary in American Television* (New York: Hastings
House Publishers, 1965), 116.

(R-Mo.), a welfare critic, championed Mitchell's cause, writing numerous letters of complaint about the program to NBC and the FCC.[37] The FCC eventually dismissed the complaint, agreeing with NBC that the documentary offered a reasonable opportunity for Mitchell to air his views and relied on credible (and mainly official) sources of information to critique those views.[38] An unsatisfied Curtis maintained that the FCC needed to clarify its fairness standards and promised to introduce legislation that would do so.[39]

Although *Battle of Newburgh* struck a blow against conservative welfare reform by helping to expose Mitchell's mendacity in the national media, it cannot be credited with stopping Newburgh's punitive welfare plan. The New York welfare board and supreme court had already done that. The documentary may have strengthened public opinion against Mitchell in Newburgh. The city's mayor, who opposed Mitchell, suggested that the NBC report may have given Mitchell's supporters a darker view of his policies than the local newspaper offered or at least the unsettling thought that 15 million Americans now thought Newburgh was economically blighted and politically backward. But Mitchell's lack of success at stopping business flight and reducing welfare caseloads, not to mention the city's weariness at the rancor and division over the issue, also diminished his popularity. Nonetheless, Mitchell survived in his post until city leaders forced him to resign eighteen months after the documentary aired, when he fell from grace after being tried on bribery charges unrelated to his welfare struggles. At the national level, the Kennedy administration was already moving in the summer of 1961 to forge a legislative truce between conservative critics and liberal defenders of public aid by advancing the "rehabilitation" model of welfare mentioned by NBC. Whereas public assistance since the 1930s had focused on supporting the incomes of the poor and creating public-sector work during lean times, the new model emphasized job training and social services as means of helping the poor get themselves off the rolls. The administration acknowledged conservative critics not only by selling its program as a way to reduce caseloads but also by requesting states pass tougher safeguards against welfare fraud and requiring states to track down parents who had deserted their children. This national policy stratagem, along with New York State authorities, held off right-wing reform efforts in the early 1960s.[40]

The War on Poverty and the Clash over *Hunger in America*

In 1964, with liberalism ascendant, the Johnson administration boldly declared its "War on Poverty," embarking on a massive expansion of federal antipoverty programs. But the War on Poverty soon opened cracks in the Democrats'

New Deal coalition of liberals, organized labor, working-class whites, and racial minorities. In addition, northern and southern Democrats divided over whether to respond to the civil rights movement's growing demands that federal antipoverty programs do more to bring economic and political equality to the South. Perhaps the most divisive aspect of the War on Poverty for all these New Deal constituencies was the administration's ambiguous promise that the poor themselves would have "maximum feasible participation" in the conception and administration of antipoverty programs.[41] This much-disputed promise reflected recognition of how local welfare bureaucracies had often abused their power over the poor by linking eligibility for aid to political and labor quiescence. However, as black civil rights organizations in particular absorbed some of the responsibility for these programs, they siphoned money and power away from the white Democrat patronage networks in the cities. In the South, segregationist local governments raised even more bitter cries against redistribution of federal funds and power from racially discriminatory welfare agencies to the black poor and their advocates.[42]

In 1967, antipoverty advocates focused on hunger as a single, pressing need that might revive broad political support for the War on Poverty. Liberal northern senators and a coalition of foundations, civil rights, church, labor, and women's groups began to investigate malnutrition, particularly in the deep South. The antihunger campaign challenged a long-standing compromise over agricultural policy and food programs. Since the New Deal, the U.S. Department of Agriculture (USDA) had administered major federal food aid efforts, but the agency's primary constituency was not the poor. Rather, its first mission was to support farmers' incomes by buying surplus crops for distribution through aid programs in the United States and abroad.[43] CBS stepped into this clash between farm and antipoverty interests with its investigative documentary, *Hunger in America,* broadcast as part of the *CBS Reports* series on May 21, 1968. Because of the complexity of the political context in which the report appeared, and because it became the most closely investigated of these documentaries on poverty, I treat it at greater length here.

Hunger in America opened with close-up portraits of children familiar from charitable appeals to feed third-world children, as narrator Charles Kuralt intoned: "Hunger is hard to recognize in America. We know it in other places, like Asia and Africa. But these children, all of them, are Americans. And all of them are hungry." In what would become one of the most disputed sequences of the film, a doctor attempted to resuscitate a newborn baby in a hospital isolette, squeezing the child's chest with his thumb in an attempt to pump air into its lungs. "Hunger is easy to recognize when it looks like this," said Kuralt. "This baby is dying of starvation. He was an American. Now he is dead. . . . Food is the most basic of all human needs," Kuralt continued. "America is the richest country in the world, in fact the richest country in history." Yet "ten million Americans, whether or not they are reached by federal aid, are hungry."

The first sequence brought viewers to San Antonio, Texas, where the city was celebrating its 250th birthday with an international exposition. The city was portrayed as "congratulat[ing] itself on its growth and progress," accompanied by footage of roller coaster rides and a tower with a revolving restaurant on top. Meanwhile, in the city's barrios, "A quarter of San Antonio's Mexican-Americans, 100,000 people, are hungry all the time." Father Ralph Ruiz, a local priest, took over the narration, telling how poor children's diets were too often limited to beans and tortillas, as he was shown walking the streets and talking with youngsters. Ruiz entered a home where he interviewed a teenager named Jerry about how hunger made it hard for him to concentrate in school. Kuralt's voice returned over images of an office dispensing surplus commodities, explaining how the USDA program served farmers' needs to dispose of excess crops, yet how the foods given to the poor were limited in nutritional value, offering an "inadequate dole." Correspondent David Culhane interviewed a Mexican American woman, emphasizing that the starchy diets of the poor meant they could be obese yet still malnourished. A social worker told Culhane that an eleven-year-old girl had been arrested for prostituting herself for food money. San Antonio county commissioner A. J. Ploch said that children went hungry because their parents refused to work, and that the situation was incurable "because if you don't have that condition, then you'll never have Indians and Chiefs, and you've got to have Indians and Chiefs." The San Antonio sequence concluded with a visit to a city hospital, where the director of social services walked Culhane through the waiting room, explaining the health effects of hunger on the city's poor. As she spoke at length about how maternal malnutrition increased the likelihood of premature births, frail infants in incubators were shown in close-ups, and the sound of crying babies could be heard. The sequence ended by returning to the image of the dying child.

In the second sequence, the scene shifted to Loudon County, Virginia, introduced with images of champagne drinkers watching a steeplechase in this "headquarters for the horsey set." Yet, Kuralt noted, "hidden away . . . are thousands of shacks where tenant farmers lead a marginal existence," and there were no federal food programs in the county to help them. Here, the impoverished were white. The county medical officer, Dr. Stephen Granger, was shown conducting a check-up of children in a poor family's home. Granger assumed the narration, explaining the irreversible brain damage malnutrition could cause in infants, and the physical effects of poor diets: "stringy hair, a pasty complexion, a dead look about their eyes." A nurse on Dr. Granger's staff interviewed another mother in her home, whose child had had nothing to eat for breakfast but gravy. Kuralt noted that "the pride of the people" posed "an additional problem" because some would probably be unwilling to accept aid even if it existed. A farmer interviewed in his home distinguished himself from "leechers" and "bums" who wanted public aid, saying, "God only helps those who help themselves." Granger explained in voice-over how farm families' diets caused premature aging, accompanied by images of a gray-haired thirty-nine-year-old woman whose child was being attended to by Granger in his office. "These people," Granger said, "with no past to be proud of and no hope for the future, seek immediate forms of enjoyment" as evidenced by "a late model television set in the living room . . . a late model baby in the crib . . . (and) empty pint bottles in the yard."

The third sequence focused on hunger in the Navajo reservation in New Mexico and Arizona, described as "nice places to visit, but the Navajo Indians have to live there." Dr. Jean Van Duzen, a white doctor who practiced on the reservation, narrated as she was shown paying a house call in a Navajo village. Accompanied by footage of a truck bearing surplus commodities and women cooking in their hogans, Van Duzen explained how the commodities program offered an unhealthy starch-heavy diet. Kuralt noted that some recipients had to walk miles to pick up their food. Van Duzen took Culhane on a tour through a hospital infant ward where Navajo babies had been diagnosed with severe nutritional diseases such as scurvy, marasmus, and kwashiorkor. She held up a number of infants, describing their symptoms as they were scrutinized in close-ups. After Van Duzen told of a girl who had died of marasmus the week before, the scene shifted to the burial mounds at the local Navajo cemetery. "I don't go there anymore," Van Duzen concluded. "There are too many people there that I know."

The final sequence was set in Hale County, Alabama, introduced by Kuralt as a place where "it has never been easy to be a Negro," and where the mechanization of cotton farming was making it even harder by reducing the need for farm labor. Dr. Raymond Wheeler was the guest narrator and interviewer here, telling of how "slow starvation has become part of the Southern way of life." He interviewed a pregnant black mother with ten children whose husband had difficulty finding work and who said she could not afford to buy food stamps. Her baby, Kuralt said, was later born malnourished and died. As footage showed blacks buying food stamps from white clerks in a welfare office, Kuralt explained that the program was unaffordable for some qualified recipients because it required them to scrape together relatively large sums of money to buy a month's or half-month's supply of stamps at once. A fourteen-year-old boy told Dr. Wheeler that he felt ashamed at school because he could not buy a twenty-five-cent lunch. The grandmother of a large sharecropping family told Wheeler that they could no longer grow corn for themselves and their livestock because their landlord had sold the land they used for corn to the government to get a farm subsidy. "White people—they don't care how you live," she concluded. "They used to treat us a lot better than they do now . . . I feel like it's because the children go to school together and do a little voting, something we never have did."

Kuralt's wrap-up from the studio emphasized that more than a thousand counties that needed food programs didn't have them. He said that the USDA had the power to increase the programs to meet emergency needs, but the agency had been so reluctant to use this power that it planned to turn back to the U.S. Treasury $227 million that could be used to feed the hungry, and that in the meantime American farmers had slaughtered and buried 14,000 hogs because there was no market for them. He argued, "The Department of Agriculture protects farmers, not consumers," and "federal food programs might be better administered by the Department of Health, Education and Welfare" or by a special commission. "In this country," he concluded, "the most basic human need must become a human right."

Context and Sources: Questioning Agricultural and Food Policy

Hunger in America emerged from a whirlwind of federal attention to hunger. By the mid-1960s, the New Deal compromise between farm and welfare interests was unraveling. Congressional redistricting since the Depression reflected the growing exodus of agricultural workers to cities, including the huge out-migration of blacks from the South. Power shifted within the Congress from rural defenders of farm subsidies to urban legislators with significant poor constituencies.[44] Massive subsidies became less politically defensible as high-profit corporate farms drove family farmers off the land and gobbled up the bulk of USDA money (by 1967, the wealthiest 25 percent of farmers got 75 percent of farm subsidies).[45] The congressional authorization and expansion of the food stamp program in 1964 represented the first time that rural conservatives failed to justify farm subsidies as proper in their own right but had to link them with promises of increased food assistance to the poor sought by urban liberals. As one historian of the food programs has written, "During the 1960s . . . the consensus over program objectives weakened." By the end of the decade, "concern about hunger and how to improve the diet of low-income consumers gained equal status in law with the earlier objective of helping the farm economy."[46]

The antihunger campaign of 1967 and 1968 was led by the Senate Poverty Subcommittee, which was dominated by liberal, urban, and northern Democrats such as Pennsylvania's Joseph S. Clark, New York's Robert F. Kennedy, and Massachusetts' Edward M. Kennedy.[47] Subcommittee hearings and field investigations drew many of their witnesses from, and helped to coalesce, social movement supporters of the War on Poverty. Foremost among them was the Citizens' Crusade against Poverty (CCAP), composed of some 125 church, labor, and civil rights organizations, which had formed in 1964 to offer political support to the administration's antipoverty efforts. The CCAP's main financial backers were the United Auto Workers (UAW president Walter Reuther chaired the group), the National Council of Churches, the United Presbyterian Church, and the Ford Foundation. The group had close ties to the Johnson administration's Office of Economic Opportunity (OEO), where CCAP executive director Richard Boone had been one of the architects of the War on Poverty, and with the staff of the Senate Poverty Subcommittee. The Ford Foundation's directors, several of whom had served in the Kennedy administration, provided additional links between the CCAP and the Kennedys on the Poverty Subcommittee.

The combined efforts of a growing number of antihunger advocates quickly made malnutrition and food programs a major congressional issue and media story in 1967. In April, the Poverty Subcommittee hearings in Mississippi concluded with television coverage of CCAP member Marian Wright leading Senators Clark and Robert Kennedy on a tour of sharecroppers' shacks. In May, the Field Foundation sponsored a trip by several physicians, led by the Harvard School of Public Health's Robert Coles, to investigate the impact of hunger on Mississippi's children. Their report was featured at another round of subcommittee hearings in July that received extensive evening network news coverage. Further studies of hunger, entailing more hearings, were begun by an offshoot organization of the CCAP, the Citizens Board of Inquiry into Hunger and Malnutrition (Citizens Board), and by the Committee on School Lunch Participation, a coalition of women's, business, civic, and church groups.[48] These hearings and reports generated many articles in the national and local print media on hunger conditions in the year before *Hunger in America* aired, as well as a Public Broadcasting Laboratory documentary.[49]

The antihunger groups met with steadfast resistance. Southern Democrats and midwestern Republicans controlled the congressional agriculture appropriations committees, where they blocked increases in USDA food aid programs by holding up funding and staved off demands by welfare advocates to participate in administering the programs. Opponents were led by House Appropriations Subcommittee on Agriculture chairman Jamie Whitten (D-Miss.), who had held the chairmanship since the early 1950s, earning the nickname "the permanent Secretary of Agriculture." The congressional conservatives were joined by state and local government officials who wanted to retain the power to regulate the poor that came with administering food aid and by the USDA bureaucrats who worked with local governments every day. The food industry repeatedly asserted its interests in protecting agribusiness and grocery store profits at the expense of the poor, refusing to develop low-cost nutrients that might compete with more expensive commodities, lobbying against government requirements to fortify basic staples with extra vitamins, and fighting congressional attempts to provide emergency food aid that might have substituted for store-bought items.[50]

In 1967, the USDA became the focus for these contending forces as Secretary of Agriculture Orville Freeman simultaneously defended the department's farm subsidies and food programs.[51] Although Freeman played an important role in winning conservative support for food stamps, he had never tried to dislodge agribusiness interests as the main clients of the department since taking the reins in 1961. He accepted the primary role of food programs as outlets for agricultural surplus and assured his overseers on the congressional agricultural committees that he would continue to protect farmers first. Despite his awareness of racial discrimination on the part of local food administrators in the South and repeated demands to address the problem, he was slow to wrest control of USDA programs from local officials. When, after its 1967 hearings, the Senate Poverty Subcommittee asked Freeman to address the food crisis in Mississippi by offering free or reduced price food stamps and stepping up distribution of free commodities, Freeman demurred. His reluctance to act came in part from the Johnson administration's indifference to the issue. For the White House, acknowledging a hunger emergency in the South would have reflected poorly on officials responsible for the War on Poverty. More importantly, dramatic expansion of food aid would have cost money at a time when the administration needed to make budget cuts to finance the Vietnam War and stave off wartime inflation.

The last element in the rise of hunger as a public issue was the Poor People's Campaign, led by the Southern Christian Leadership Conference (SCLC), which adopted many of the recommendations of the food aid reformers and presented them as demands to the USDA in May 1968, just as *Hunger* aired. The Poor People's March on Washington, which began just a month after the assassination of the SCLC's Martin Luther King Jr. sparked black uprisings in many cities (including the nation's capital), focused much of its energy on negotiating with the USDA to improve food programs. The campaign shared leadership with the civil rights groups involved with the CCAP.[52]

Hunger in America represented a close collaboration between CBS and the antipoverty officials and movement groups attempting to influence the USDA. The documentary relied heavily for its inspiration, sources, locations, and estimates of the severity of hunger on hearings conducted in Congress and in the field by antihunger advocates with ties to the Senate Poverty Subcommittee. It was important that the hunger groups were legitimated by their cooperation with the Senate Subcommittee. Previous protests by forces without congressional backing were not covered as extensively by the national media and had little effect.[53] The CCAP and other advocates came to national attention largely through their appearances at Senate hearings. In short, congressional sanction was needed before the media took note of the hunger issue. The CBS report was inspired not by the movement groups but by a suggestion from Senator Robert F. Kennedy to the documentary's executive producer, Don Hewitt, at a cocktail party in 1967.[54] By this time Kennedy was already helping to lead Senate efforts to increase food aid. His staff's close relationship to the CCAP reformers gave the activists a congressional imprimatur they would not have enjoyed otherwise.

The CCAP and its spin-off group, the Citizens Board, provided many of the sources and locations for CBS. According to one historian, by June 1967 the CCAP offices were "a mandatory stopping off point for journalists who wanted to write stories about hunger in the South"[55] and who needed the contacts, quotes, and information the group could provide. Citizens Board research trips and hearings on food aid in 1967 and 1968 included the Navajo reservation of Arizona, the barrios of San Antonio, and Birmingham, Alabama (including rural areas such as Hale County), all of which became locations for the CBS report. The San Antonio hearings, held over a month before CBS crews visited the city, drew testimony from the same doctors and social workers at the city hospital who were later featured in *Hunger in America.*[56] County Commissioner Albert Pena, who CBS later cited as the source of its estimate of the number of hungry people in the city, was a CCAP board member. Guest narrator Father Ralph Ruiz belonged to a group that sponsored the Citizens Board's San Antonio hearings, and he testified there. He also played an important role in defending the documentary, testifying at a December 1968 hearing of the U.S. Commission on Civil Rights in San Antonio that congressional investigators of the documentary were harassing people who appeared in the program.[57] Dr. James P. Carter, a Citizen's Board member, had visited the Navajo reservation and testified to the presence of kwashiorkor and marasmus cases in the hospital where Dr. Van Duzen worked.[58] Dr. Raymond Wheeler, CBS's guest narrator and interviewer in the Hale County sequence, was also a member of the Citizens Board. Of the four sites featured in *Hunger in America,* only one, Loudon County, was not a focus of the group's hearings or research trips.

CBS's estimate of the magnitude of hunger conditions and its focus on the impact of hunger on children also were influenced by the food aid reformers. The question of how widespread malnutrition was became one of the central points of struggle between conservative antiwelfare forces, the USDA, and Senate liberals in 1967, and it was at the heart of the subsequent investigation of *Hunger in America.* The documentary repeatedly put the number of hungry and malnourished Americans at 10 million, acknowledging as its source for this figure the Citizens Board report, *Hunger U.S.A.,* published a month before the documentary aired. CBS's emphasis on children as the victims of malnutrition seems to have been based in part on the first 1967 study of hunger conditions in the South, *Children in Mississippi,* conducted by the Field Foundation doctors. The doctors decided to go to Mississippi after the Kennedy-Clark hearings in April, and their testimony about emergency conditions there dominated the Senate Poverty Subcommittee's widely televised summer hearings. Bill Leonard, who led CBS's documentary unit at the time, recalled the doctors' report as particularly influential on *Hunger in America.*[59]

Reaction and Impact: Congressional and USDA Response

Hunger in America quickly became caught up in the political battle over food aid. Advocates of expanding aid cited it approvingly, entering a transcript of the documentary in the *Congressional Record* and arranging Capitol Hill screenings.[60] However, *Hunger in America* was soon investigated in three forums: the USDA, the House Agricultural Appropriations Subcommittee, and the FCC.

USDA secretary Orville Freeman was the first to lash out at CBS. In a press conference and in public letters to CBS president Frank Stanton and Representative Carl Perkins (D-Ark.), Freeman assailed the documentary as "a travesty on objective reporting," faulting it for presenting "a distorted, oversimplified and misleading picture of domestic hunger and what is being done to combat it."[61] First, Freeman alleged "gross errors of fact" in CBS's representation of the surplus commodities program. Although the commodities program distributed extra food, Freeman argued it was unfair of CBS to say that this was food "nobody else wants." The secretary complained about CBS's characterization of the food program as having "not changed since it was instituted in the 1930s," claiming he had expanded the range of foods distributed through the program and that the USDA now directly distributed commodities in a handful of counties reluctant to participate in the program.

CBS, he alleged, also understated the number of people served by federal food programs and overstated the number of counties that lacked them. If Freeman had not done more, he claimed it was because Congress had not allocated more money for antihunger work, and local governments were often unwilling to participate. In his second line of argument, Freeman assailed CBS for "ignoring—or suppression—of known facts and individual cases presented as general truths." CBS, he said, ignored that the USDA had lowered the price of food stamps in the past year and that many children participated in the school lunch program. As for the funds the USDA had turned back to the Treasury, Freeman claimed these could not be used for food stamps (a much-disputed point in his appearances before the Senate) and that his decision not to use the money for other food aid was based on his "judgment of priorities in the effort against hunger and poverty." Finally, he added an addendum to individual cases presented in *Hunger in America,* claiming that, based on their stated incomes in the documentary, the two Alabama women would pay less for food stamps than they claimed. In short, Freeman faulted the documentary for factual errors, lack of balance, and misrepresenting individual cases as the norm. He asked CBS for equal time under the fairness doctrine to respond to the network's charges.

Freeman attacked CBS for several reasons. Although he was sympathetic to expanding food aid, he was unwilling to risk siding with Senate liberals if it would put him in bad stead with the agricultural committees and the Johnson administration, who held more control over his political fate. Between Congress and the administration, the latter was more likely to support new aid, but Johnson was preoccupied. Despite repeated urging from liberal White House advisors to increase food aid, the president was unwilling to ask Congress for anything that might jeopardize his top legislative priorities in the early summer of 1968: a tax bill to fund the Vietnam War and efforts to curb war-related inflation. Freeman, a former governor of Minnesota, had become a leader in Hubert Humphrey's campaign to succeed Johnson. Humphrey tried to broker a behind-the-scenes deal with the Poor People's Marchers, but Johnson rejected it.[62] Therefore, Freeman could not give food aid reformers what they wanted. Second, USDA's liberal critics had intensified their pressure on the department, which had become the target of so much faultfinding in the months prior to *Hunger in America* that Freeman had to start defending his agency publicly. The Senate Poverty Subcommittee reconvened hearings on the department the same week *Hunger in America* aired. The secretary had become the focus of intense public scrutiny and had to defend his own record and shift blame for hunger elsewhere.

Why did Freeman publicly assail CBS, rather than his other critics? Cer-

tainly, he shared a widespread view of network television as uniquely powerful and persuasive, offering more of a national platform for attacks on the
USDA than his other critics had. "Many have advised me against making any
reply to CBS in this matter," he commented. "I have been told that no public
official, regardless of the merits of his case, can expect to win an argument
with a powerful television network. I believe this is true."[63] Yet, more importantly, he could not mount a vigorous public denunciation of Senate liberals
and antihunger advocates without further alienating key Democratic party
constituencies. His response to the food aid reformers' studies was tame in
comparison with his bristling at CBS. He negotiated carefully with the Poor
People's Campaign, offering free food to the marchers who camped on the
Washington mall for over a month and avoiding personal attacks on their
leaders. Rather than censure the Poor People's demonstrations directly, he
cited *Hunger in America* for threatening to "disillusion, disappoint and dis-
enchant" the poor, an act that "can only serve to increase the bitterness and
the unrest that so disturbs American society today."[64] Attacking the Senate
Poverty Subcommittee would have been political suicide, particularly after
the June 6 assassination of Robert F. Kennedy aroused public sympathy for
one of the Senate's leading critics of the USDA. Thus, *Hunger in America*
emerged as the most politic target. In a June 28 memo to President Johnson,
the secretary noted that his "counterattack" on the documentary "has given us
at least a sounding board, for my charges have captured attention and some of
the real facts are coming to public attention. In the process, I believe people
will become aware of all the things we have done and are doing to meet the
food requirements of the needy."[65]

    In its response to Freeman, CBS defended the documentary yet gave the
secretary a minimal chance to rebut it so as to avoid triggering FCC intervention. CBS president Frank Stanton praised the report as a "hard-hitting
job of investigatory reporting" on a "critical and shameful national problem,"
deflecting attention from the program's origins in the work of the food aid
reformers.[66] Disregarding the bulk of Freeman's letter, Stanton claimed that
the secretary "did not appear to be concerned so much with the existence of
any significant inaccuracies" in the report as he was with attributing hunger
to congressional and local inaction rather than to the USDA. "The issue of
hunger in America," Stanton replied, "transcends the superficial issue of assessing blame for its continued existence." Thus, Stanton attempted to refocus
attention on the urgency of hunger, place CBS above the political fray over
the issue, and mark the secretary's objections as self-servingly political. At
the same time, CBS's owned-and-operated St. Louis affiliate, KMOX, quickly
invited Freeman to air his views, which were edited by the station and fol-

lowed by a response from the documentary's producer, Martin Carr. But CBS did not run these remarks nationally, failing to satisfy Freeman's request for equal time on the network. Instead, CBS News president Richard Salant appeared on the network's evening newscast to announce that the network would consider Freeman's request and to defend the documentary's "accuracy and responsibility." Stanton quickly refused to make equal time available, noting that "such an obligation can only arise under Section 315 of the Communications Act relating to appearances by candidates for public office." Yet Stanton also promised to "continue to provide news coverage of the differing views on the issue of hunger." This promise could be used later as evidence of having satisfied the FCC's fairness doctrine. Indeed, when *Hunger in America* was rebroadcast in June, it was followed by a short postscript, including a statement by Freeman about actions taken by the USDA to remedy the problems shown in the program. CBS's careful strategy seems to have dissuaded Freeman from pursuing the matter with the FCC; he did not ask the commission to rule on whether he deserved more rebuttal time.[67]

Congressional conservatives on the agricultural appropriations committees also picked up the torch against *Hunger in America.* Congressmen Jamie L. Whitten and Odin Langden (R-Minn.), chairman and ranking minority member respectively of the House Agricultural Subcommittee, ordered an investigation two days after the documentary aired. The subcommittee used agents on loan from the Federal Bureau of Investigation (FBI) to visit each area covered in the documentary, interviewing welfare personnel, social-service providers, the poor who appeared on the program, and their landlords and family members. Whitten later justified the investigation by explaining, "If what's said is true, then we need to correct it. If not, we need to stop folks from making wild charges."[68] The subcommittee maintained that the probe was handled independently and was "completely objective."[69] However, Citizens Board affiliates and others suggested that it was intended to discredit their work from the start and that FBI agents intimidated the poor, searching their kitchens for food.[70] Although the probe focused on the accuracy of "malnutrition allegations" in many recent studies of hunger, the subcommittee devoted the bulk of its attention and public comments to the CBS report. When Whitten released the report at a hearing in May 1969, he read into the record the long section dealing with *Hunger in America* "to indicate the complete lack of objectivity in these TV programs on alleged hunger conditions."[71]

The congressional probe was clearly part of a political counteroffensive to reframe hunger issues in conservative terms. The thrust of the Whitten report was to argue that the families shown by CBS were either now receiving assistance from welfare and food programs, or were ineligible, or that their poverty and hunger could be blamed on parents' drinking, abandonment of their children, unwillingness to work, and ignorance of proper nutrition. Whitten had been nettled by a *CBS Evening News* report that had aired just three weeks before *Hunger in America*. The story examined Marks, Mississippi, the launching point of the Poor People's March, and a town in Whitten's district. Citing a constituent's letter to him, Whitten accused CBS of staging scenes of poverty to overemphasize deprivation among the town's blacks, and he filed a news distortion claim against the network with the FCC.[72] Other congressional conservatives joined Whitten's attack on the House floor, defending farm subsidies, excoriating welfare, and defending their own districts when they had been portrayed as sites of hunger.[73]

Finally, the FCC investigated *Hunger in America*. The commission did not consider whether the documentary violated the fairness doctrine, which concerned the presentation of contrasting viewpoints, but whether it had "slanted" or "staged" the news. Had Freeman or Whitten brought the complaint against CBS, fairness could have been the issue, but the focus on "slanting" emerged in response to a complaint by Representative Henry Gonzalez (D-Texas), who repeatedly denigrated the documentary in the *Congressional Record* for over a year after *Hunger in America* aired. Gonzalez, who was angered by CBS's portrayal of his home district in San Antonio, held the program up as an example of the deceptive power of network news and the need for new legislation to regulate the networks more fully and directly.[74] Although the FCC found that the San Antonio baby doctors failed to resuscitate at the beginning of *Hunger in America* had not died of malnutrition, it accepted CBS's explanation as having relied on hospital officials for the cause of death, and the commission dismissed the complaint.

Hunger in America certainly garnered a public response, which CBS personnel and other journalists trumpeted as stimulating private charity and political reform. The network claimed it received over five thousand letters from viewers, the majority favorable, many including cash donations to the poor.[75] According to CBS's Bill Leonard, the Alabama teenager who could not afford a school lunch got "enough money through viewers' donations to eat decent lunches for well over a year."[76] For reasons known only to themselves, some charitable Minnesotans sent San Antonio's hungry some 36,000 packages of pudding.[77] Journalists also attributed wider political change to the documentary. When *Hunger in America* won a special George Foster Peabody award for broadcast journalism, the awards committee praised it as having "goaded our nation to action—to begin to feed its hungry."[78] Leonard later claimed that food aid advocates' studies "attracted no popular attention. It took television to open the eyes of the country."[79] Many journalists credited

Hunger in America with pushing the USDA and Congress to expand food aid dramatically.[80]

Although the CBS report assisted food aid reformers, there is little reason to believe that a single documentary had such a significant and immediate political impact. First, this view ignores the numerous hunger studies and Senate hearings that predated CBS's involvement as well as the pressure mounted by the Poor People's Campaign, which also drew public attention to hunger at the same time the report aired. Second, if food aid advocates effectively rallied public support through the media, *Hunger in America* was one of many reports on malnutrition at the time. It was not even the only television coverage of the issue, which the Senate Poverty Subcommittee had pushed on to the networks' evening news agenda and public television. Third, and most important, the political system did not respond substantively in 1968, when food aid reform was minimal. Reformers managed to expand the range of foods available through the commodities program, to win a $43 million increase in the school lunch program, and a $55 million rise in food stamps. But these were relatively small changes in funding levels compared with the broader aims of antipoverty advocates. In 1968, Congress did not liberate food stamps from the USDA and refused to authorize the program on an open-ended basis, allowing agriculture supporters to continue holding food programs hostage to preserving farm subsidies. The larger expansion and permanent authorization of food stamps came in the following two years as a result of intense pressure on the Nixon administration by a range of political forces, especially the Senate.[81] One hour of CBS's time was not enough to bring food programs into the welfare system. It took long-term efforts by a coalition of health professionals, labor and civil rights groups, and congressional liberals to enact these changes, efforts that gave birth to *Hunger in America* and long outlasted it. Certainly the documentary generated broader public attention to the issue, but it is impossible to separate its impact from other media coverage and political activism before, during, and after the report aired.

If CBS escaped congressional and FCC oversight, the flak generated by *Hunger in America* helped to diminish the report's impact somewhat. Producer Martin Carr claimed to have spent the year after the report aired doing little else than working with network lawyers to defend his work, and his departure from CBS the following year was reportedly spurred by frustration at the dueling over *Hunger in America*.[82] In 1971, Vice President Spiro Agnew revived the charges against *Hunger in America* in a speech denouncing CBS documentaries for alleged liberal bias and news staging.[83] Three years later, when CBS announced it would air the program again, the conservative media watchdog Accuracy in Media protested that it should not be shown unless the dying baby sequence was omitted or CBS admitted that it had incorrectly identified the child's cause of death.[84] CBS canceled the rebroadcast.

Framing Poverty

I have argued that all three controversial reports on poverty emerged from government efforts to assist the poor and relied on official sources and policy perspectives on these issues. However, full exploration of whether these reports were indexed to the range of debate among mainstream political elites at the time requires closer attention to the documentaries' ideological and policy framings of poverty. To understand their ideological frames, we need to examine how the reports characterized the problem of poverty, attributed causes and responsibility for it, and evaluated the morality of actors in these controversies. To grasp the policy frames, we need to consider the reports' proposed or implied solutions to the specific problems they addressed.

Conservative, Critical, and Liberal Frames

These reports had to negotiate a position among competing framings of poverty at the time. Despite the shifts in policy, it is possible to identify three enduring framings of poverty and hunger in the 1960s: conservative, critical, and liberal. Although participants in poverty debates at times drew on elements of more than one frame, these stances can be distinguished if we consider them as ideal types that structured most public discourse about the issue at the time.[85]

Conservative ideology could be found in the early 1960s attacks on welfare abuses by Mitchell and others as well as in congressional attacks on the War on Poverty and food aid, especially by those who represented farmers' interests. To the extent that conservatives construed poverty as a problem at all, it was a problem of human nature and its causes could be found in individual character defects of poor people: poverty stemmed from the poor's ignorance, hedonism, and sloth. As House Agricultural Committee chair W. R. Poage (D-Texas) explained hunger in 1968: "The basic problem is one of ignorance as to what constitutes a balanced diet, coupled with indifference by a great many persons who should and probably do not know . . . [There is] deliberate parental neglect . . . relief clients are virtually ineducable."[86] If there were victims, they were the children of irresponsible parents, the employers who needed parents' labor, and the working taxpayers who supported them. Occasionally, the poor themselves might be seen as victims of a welfare system that allegedly destroyed their initiative, but human frailty could not be cured by government. Conservative solutions, such as Newburgh's plan, involved limiting the duration and amount of public aid, in part because the intransigent human nature of the poor meant that no amount of good will would dispel poverty fully. As Senator Strom Thurmond put it, "There has been hunger since the time of Jesus Christ and there always will be."[87]

Clearly, the poverty documentaries drew on conservative ideology largely to refute it, and none of the reports endorsed conservative policy solutions. In *Harvest of Shame,* the Farm Bureau president who called migrants "practically unemployable" and the farmer who maintained that they liked to travel because they had "a little gypsy in their blood" were opposed by the entire thrust of the documentary. *Battle of Newburgh* dismantled Mitchell's case for curbing welfare. *Hunger in America* featured just two sources that blamed malnutrition on lazy parents in brief interviews. The San Antonio County commissioner interviewed seems to have been chosen for his extreme views; he not only rejected food aid to children but questioned the need to educate them beyond the eighth grade and claimed hunger would always exist because "you've got to have Indians and Chiefs." As the commissioner attempted to frame the cause of hunger as poor fathers' unwillingness to work, reporter Culhane repeatedly asked questions about the effect of hunger on children. The tenant farmer who called welfare recipients "bums" was introduced by Kuralt as an example of "an additional problem in Loudon County: the pride of the people." After the farmer claimed that he could help his children himself, Culhane responded skeptically, "Granted that you *try,* but really now, doesn't it sometimes happen that you can't afford something that you know they should have?"

A second, critical ideology could be found among critics of the limits of the War on Poverty and the USDA among the left and in civil rights groups, especially with the onset of the Poor People's Campaign. They traced the causes of poverty and hunger not to individual deficiencies but to an economic system in which employers, landlords, and grocers exploited the poor. Poverty was a problem of injustice, inequality, and oppression. Welfare was more often framed in this ideology as a system for regulating the poor, a mechanism for maintaining political order in, and control over, the destitute and unemployed. The history of welfare was seen as a "record of periodically expanding and contracting relief rolls as the system performs its two main functions: maintaining civil order and enforcing work."[88] This critical discourse emphasized the causes of rural poverty in the welfare state's complicity with the "most feudal systems of agricultural peonage," pointing to how welfare payments increased to keep agricultural workers alive during the winter, then declined during the growing season to force them into subsistence-wage farm jobs.[89] These critics were more likely to portray southern governments' withholding of aid as an attempt to drive surplus black labor out of the region through starvation.[90]

This view faulted the USDA and Congress for "converting programs to feed the poor into disposal systems to relieve market gluts and protect profits" and emphasized that farm policy primarily served "the large producer, the commercial and corporate farmer."[91]

Although critical voices often mounted a radical analysis of capitalism, their proposed solutions were best characterized as a mix of European social democracy with the participatory ethos of the early War on Poverty.[92] The recommendations of *Hunger U.S.A.* and the demands presented to the USDA by the Poor People's Campaign in June 1968 are good examples. The Citizens Board authors limited their calls for reform to extending emergency food aid to areas most in need, increasing funding and loosening eligibility criteria for hunger programs, funding more research and training on nutrition in medical schools, and shifting responsibility for food aid from the USDA to the Department of Health, Education, and Welfare.[93] The Poor People's Campaign echoed these recommendations but went beyond them in demanding greater "involvement of the poor in planning and evaluating poverty programs," doubling funds for minority-owned farm cooperatives, revising the USDA's acreage diversion policy (presumably to allow sharecroppers to grow food for themselves in unused land), and distributing USDA funds to aid poor farmers more equitably.[94] These demands suggested that organization and political empowerment of the poor were necessary solutions to poverty as well, and they presented the poor as potential producers of their own food rather than simply as dependent on government food distribution.

This critical view was also rarely heard in the controversial poverty reports, at least after *Harvest of Shame.* In this initial report, Secretary Mitchell, labor and religious leaders, and Murrow repeatedly presented the migrants as exploited by farmers and crew leaders, and Murrow noted that American consumers enjoyed lower food prices as a result. Murrow explained that the documentary was being aired over the Thanksgiving holiday because he wanted viewers to know how the people who harvested their food were treated. However, *Battle of Newburgh* did not present civil rights activists' view that the city's welfare reform effort was an attempt to quash rising black political aspirations. Huntley presented the city's controversial urban renewal efforts as progress and did not mention blacks' resistance to their displacement from downtown. In *Hunger in America,* Kuralt adopted the Citizens Board's view of the commodities program as serving farmers first, "consist[ing] largely of dumping excesses rather than providing essentials." In his wrap-up, he noted that one reason for resistance to boosting food aid was that "surplus commodities means less food purchased in local stores." A black mother in the South suggested briefly that local officials wouldn't raise food aid because black children were attending white schools and voting. But the documentary spent no more time than this exploring how these and other political-economic interests (such as agribusiness companies or middle-class consumers) benefited from restricting aid and keeping farm wages low. By contrast, other exposés of hunger—such as the Citizens Board's *Hunger U.S.A., Des Moines Register* journalist Nick Kotz's book *Let Them Eat Promises,* and the Public Broadcasting Lab's documentary *Hunger American Style*—paid more attention to critiquing the larger causes of hunger and were more willing to locate responsibility in identifiable "villains."[95]

A third, liberal ideology was shared by the Johnson administration and many congressional supporters of a limited War on Poverty and echoed in USDA secretary Orville Freeman's analysis of food programs. This approach was common among those who supported expanding services and increasing benefit levels while minimizing structural changes that boosted participation by the poor and poverty groups in defining and administering programs. Here, the causes of poverty and malnutrition were defined neither as individual character flaws nor as the outcome of an unjust political economy but as isolation from the economic mainstream. The central image of the problem presented the poor as trapped in a self-perpetuating "cycle of poverty," in which lack of skills and opportunities led to low incomes, which led to long-term welfare dependency and living in ghettos, which led to absorbing a "culture of poverty."[96] The poor were generally portrayed as sympathetic victims who deserved assistance in breaking out of this cycle. Yet, because of the need to circumvent political opposition, liberal discourse generally did not identify the interests at stake in redistributing wealth and economic opportunity, attributing responsibility for poverty not to any particular economic or racial groups but to diffuse, impersonal forces like the "cycle."[97] If poverty was portrayed as a moral disgrace in a land of abundance, there was little attempt to argue that those who enjoyed plenty were responsible for impoverishing others. As Frances Fox Piven and Richard Cloward observed, the liberal approach framed responses to poverty in the confident, professional language of medicine and social science, "which lent an aura of scientific authority to what might otherwise have been perceived as political rhetoric."[98] Poverty and hunger were "maladies," "scourges," or "social ills" that could be "eradicated" or "cured." Liberal solutions suggested that government funding had to be increased, administrative roadblocks had to be overcome, and the efficiency of social-service and welfare programs had to be improved. For example, in a June 1967 review of domestic food programs prompted by the Senate investigations, Secretary Freeman identified the principal weaknesses of these programs as stemming mainly from "administrative," "informational," and "educational" problems shared by all levels of government and the poor themselves.[99]

Over time, the documentaries increasingly framed poverty in liberal terms. *Harvest of Shame* was only partially characterized by this perspective. As noted, the report portrayed migrants' plight in a critical vein as a problem of exploitation by growers that benefited consumers. True, the report did not explore the historical origins of policies that allowed farmers to pay their workers so little, denied migrants public aid, and blocked unionization.[100] In this omission, the documentary may be said to have erased political responsibility for exploiting migrants, presenting government in a liberal light as the cure rather than the cause of poverty. But there was little couching of the causes of migrant penury in a cycle or culture of poverty. The documentary's policy solutions mixed critical and liberal approaches. The extended, positive treatment of unionizing efforts suggested collective action by the poor was necessary to wrest some control from growers. However, Murrow's conclusion endorsed the weaker Eisenhower presidential commission's recommendations rather than attempts to restructure farm labor markets more dramatically through Senator Williams' call for a minimum wage for agriculture and ending the bracero program. Nor did *Harvest of Shame* advocate struggling against the exploitation of immigrant labor, which was presented simply as a threat to American migrants.

In *Battle of Newburgh,* a liberal image of the poor as sympathetic victims of unavoidable circumstances such as illness and unemployment, but not oppression, prevailed. It suggested that the rehabilitation model of welfare that had emerged under the Kennedy administration as a liberal-conservative compromise was the best solution both for reducing poverty and the welfare rolls. Drawing on cycle-of-poverty imagery, Huntley said that services and other aid to the poor had helped them "to become independent, breaking the chain of second generation welfare families," and "freeing people from dependency."

Similarly, *Hunger in America* mostly framed poverty in liberal terms. Introducing each segment, Kuralt presented sympathetic victims of poverty yet refused to locate responsibility for their condition in any identifiable social group or interest. San Antonio's Mexican Americans were poor because they "faced a language barrier, and like most poor people, they suffer from lack of skills and unemployment." As for the Navajos: "The West was theirs once. They were nomads and their home was vast. Now they have an arid reservation." For southern blacks, "Cotton has been a misery, but at least it's been a meal ticket. Now it's not even that. The machines have taken over. . . ." Who raised the language barrier, who now owned the West and how they got it, who imposed the misery of "cotton" and machines was not explored. To the extent that the documentary named causes of hunger, it blamed the cycle of poverty and the failure of food aid programs to break it. Dr. Granger's discussion of his Virginia patients drew most clearly on this rhetoric:

> These people, with no past to be proud of and no hope for the future, seek immediate forms of enjoyment . . . a late model television set in the living room . . . a late model baby in the crib . . . empty pint bottles in the yard. All these things are signs of the short term. With no real prospects in life, they turn to the few pleasures they can find. Often the only creative thing a woman can do in these circumstances is to have a baby, and then to have another one. And so they do. The children grow into the image of their parents, and like their parents, they will be old before they should be. Surrounded by prosperity, these people share in none of it. The misery in their lives is a constant. The sameness stretches from one day to the next, one year to the next, one generation to the next.

The solution, according to *Hunger in America,* was to bring the food programs into the welfare system proper by transferring them to the Department of Health, Education, and Welfare or a special commission. This was certainly in line with the demands of food aid reformers, but it omitted their calls to change the welfare system itself by offering the poor and their advocates a greater role in defining needs and administering benefits.

Liberalism and Participation of the Poor

All three documentaries' use of narration and point of view also embodied the ambivalence within liberal ideology about extending power to the poor to define welfare needs and the causes of indigence. This ambivalent framing paralleled the intense struggles over "maximum feasible participation" by the poor in the War on Poverty, struggles over whether the poor should be considered authors as well as objects of welfare policy. Each report offered more space for the poor to speak about their own conditions through longer interviews than the evening news permitted. But few interviewees were invited to talk about the roots of poverty or in terms that suggested a larger political critique of public aid. Rather, the poor were limited to the familiar role that they most often play in sympathetic mainstream treatments of poverty: as victims who testify about personal experience to illustrate or dramatize a larger point made by experts or journalists. In this sense, the documentary fit what Brian Winston has called "the victim tradition" typified by the social documentaries of the 1930s. Winston critiques this tradition because it "substitutes empathy for analysis, it privileges effect over cause, and therefore it seldom results in any spin-offs in the real world—that is, actions taken in society as a result of the program to ameliorate the conditions depicted."[101] Except for the union meeting in *Harvest of Shame,* the poor were presented in all three documentaries largely through interviews set against the iconographic and stereotypical backgrounds of rural poverty (interiors of shacks, the fields, amidst large families), rather than testifying at hearings or organizing to take part in efforts such as the Poor People's Campaign.

Hunger in America provides an especially rich example of liberalism's conflicted stance toward empowering the poor. Although the report offered little chance for substantial participation by the poor in framing food problems, it adopted four guest narrators, all professionals who ministered to the indigent. This was extremely rare. Television documentaries of the 1960s almost never shared narrative power in this way because doing so contradicted the networks' interest in cultivating recognizable star journalists. Sharing the narration also conflicted with the networks' jealous preservation of editorial control over documentaries, a pattern established in the early 1960s in the name of guaranteeing professionalism and objectivity.[102] Guest narrators potentially undermined journalists' role as omniscient mediators between audiences and the personal experiences of the "man on the street" or the technical knowledge of experts.[103] Nonetheless, *Hunger in America* turned over the narrative voice to Father Ruiz in San Antonio, Dr. Granger in Virginia, Dr. Van Duzen in Arizona, and Dr. Wheeler in Alabama. Kuralt introduced them as legitimate and authentic representatives for the indigent because of their personal experiences and professional knowledge gained from treating the poor on a regular basis.[104] They spoke mainly from a professional standpoint about the hungry rather than from the point of view of the poor themselves or even as political advocates for increasing food aid (despite the fact that Ruiz and Wheeler were directly affiliated with the Citizens Board, which CBS did not mention). The guest narrators, three of them doctors, identified the causes of hunger in mostly medical terms (too much starch, too little protein, insufficient calories) and did not advocate solutions. The narrators offered CBS a way of bringing viewers closer to the poor without taking the politically riskier step of allowing the poor themselves to assume narrative power.

The reports' point of view also contained participation by the poor, relegating them more to an object than a subject of poverty policy. In these reports, the typically intrusive and interrogatory point of view of television journalism overlapped with the welfare systems' methods of examining the poor. Many of the journalists' interviews with the indigent involved establishing the legitimacy of their claims to aid. Typical of these interviews was Dr. Wheeler's questioning of an expectant black mother in Alabama in *Hunger in America:*

DR. WHEELER: What did you have for dinner today?

MRS. ZANDERS: I didn't have any dinner.

DR. WHEELER: You're going to have a baby before long?

MRS. ZANDERS: Yes sir.

DR. WHEELER: What kind of food do you eat?

MRS. ZANDERS: Rice. Chicken sometimes.

DR. WHEELER: What else do you eat?

MRS. ZANDERS: That's all. And water.

DR. WHEELER: Mrs. Zanders, what does your husband do for a living?

MRS. ZANDERS: He gets jobs in hay fields.

DR. WHEELER: In hay fields?

MRS. ZANDERS: Yes.

DR. WHEELER: How much does he make when he's working?

MRS. ZANDERS: From three to four dollars a day.

DR. WHEELER: Three to four dollars a day?

MRS. ZANDERS: Yes sir.

DR. WHEELER: And he hasn't worked now in three or four weeks?

MRS. ZANDERS: Yes.

DR. WHEELER: Do you get food stamps?

MRS. ZANDERS: No sir, because I'm not able to get them.

DR. WHEELER: Why not?

MRS. ZANDERS: I ain't got them this month. They cost $70 and I don't have it.

DR. WHEELER: Have you asked for any help from anyone in raising the money to buy those stamps?

MRS. ZANDERS: No sir, there ain't no need.

DR. WHEELER: Why?

MRS. ZANDERS: They ain't going to give it to you.

DR. WHEELER: Have you been down to the Welfare Department and talked to them, or has your husband?

MRS. ZANDERS: No, sir, the last time I went to Welfare the lady told me—said if you have a living husband that they can't give you no help.

DR. WHEELER: Even if he's not working?

MRS. ZANDERS: Yes sir.[105]

Although the thrust of this segment was to suggest that food stamps failed to meet the needs of a legitimate aid recipient, it did so through the same interrogative methods and the same questions Zanders would have faced in a welfare office. Unable to speak except to answer Wheeler's demands for information, her role was to prove that she met most welfare eligibility criteria: mother needs food to feed (unborn) baby, family lacks male jobholder, client has applied for aid. She was not asked to comment on whether these criteria were valid, which was a job reserved for Kuralt and professional or political sources. None of the reports offered the opportunity to the poor to challenge the way that the welfare system, in Nancy Fraser's words, "tends to translate political issues concerning the interpretation of people's needs into legal, administrative, and/or therapeutic matters." Like welfare officials, CBS and its guest interviewers tended to position the poor as "passive client or consumer recipients and not as active co-participants involved in shaping their life conditions."[106]

The documentary's point of view partook of the medical and judicial systems' positionings of the poor as well. Hospital and clinic segments in which social workers and doctors explained the mental and physical effects of hunger on newborns consisted of numerous extreme close-ups of infants' distended bellies, protruding ribs, and sagging flesh. These shots followed the logic of the medical textbook, presenting depersonalized evidence of kwashiorkor, marasmus, and other hunger-related ailments. Doctor's hands pried open children's mouths to reveal gum disease and held passive infants up for the camera, fingering their ribs and legs ("You can't feel a good muscle mass and the thighs show a lot of flabbiness").

At times, *Hunger in America* viewed poverty's effects on children with an intrusive medical gaze.

Yet it was when *Hunger in America* intersected with the judicial system that its treatment of the poor became most intrusive and demeaning. Kuralt introduced one San Antonio segment by saying, "Hunger is never so devastating as in a child, never so horrifying as in what it may drive a child to do." An assistant probation officer (identified by CBS as a "social worker") was shown kneeling next to a young girl sitting at a table and burying her face in her hands. The camera followed the probation officer as she rose and took a few steps away from the table, where CBS's Culhane was waiting. At Culhane's prompting, she explained that the eleven-year-old girl had been arrested for prostituting herself to make money for food. The camera panned back to examine the girl, who desperately tried to hide her face by turning away. The girl clearly appeared unwilling to take part in the program, and CBS seemed to take no measures to get her permission, protect her identity, or let her speak anonymously for herself.[107]

Responsibility: Victims, Villains, and Viewers

These reports also fit squarely within a mainstream liberal tradition of representing poverty in the way they attributed responsibility for poverty and offered moral evaluations of the poor. Any attempt to construct an image of the worthy poor must contend with four long-term ideological distinctions in American welfare policy that separate the "deserving" and "undeserving" indigent. The first differentiates between the disabled and the able-bodied. Policy makers have tended to view the able-bodied more circumspectly because of twin assumptions that those who are capable of work ought to take any available job and that the American economy provides jobs to all who seek them. The figure of the able-bodied welfare applicant has been particularly troublesome in the United States because it is a reminder of the market economy's inability to provide full employment at a living wage.[108] A second distinction that follows from the difference between the disabled and abled is between adults, on the one hand, and children and the elderly, on the other. Because the latter are officially excused from the labor market, they are more likely to be considered as the innocent poor.

The deserving poor have also been distinguished along racial and gender lines. Especially since the early 1960s, welfare opponents have attempted to undermine white support for welfare programs by identifying the undeserving as people of color, construing higher rates of poverty among nonwhites as stemming not from historic discrimination but from the "culture of poverty" or from genetic inferiority.[109] Finally, the American welfare system differentiates between male- and female-oriented programs.[110] A "masculine" set of programs (including unemployment and social security) is designed to compensate for failure in the primary market for male labor power, and its benefits are considered "entitlements" based on participants' claims as members of the paid workforce. Recipients are more often characterized as getting "deserved" compensation, as earning back what workers and employers "paid in" to the program, in short, as rights-bearing individuals. These programs require less intrusive and demeaning efforts by recipients to prove their eligibility. Benefits tend to be paid in cash, allowing recipients to be free consumers. By contrast, a second set of "feminine" programs (such as food stamps and the formerly named Aid to Families with Dependent Children) are designed to compensate for family failures, understood as the absence of a male breadwinner. These programs are "means-tested," based on participants' abilities to meet state-defined definitions of need, as unpaid or low-income workers and parents. They require more intrusive and demeaning efforts by recipients to prove eligibility. Recipients are more often stigmatized as being "on the dole" and benefiting from "government largess." Benefits tend to be in-kind and earmarked for specific purposes, depicting recipients as potentially irresponsible wards or clients of the state.

All three reports negotiated rather than challenged mainstream divisions between the worthy and unworthy indigent by emphasizing poverty's effects on children and the elderly. All of David Lowe's interviews with migrants in *Harvest of Shame* focused on farm workers' inability to provide decent food, care, housing, and education for their children. *Battle of Newburgh* followed the same approach, adding a focus on the elderly as the primary recipients of aid in the city. One of the report's central indictments of Mitchell's tactics was its depiction of elderly aid recipients forced to struggle down to the police station to verify their eligibility before receiving their checks. Newspaper advertisements for *Hunger in America* featured a single image of the dying child that opened the program, captioned "This Baby Is Dying of Hunger." The guest narrators and almost every parent interviewed discussed the effects of malnutrition on children rather than adults. CBS presented only one able-bodied man in poverty, and he was the Loudon County tenant farmer who rejected welfare recipients as "leechers." When guest narrators explained the poverty of mothers and grandmothers, they attributed it to unemployed husbands. Even when the narration generalized about the scope of hunger among all Americans, the accompanying images were of children. For example, when Kuralt noted that 100,000 "people" were hungry in San Antonio, and when he said that 10 million "Americans" were hungry, viewers saw images of impoverished children. Almost entirely lacking adult male welfare recipients, these reports constructed public aid as targeted toward children and the elderly. In doing so, the documentaries directed attention away from recipients who could have been considered "illegitimate" within the ideology of the American welfare system, but the reports did not challenge that ideology.

The reports also observed, rather than contested, the gender distinctions of welfare ideology. The documentaries depicted the feminine poor almost exclusively as mothers, whose primary claim to aid was based on the need to provide for their children rather than for themselves. The many mothers interviewed were not asked what they ate for breakfast that morning or would eat for dinner that night, but about what their children were eating. When the programs raised the issue of women's health, it was almost always to point to the consequences for their babies. In *Hunger in America,* for example, Kuralt commented over a montage of infants in the San Antonio hospital maternity ward, "Malnutrition—a problem for the mother—can become a tragedy for her baby."

However, the documentaries carefully challenged growing attempts to racialize poverty discourse by conservative critics of public aid. *Harvest of Shame* equated migrancy with slavery, not with a culture of poverty, portraying black and white farm workers as exploited labor. If the documentary portrayed imported Mexicans as a threat to American workers, it failed to extend its sympathies across citizenship, not racial, lines. Mexican Americans were shown taking part in the AFL-CIO meeting. *Battle of Newburgh* maintained that most blacks had moved to Newburgh in search of work rather than a handout, made it clear that most of the town's public aid recipients were white, and presented more white than black interviewees discussing their welfare needs. The report countered Mitchell's image of lazy and oversexed African Americans, albeit largely through footage of black children working after-school jobs and the school superintendent's contention that black youngsters could learn just as well as whites if given equal facilities. The racially integrated school Christmas pageant served as the key moral symbol of tolerance in the report, presenting the provision of public aid as the Christian thing to do. The structure of *Hunger in America* displayed a range of food aid recipients by race and ethnicity, including Mexican American, African American, Navajo, and white poor. When it traded in culture-of-poverty discourse, as in Dr. Granger's soliloquy on empty liquor bottles in the yards of the poor, it applied this frame to the white farmers of Virginia. Granted, the documentary focused on blacks in the South, where the legacy of slavery and ongoing segregation likely provided more sympathetic victims for white audiences, rather than urban blacks, who were the most politically controversial constituency of the War on Poverty. However, in none of these reports were blacks more often used to illustrate problems with welfare and whites more often used to illustrate the deserving poor, as Martin Gilens has found in other media coverage at the time.[111] On the contrary, these investigative reports neither portrayed African Americans as undeserving of public aid nor airbrushed them out of their images of the deserving poor.

The reports' visual language drew on an American tradition of persuading middle-class viewers to address the needs of the worthy poor. This humanist social documentary legacy includes Jacob Riis's Progressive-era images of urban tenement dwellers, Lewis Hine's photos of immigrants and children in New York in the 1910s and 1920s, the New Deal Farm Security Administration (FSA) images of rural poverty, and appeals for international aid associated with the Kennedy era New Frontier foreign aid programs and private charities such as CARE. The tradition is also evident in fiction films of the 1930s about rural poverty, from *The Grapes of Wrath* to *Sullivan's Travels*. This aesthetic strongly influenced *Harvest of Shame*, which Murrow introduced as "a 1960 *Grapes of Wrath.*" Executive producer Fred Friendly directed the report's editor to include shots of migrants that were reminiscent of 1930s photos of displaced farm families.[112] The New Deal and CARE aesthetic shaped the presentation of interviews with welfare families in their homes featured in *Battle of Newburgh* and especially *Hunger in America.* In the latter report, several of the segments set in the homes of poor families began with an establishing still shot of mother and children posed on a porch, couch, or bed, into

In *Harvest of Shame*, David Lowe arranged a migrant family into a tableau familiar from Depression-era photographs of poverty.

which entered a guest narrator who began an interview or medical checkup. The composition of these tableaus is familiar from the FSA photos of tenant farmers and migrants in their shacks made by Walker Evans, Ben Shahn, Dorothea Lange, and others.

In each shot, a mother, sitting in the center of the frame, stares off camera with a grim, determined gaze, surrounded by her children. At other points in *Hunger in America,* the narration paused to allow the audience to contemplate almost still images reminiscent of FSA photos. A Virginia boy squatted facing the camera next to an iron pot-bellied stove on a dirty kitchen floor, eating his meal from a tin plate. Another boy was shown in silhouette from behind, staring out of a screen door in his kitchen, one hand resting on the door frame, as if "trapped" by his poverty—a common framing device in this tradition.

In the San Antonio hospital, a close-up of an elderly woman who looked steadily but worriedly off camera with her hand lifted to her mouth was remarkably similar in its subject matter and composition to Lange's famous "Migrant Mother, Nipomo, California" (1936). *Hunger in America* and *Harvest of Shame* featured numerous close-ups of children staring directly at the camera, with vulnerable yet wary eyes, traces of skin disease on their cheeks, impassive to circling flies. These images reproached the middle-class viewer using the same techniques as appeals for international aid to poor children. Images of infants focused on the distended bellies familiar from such appeals.

Hunger in America framed children as trapped in a cycle of poverty.

This visual language, with the potential to trigger associations with historic public-private campaigns to aid the poor—from the Progressive era to the New Deal to the New Frontier—may have been the reports' most persuasive argument for expanding food programs.

✿   ✿   ✿

All three controversial documentaries on poverty were framed squarely within the sphere of legitimate controversy, growing out of conflicts between and within the major parties over the federal safety net for the poor, especially as it related to farm politics and civil rights. In each case, the journalists framed poverty in liberal terms, advocating policy solutions that could be presented as mainstream and even bipartisan, while avoiding more far-reaching alternatives proposed by government and social movement actors such as civil rights and antihunger groups. These investigative reports generally presented the poor neither as the villains of conservative ideology nor as the potential political actors of critical ideology but as innocent and mainly passive victims. The reports paid little attention to the historic and political origins of poverty, relying mainly on the point of view of professionals who worked with the poor and official advocates for them more than on the poor themselves or on relevant movement sources. In response, local and congressional forces attacked television reporters' fairness and accuracy as part of larger struggles over poverty policy. Network critics brought FCC and congressional probes and threatened to regulate television news more strictly. These conflicts arose repeatedly during a decade of unprecedented experimentation, expansion, and redefinition of federal antipoverty programs.

As noted in the introduction, the dramatic growth of network documentary in the early 1960s was identified with gaining public consent for the Kennedy administration's activist foreign policy. The New Frontiersmen and network journalists made the global competition between communism and capitalism a central documentary topic. These reports, officials hoped, would cure Americans of their isolationism and teach them of the need for world leadership. However, foreign affairs documentaries, at first broadly championed by government, corporate, and media elites, became an increasing source of friction between them. Some documentaries provoked official concern not because they challenged policy but because television journalists began to intervene in Cold War stories more directly in search of exclusive coverage of unfolding events. In doing so, journalists encroached on the ability of the foreign policy apparatus to conduct its affairs in secrecy and manage public opinion at home and abroad. Other reports ran afoul of Cold War hawks as reports began to echo the foreign policy community's own growing criticisms of the war in Southeast Asia and the burgeoning power of the military in the United States. Elite support for television documentaries broke down not because of journalistic adversarialism but because of journalistic adventurism and the splits that beset U.S. foreign policy at the time.

American policy differences sparked skirmishes over many Cold War investigative reports. Pennsylvania representative Daniel J. Flood attacked *Panama: Danger Zone* (NBC, 1961), which included demands on the United States to relinquish its control of the Panama Canal Zone, for treating "a theme hostile to the United States." For Flood, the report showed that the networks were "subversive forces" and the Kennedy administration was losing control of the Caribbean.[1] Florida senator George A. Smathers criticized *Trujillo: Portrait of a Dictator* (CBS, 1961), on Dominican Republic ruler Rafael Trujillo, as an irresponsible attack on a Caribbean ally.[2] The report featured American

business interests and Smathers himself crediting Trujillo with economic development and anticommunism but also dissidents who detailed corruption
and human rights abuses and Representative Charles O. Porter (D-Ore.),
who said "the bloody, black era of Trujillo is nearly ended," and that the
United States would not send Marines to protect him from revolution. The
documentary reflected competing American views of the dictator, from whom
the Kennedy administration distanced itself before Trujillo's domestic opponents assassinated him in 1961 with CIA approval.[3] As part of Senator John
McLellan's investigation of alleged favoritism in awarding contracts for the
TFX aircraft, the senator subpoenaed unused film from *McNamara and the
Pentagon* (CBS, 1963). McLellan demanded to review comments on the issue
to CBS made by Defense Secretary Robert McNamara, with whom the senator was dueling at the time. CBS successfully refused to give up the outtakes.[4]
News reports on the Vietnam War generated official resistance throughout
the conflict. The most famous of these brouhahas was Morley Safer's *CBS
Evening News* story about Americans sacking the village of Cam Ne, which
included shots of troops using their cigarette lighters to burn terrified civilians'
huts. President Johnson immediately called CBS president Frank Stanton
to excoriate Safer as a "communist" who "just shat on the flag," and had the
reporter's background investigated for evidence of communist leanings.[5] The
Defense Department pressured CBS to recall Safer from Vietnam, but the
network resisted. However, three other Cold War reports generated more
intense government probes, intervention, and threats of further regulation
of news than any other documentaries of the time.

Journalistic Trespassing: *The Tunnel*

In the summer of 1961, the Soviet Union and East Germany precipitated
a major Cold War crisis when they raised the Berlin Wall to stanch a growing flow of refugees to the West. The flight of the mainly young, educated,
and professional refugees threatened the viability of the East German state,
which had stagnated politically and economically. West Berliners protested,
fearing that the Soviet Union would make good on its long-term demand for
the eviction of Western troops—British, French, and American—that had
administered separate sectors of Berlin since the end of World War II. The
Kennedy administration accepted the wall as the price of preserving West
Berlin's independence from the Soviet sphere of influence and avoiding war
with the USSR. West Berliners began to dig secret tunnels beneath the wall
as escape routes for refugees from the East. College students financed by the
West Berlin government, West German nationalist parties, and media organi-

zations did much of the digging.[6] In 1962, when the U.S. State Department learned that both CBS and NBC were filming the digging of different tunnels, the department pressured the networks not to participate in such projects. CBS complied, but NBC finished its secret report, shooting footage of refugees crawling out from an underground passageway into West Berlin.

NBC's ninety-minute saga, *The Tunnel,* told the story of the diggers against the background of the divided city. It opened with the three student leaders of the tunnel project strolling around and surveying the Berlin Wall. They were described by reporter and narrator Piers Anderton as "planning the most daring refugee rescue operation in Berlin's history." Images of refugees, shot in telephoto lens, showed them entering a tenement on the eastern side of the wall. "They go 140 yards to West Berlin and a free future," said Anderton over a tracking shot through the tunnel.

Throughout, the documentary entwined brief contextual material on the history of the wall with its main focus: the diggers' struggles to complete the tunnel. Anderton told how the East Germans erected barbed wire through the city at first and narrated dramatic film clips of early escapes by men and women leaping from windows on the eastern side into safety nets on the western side below. He related how the East Germans then built a permanent, concrete wall and began demolishing buildings close to its eastern side to frustrate escape attempts. Anderton profiled the tunnel leaders—two Italian engineering students and a German, all studying in West Berlin. Others joined them to help friends and family members escape to the West. The report detailed their plans for building the tunnel as the students pored over maps and sketches and began the digging in the basement of a bomb-damaged building. Anderton contrasted life in East and West Berlin and told the stories of would-be refugees shot by the Vopos, the East German guards who patrolled the wall. The report outlined the rising tensions in the city as the diggers worked through the summer of 1962 and showed a highly publicized incident in which a student attempting to scale the wall was shot down by the Vopos and left to bleed to death. Secretary of State Dean Rusk's June visit to the city to pledge support for West Berlin's independence and declare that "the wall must go" was also shown.

However, most of the documentary followed the hardships of digging the tunnel. Obstacles and setbacks to the project were detailed: recurring flooding in the tunnel, a student leader rushed to the hospital for an emergency appendectomy, a coworker captured in the East recruiting refugees for another tunnel underway at the time, fears that he would reveal the student tunnel's location when interrogated. The report showed each phase of the project as well: the planning, engineering, and digging, the students' trips to East Berlin to contact and collect the refugees, the escapees emerging on the Western side of the tunnel muddy and scraped to triumphant soundtrack music. "Only the faces of those who clearly consented are shown," said Anderton. "These are ordinary people, not trained or accustomed to risk," he noted. "What must they be leaving to risk this?" One of the diggers reunited with his wife and child, who came through the tunnel. "Tonight for the first time he held his baby," said Anderton. In the report's coda, a rescued German friend serenaded the diggers in Italian at a restaurant. Outside the restaurant, Anderton told how the tunnel had filled with water and had to be closed, but "there will be other young men, and other tunnels."

Context and Sources: Students and the Berlin Crisis

The Tunnel was one of the few controversial reports in this study that relied little on U.S. government sources. Aside from the brief clip of Rusk denouncing the wall, NBC focused on the students. Producer Reuven Frank told Anderton that he wanted stories on refugees and the tunnels, saying, "Don't worry about getting any permission. Go ahead and do it. I'll pay the bill."[7] Anderton put the word out to students that NBC was looking for a tunnel to film. The project leaders and their colleagues had run through their initial funding from West German government sources before the tunnel was halfway completed. NBC agreed to give the students approximately $12,000 for what Frank called the "film rights" to the story, although the documentary producers understood that the money was used to enable the story, paying for wood, pumps, and other supplies that allowed the digging to go forward.[8] Frank guarded the project from the authorities (and rival journalists) with as much secrecy as the diggers, instructing NBC personnel not to discuss it on the phone and transporting the film out of Berlin only after all shooting was completed, and in his own handbags. Although the film used no interviews, its major sources were the students themselves as well as the NBC journalists' understanding of the Berlin crisis.

The Kennedy administration's response to what it saw as the Soviets' first test of the new president's resolve in Europe was by no means easy for journalists to read at the time.[9] Caught by surprise when the East Germans began building the wall, the administration's public position was to demand that the wall be removed and assert that Western powers would not leave Berlin under Soviet pressure. Kennedy moved a small but symbolic contingent of 1,500 troops to the city to show American commitment and sent high-level emissaries such as Rusk and Vice President Johnson to the wall to reiterate U.S. policy. The administration exploited Berlin's propaganda value continually. As the refugee crisis worsened for the East, Edward R. Murrow's United

States Information Agency distributed stories entitled "West Berlin Today—A Refugee a Minute," accusing the communists of violating Berliners' right to govern themselves and failing to meet their economic needs. The administration took full advantage of the wall as a symbol of the Eastern Bloc's need to constrain its people's freedom and to stop them from voting with their feet for capitalism and democracy. This public position also attempted to inoculate the administration against Republican charges that it was soft in negotiating with Soviets over Berlin.

However, the administration's private position was that the wall was an acceptable solution to the Berlin crisis. Kennedy and his state department advisors were not willing to risk war with the USSR over Berlin. As the president said privately, "a wall is a hell of a lot better than a war."[10] Rusk told American diplomats the administration did not want to see a destabilizing East German revolt against Soviet rule and "We plan, therefore, [to] do nothing at this time to exacerbate [the] situation."[11] Senator J. William Fulbright (D-Ark.), the leading Democratic foreign policy voice in Congress, shared this view, saying on national television during the 1961 crisis: "I don't understand why the East Germans don't close their border. I think they have a right to close it."[12] In addition, the administration in some ways preferred a divided Germany to West German aspirations to reunify the country since Kennedy and other NATO allies remained suspicious of German nationalism and desire to acquire nuclear weapons. Nonetheless, Bonn had to be handled carefully. Kennedy's advisors feared that if German hopes for reunification were challenged by the loss of Berlin, it could push West Germany either to ally with the USSR or, more likely, to provoke an attack by the Russians designed to draw NATO into a war. Kennedy instructed Rusk to "Protect our support for the *idea* of self-determination, the *idea* of all-Germany, and the *fact* of viable, protected freedom in West Berlin."[13] West German leaders, especially in Berlin, felt betrayed by the American position and attempted to sabotage negotiations with the Soviets in the spring of 1962, driving "American–West German relations [to] their lowest ebb in post–World War II history," according to one historian.[14]

Framing the Cold War: Through Berlin's Eyes

This uncertain policy environment helps to explain the documentary's framing of the Berlin crisis and the State Department's surprisingly negative reaction to the report. *The Tunnel* viewed one of the most significant crises of the Cold War not simply from the standpoint of the West, or of the United States, but of Berlin. In the report, the problem was not managing superpower rivalry without war but the wall's harsh division of the city's families and friends. The cause of this division was traced to East Germany's repression of its people, which was largely unexplained, and their desire for freedom, which was mainly construed as freedom of movement and association (rather than desire for political freedom or economic reasons for crossing to the West). The solution was to aid individuals in their escape. This highly localized and personalized frame came from the producers' decision to focus tightly on the students' tunnel project rather than the surrounding policy context. The producers likely did so in part because they had exclusive access to a dramatic story that many journalists wanted, and NBC had paid to get it. But focusing on the tunnel made political sense for the journalists as well. As NBC's regular Berlin correspondent, Anderton could not have been unaware of West German resentment of the United States for accepting the wall, which was expressed in German newspapers as well as on the streets of Berlin. Framing Berlin as a policy problem could not have avoided discussion of this anger, which would have been a good deal more likely to have alienated American policy makers and viewers than the paean to freedom that *The Tunnel* became.

The report's moral treatment of its subjects was very much in keeping with American World War II and Cold War propaganda. When the documentary contrasted the two Berlins, it depicted the West through images of children playing and bustling sidewalks filled with shoppers, accompanied by upbeat music. "But the eastern sidewalk is blighted by the wall," said Anderton, over somber music and images of overgrown grass and guards "who shoot to kill." On one side sat the vibrant, capitalist West and on the other the repressive, communist slums. Because the report restricted its field of vision to the wall and what could be seen from its western side with a telephoto lens, the Vopos provided its villainous symbols of repression rather than the East German or Soviet policy makers who stationed them there. The guards were shown holding their guns grimly, framed through barbed wire, patrolling the other side of the Iron Curtain. They were shown in close-ups of their black boots striding across the pavement, reminiscent of images of marching German troops during the Second World War, as heirs to the Nazi past. The victimized East Berliners appeared in profiles of escapees who had been killed trying to cross the wall and the potent symbol of brutality of the young student left to die at the base of the wall.

By contrast, the student engineers and their tunnel epitomized the West's technological prowess, work ethic, and youthful innocence—frequent themes of American propaganda in the 1950s.[15] Producer Frank explained that the report's extensive attention to the construction of the tunnel had aimed to show the students' commitment during hard, monotonous months of work.[16] One sequence showed the diggers fighting to save the tunnel from flooding after a water-main break. Anderton spoke of "mud everywhere, like war; fungus from wet clothes, like war." One of the Italian project leaders then became a kind of "casualty" when Anderton followed the war similes with the description of the student being rushed to the hospital (albeit to have his appendix removed). The many shots inside the dark tunnel itself connected the students' efforts with those of World War II resistance fighters in the sewers of Warsaw and other European cities.

For Americans squeezing into fallout shelters during practice drills for a nuclear attack, the tunnel may have had a different resonance. Frank wrote that "living close to such attractive, dedicated young people," the reporters "strained . . . to hold strictly to their roles as disinterested onlookers."[17] Indeed, the report declined to include the less-than-heroic moments in the students' work. Fearful that one of the diggers was a spy, they held him under armed guard until the escape was over. In the aftermath, the diggers argued publicly over whether their leaders had kept some of the money that NBC gave them to build the tunnel. Instead of portraying any of this, the reporters arranged

NBC reporter Piers Anderton (*left*) and camera operator Peter Dehmel (*right*) confer with a student leader of the digging under the Berlin Wall, captured in *The Tunnel*. From A. William Bluem, *Documentary in American Television* (New York: Hastings House Publishers, 1965), 143.

the restaurant party shown at the end of the documentary, presenting a happy reunion of the group for the camera despite the friction within it.[18]

Reaction and Impact: Controlling the Fallout from Berlin and Cuba

The State Department moved to keep *The Tunnel* off the air shortly after it learned about the project in October 1962. NBC president Robert E. Kintner recalled the controversy as "NBC's worst encounter with the government," adding that the State Department pressure was "unremitting for a month."[19] The State Department objected that airing the report would be "irresponsible" and "not in the national interest" because it "would complicate the Berlin situation."[20] According to Frank, when Secretary of State Dean Rusk met with him and NBC News president William R. McAndrew to ask them to shelve the film, Rusk said that had the tunnel been compromised, it would have been embarrassing if the East Germans had found American journalists in it.[21] NBC decided not to air the report in October. Frank later accused Kintner of pulling the documentary for fear that offending the administration would jeopardize parent company RCA's military contracts, and the producer resigned. McAndrew convinced Frank to wait until tensions abated, and NBC decided to air the report on December 10.

Why did the State Department attempt to curb a documentary that so effectively advanced America's Cold War ideological framing of communism? Kintner and Frank suggest several reasons. First, Kintner notes that the department claimed the West Berlin city council protested the film. But he writes that the Germans were only concerned that the report not reveal the identities of any refugees against their will, which might have left family members still in East Berlin vulnerable to reprisal. Once NBC showed that the film would not do so, in mid-October, the West German and West Berlin governments publicly endorsed airing the report.[22] Frank raises media jealousy and State Department embarrassment as possible reasons. He notes that rival journalists in Berlin tipped off the State Department to NBC's involvement in the tunnel and that CBS quit its similar project at the department's request. Thus, the department was unhappy that NBC had ignored its authority and was determined to show that such behavior would not be rewarded with an exclusive story. Recognizing that there was likely a larger explanation for the extraordinary pressure on NBC than media politics, Frank also suggests that the department was protecting intelligence sources. He says thirty people came through the tunnel the day before it flooded who were not known to the diggers and speculates that they were American or German spies "coming in from the cold." This would explain why Rusk was concerned that their faces be blacked out on the film and why the State Department dropped its opposition to the documentary when it found that NBC had no footage of these people.[23]

However, the larger political context offers perhaps the most compelling reasons why the State Department wanted to keep the report under wraps. If *The Tunnel* fit American Cold War ideology, it exceeded the administration's policy frame in Berlin. In October 1962, Cold War tensions reached their apex as the administration faced not only the lingering crisis in Berlin but the discovery of Russian missile sites in Cuba. The report might not simply have been seen as NBC's humiliating the USSR at this sensitive time. If the Soviets perceived the American network's extraordinary involvement in the story as supported or encouraged by the administration, the Soviets might have added the incident to a list of actions that could be presented as disturbing the fragile status quo in Berlin. On the domestic front, the administration had little reason to be enthusiastic about a documentary that not only appealed for sympathy for Berliners but might have elicited stronger demands for action against the wall than Kennedy was prepared to take. This was a real possibility during a midterm election season in which Republicans continually attacked the administration's response to the Soviets in Berlin and Cuba as soft on Communist aggression. These attacks resonated widely in the press before journalists rallied round the president during the late October missile crisis.[24] Furthermore, both superpower leaders saw the Berlin and Cuba crises as linked. Soviet diplomats hinted that trading their Cuban missile presence for total control of Berlin was a possible solution. Even if Kennedy did not seriously consider this option, he feared that an attack on Cuba would spark a Soviet takeover of Berlin and that European allies would denounce the United States for sacrificing their interests.[25] At this moment, before the Republicans and the press quieted their criticism and the Soviets backed down and withdrew their missiles, there was little for the Kennedy administration to celebrate in a report that stirred public passion against Soviet control of Berlin.

After it finally aired, *The Tunnel* was received triumphantly in the United States, but it had no further effect on the Berlin situation. Thanks in part to the State Department's advance publicity and public attention to international affairs after the missile crisis, *The Tunnel* beat *I Love Lucy* in the ratings and won an Emmy for Program of the Year. Murrow's USIA distributed it internationally as a testament to the repressive nature of communism. Unsurprisingly, the USIA version did not mention U.S. government attempts to suppress the report. Kennedy traveled to Berlin in 1963 to deliver his famous "I am a Berliner" speech, declaring solidarity with the city's people but not committing the U.S. to any policy change toward the wall. The following year, the West German government withdrew support for the tunnel projects as too provocative after an incident in which tunnelers killed a Vopo who discovered them on the eastern side of the wall. The East Germans demolished more buildings on their side of the divide, creating a no-man's-land too long to dig beneath. And the wall stood for almost thirty years.

Journalistic Adventurism: *Project Nassau*

In 1966, CBS journalists injected themselves even deeper into the conduct of foreign policy than NBC had done in Berlin, helping to fund a secret, ill-fated plot to invade Haiti and Cuba. CBS spent over eight months documenting and paying Haitian and Cuban exiles in the United States who planned to depose the government of Jean Claude "Papa Doc" Duvalier and then launch a subsequent invasion of Cuba to unseat Fidel Castro. CBS dropped the report, entitled *Project Nassau,* when, according to CBS executives, they began to suspect that the exiles were staging scenes for the cameras and simply trying to extract money from the network. The plotters were arrested in Florida in early 1967 and convicted of violating the Neutrality Act and arms smuggling laws. This documentary that never aired eventually became one of several reports investigated by Representative Harley O. Staggers (D-W.Va.), chair of the House Interstate and Foreign Commerce Committee and of its Subcommittee on Investigations.[26]

Although CBS never produced a finished report, the Staggers subcommittee subpoenaed a draft version almost thirty minutes long, which indicates some of what the documentary covered.[27] The draft began with an interview of three conspirators—a former Haitian colonel, a former Haitian minister of education, and a Cuban priest—in a New York apartment discussing their plans to assassinate Duvalier, who was shown in interspersed clips. The next sequence described how arms smugglers connected to the plot transported weapons between safe houses. Mitchell WerBell III, a Georgia arms dealer who presented himself as a leader of the invasion team, narrated footage of arms being packed and trucked between houses in the area of Miami, Florida. Interviews with the plotters followed, including one with Rolando Masferrer Rojas, a Cuban exile and a leader of the invasion effort, wearing pantyhose on his face as a disguise. CBS producer Jay McMullen asked Masferrer whether such a large arms cache could be purchased and exported from the United States without government knowledge. Masferrer said the government might know about the arms, "but our general ends of fighting dictatorship in the Caribbean agrees with the general known policies of the United States government." Over images of a speedboat being pulled on a trailer, WerBell said the weapons would be transferred from this craft to a "mother ship" at sea before the invasion. The report then stepped back in time, showing guns loaded into the speedboat at WerBell's Georgia farm for transport to a Florida yacht club where WerBell described the main ship to be used in the invasion. In interviews, a former Haitian official said the U.S. government divided over whether to support exiles like himself in taking up arms against the Duvalier regime while the Haitian leader of the plot, Father Jean Baptiste Georges, said that the United States was "rather sympathetic" to his efforts. A military training sequence set in rural Florida followed, in which a former marine sergeant drilled the would-be invaders in riflery. One soldier's rifle exploded, and he was shown being taken to the hospital with a severe eye injury. Father Georges spoke of his prior attempts to invade Haiti. Interviews with the soldiers described the aircraft they would fly in this attempt. A pilot, asked whether he had seen any evidence that the U.S. government disagreed with the invasion, said he had not, and in a final interview Masferrer claimed twenty of his men were CIA agents.

Context, Sources, and Framing: U.S. Foreign Policy in the Caribbean

CBS stumbled into ambiguous U.S. policy toward Cuba and Haiti at the time. In Cuba, the Kennedy administration's failed attempts to overthrow Fidel Castro through the Bay of Pigs invasion and covert assassination plots had come and gone. Sensing the building opposition to Duvalier's bloody rule in Haiti, the Kennedy administration cut off military and economic aid in 1963. This aid flowed heavily to the Duvalier government until the early 1960s to prevent communist infiltration, secure Haitian support for U.S. policy in international organizations, and protect American citizens and property in Haiti.[28] Relations with Haiti thawed slightly under President Johnson, but the CIA continued to help groups trying to unseat Duvalier in part because the country remained a strategic launching point for invading Cuba. Haitian and Cuban exiles made alliances in a number of invasion schemes in the 1960s, at least a half a dozen supported by the CIA.[29] In addition, arms smuggling by exiles from both countries set U.S. government agencies at odds. The State Department backed federal prosecutors in indicting a group responsible for smuggling war planes from the United States to Haiti in 1964, but the case was dropped apparently because the CIA protected a former agent who had been involved.[30]

CBS's sources and journalists reflected the uncertainty about clandestine American policy toward the Caribbean. Masferrer, the military leader of the invasion, had been a senator, publisher, and captain of a feared private army in pre-Castro Cuba and was a veteran of several fruitless attempts to invade Cuba. WerBell had worked for the OSS, the CIA's forerunner agency during World War II, and was an international arms merchant with a network of Latin American contacts. Both repeatedly implied to CBS that they had CIA backing.[31] Masferrer and Georges later claimed to have met with President Johnson's Latin America expert on the National Security Council and received his approval of the invasion.[32] Most of the journalists who worked on the report, including several freelancers, also briefed government agencies on the exiles' activities at the same time, speaking with the CIA, FBI, the White House, and the Customs Bureau. It is not clear whether the journalists did so to inform the authorities of the invasion and their role in it, as the journalists later claimed, or to protect themselves from charges of having concealed illegalities and test whether the plot enjoyed federal government support, as the House investigators generally interpreted these overtures.[33]

The CBS draft report also framed the invasion ambiguously. Certainly, McMullen took pains to present evidence of government support for the coup through the claims of Masferrer, Georges, and others. If true, these revelations would have been embarrassing for American foreign policy, which publicly denied fostering unrest in the Caribbean. Much of the draft documented the mechanics of gunrunning, reflecting McMullen's original interest in this topic before he learned about the invasion plot. But the draft does not indicate whether the main problem presented would have been illegal arms smuggling or the Haitian and Cuban regimes. There was no historical context given on either regime that might have framed the causes or justice of the plotters' efforts, and it is unclear whether the exiles would have been shown as heroes or outlaws.

Reaction: The Courts and House Probe

CBS's adventure collapsed into a mire of prosecutions and congressional hearings into the journalists' conduct. The man injured in the riflery training incident sued the network for damages, claiming to have been hurt while employed by CBS, as the network was helping to finance the operation. CBS settled the case out of court, paying the man $15,000.[34] The Justice Department successfully prosecuted the coup leaders for violating the Neutrality and Munitions Control Acts. The CBS reporters were not included in the case because prosecutors decided there was insufficient evidence of their guilt.[35] The question of whether the coup was initially supported or tolerated by the United States was never answered satisfactorily. In the aftermath, the CIA predictably denied any connection to WerBell, and he to it. Yet the Justice

Department mysteriously dropped him from its case against the plotters, refusing to say why publicly. At least one account of the case suggests that the CIA intervened to protect him and that the Justice Department had a policy at the time of allowing the agency to block prosecutions of intelligence assets on national security grounds.[36]

Representative Staggers's House subcommittee investigated the incident in 1969–70 as part of a series of probes into television investigative reporting practices. The subcommittee held seven lengthy and secret hearings, justifying their closure to the public as protecting CBS's credibility and ongoing court proceedings from undue impact, although national security may also have been a concern.[37] The subcommittee concluded that CBS had staged the military training exercise and some scenes of arms smuggling for the cameras. The probe found that the network had injected several thousand dollars into the conspiracy that assisted in illegal arms shipments. According to the subcommittee, the journalists paid the plotters for access and provided them with equipment, such as the boat to be used in the invasion shown in the CBS draft of the report. The House report noted that CBS hired WerBell as a "consultant" on the project with knowledge that he was procuring arms for the group and gave him $1,500 to go to the Dominican Republic and ask his military contacts for permission to site a base for the invasion there. The subcommittee also accused the network of failing to notify federal authorities about the impending coup.[38] Staggers and his colleagues concluded that legislation was necessary to "protect the public against falsification and deception in the preparation and presentation of purportedly bona fide news programming, and . . . prohibit the practice of news media involvement in criminal activities."[39] An additional statement signed by nine representatives called on Congress to regulate network news immediately and for the FCC, when it considered whether to renew the licenses of CBS's owned-and-operated stations, to consider the network's conduct in this case.[40]

In its defense, CBS argued that its journalists had not authorized any staging, that they learned only later that the plotters had concocted some scenes for the cameras, and that these revelations played a part in the network's decision to cancel the report.[41] CBS maintained that it did not support the coup financially but merely paid the invaders for film rights to their story and costs associated with providing information. The network also maintained that its contacts with government agencies during the course of the project led it to believe that the authorities knew of the exiles' plans and approved of CBS's filming them, "although we could not be certain that all elements of the government were acting in unison." CBS News president Richard Salant wrote to Staggers: "As the story developed, the producer did not know whether he was dealing with a situation involving gun-running, an attempted invasion of Haiti which the United States government knew about and approved, an attempted invasion about which the government knew and would stop, or a group of people who had no intention of even attempting to invade but were merely raising funds from the refugee communities under the false promise of 'freeing' their homeland." Regardless of the nature of the operation, CBS asserted that it had a right to cover illegal events. Salant wrote that "Investigatory journalism is a vital function of a free press and of a free society," and that this included "reports on flouting of the law."

The FCC responded to Staggers's request for comments on the House probe, taking little action.[42] The commission said it requested CBS's policy on supervising investigative journalism projects and asked whether the network would institute changes as a result of the House inquiry. In particular, the FCC asked whether the network had devised a policy on notifying government officials of its activities when they involved covering lawbreaking. But the FCC waited almost eighteen months to respond to Staggers. In the interim, CBS had already revised its guidelines in response to Staggers's probe of *The Selling of the Pentagon*. The commission declared itself satisfied with these revisions as long as they were properly implemented. The FCC also noted that because the program was never aired, it did not raise concerns about deceiving the public. The commission noted that CBS personnel had notified authorities about the invasion, although it admitted that the most forthcoming of them were a freelancer and a cameraman, who was reprimanded by CBS for notifying the Customs Bureau without telling the network.

Whether CBS was duped by a ragtag army or by the government, the network's problems in relation to *Project Nassau* came not only from its questionable news-gathering ethics but also from its remarkable closeness to a story that touched on U.S. interests in the Caribbean. CBS's drive for an exclusive behind-the-scenes account of a coup was attacked as an intrusion on government prerogatives to conduct foreign policy. It is not clear that the report would have challenged that policy or merely documented what the network thought, or hoped, was a government-approved invasion. It is clear that CBS did more than make arm's-length payments for "film rights," contradicting its own prior public relations on this issue. During the controversy over whether or not to air *The Tunnel*, CBS sources noted that NBC had given money to the West German diggers they were covering and claimed that their network would never pay for news in this way.[43]

Military Propaganda and Vietnam: *The Selling of the Pentagon*

In contrast to *The Tunnel* and *Project Nassau*, the *CBS Reports* February 23, 1971, documentary, *The Selling of the Pentagon*, directly attacked an aspect of Cold War foreign policy, although it did so mainly by focusing on its domestic impact. The report's objections to military public relations as wasteful and deceptive drew heavy criticism from the Nixon administration, the Department of Defense, and many members of Congress. In response to the documentary, Congressman Staggers's subcommittee launched a punitive investigation of television news editing practices, charging CBS with deceiving the public by misrepresenting statements by two military spokesmen. When network president Frank Stanton refused to release subpoenaed materials related to the documentary to Staggers's investigators, Stanton narrowly escaped being found in contempt of Congress and possibly jailed. Needless to say, this was a remarkable moment in the recent history of U.S. government–media relations. Most accounts inaccurately portray the battle over *Selling of the Pentagon* as a simple First Amendment struggle between government and an adversarial news media aggressively playing the watchdog on government abuses.[44] Indeed, the controversy has become a central example for those who characterize the late 1960s and early 1970s as a time of intense conflict between press and state. In reality, neither the media nor the government were unified in their response to the documentary. Rather, opinions clashed within both institutions at a time of conflict over the Vietnam War, First Amendment issues, and the growing power of television news.

Produced by Peter Davis and narrated by Roger Mudd, the report was structured as a three-part exposé of Pentagon public relations techniques. Part 1 presented the range of direct contacts between the Pentagon and the American public, estimating the costs to taxpayers and the number of citizens exposed to military public relations. Public weapons displays were represented by footage from a parade and a firepower presentation at Fort Jackson, South Carolina, where boys enthusiastically imitated the soldiers, riding tanks and pretending to fire weapons. Mudd noted that an Army public relations officer estimated the display's price tag at $22,000, but a weapons officer put it at $2 million. Public lectures to church and civic groups by several traveling colonels were excerpted, revealing them discussing foreign policy implications of the war in Indochina, a violation of Army regulations. A shopping mall display in St. Paul, Minnesota, exemplified the Pentagon's use of traveling exhibits. Although the Army claimed only to provide these on request, the mall manager told reporters he was approached first by a local recruiter. Other examples included aerial displays by the Air Force Thunderbirds, which Mudd characterized as "an elaborate commercial for air power," and a Green Beret demonstration of hand-to-hand combat, followed by footage of children imitating the marines' fighting. Finally, the cameras followed along on a special VIP tour of the latest weapons, arranged for specially invited "major taxpayers" by the Pentagon's Joint Civilian Orientation Conference. In interviews, these "influential citizens" told how impressed they were with the military, and Mudd told viewers that the civilians were allowed to fire weapons, which "CBS was not permitted to film." Throughout the first section, CBS showed that Defense Department public relations techniques violated official regulations, were expensive and widespread, and that they aggressively militarized American culture.

Part two scrutinized the Pentagon's film library. Mudd began by noting that although the Defense Department claimed to eschew propaganda, its stridently anticommunist films told a different story, including its most recent efforts "made after the thaw in Cold War politics." After summarizing the costs and reach of these films, Mudd went on to explore the connections between Hollywood and the Pentagon. Stars such as Jack Webb, Robert Stack, and John Wayne were shown narrating excerpts from anticommunist films, and Pentagon cooperation in making promilitary features such as Wayne's *The Green Berets* was detailed. The use of journalists as narrators in these films was also revealed through clips of NBC anchor Chet Huntley and CBS's own anchor, Walter Cronkite. Viewers saw a particularly lengthy excerpt from *Red Nightmare*, a Pentagon fiction film that depicted a Soviet takeover of a small American town and the conversion of the populace into quasi-robotic communists. Mudd summarized the case against the films as perpetuating an outdated Cold War image of expansionist, monolithic communism. "It has been more than a decade since the national policy of peaceful coexistence replaced the harsher rhetoric of early Cold War years," said Mudd. Yet for Pentagon filmmakers, he added, "1946 seems to have lasted a generation."

Defense Department manipulation of the news media was the focus of part three. Mudd characterized news as "the widest, most penetrating of all contacts the Pentagon has with the public." At a Pentagon press briefing, a military spokesman was shown dodging reporters' questions. National security reporters and former Pentagon public information officer Jack Tolbert discussed the obstacles to covering the military: reporters' inability to establish alternative sources, the vast size and resources of the Defense Department, and the lack of demand by media managers and executives for critical coverage of military issues. *Washington Post* reporter George Wilson maintained that only public scrutiny of nuclear weapons systems "can keep technology from running us right onto the road to Armageddon, and I think that points

Selling of the Pentagon criticized Defense Department propaganda films such as
Red Nightmare, narrated by *Dragnet* star Jack Webb.

up why more coverage of the Pentagon is desirable." A Mudd interview with
Assistant Secretary of Defense Daniel Henkin concluded with a dispute over
who was more responsible for staging the news—the media or the military.
The Pentagon's Hometown News Center was shown blanketing the local media with the military's side of the story, in part by helping sympathetic congressional figures to make TV reports for stations in their districts. Sergeant
Thomas Demitor, a Defense Department cameraman, told how he helped
stage television footage for the news media, including a misleading report
suggesting South Vietnamese patrols were replacing U.S. soldiers in the field
as part of the Nixon administration's declared policy of "Vietnamizing" the
war. Mudd dissected daily Saigon press briefings, the infamous "Five O'clock
Follies," debunking the military-speak used there by translating terms such as
"protective reaction" and "defoliation." Tolbert returned to say that the war
would have been impossible without public relations. Mudd's wrap-up noted
that the documentary had presented "only a fraction" of the military's public
relations apparatus, which showed little sign of curbing its excesses despite a
Nixon administration directive to cut back on nonessential public relations.

Context, Sources, and Framing: The Cold War and Vietnam

By the early 1970s, the Johnson and Nixon administrations had pursued a two-track strategy aimed at thawing relations with the USSR, and more quietly with China, yet avoiding a humiliating defeat in Vietnam, where American forces had bogged down in intractable conflict. The first track reduced the likelihood of nuclear confrontation between the superpowers through arms control. The second, less successful, had destroyed Johnson's resolve to seek reelection and divided American elites. The Tet offensive and other setbacks raised questions about whether the war was as winnable as the military and the Johnson administration had promised. Some foreign policy and business elites, most notably Senator J. William Fulbright's Senate Foreign Relations Committee and some of President Johnson's closest advisors, grew disillusioned with the war's economic and political costs.[45] Popular protest spread from the New Left to the moderate "moratorium" wing of the antiwar movement.

Because CBS's critique of Pentagon propaganda emerged at the height of differences over the Vietnam War and because of the propaganda's apparent contradiction with pursuing détente in the Cold War, it makes sense to understand the network's framing of the subject with reference to the Vietnam conflict. Policy hawks construed the problems of the war as checking the spread of communism, demonstrating American resolve to protect national security, and overcoming weak-kneed and isolationist tendencies at home.[46] For hawks, lack of commitment to win in Vietnam was caused by the rising critical culture of the 1960s, especially as that culture infected the news media. Journalists undermined the war effort by violating military restrictions on battlefield coverage, televising casualties on a nightly basis, amplifying the message of antiwar protesters, and sabotaging diplomatic initiatives by leaking dissenting government views and splitting public opinion. Hawks drew on the moral language of the early Cold War, portraying communism as inherently expansionist, godless, and repressive and policy doves as naive, unpatriotic, or weak-willed dupes. Policy makers, hawks argued, should increase the war effort, restrict media access to information, and suppress domestic dissent.

By contrast, radical war critics, such as the New Left, saw the problem of Vietnam as American intervention in a civil war on the side of an illegitimate government. The causes were American imperialism and anticommunism, driven by the needs of the military-industrial complex and of multinational corporations for cheap labor, raw materials, and markets. The news media supported the war effort by staying too close to the views of official sources prosecuting the war, swallowing misinformation whole or balancing plausible evidence of American failure and culpability with pro-war propaganda. In this view, the primary villains were the national security state and the defense industries, abetted by the mainstream news media. The main victims were the Vietnamese. Policy responses ranged from shutting down the war effort through protest to revolutionary transformation of American capitalism and imperialism.[47]

Moderate war critics offered a third frame.[48] For them, the problems were that the United States was expending too much American money and blood in a country that had little bearing on national security. The war was being waged unsuccessfully, guided by an ineffective and incoherent policy. The causes were the Pentagon's and president's unchecked power and their deception of American citizens to save face in a fruitless war. Mainstream doves tended to emphasize the war's moral costs at home in weakening democratic control of foreign policy, sapping funds from social programs, sparking violent clashes between protesters and police, and celebrating aggression. Vietnam, said Senator Fulbright, was "poisoning and brutalizing our domestic life."[49] Mainstream policy solutions included a negotiated truce in Vietnam, full pursuit of détente with the USSR and China, reducing the defense budget, and curtailing the powers of the president and Pentagon to make war without congressional approval.

The most careful studies of Vietnam coverage suggest that the news media as a whole took their cues on framing the war from political and economic elites and that substantial dissent in Congress, the military, and the executive branch were preconditions for critical media reporting. Thus, news reports rarely expressed skepticism about the war effort during the buildup of American forces from 1960 to 1967, when the Kennedy and Johnson administrations were united behind the effort and congressional acceptance of the conflict was at its height. However, several of these studies have shown how the news media began to include antiwar frames after 1967, giving more favorable coverage to moderate critics and legitimating other sources besides administration officials.[50] Congress's reassertion of its role in foreign policy may have been most important to the tenor of news coverage, offering journalists regular dissent by official sources of opposition.[51] By the time CBS began work on *The Selling of the Pentagon,* the Senate had passed two amendments aimed at stopping the Nixon administration from increasing U.S. involvement by prohibiting the use of American ground combat forces in Cambodia, Laos, and Thailand. The Senate had narrowly defeated an amendment to cut off funds for the conflict contingent on the return of American prisoners of war.

This post-1967 frame legitimated moderate war critics, not radicals. Todd Gitlin summarized it as, "the war is unsuccessful, perhaps wrong; but ending it is the task of responsible authorities, not radical movements."[52] Daniel Hallin found news coverage in this phase continued to construct the problems raised by the war in technical terms, examining the coherence of policy rather than questioning core Cold War principles such as the rightness of the American foreign policy system and the benevolence of American world leadership. Accounts of the war's impact continued to focus on what it was doing to Americans, not to Southeast Asians. Crucially, the news media often reported with a straight face Nixon administration claims about "Vietnamizing" the war by handing combat duties over to the South Vietnamese Army. Thus the thrust of news reports may have been to normalize the problem of the war, reassuring Americans that "we are on our way out," at a time when the United States was opening up new fronts in Cambodia and Laos and increasing bombing to record levels.[53] Robert Entman and David Paletz argue that during the Nixon phase of the war, the news media often gave "support by omission" when they failed to report evidence that the administration was expanding the fighting even as it claimed to be disengaging.[54]

Most television documentaries appear to have stayed within the confines of these larger framings of the war, failing to realize the greater critical potential of the long-format investigative report. A study of CBS documentaries and news specials on the war from 1965 to 1969 revealed that these programs relied mainly on government and military sources responsible for the war effort until 1968. In that year, the main sources became network correspondents themselves, then congressional and military sources. Throughout the period, CBS documentaries focused heavily on the theme of U.S. foreign policy considerations.[55] A closer textual study of CBS documentaries on the war found that, with a few exceptions, these reports were marked by an ethnocentric concern with the war's impact on U.S. prestige and interests, a view of Vietnam as backward and in need of development by the West, and an absence of moral criticism of the war.[56]

Context, Sources, and Frames: Senator Fulbright Views the Pentagon

Once again, preexisting conflict among policy elites was reflected in *Selling of the Pentagon*. The report drew its statistical portrait of the scope and costs of military public relations from a series of addresses made by Senator Fulbright on the Senate floor in 1969, published a year later as *The Pentagon Propaganda Machine*. CBS also relied on research prepared for a Twentieth Century Fund report by Adam Yarmolinsky.[57] Yarmolinsky had been a special assistant to former secretary of defense Robert McNamara, who had lost faith in the war several years earlier. Although the Pentagon stated its annual public relations budget as $30 million per year, *Selling of the Pentagon* also used Yarmolinsky's estimate of $190 million. When CBS aired a special one-hour follow-up debate on issues raised by the documentary, it invited Yarmolinsky and Fulbright to represent Pentagon critics. The documentary also featured former military employees such as Sergeant Demitor, who told of staging news on the Defense Department's behalf, and Pentagon public information officer Tolbert, who indicted propaganda for prolonging the war. However, despite Mudd's assertion in the opening narration that "We sought . . . no politicians pleading special causes," the CBS report leaned most heavily on Fulbright's views. Although the documentary did not even mention the senator, producer Peter Davis met with Fulbright's staff during the course of his research, and the head of the network's documentary unit at the time later noted that Fulbright's work was the basis for *Selling of the Pentagon*.[58]

CBS closely echoed Fulbright's framing of the problems of Pentagon public relations and the examples he raised.[59] Both CBS and the senator attacked propaganda as wasteful, objecting to the costs of military exhibits mounted at shopping malls, the VIP tours of military bases, and air shows. Both assailed military speaking tours for breaching regulations against soldiers advocating foreign policy positions, and both singled out General Lewis Walt as a prime offender.[60] Both took issue with the militarization of American culture, complaining about Defense Department motion pictures (citing some of the same films) and Pentagon subsidization of feature films made by friendly Hollywood figures (both used Wayne's *The Green Berets* as an example). Both portrayed military public relations as manipulating public opinion through the news media and drew on a legion of common examples. These included Sergeant Demitor's evidence that the military fabricated events for news reports. They included the Pentagon's Hometown News Center and its cooperation with friendly politicians, illustrated by the same example of how the Pentagon had provided Major James Rowe, a hawkish former prisoner of war, for congressional figures to interview for news stories. They included characterizing media managers as too quick to accept military claims and faulting broadcast executives for airing Pentagon films as a cheap way to fulfill their public-service obligations. They included the public relations campaign on behalf of the antiballistic missile system as an example of the military's ability to sell the public and Congress on expensive and unnecessary new weapons. Like the senator, CBS compared the Pentagon's efforts to slick and misleading advertising. *The Selling of the Pentagon* not only repeated the charges made in *The Pentagon Propaganda Machine* but did so in roughly the same order.

The documentary, like Fulbright, portrayed the Vietnam War as an ongoing sales job that posed a danger to the country. In the documentary, Tolbert attributed Americans' consent to embark on the war to Pentagon propagandizing and warned that were the public relations efforts' "pervasiveness to continue, that frankly it could lead us to another Vietnam." Departing from most news coverage at the time, the report undermined Nixon administration claims about Vietnamizing the conflict. There was Sergeant Demitor's story about how he shot footage of a staged South Vietnamese patrol to replace actual combat footage of American troops active in the same area. Demitor admitted the switch "would lead someone to believe that the Vietnamese were doing the majority of the work." There were telltale bits of editing, such as the bridge between the segments about the traveling colonels pitching American involvement in Vietnam and the shopping mall display. Colonel John McNeil defended continuing the American presence in Southeast Asia, saying that when the United States put half a million men in Vietnam, "we placed the national interest at stake when we did that." The next cut was to a close-up of a blinking warning light on a control panel at a shopping mall exhibit that read "Nuclear Attack on the U.S." The administration's claims that it was winding down the war contrasted sharply with the colonels' advocacy and the suggestion that the military was dragging the country to the brink of nuclear conflict—perhaps a reference to rumors that the administration considered using tactical nuclear weapons, which Fulbright publicized.[61] In addition, the report repeatedly undermined hawkish attacks on war critics. An Army colonel who dismissed "the college students" as "sincere" but ignorant of "the history of other things like this" was presented as violating Defense Department policy by "promot[ing] American presence in Southeast Asia" and doing so "at taxpayer's expense." *Dragnet* star Jack Webb's condemnation in an excerpted Defense Department film of youth who "openly advocate abandonment of Vietnam to communism" was framed as part of an outmoded Cold War logic. Mudd dryly noted that the film contained "scenes of war protesters tinted red for emphasis." Major Rowe's attack on peace protesters as the equivalent of the "Viet Cong" was introduced as an example of how the military story got a "free ride" in the local media by using friendly members of Congress, such as the one who interviewed Rowe for his home district television stations. Although antiwar movement spokespeople were not interviewed in the documentary, their attackers were discredited.

CBS also drew on Fulbright's assessment of the causes of military self-promotion. The root of the problem for Fulbright was the "uncontrolled size of the military establishment" and not simply its budget but its growing power in foreign and domestic policy.[62] Similarly, in the CBS report's conclusion, Mudd said, "This propaganda barrage is the creation of a runaway bureaucracy that frustrates attempts to control it." Fulbright also saw misleading propaganda as rooted in the Pentagon's "ideological obsession with communism," which it perceived as monolithic despite friction between the Chinese, Soviets, and North Vietnamese.[63] Likewise, the documentary devoted great attention to how Defense Department films, in their "obsession with monolithic communism," perpetuated an early Cold War image.

The senator and CBS drew on the common moral worldview of moderate antiwar forces. Both presented the military as victimizing Americans, not only by milking them as taxpayers but also by depriving them of sovereignty as citizens. Fulbright argued that democratic values were diminished when the military concealed information in the name of national security and propagandized Americans.[64] CBS took up this theme from the start when Mudd told viewers, "Nothing is more essential to a democracy than the free flow of information. Misinformation, distortion, propaganda all interrupt that flow. They make it impossible for people to know what their government is doing, which, in a democracy, is crucial." In his wrap-up, Mudd suggested that "the news restrictions on the current invasion of Laos raise the question whether the public's right to know is being served or thwarted."

The documentary also expanded on Fulbright's warnings about how "the mindless violence of war has eaten away at our moral values as well as our sensitivity."[65] As in so many poverty documentaries, CBS handled a politically sensitive issue by pointing to its harmful effects on children. In the Fort Jackson sequence, children came to stand in for the "lost innocence" of Americans made mad with killing and the potential for self-destructive violence unleashed by war. The weapons display ended with a grand finale in which soldiers fired off all of their guns to impress the crowd. Mudd noted that it was known as the "mad minute" and added, "It would be hard to argue with that description." Shots of soldiers firing machine guns were intercut with images of children in the crowd covering their ears, some looking frightened. Boys crawled over the tanks used in the demonstration, struggling with each other for the best seat. "Get off," yelled one. "What are you doing?" asked another. "I'm going to shoot you," replied the third. The audience that cheered marines demonstrating hand-to-hand combat was mostly children, who gasped as one soldier was flung at their feet, almost upending several youngsters. The sequence concluded with footage of boys imitating the marines' fighting, until one boy began to cry.

The final image of the documentary was of a young boy peering at the camera through the barrel of a cannon. The VIP tour sequence also raised questions about the celebration of violence. Cigar-smoking men cheered firepower demonstrations from a grandstand as if they were watching a football game and snapped tourist pictures of soldiers arrayed on either side of their

Selling of the Pentagon attacked the military for glamorizing violence by showing children watching, then imitating, a Marine display of hand-to-hand combat.

open car as a military announcer described the components of an infantry battalion. Interviews in which the VIPs attested to their enthusiasm for the demonstrations were repeatedly interrupted by huge blasts from off-screen, eliciting nervous smiles from interviewees. Throughout, the documentary offered visual correlatives to Mudd's portrayal of military violence as "out of control" and therefore dangerous to Americans themselves. Mudd closed by condemning the demonstrations of materiel as "violence made glamorous" and the displays of "expensive weapons advertised as if they were automobiles."

The report departed somewhat from Fulbright's work by devoting more attention to how the news media themselves were victimized by Pentagon manipulation. By presenting the news media as overmatched, CBS avoided the hawks' vision of journalists as potent adversaries of the war or radicals' critique of the media as complicit collaborators. As noted, news media vulnerability to military staging was a central problem posed by the documentary. *The Selling of the Pentagon* thus served as a kind of riposte against charges that television journalists were to blame for faking the news—charges levied against a range of stories, from Morley Safer's 1965 report on the burning of Cam Ne to coverage of the protests outside the 1968 Chicago Democratic Convention to the numerous charges against documentaries. Viewers were encouraged to mistrust military film from the report's opening sequence, which began with a brief montage of war footage, replete with screaming jets, fiery explosions, and medics aiding wounded troops. Mudd then informed viewers that the "battle" they were watching was actually a military exercise held in North Carolina to impress an American audience. Thus, Mudd added, "it was also an exercise in salesmanship—the selling of the Pentagon." The title recalled *The Selling of the President,* Joe McGinnis's 1968 book on the image makers behind the presidential campaigns, signaling viewers to expect the same kind of exposé of public relations mendacity on behalf of the Pentagon. The report then suggested the military's communications power outweighed that of the networks by showing bar graphs comparing the estimated $190 million Pentagon public relations budget to the $146 million spent annually by all three network news departments combined. The report sowed further seeds of doubt about the credibility of military footage, from Sergeant Demitor's admission of staging combat footage to a montage during the VIP tour sequence that showed military photographers taking souvenir pictures of their guests furiously paddling in a boat that was safely beached at the time to Tolbert's story of carefully briefing pilots to ensure that each told reporters that the air war was going well. Eventually, the question of staging sparked a confrontation between Assistant Secretary of Defense Henkin and interviewer Roger Mudd. Henkin said, "There undoubtedly have been times when certain actions have been staged. I think this is true of all TV news coverage; after all, this interview here is being staged . . . props were set up, arrangements were made. You and I did not just walk into this room cold. Arrangements were made for it." Mudd retorted, "Well, we wanted to film in your office but your people said let's go into the studio—so we didn't stage it." This confrontation was the capstone of an argument developed throughout *Selling of the Pentagon* that the military was the most powerful and manipulative news manager.

The report was most careful to present CBS itself as a victim of Pentagon deception. After Tolbert told of briefing the pilots for a network documentary that presented the Pentagon's view of the war "as good as if we had done it ourselves," Mudd said he was "duty bound" to ask which network had been used, and Tolbert replied that it was CBS.

More ticklish was the report's inclusion of a 1962 propaganda film narrated by the network's own anchor, Walter Cronkite. In the film clip, Cronkite warned that "Starting in World War II the aggressive Communist tide has spread in Europe and Asia to engulf its neighbors." This was accompanied by the plodding, ominous music favored by Defense Department filmmakers as

In *Selling of the Pentagon,* CBS anchor Walter Cronkite was shown narrating a Defense Department propaganda film that superimposed Cuban leader Fidel Castro's face on a map of the Caribbean, as Cronkite told viewers that "whiskers do not hide the naked face of dictatorship."

well as the requisite map of Europe showing a red tide advancing westward like blood. "Communist China," Cronkite continued over images of marching soldiers, "even now has plans to dominate Asia by mass murder, destroying ancient civilizations." A Soviet hammer and sickle was then superimposed over the Chinese soldiers. Cronkite and Bill Leonard, who oversaw CBS's documentary unit, initially opposed using the clip, but producer Peter Davis argued successfully that the Defense Department knew that he had requested the footage from its film catalogue and that the Pentagon would exploit the omission of Cronkite to attack the network's credibility.[66] *The Selling of the Pentagon* quickly minimized potential criticism of Cronkite from antiwar critics, while defending his flank against hawks, by saying that he, Huntley, and other journalists "volunteered their talents . . . for patriotic reasons" and that "even though Walter Cronkite and Chet Huntley may now disagree with the intent of the films they narrated, even though the roles of journalist and government spokesman are incompatible, the films grind on and on." Later, journalism and government were restored to their proper roles as adversaries yet fellow loyal Americans when contemporary reporters were shown at a Pentagon briefing. Journalists fired questions at evasive Deputy Assistant Secretary of Defense Jerry Friedheim in what Mudd described as a "formal confrontation" between the press and "a careful and respected adversary." (Ironically, Friedheim, like many Pentagon public affairs personnel, was himself a former journalist and one who returned to the media after his stint at the Pentagon.)

However, the documentary did incorporate Fulbright's suggestion that broadcast executives (not journalists) had at times been too close with the Pentagon, as well as a bit of the radical critique of media complicity. Mudd noted that broadcasting leaders were among the beneficiaries of VIP junkets to inspect military hardware and that "at least 356 commercial and educational television stations have presented [Army propaganda films] as part of their public service broadcast time." Mudd also complained that "over 95 percent of the news bureaus in Washington do not even assign a reporter regularly to the Pentagon. More newsmen cover the pennant race than the arms race." George Wilson of the *Washington Post* then blamed not only the Pentagon for barring access to military news but "the lack of demand from the editors, both of TV and of the newspapers generally." This kind of self-criticism was rare for network television at the time. It acknowledged that institutional priorities shaped news-gathering decisions more than journalists did. If it did not make a clean breast of all kinds of Cold War collaboration between the media and the military, the report suggested media managers and owners contributed to benighting the public by accepting subsidized military misinformation and showing little interest in questioning its accuracy.[67]

If CBS embraced Senator Fulbright's ideological framing of Pentagon public relations, the report declined to propose specific policy solutions. Mudd restricted his closing comments to the Nixon administration's unfulfilled order to curb vaguely described "inappropriate promotional activities." By contrast, Fulbright had called for legislation that would cap Defense Department public relations spending, require regular reporting of Pentagon promotional activities to Congress, eliminate most of the activities described in Fulbright's book and the CBS report, and require the State Department to clear all Pentagon films, speeches, and other materials related to foreign policy. Most of all, Fulbright raised the need for a "central attack on the previously uncontrolled size of the military establishment" and its power.[68] Had CBS been willing to cite its main source, it could have raised the same recommendations, but to do so would have left the documentary open to charges of partisanship. Interestingly, none of CBS's critics in the Congress or the administration would publicly attack the documentary on the grounds that it represented Fulbright's position, perhaps because doing so would have required acknowledging critics' own partisanship on behalf of the Pentagon and the war.

To be sure, CBS did not normalize the problem of military propaganda by suggesting that the authorities were handling the problem. Mudd's wrap-up noted that the Nixon administration had issued a directive to all executive branch departments instructing them to cut unnecessary public relations spending, but that the Pentagon had told CBS it would trim public relations personnel but not activities. "To date," Mudd intoned, "not a single activity shown on this broadcast has been eliminated." He then went on to describe several weapons displays and lectures planned for the next few days. If the Nixon administration was suggested as the legitimate force to curb Pentagon excesses—and it was rather carefully shielded from the broadside against the military—little was being done to solve the problem. It may be said that this was merely a veiled jab at the administration's handling of the problem and one that reinforced the principle of presidential legitimacy and accountability. But to reduce the report to a defense of presidential authority would be to ignore the bulk of Mudd's closing statement and of the documentary as a whole, which built an institutional critique of the military, not the presidency.

In sum, *The Selling of the Pentagon* in some ways pushed the limits of the moderate antiwar frame and network news criticism at the time. The documentary's broad-ranging critique of the many problems raised by military propagandizing on behalf of the Vietnam War, the skepticism about the Vietnamization policy, and the account of Pentagon-media relations exceeded the frames of much wartime coverage. *The Selling of the Pentagon* questioned normally unproblematic beliefs about the soundness of the U.S. foreign policymaking process and the subordination of the military to civilian control. Many reviewers, opponents and defenders of the documentary, would later comment on the power of its portrayal of military promotion as desensitizing Americans to violence. Significantly, much of this moral criticism emerged from montage sequences (of the boys imitating the Green Berets, for example) rather than being stated directly in the narration, and much of it focused on children as the victims. The report admitted some media complicity, by executives, in Pentagon propaganda. Nonetheless, most of the report skillfully illustrated Senator Fulbright's criticisms of the Pentagon, indicating that the report was no simple example of media adversarialism toward government but depended on prior conflict among political elites. The documentary largely relied on the moderate antiwar frame, showing American taxpayers and citizens as the victims of propaganda while ignoring what the selling of the war in America had wrought upon the people of Southeast Asia.[69] Radical antiwar protesters' views were absent. The report offered no controversial policy prescriptions by avoiding any concrete recommendations.

Reaction and Impact: Conflicts over Militarism and TV's First Amendment Rights

Just as elite opinions were divided over the war and the growth of the military-industrial complex in 1971, so they were over media-state relations. These struggles erupted in the controversy over *The Selling of the Pentagon*, generating the most intense and widespread response among government to any of the reports in this study. The significance and complexity of the controversy warrant greater attention than probes into earlier reports. Understanding the struggle over the documentary requires some background on the Nixon administration's jeremiad against the news media as well as close attention to how the administration, the Pentagon, Congress, and the FCC responded to the report.

The administration's attack against what it saw as the liberal establishment news media was already in full swing by the time the report appeared. Although previous administrations had regularly called publishers and network presidents to complain about coverage, this was the first time an administration made an extended public assault on the media as an institution. Daniel Hallin notes that "the political environment during the Nixon years was exactly the kind of environment in which a president is likely to have trouble managing the news."[70] Nixon did not enjoy an elite consensus on foreign policy. His administration was itself divided, pursuing an erratic course of expanding and limiting the war. By the early 1970s, Nixon was advancing a policy of détente toward the Soviet Union and China yet continuing to defend the war in Southeast

Asia in part through the early Cold War framework of deterring the spread of expansionist communism. Because decision making was highly centralized in the White House, even senior policy makers were unsure of where the administration stood, and often they could only participate in debate through the media. Nixon's personal hostility to the news media probably contributed to the administration's hypersensitivity to news coverage, although this reductive "personal grudge" theory has been overemphasized.[71] Nixon was hardly alone in his hostility, especially towards network television. The perceived power of television news, which had become the primary source of news for Americans during the 1960s, made it of special concern to Congress as well and for politicians of both parties, as the *Selling of the Pentagon* investigation made clear.

The administration's offensive against the news media, as has been widely discussed elsewhere, was a multifaceted system of punishments and rewards designed to preserve the deferential attitude of the early Cold War media toward the executive branch.[72] The Nixon FCC made economic strikes on the networks, threatening antitrust investigations, promoting cable television as a competitor to broadcasters, and banning the networks from owning and syndicating most of their prime-time programming. Nixon authorized the wiretapping of his own aides and four news reporters to stem news leaks. Through Vice President Agnew in particular, the administration launched a public relations campaign against "liberal" bias in the media (including organizing letter writing drives to complain of bias), and against "instant analysis" of the president's television addresses by network commentators. The administration tried to organize conservative broadcast affiliates to oppose network news "liberalism" as well. It used the FBI to harass the alternative press by breaking into their offices, destroying materials, and setting fires, and financially hobbled the Public Broadcasting Service as punishment for its perceived leftward tilt. It used exclusive press briefings to punish critical journalists and reward supportive ones. It wined and dined reporters and editors to win their favor and had the Internal Revenue Service audit some who refused to give it. The administration was particularly concerned with television, given its perceived power, and by 1971 CBS was its least favorite network.[73] It was in this tense environment that *The Selling of the Pentagon* emerged, but the administration moved slowly to discredit it since the Defense Department and its congressional supporters took up the sword initially.

Defense Department officials used their considerable powers to build a public relations blitz against CBS. On the evening of the broadcast, the Pentagon made thirty copies of *The Selling of the Pentagon* and distributed them to members of the military who might be able to find fault with it.[74] The

Defense Department quickly issued detailed attacks on CBS's "misrepresen-
tations," from the editing of the interviews with military spokesmen down to
overstating the number of offices in the Pentagon. These were printed in major
newspapers around the country within a week of the first broadcast.[75] The
Defense Department prepared special pamphlets attacking the documentary
and delivered them to every member of the Washington press corps. It issued
a letter to every CBS affiliate attempting to sow their dissension against the
network by pointing to "some very serious allegations against the personnel
of local TV stations" made by a CBS journalist in a radio panel discussion.
The unnamed journalist had said, according to Henkin, that local broadcasters frequently aired Pentagon press releases and films uncritically because
they were "cheap time filler for all those munificent station managers out
there."[76] The Defense Department also hinted it would deny routine forms
of access to CBS News. Defense secretary Melvin Laird refused to submit
to recorded interviews with CBS for some time, and Vietnam correspondent
Morley Safer could not get military interviews and transportation during the
controversy.[77]

Yet even the Pentagon sent mixed signals about how severely the network
ought to be punished. The department's top public relations officers, Jerry
Friedheim and Daniel Henkin, were lukewarm about the public campaign
against the documentary. The day after the broadcast, Friedheim wrote White
House deputy director of communications Jeb Magruder recommending no
further action against CBS.[78] Henkin, whose misquoting in *The Selling of
the Pentagon* became the main focus of the congressional probe, faulted the
documentary's accuracy at a hearing during the congressional investigation.
But he was so reluctant to support the House investigators' probe that one
congressman noted that Henkin was a former journalist and accused him of
"hedg[ing] a little bit for the 'brothers.'"[79] Henkin declined to support the
House subpoena of outtakes and materials used to prepare the documentary or
the eventual contempt citation, citing CBS's First Amendment rights. Henkin
and Friedheim's reluctance may be attributed to their experience as journalists or, more likely, to their understanding that the congressional probe was
unlikely to succeed and might alienate further the reporters they had to face
every day.

Congressman Staggers launched his investigation of the documentary at
the request of House Armed Services Committee chair F. Edward Hébert.[80]
Hébert, who was shown in *The Selling of the Pentagon* interviewing Major
Rowe for a television report aimed at his home district, was incensed at CBS
for representing him as a one of the "sympathetic Congressmen" the Pentagon
used "to counter what it regards as the anti-military tilt of network report-

ing." On April 7, 1971, Staggers went on a fishing expedition, issuing a broad subpoena of all materials related to the documentary, including unused film clips and internal files. He seconded Hébert's complaint to the FCC and asked the commission to investigate whether CBS had violated the fairness doctrine by failing to balance the broadcast's criticism of the Pentagon with sources supportive of Defense Department public relations. Staggers also charged the report with deceptive editing.

The House investigation would eventually center on two interviews with military spokesmen. Using transcripts and a tape of the documentary provided by the Pentagon, Staggers found that pro-war remarks by a Colonel John Mc-Neil had been edited out of sequence. The documentary introduced McNeil's statements as violating military rules that forbade personnel from speaking about the foreign policy implications of U.S. involvement in Vietnam. McNeil's domino-theory warnings about encroaching Chinese power in Southeast Asia, which were shown to have been assembled from six different points in his speech, had been made to seem continuous by editing them with alternating shots of his audience. Particularly egregious for critics of *The Selling of the Pentagon* was that McNeil was quoting Prime Minister Souvanna Phouma of Laos in several places, but these remarks were presented as the colonel's own words. The second interview, with Assistant Secretary of Defense Henkin, was also attacked for rearranging the sequence of his remarks. Henkin had defended military public affairs as fulfilling the public's right to know about how their money was being spent and about the armed forces' response to drug problems and racial conflicts within the services. Mudd asked whether the sergeants standing next to rockets at state fairs were really passing out information about the military's drug and racial problems. Henkin answered: "No, I didn't—wouldn't limit that to sergeants standing next to any kind of exhibits. I knew—I thought we were discussing speeches and all." In the documentary, Henkin's answer appeared as: "No, I wouldn't limit that to sergeants standing next to any kind of exhibits. Now, there are those who contend that this is propaganda. I do not agree with this."[81] Henkin's ending comment had been spliced on from a previous question, omitting his misunderstanding of Mudd's question. The effect was to make his denial of Pentagon propagandizing appear less than credible since it followed an apparent admission that information about problems in the military was not circulated publicly.

The House subcommittee seized on the two instances of sloppy editing to punish CBS for attacking the Pentagon. Mindful of the political dangers and First Amendment issues raised by his investigation, Staggers maintained that his subcommittee was restricting its inquiry to the "clear, definite, and objectively ascertainable" question of whether "television news documentary programs [are] engaging in factually false and misleading filming and editing practices."[82] There are a number of reasons to doubt Staggers's claim. First, the subcommittee did not need the outtakes it repeatedly subpoenaed to prove that CBS had juggled Henkin and McNeil's statements since the Defense Department had quickly provided House investigators with transcripts of both interviews and a tape of the program. Second, the juggled interviews were a rather thin pretext for a great deal of congressional activity. A glance at the full transcript of Colonel McNeil's speech reveals that CBS's editing was true to the spirit if not the letter of his remarks.[83] If McNeil was citing Souvanna Phouma, he was clearly endorsing Phouma's views. And McNeil himself edited selectively from Phouma. The colonel, quoting from a U.S. News and World Report article, cited Phouma when he warned that the fall of Vietnam to the communists would make it difficult for other Southeast Asian nations to resist them, but he omitted his warning *against* spreading the war into those countries.[84] As for the Henkin interview, it was indeed edited to make him seem even more misleading, but this was little justification for a full congressional probe. Third, the subcommittee claimed it was looking into another documentary as part of a larger probe of news misrepresentation. This was NBC's Say Goodbye, which examined the hunting of endangered species. Yet the House investigators quickly dropped any pretense of probing the documentary after its producers complied with a similar subpoena for outtakes, despite evidence that footage of a polar bear being shot with tranquilizing darts in an effort to tag and track it was represented as a hunting scene. Fourth, during the subcommittee's hearings, members quickly strayed into browbeating CBS representatives about the lack of "balancing" perspectives in TV news generally rather than sticking to their professed interest in whether the Selling of the Pentagon documentary was "factually false."[85]

In response to the subpoenas, CBS refused to supply more than a transcript and a print of The Selling of the Pentagon as broadcast, citing a number of free-speech arguments. The network maintained that the First Amendment applied to broadcast news as well as print and that the subcommittee violated it by attempting to "apply a presumed objective criterion of truth, both to the product of journalism and to the very heart of the journalistic process."[86] The network pointed to the potential "chilling effect" of such direct congressional oversight on the ability of journalists to report on government. CBS also claimed that the subpoena violated reporters' privilege, which offered the print media some legal protection against revealing their confidential sources. CBS likened their outtakes to a print journalist's notes and maintained that divulging them might expose CBS's confidential military sources to reprisals.

CBS's refusal was a response to an unprecedented number of subpoenas served on news organizations in the previous three years. Increasingly, these orders demanded unpublished material such as outtakes. The wave of several hundred subpoenas began with the congressional and judicial probes into the clashes between antiwar protesters and the Chicago police at the 1968 Democratic National Convention. The Department of Justice and others commandeered film, photos, and notes to identify suspects, and congressional investigators demanded the same materials to determine whether the news media had help stage or inspire the protests. Afterwards, prosecutors of the Black Panthers and Weathermen faction of the New Left began demanding media materials to build their cases. Civil liberties groups, journalists, and FCC commissioner Nicholas Johnson faulted the major media for becoming de facto investigatory agents for the government by complying with the subpoenas and for breaking promises of confidentiality to their sources by divulging their identities.[87] A particularly embarrassing moment for CBS came in 1970 when federal agents swept through the newsroom without resistance, seizing confidential materials related to a *60 Minutes* segment on the Black Panthers. Previously, CBS had handed over materials related to two documentaries, *Project Nassau* and *Pot Party at a University,* to the Staggers subcommittee. By February 1970, a number of national news organizations finally began opposing the subpoenas, including *Time, Newsweek,* the *New York Times,* and CBS. Over the course of the year, Attorney General John Mitchell and media organizations negotiated publicly, issuing statements about when it was acceptable to subpoena reporters' notes. When the *Selling of the Pentagon* controversy broke, CBS saw it as an opportunity to squelch future demands for notes and outtakes.

The White House pursued a two-track strategy in relation to the documentary controversy: one public, the other behind-the-scenes. Publicly, administration officials condemned the documentary as deceptive and unpatriotic, yet they appeared to take a limited role in the campaign to investigate it. Vice President Agnew, who had avoided public criticism of the news media since his initial speeches against the "nattering nabobs of negativism" in 1969, took the opportunity to renew his attacks on negative coverage of the military, the elitism of eastern establishment journalists, and television news staging. On March 9, 1971, Agnew told local reporters in New Orleans that the documentary was "a disreputable program" and commended the Pentagon for "defend[ing] the country a lot better than CBS is doing at the present time."[88] On March 18, before a Republican Club audience in Boston, he devoted an entire speech to an extended attack on the credibility of CBS News, focusing on past staging allegations against its documentaries, including *Hunger in America* and *Project Nassau.* He derided *The Selling of the Pentagon* as the latest example of CBS's staging and distortion of the news, and as "a subtle but vicious broadside against the nation's defense establishment."[89] Agnew would continue to tilt at the broadcast in the coming months, allowing Nixon to stay above the fray. However, the administration did not openly pursue the matter further. Nixon declined to support the House investigation publicly, saying at a press conference that he took "a very jaundiced view" of subpoenaing reporters' notes and "of government action which requires the revealing of sources," except when they had information about serious crimes.[90] Nonetheless, National Security Advisor Henry Kissinger told Secretary of Defense Laird that Nixon was pleased with the Pentagon's "outstanding job of dealing with your interrogators" about the charges raised in *The Selling of the Pentagon*.[91] The White House's public strategy allowed Nixon to take a rare stand for press freedom while letting a congressional subcommittee discredit CBS instead. Thus the administration's interests were served both by the House pressure for favorable military reportage and by the White House's ability to appear more tolerant of media criticism than the Democratic Congress.

The administration's public stance may have been influenced by internal conflicts over escalating attacks on the news media. Communications director Herbert Klein claims to have convinced Nixon not to support the subpoena.[92] In a news briefing, Klein repeated Nixon's contention that the administration saw the subpoena as "an infringement on freedom of the press," yet Klein seems to have displeased the president by continuing to weigh in on the side of the media.[93] When Nixon was alerted to Klein's defense of CBS by an item in the confidential daily news summary circulated to the president and top White House staff, he wrote in the margin that Klein "should stay out of it."[94] Foreign policy advisor John Scali, a former ABC correspondent recently hired by the administration, urged the president in a confidential memo to reign in Agnew's assaults, warning that the increasing polarization between the White House and the media would encourage more skeptical reporting of the administration's foreign policy initiatives.[95] Even Patrick Buchanan, who wrote many of Agnew's broadsides against news bias, raised questions about pursuing *The Selling of the Pentagon*. In his daily news summary circulated shortly after the documentary aired, Buchanan noted that "a major counterattack would also serve as fodder for Fulbright, [Senator] Proxmire, et. al., who have been very critical of DOD's PR operations in the past . . . Kids playing with guns and business leaders watching war games are hard to defend—and maybe they shouldn't be, but it's outside my purview to so determine."[96]

Nonetheless, the White House played a larger role than previously known, mainly through behind-the-scenes activities against CBS. Special assistant to the president Charles Colson, the administration's main negotiator with the networks throughout this period, followed the controversy very closely and was the driving force behind a subterranean campaign to discredit the documentary. Colson urged the Defense Department to use the fairness doctrine to demand airtime from CBS for a response to *The Selling of the Pentagon*. In a memo to White House press secretary Ron Ziegler, Colson wrote: "My judgment is that the half-hour could be used very effectively—not only to set the record straight, which is of secondary importance, but also to devastate CBS' reporting techniques, and particularly the credibility/integrity issue . . . We are entirely on solid ground and therefore should not in any way be reluctant to press our case (through the Pentagon, of course)."[97] After an article questioning the documentary's editing techniques appeared in *Air Force* magazine, Colson instructed an assistant to "get all of the other military auxiliaries—Navy League, VFW, etc. to do similar things in their publications."[98] Later, he urged another subordinate to publicize FCC chair Dean Burch's criticisms of *The Selling of the Pentagon* but to "be sure not to have it in anyway traceable back to the White House, and be sure whoever writes the story really sticks it in to CBS as they deserve."[99] Most significantly, Colson sent yet another assistant, Alvin Snyder, to undermine CBS at the National Association of Broadcasters (NAB) Convention in March. Colson later praised Snyder, a former CBS News employee, for helping to write and publicize surprise assaults on network news bias that were inserted into speeches delivered to the NAB by Secretary of Housing and Urban Development George Romney and cartoonist Al Capp. Snyder also circulated an editorial from *Barron's National and Financial Weekly* that concluded that CBS News was so deceptive that it had "forfeited its access to the nation's airwaves."[100] Colson's deputy arranged for tapes of purportedly biased CBS coverage of Laos to be shown to convention attendees and leaked to the press that CBS affiliates were pressuring the network to be less critical in its news coverage of the administration and the war. Most importantly, Colson noted, Snyder did "all of this without getting caught."[101]

The controversy marked the debut of a new and significant source of right-wing attempts at quasi-private regulation of the news media. This was Accuracy in Media (AIM), which emerged in the early 1970s from a study group known as the Council against Communist Aggression and Alexis de Tocqueville Society. AIM's origins and ties to conservatives in government and journalism will be discussed in later chapters. It is enough to note here that *The Selling of the Pentagon* was AIM's first major target, and that the group was welcomed into being by the documentary's opponents in Congress and the conservative media. On March 20, AIM sent a seven-page letter to CBS asking the network to reply to the charges against it and eventually prepared the kind of rebuttal to *The Selling of the Pentagon* that would become characteristic of its later examinations of media content. It was a microscopic analysis of "inaccuracies" in the CBS report, most of which echoed the Pentagon's faultfinding. Hébert later inserted AIM's "Analysis of CBS Answers" to the group's complaints into the *Congressional Record.*[102] Reed Irvine, AIM's chairman, also laid out the case against CBS in the *National Review.*[103]

The FCC followed the White House by refusing to use its regulatory powers yet condemning *The Selling of the Pentagon* and disparaging CBS's credibility. The FCC's deliberations appear to have been contentious, with the three Democratic-appointed commissioners siding firmly with CBS while Nixon appointee and chairman Dean Burch attempted to win the three Republicans' consent for denouncing the network. Among the FCC staff, General Counsel Henry Geller opposed the complaints while William Ray, who led the Broadcast Bureau's Complaints and Compliance Division, recommended a full investigation of the staging charges.[104] In late March, well before the FCC reached its decision, liberal commissioner Nicholas Johnson wrote a syndicated article defending the CBS documentary and excoriating the broader Nixon administration attacks on the news media.[105] Burch rebuked him for commenting publicly on a pending case, and Johnson countered in comments appended to the FCC's ruling. Despite the internecine political struggles, the commission did not appear to consider seriously an investigation of CBS. Instead, the conflict was over whether or not to retain in the final ruling Burch's strong language faulting the network, such as his comments on CBS's "sheer hubris . . . overweening pride and even arrogance that simply will not allow of the possibility that error may have occurred."[106] Burch's accusation, excised by the majority, was later leaked to the news media.[107] In its ruling, the commission rejected a probe as violating broadcasters' First Amendment rights, citing the FCC's prior decisions on complaints spurred by coverage of the 1968 Democratic convention and *Hunger in America,* in which the FCC had decided that it could not "lay down some precise line of factual accuracy" for network journalism.[108] In addition, the decision noted that CBS had not violated the fairness doctrine because it had repeatedly allowed the documentary's critics to respond. The network offered its foes even more reply time than it had during the *Hunger in America* controversy. At the end of a March rebroadcast of *The Selling of the Pentagon,* Agnew, Hébert, and Defense Secretary Laird appeared to express their views (followed by a CBS rebuttal by Salant). The network also aired an hour discussion of the documentary in April featuring two military spokesmen facing off against Yarmolinsky and Fulbright. And CBS devoted an hour of *Face the Nation* to two members of the House Commerce Committee in July, just before the House contempt vote.

On June 29, Staggers's subcommittee voted unanimously to hold CBS president Stanton in contempt of Congress for refusing to provide the subpoenaed outtakes. Although CBS would not publicly admit error, two days later it conveniently issued a revised standards and practices manual for news and sent a copy to every member of the full Commerce Committee, who would be voting on whether to confirm the contempt citation. In it were three new items: (1) if answers are responding to questions other than the immediate one, the broadcast must so indicate in narration; (2) if excerpts from speeches are used out of their original sequence, this must be indicated; (3) transcripts of the entire interview will be made available to the interviewee on request.[109] Nonetheless, the Commerce committee voted 25 to 13 against Stanton and CBS. The citation headed for a full House vote, where a committee's recommendation for contempt had never been overridden before. Stanton would have to hand over the outtakes or face a possible jail sentence. He narrowly escaped this fate when the House voted 226 to 181 to recommit the motion to committee, effectively killing it. Republicans and Democrats voted in about the same proportions on both sides of the issue.

Why did the House break precedent and reject one of its committee's recommendations for contempt? A number of explanations are possible. First, as Senator Fulbright, a few representatives, and CBS itself had argued, no one had disproved the documentary's main thesis, and it found some support in the Congress among those who wanted to cut the Pentagon budget (*The Selling of the Pentagon* is probably the only documentary entered into the *Congressional Record* three times by three different supporters).[110] But defenses of the documentary's accusations grew sparse before the House vote. Of the thirteen Commerce Committee members who signed the minority report, only Robert O. Tiernan (D-R.I.) actually praised the documentary for exposing abuses by the military, in a separate opinion.[111] In the House debate, more than twenty-five representatives rose in opposition to the citation, but only Michael J. Harrington (D-Mass.) spoke favorably of CBS's criticism of the Pentagon. Hastings Keith (R-Mass.), who introduced the motion to recommit the contempt citation, submitted a bill two days later aimed at increasing the FCC's authority to punish broadcasters who willfully deceived the public. Hence, support for the documentary's unmasking of the Pentagon probably does not explain the majority of votes for CBS.

Second, some maintain that a deal was struck between the White House and the network, turning around some Republican votes in exchange for kinder coverage of the president.[112] Stanton would later deny asking the administration for help, but the White House did indeed seem to think that CBS had offered them a deal. The network hired Alexander Lankler, an attorney and chair of the Maryland Republican Party, to negotiate with the White House in the days leading up to the House vote. Colson aide Henry Cashen reported that he had told Lankler that

> the Administration would like to use Lankler as a conduit through which we could get to CBS on those matters which we think important to the country . . . In this regard, Stanton has agreed that if he is aware of what the Administration considers high priority, he will convey this either through himself or Cronkite as important to CBS with the hope that those particular issues will be conveyed in the manner we desire. Obviously there are no blood agreements to the above described, but based upon my conversations with Lankler, CBS has given a very firm commitment that if we can turn the Republicans on the Hill off, they will do whatever possible to deliver based upon *their* initiated offer. Further, they have also indicated that if a particular story surfaces which they deem of extreme importance, they would like to use Lankler to let us know that they are zeroing in on a particular issue, and in this regard, would like to talk to the Administration before the story breaks.[113]

When Stanton met with Colson two days after the vote to offer thanks, Colson pressured him to make sure CBS covered the administration's side of a number of issues, including prisoners of war, the president's popularity ratings, unemployment, and the economy. Colson claimed, "On all of these points Stanton acknowledged that we have been very badly treated. I couldn't get him to argue on a single point."[114] When Colson doubted Stanton's ability to intervene in the news, saying that he couldn't imagine Stanton calling Roger Mudd to correct a report, Stanton allegedly replied, "No, I wouldn't call Roger Mudd, but I would certainly call the President of CBS News and raise hell." In Colson's eyes, CBS did seem kinder to the administration in the near future. A week after his meeting with Stanton, Colson wrote to chief of staff H. R. Haldeman, citing a number of favorable CBS News reports and concluding, "There are some pretty good initial indications that Frank Stanton is in fact delivering on his commitment last week."[115]

This back-room dealing between the administration and CBS is significant because it reveals that the network did not simply resist political pressure and muddies the image of Stanton as a staunch defender of broadcast freedom who stood up to Congress and the White House. This image prevailed in the media at the time and has been inflated in historical accounts written since then.[116] However, the bargaining was not a major reason for the House vote. Colson hardly expected CBS's more favorable stance toward the White House to last long, and he was soon threatening the network in more dire terms for its coverage of administration policy and of the Watergate scandal.[117] More importantly, explaining the House vote as the result of a pact between the White House and CBS is insufficient because both the administration and the House had more significant reasons to avoid the confrontation, and House members were not merely beholden to the president. White House aides themselves suspected that their intervention had little bearing on the House vote but moved to exploit the appearance of helping Stanton to wring better coverage from CBS. On the day after the vote, Colson wrote Haldeman that White House aide Clark MacGregor "is convinced, as am I, that whether we had lifted a finger or not the contempt citation would have been defeated. So I believe we are getting credit for nothing."[118]

The third, and more important, reason for the House vote was an intense lobbying effort mounted by CBS that must have left representatives concerned about risking their own future coverage, especially by their local CBS affiliates, by voting against the network.[119] As the contempt citation moved from a threat to a reality, CBS affiliates and other broadcasters began to fear that it would set a precedent encouraging further investigations into local as well as network news.[120] As an adviser to a top House Democrat wrote in a confidential memo, "the politics of the situation is such that now the Democrats are fighting the networks and the Republican Administration is defending them. I realize that castigating CBS is good politics [in your home state] but nationally it's something else."[121] Several representatives complained that broadcasters in their home districts threatened to try to drive them from office by giving increased coverage to opposing candidates.[122] In the end, the lobbying and the administration's public position discouraged the House leadership from supporting Staggers.

Fourth, and perhaps most importantly, both the White House and Congress had reason to fear that a contempt citation would be overturned in the courts. Just two weeks before the vote, the administration had waged a very strenuous, public, and unsuccessful battle to stop publication of the Pentagon Papers. While the Supreme Court was divided, its decision to allow publication could be seen as signaling judicial support for the First Amendment rights of publishers over government censorship to protect national security. The administration's failure in this case could have been cause enough not to risk losing another public battle with the news media by lobbying the House against CBS. Similarly, the House was influenced by two other recent legal decisions expanding the First Amendment rights of journalists. In a landmark reporters' privilege case, a federal appeals court had upheld the right of *New York Times* journalist Earl Caldwell to refuse a grand jury subpoena of his notes for stories on the Black Panthers, who were then under investigation. The ruling, later reversed by the Supreme Court, suggested that the courts might sympathize with the ability of journalists to withhold their notes on confidential sources and controversial matters from government scrutiny. In addition, the Supreme Court had just issued its *Rosenbloom v. Metromedia* decision, which extended broad protection against libel suits brought by figures involved in matters of public interest. The ruling explicitly applied these protections to broadcasters as well as the print media, suggesting that broadcast news ought to enjoy the same constitutional protections as their counterparts at newspapers and magazines. The legal opinion CBS submitted to Staggers's subcommittee relied heavily on these two cases, as did the minority report of the Commerce Committee, which was cited repeatedly during the full House debate.[123] While the minority report's authors offered no ringing defense of broadcasters' free-speech rights, they feared that *The Selling of the Pentagon* was a weak case to use as a test of Congress's investigative powers over broadcasting. They argued that the contempt citation was unlikely to survive judicial review since the subcommittee did not appear to need the outtakes and its hearings strayed into government oversight of CBS's editorial position. The courts might not only let CBS off the hook in this case but curtail Congress's power to investigate broadcasting. As the minority report warned, "we might lose some of our authority to act properly in the future by acting improperly here."[124]

The more intriguing question may be why so many members of Congress voted *for* the citation, knowing that it could have led to jailing a network president. In the House debate, a decade's worth of frustration with network news poured forth. War supporters agreed with the Cold War rhetoric of critics such as Hébert, who branded *The Selling of the Pentagon* as "un-American." Others appeared to want to punish all the networks for perceived "liberal bias" in coverage of other issues. For southerners, resentment remained over television reporting on the civil rights struggles of the 1960s. John R. Rarick (D-La.) attacked the networks for not defending the free-speech rights of WLBT, the Jackson, Mississippi, station denied a license renewal on the grounds that it "did not program its TV coverage to conform with the racial proportions of the community," in Rarick's words. He also complained of the networks' indifference to the rights of southerners to display the Confederate flag and play "Dixie" on the air.[125] Jack Edwards (R-Ala.), although voting against the contempt citation, decried the way CBS "has maligned the South, colored the news."[126]

If the rhetoric of representatives who spoke out against the networks on the House floor is a fair indicator, the most important reason for their vote against CBS was the fear of unaccountable and powerful networks defining the political landscape. Many wanted to raise a cudgel against television news for depriving politicians of some control over shaping their images and advancing their views to their local constituencies. John H. Dent (D-Pa.) told how he had spent two days before television cameras while working in a glass factory, expecting to have the "starring performance" in a documentary on trade issues, but he was disappointed when he was only briefly featured. Chet Holifield (D-Calif.) complained of two instances in which he was interviewed at length but only briefly shown for documentaries that were "biased" against his views in support of nuclear energy. Henry Gonzalez (D-Texas), who took the opportunity to renew his attacks on CBS's *Hunger in America* for disparaging his home district, expressed this fear of growing network power in passionate if mixed metaphors when he warned that "we live in the world where the baleful eye of CBS reigns with a mighty hand."[127]

In sum, the political reaction to *The Selling of the Pentagon* was not monolithic but divided between supporters and defenders of the war, of the documentary's critique of military public relations, and of broadcasting's First Amendment rights. Perhaps most important, network news critics in the administration and the House differed over tactics as well, as some considered the subcommittee's case against CBS too weak to pass judicial scrutiny. In the end, however, the investigation was successful at diverting congressional attention from the subject of the documentary—the selling of the Pentagon. By investigating CBS's small manipulation of two military spokesmen, the Commerce Committee and the Department of Defense forestalled another possible congressional inquiry—one into how the military manipulated and withheld information. Such an investigation easily could have been appended to a number of ongoing congressional probes of the war effort. Indeed, several members of Congress made inquiries to the Pentagon asking for a reply to CBS's charge that it had ignored Nixon's orders to cut public relations spending.[128] The Government Accounting Office audited the costs of the VIP tour shown in *The Selling of the Pentagon* at the request of one House member and found the tour costs were five times more than the Pentagon had claimed.[129] Yet the inquiries stopped there. Even after the Defense Department had been shown as violating a presidential order, even after the Southeast Asian war had become a political liability for the administration and the Congress, they shared more of an appetite for a full-scale investigation of a news network than of Pentagon public relations.

In the end, the documentary changed little. During the House probe, the Defense Department announced it would review its film catalogue and remove some of its harshest Cold War products and claimed to be cutting the public relations budget. There is little reason to believe that anything was trimmed in response to the documentary, however. By the mid-1970s, the Pentagon put the official costs of public relations at $24 million, a ninefold increase in fifteen years.[130] By the mid-1980s, the admitted budget had grown to $100 million.[131] Both figures are almost certainly understated given the practice of concealing public relations spending under other budget lines, such as "recruiting costs."[132] Nor did the media pay any more attention to the Defense Department. The number of correspondents there on a regular basis remained small in the mid-1970s, with thirty-seven full-time correspondents registered of which only ten to twelve represented the general-circulation media.[133] Since the Vietnam War, the Pentagon's grip over wartime news grew tighter, with the institution of a press pool system during the invasions of Grenada, Panama, the Persian Gulf, and Iraq. The lesson of Vietnam for the military has been to control media criticism of war by restricting access to the battlefield through the press pool system and enforcing stricter censorship via "security reviews" of all reports from the front. The major media, for their part, have not mounted much of a challenge to the new military restrictions during brief, "popular" wars, failing to join in a lawsuit brought by alternative news organizations that challenged these controls during the Persian Gulf War.

CBS and television journalism gained little from the controversy, except perhaps an appreciation for the network's lobbying power. If the affair helped to establish in the minds of some in Congress that television outtakes should have the same First Amendment protections as print journalists' notes, the Supreme Court quickly undermined protections for both when it ruled a year later that reporters had no constitutional right to resist subpoenas.[134] The House vote signaled an unwillingness to intervene too directly in the networks' editing decisions, yet it did not put the matter to rest. In the near future, the networks would be faced with various "truth in news" bills attempting to legislate guidelines for news editing and further hearings on staged news by Staggers's subcommittee. But Staggers's extraordinary attention to television documentaries lessened after his political defeat over *The Selling of the Pentagon,* and the affair probably helped to push him out of his committee chairmanship (as discussed in chapter 6).

At the same time, the Pentagon and congressional pressure seems to have had some chilling effect on the network's news division. CBS's Washington bureau chief admitted fearing that his coverage of the congressional probe would be scrutinized closely, so he ran extended stories on the principal congressional foes and the hearings, carefully editing Staggers's statements to clean up his verbal stumblings.[135] CBS paid a large price for the documentary. *The Selling of the Pentagon* cost $150,000 to make and about $3 million in legal expenses to defend, according to one CBS lawyer.[136] Of CBS's attitude toward the documentary, Peter Davis recalls that "they were eager to do it, proud of it after it was done, and they didn't want to do it again," and he remembers "a kind of chill in the air afterwards . . . for a little while for some people who wanted to be investigating government programs."[137] The affair may help explain why CBS refused to accept a copy of the Pentagon Papers from Daniel Ellsberg, who offered the famous classified study of the origins of Vietnam War policy to the network at the time. Ellsberg claimed that CBS was reluctant to take the papers because it was already embroiled in the House investigation.[138] CBS documentarians did not return to the Defense Department until a September 1974 report, *Peace and the Pentagon*, which concluded that the military's image had improved and military forces "are in much better shape than they were twelve months ago."

✦ ✦ ✦

Controversial Cold War documentaries rarely challenged consensus ideological beliefs about America's right to exercise superpower status or policy positions on which Washington leaders substantially agreed. Rather, these reports ran afoul of government forces for entangling themselves in areas where Congress disputed policy or where officials sent mixed signals about their position. In each case, executive branch rhetoric and covert policy conflicted. Kennedy talked tough on the Berlin Wall but accepted it. Johnson appeared to retract support for overthrowing governments in Cuba and Haiti, yet the CIA continued to support exile incursions. Nixon promised to scale down American involvement in the war in Southeast Asia yet expanded it, and promised to trim Pentagon public relations to little effect. If television journalists reflected government dissensus, they grew more aggressive in documenting it by seeking stories through novel means, including paying foreign policy actors for exclusive access. The growth of investigative reporting on the Cold War is better understood as a shift toward media adventurism, not adversarialism.

Broadcast news critics often attacked reports that turned a critical lens on business's treatment of consumers in the 1960s and early 1970s. The era was marked by a rising consumer politics and a special relationship between the news media and consumer advocates in government, social movements, and the professions. Business moved to protect its image from the challenge of consumerism and media coverage of it. The conflicts that emerged can be seen in the origins, framings, and impacts of the two most heavily investigated muckraking reports on consumer issues: *Banks and the Poor* (PBS, 1970) and *Pensions: The Broken Promise* (NBC, 1972).

The Regeneration of Consumerism

Many observers have remarked on the long-term transition in postwar America from political movements organized around production, principally the labor movement, to those concerned with issues of consumption or quality of life.[1] Although consumer organizations arose to support Progressive era food and drug safety legislation at the turn of the twentieth century and to conduct product testing and campaigns against deceptive advertising in the 1930s, the movement quieted thereafter. Mark Nadel suggests some of the reasons for its revitalization in the 1960s.[2] The marketplace had become increasingly complex, impersonal, and removed from consumer control. Intricate products grew more difficult and costly to repair, prescription drugs became more potent and potentially dangerous, and burgeoning traffic and accidents sent auto insurance rates soaring. Americans increasingly relied on consumer credit, but computerized billing errors undermined credit histories and distanced consumers from human billing clerks. Consumer protection especially attracted Democratic presidential administrations and congressional figures because it offered a set of issues that spoke to middle- and working-class constituencies while being cheaper to implement than environmental controls and the War on Poverty. Finally, consumerism was a potential consensus issue at a time when the Democrats in particular were divided over Vietnam and civil rights. No potential constituency was broader than consumers.

Congress and the executive branch were already discovering consumer issues before Ralph Nader's emergence in the mid-1960s, first as a champion of auto safety regulations, then as the creator of a range of consumer and public-interest law groups from 1968 onward. Indeed, Nader began working on the auto issue as a staff member at the Department of Labor and a consultant to congressional committees. As early as 1962, the Kennedy administration appointed a Consumer Advisory Council, and Congress passed significant safety amendments to the Food and Drug Act. From 1965 onward, when Lyndon Johnson made consumer protection a major part of his legislative program, presidents legitimated the issue through annual messages to Congress endorsing and proposing new consumer legislation. Congressional activity on consumer issues during this decade peaked between 1966 and 1968 with the passage of major laws on auto safety, meat inspection, fair packaging, and truth in lending. In short, the turn toward a politics of consumerism was already evident within the federal government, and among political elites themselves, prior to the rebuilding of a broader consumer movement.[3]

By the late 1960s, a loose, mainstream, liberal coalition had built around consumer interests. It included northern Democrats, especially a handful of activist policy entrepreneurs in the Senate, and their counterparts at the state and local levels. The consumer coalition included Ralph Nader's public-interest law groups and citizens' organizations, which were supported not only by major foundations but also by the pro bono activities of large mainstream law firms. The coalition included older organizations such as Consumers Union and the groups that gathered under the umbrella of the Consumer Federation of America (CFA) in 1967. Organized labor played an important role. The AFL-CIO often provided research and lobbying in support of consumer interests, and several of its member unions were active in forming the CFA. "Until 1970," Nadel notes, "there was no important issue on which the primary consumer groups and the unions were divided."[4] Civil rights and antipoverty advocates turned toward consumer issues toward the end of the 1960s as they confronted the causes of economic inequality in the exploitation of ghetto residents by merchants and credit providers, who were frequent targets of black rage during the urban riots of the decade.[5] By the end of the 1960s, the courts became more receptive to tort suits brought against businesses for a range of offenses against consumers, and a variety of legal decisions expanded consumers' ability to bring class-action suits.[6]

The political appeal of consumerism also depended on its initial address to a mainly middle-class constituency and its low costs to business.[7] Most of the legislation that passed in the 1960s conferred collective benefits, dealing with aspects of consumption that affected a broad strata of consumers relatively equally. Provisions that might have benefited the poor disproportionately or that substantially shifted power from sellers to buyers rarely survived in the final versions of bills. This was despite the greater needs of low-income households for consumer protection, given that they were likely to pay more for basic goods and services, were more susceptible to fraud, and could least afford it.[8] Health and safety provisions, such as those imposed on the auto and drug industries, protected all buyers of these products without reducing prices. The costs of such legislation to business were low and easily passed on to consumers because regulations usually applied similarly across an entire industry. Indeed, to the extent that purchasers absorbed the costs of regulation through higher prices, the poor paid a regressive "tax" for increased safety. Nor did most consumer laws significantly alter power relationships between corporations and consumers, as there were few criminal sanctions for corporate violators.

Consumerism, the Media, and Business

Consumer politics held a special legitimacy and appeal for the news media. Most importantly, official Washington had signaled that consumerism was within the pale of acceptable criticism of business. Nadel found that Congress, especially the staffs of the Senate reformers, was the most significant source for consumer reporters in the late 1960s, via press releases, interviews, and hearings.[9] Michael Pertschuk, aide to Senator Warren Magnuson, a leader on consumer issues and chair of the Senate Commerce Committee at the time, has written that, at the time, "I could safely *assume* that virtually *any* national reporter assigned to cover the story of some piece of consumer legislation or other would be unabashedly sympathetic with the aims of the legislation, though they were hardly all consumed with anti-business animus."[10] The consumer movement also enjoyed credibility with the news media that other challengers to business did not. Consumer advocates associated with Nader's groups looked and sounded like young professionals; they were generally white, clean cut, well-spoken, and educated at elite colleges and law schools. Often lacking an organized constituency, the consumer movement relied especially on generating public and official support through media coverage. Thus, they observed Washington's political and journalistic rules, producing clear sound bites, vivid testimony evoking moral indignation, and footnoted research reports rather than staging demonstrations. They shared journalists' interests in opening up administrative decision-making to public scrutiny, funneling leaks about backstage lobbying by business interests to reporters and working on behalf of the Freedom of Information Act and other open government measures.

Consumer advocates were not the only sources of more critical business reporting in the 1960s and early 1970s. Governmental changes also account for the shift in business reporting on television. The late 1960s and early 1970s mark one of the brief periods in twentieth-century American history when corporations' grip on the political agenda weakened somewhat. New executive branch agencies with missions to watch over business debuted, including the Equal Employment Opportunities Commission (1965), the Occupational Safety and Health Administration (1970), the Environmental Protection Agency (1970), and the Consumer Products Safety Commission (1973). Some existing agencies set themselves to regulate corporate abuses with renewed vigor, most notably the Federal Trade Commission, which cracked down on misleading advertising. Finally, the Justice Department turned briefly toward stricter enforcement of antitrust law in the late 1960s in response to an unprecedented wave of acquisitions, mainly by corporations that were already the largest in the land. At least in a few high-profile cases, including International Telephone and Telegraph's attempt to suck up ABC, the department brought to public attention this concentration of economic power and its consequences in price-fixing, bribery, and political influence. Much of the bad news about business emerged from broadcast journalists' traditional job of following what happened in congressional hearing rooms and the federal bureaucracy.[11]

In addition, we need not assume that the media perfectly reflected changes in the world outside to acknowledge that there was little good economic news at the time. Recession in 1969–1970 and the oil price shocks of 1973–1974 plunged the economy into its worst decline since the Depression. Contrary to every mainstream economist's expectations, interest rates, inflation, and unemployment rose simultaneously, spurred by the lingering costs of the Vietnam War, the Great Society's domestic programs, and the energy crisis. The end of the American economy's long postwar boom did not bring forth huzzahs for its corporate managers.

The changing economics of the broadcasting industry also help explain the shift in business reporting. In the 1950s, news and documentary programs were typically funded by a single sponsor who exercised great influence over the program. As television production grew more expensive and the networks demanded greater control over their programming, financial support shifted from sole to multiple sponsors. Thus, individual corporate advertisers' control over programming weakened; the era in which a network's major public affairs offering consisted of the *Camel News Caravan* was over. The emergence of television as a national advertising medium made it indispensable to major corporations, regardless of how they were portrayed by each program in each instance. No major corporation could afford to pull its advertising from television for long, and if one did another advertiser quickly filled its place. Demand for television time was such that broadcasters suffered little even when an entire industry that advertised heavily left the airwaves, as the cigarette companies did after being banned by law in the early 1970s. This is not to say that the needs of corporate advertisers as a whole did not influence programming deeply, but the demands of any one company for favorable treatment were less likely to be honored by the networks than in the days of direct sponsorship.

In response to a soured economy, a more activist federal government, and the revived consumer groups, business leaders launched a campaign to manage the political and media environment in the early 1970s.[12] Corporate attempts to control the news media did not emerge from a central headquarters, but had a common message about reporters' liberalism and economic naïveté and shared targets in the elite print media and television news. Business vastly increased its advocacy advertising, hoping to personalize the corporation, promote an image of social responsibility, and generate opposition to unfavorable regulation. By 1975, corporations spent $100 million on advocacy advertising, "aiming as much as a third of their total advertising expenses toward people as 'citizens' rather than as 'consumers,'" as Michael Schudson put it.[13] Business organizations such as the Advertising Council launched "educational" campaigns to increase "economic understanding," defined as "hav[ing] a more positive attitude toward the system . . . a more favorable attitude toward business . . . [and] less desire for government regulation of economic activities."[14] At the same time, corporate and conservative foundation money created a new array of think tanks to provide the political system and the media with policies, studies, opinion pieces, and expert sources. Funds also flowed to researchers who raised questions about media ethics or investigated journalists. Businesses directly cultivated journalists by sponsoring forums for corporate leaders and reporters, endowing university training programs in economic reporting, and offering awards for the right kind of business journalism. Corporate sponsors also quickly involved themselves in public television.

Conservative political forces and corporate interests converged in Accuracy in Media (AIM), the news watchdog group that attacked *The Selling of the Pentagon* and the documentary on pensions discussed in this chapter.

Founded in 1969, AIM became increasingly active after incorporating in 1971 as its budget grew from just over $5,000 in that year to over $1.1 million in 1981.[15] Its first activities involved producing mailings, newspaper advertisements, and letters to the editor that attacked the accuracy of coverage as well as bringing fairness doctrine complaints to the FCC. AIM's campaigns reflected the interests of its government and business advisors, officers, and funders. Prominent among them were anticommunists and Vietnam War advocates, including supporters of the defense industry and intelligence agencies, former military leaders, defense academics, and Cold War foreign policy officials.[16] Business advisors and contributors included representatives of nuclear power, investment and commercial banking, oil, food, chemicals, steel, manufacturing, and the American Medical Association. AIM's chairman was Reed J. Irvine, an economist in the Federal Reserve Board's Division of International Finance and chief of its International Development Section, who continued to work in government for several years while serving at AIM. AIM also drew support from within the communications industry, undermining its own sweeping generalizations about the liberal media. The group's contributors included Walter H. Annenberg, owner of *TV Guide*, and Edward Willis Scripps II, owner of the Scripps League of Newspapers. Its advisory board members included Alphons J. Hackl, whose Acropolis Books published conservative media criticism, and John E. Tilton, former president of the Suburban Press Foundation.

To be sure, particular industries had brought pressure in response to network investigative reporting that touched their interests throughout the 1960s, but their efforts were generally more isolated and short-lived than AIM's. Aside from the American Farm Bureau Federation's attacks on the reports on food policy discussed in chapter 1, chemical manufacturers disputed claims about the health dangers of pesticides made in *The Silent Spring of Rachel Carson* (CBS, 1963); funeral home operators assailed *The Great American Funeral* (CBS, 1963) for characterizing the industry as preying on the grieving; tobacco companies objected to *The Teenage Smoker* (CBS, 1962) for drawing the link between smoking and cancer; and the American Medical Association accused both *The Business of Health* (CBS, 1961) and *What Price Health?* (NBC, 1972) for tilting toward congressional advocates of national health insurance.[17] These disputes were resolved without FCC or other government probes as the networks either refused to alter their reports or provided reply time to their critics. AIM now offered a source of growing expertise on bringing sustained regulatory pressure to bear on broadcasters. Best of all, as a nominally independent organization, AIM offered some insulation from charges of self-interest that direct industry attacks on reports did not.

By the early 1970s, the ideological positions of consumer advocates and business had solidified. For consumer advocates, the problem was business's exploitation of the public by limiting information about products, committing fraud and deceptive advertising, disregarding consumer safety, and engaging in anticompetitive behavior.[18] The causes were often identified as excessive corporate power and lack of government action. The scale of mammoth corporate and government bureaucracies limited their responsiveness to individual needs. Industry self-regulation was, in the words of the National Commission on Product Safety, "legally unenforceable and patently inadequate."[19] More critical consumerists such as Nader attributed government quiescence to the corporate capture of agencies created to regulate industry. Civil rights groups stressed racial discrimination as an independent cause of harms to ghetto consumers. The moral world of consumerism emphasized the innocence and vulnerability of all consumers, but especially the poor, and the culpability of insensitive, profit-minded businesses and uncaring or compromised regulators. The Kennedy administration articulated mainstream consumerists' typical policy solutions in the early 1960s when it called for strengthening consumers' rights to safety, to information about products, to choice in the marketplace, and to be heard in government regulatory proceedings.[20] More critical voices in the consumer movement later added strengthening citizens' legal abilities to sue for damages, more vigorous antitrust efforts, and an economic vision of smaller and more democratically owned and operated businesses and cooperatives.

For their part, business advocates replied by portraying the problems of the marketplace as threefold.[21] Exploitation, they argued, was limited to a few bad actors in any industry. In addition, business arguments pointed to some consumers' ignorance about the proper use of products and portrayed undesirable effects of consumption as stemming from consumer demand, to which the market merely responded. The consumer movement was itself part of the problem. Its ascetic culture would deprive Americans of choice in the marketplace. The movement set unreasonable standards of zero risk and total information about products when the effects of many products could not be known or predicted. The movement missed the positive side of advertising, which increased competition by providing price information and by helping to differentiate products' attributes. Business's defenders also painted regulation as problematic because it invariably raised more costs to consumers than benefits, especially by stifling innovation, efficiency, and competition. The root of these problems generally lay in government and consumer advocates' bid to rule the market, usurping the legitimate decisions of producers and consumers. A more sophisticated account of the causes emerged in postindustrial theorists' suggestion that a "new class" of knowledge workers—academics, professionals, political advocates, philanthropists, and journalists—was staking a claim to leadership through social movements and an expanding government.[22] Irving Kristol warned *Wall Street Journal* readers of the moral threat they posed, from this point of view:

> [One] should understand that the members of this class are "idealistic" in the 1960's sense of the term—i.e. they are not much interested in money but are keenly interested in power. Power for what? The power to shape our civilization—a power that, in a capitalist system, is supposed to reside in the free market. This "new class" wants to see much of this power redistributed to government, where they will then have major say in how it is exercised. . . . [They] are convinced they incarnate "the public interest" as distinct from all the private interests in society.[23]

In short, the new class were self-serving, power-hungry advocates of government regulation. Business advocates' policy solutions typically involved limited enforcement of existing regulations, preferably at the state or local rather than the federal level, consumer education, and voluntary industry self-regulation.

Financial Reform, Public Television, and *Banks and the Poor*

On November 9, 1970, the fledgling Public Broadcasting System aired *Banks and the Poor,* a report that exerted little impact on the banking industry but played an important role in shaping the future of public television. The documentary was produced by Morton Silverstein for National Educational Television (NET), then a major program supplier to public broadcasting. In its introductory sequence, the documentary announced that it would examine the claim that "the banking industry has paid special attention to the needs of the disadvantaged," made here by David Rockefeller, chairman of Chase Manhattan Bank.

Banks and the Poor began by criticizing the industry for perpetuating slum housing conditions. It incorporated a Savings and Loan Association television commercial that boasted that "if you combine the total assets of the twenty-five largest industrial corporations, it would still be $7 billion less than the assets of savings and loans." The report's unseen narrator noted that although these institutions were federally chartered to be the main source of housing credit in the country, the House Banking Committee estimated that banks had used less than 1 percent of their funds to finance low-income housing. Over images of run-down urban streets, the report said that a congressional committee found that banks lent the bulk of their housing funds to absentee landlords, "in this case a euphemism for slumlords." House Banking Committee chairman Wright Patman said in an interview that he wished bankers would realize that, "since it's the people's money . . . that we're using, certainly we should take care of their housing." Another commercial told viewers, "your local savings and loan wants you to save for the good things in life," over soft-focus images of upscale cars and homes. The report contrasted the advertisement with a black family living in an overcrowded, dilapidated Washington, D.C., tenement, whose landlord was also a director of the savings and loan that had financed his purchase of the building.

The scene shifted to Philadelphia and New York to present more evidence of banks funding what the congressional committee called "predatory slum speculators" instead of poor homebuyers. The savings and loan industry's response was presented through a letter to Congress defending its record of lending to low-income homebuyers, calling for government-backed home loans for the poor, and noting that the industry's lending was affected by growing inflation and tight credit. The report then showed a Chase Manhattan Bank commercial touting its participation in a $100 million lending pool to revive the Bedford-Stuyvesant neighborhood. A NAACP Legal Defense and Education Fund attorney interviewed walking through the blighted neighborhood said that only $8 million had been loaned thus far and that the pool would not help 80 percent of the area's families because they could not afford to buy homes. As the report showed a billboard in the neighborhood claiming, "You have a FRIEND at Chase Manhattan," the attorney dismissed the lending program as a "game perpetrated by the rich and powerful on the poor and helpless." The report then constructed from separate interviews a "debate" between Patman and Rockefeller over the propriety of Chase Manhattan's financing gambling casinos when it was slow to fulfill its commitments to affordable housing. Rockefeller attributed Patman's animus toward banks to having been turned down for a loan in his youth, which Patman denied. The segment ended by contrasting footage of beachgoers at the Resorts International casino in the Bahamas, financed by Chase Manhattan, with the rubble of the Washington, D.C., tenement, which was torn down to make way for luxury apartments.

The program then criticized banks for refusing to extend credit directly to low-income borrowers, instead funding high-interest finance companies from which the poor were forced to borrow instead of the banks. A commercial for full-service banks promising checking and savings accounts and loans gave way to a Harlem Legal Aid Society lawyer contrasting the banks' intimidating paperwork and cool reception to low-income loan applicants with finance companies' welcoming atmosphere and exorbitant interest rates.

Hidden-camera footage showed a black man applying for a loan at Beneficial Finance, where he was quoted a 25.5 percent interest rate, more than double what banks charged. The lawyer explained that it was more efficient for banks to provide credit to the finance companies than to numerous individuals and that it was legal, but that it allowed banks to shirk their obligations to the community. Patman excoriated the practice while the president of the American Bankers Association defended the finance companies as legitimate businesses, regulated by the states, and filling a niche in making small loans.

In the next segment, banks were accused of buying loans originated by the finance companies, unscrupulous home improvement contractors, and "ghetto merchants." A black Philadelphia woman watched her home auctioned by a bank to pay off a delinquent car loan she had cosigned for her brother. Outside a bank in the same city, the Consumers Education and Protection Association (CEPA) demonstrated against abusive debt collection practices. Two customers read from notes for them left by collection officers calling the borrowers "idiots" and "pigs" and threatening "to tell everybody that you are not worthy of trust." A spokesman from the bank said that it had apologized to the customers for these isolated incidents and the bank was acting to eliminate them in future. CEPA representatives said they had heard numerous such complaints. Outside a furniture store, New York City Commissioner of Consumer Affairs Bess Myerson Grant discussed banks' purchases of consumer credit contracts from dealers in shoddy merchandise. She noted that even if the goods turned bad, the consumer was obliged to keep making payments to the bank, who was not obliged to honor warranties on the product. Hidden cameras captured an aluminum siding salesman's pitch to an undercover employee of Grant's department while Grant analyzed the salesman's deceptive techniques. She said that if the law did not require borrowers to pay off loans for poor goods and services, banks would stop buying loans from fly-by-night contractors and shady merchants.

Finally, the documentary suggested that banks had been able to disregard the social consequences of their lending policies because of the power of the Washington banking lobby and because legislators were violating conflict-of-interest rules by voting on banking laws despite having financial stakes in the industry. After Patman introduced the problem, Louis M. Loeb of the Bar Association of New York said legislators should remove such conflicts of interest. Over shots of statues of American Revolutionary War heroes in the U.S. Capitol, Loeb quoted Plato's *Republic* to the effect that legislators should avoid dealing in money ("And this shall be their salvation, and they shall be the saviors of the state.") The report noted that Treasury Secretary David Kennedy continued to receive a pension from the bank he had run that was roughly equal to his current federal salary. As "The Battle Hymn of the Republic" played in the background, the report scrolled over shots of the Capitol a list of almost one hundred names of representatives and senators with ties to banks as shareholders, directors, consultants, or lawyers to the industry. The report noted several policy reforms that "might enable an affluent nation and its banking industry to better serve the needs of the poor."

Context and Sources: Bank Reform

In the years before *Banks and the Poor* aired, Congress and a host of reformers had made banking a central consumer issue. The documentary reflected their efforts to address each of its central concerns: low-income housing, fair credit practices, and congressional conflicts of interest.

As noted in *Banks and the Poor,* the report drew its analysis and examples of banks' responsibility for housing problems from congressional sources. In addition to Patman's criticisms, the documentary cited the congressional ad hoc subcommittee report that decried bank lending to absentee ghetto landlords and real estate speculators who failed to maintain their buildings. The House Judiciary Committee had delved deeply into Chase Manhattan's relationship to the Resorts International casino in public hearings in 1969 as part of an antitrust probe into Chase's attempt to take over Pan American Airways.[24] Patman's proposed law to limit the growth of bank holding companies, which passed Congress over two months before the report aired, required banks to divest themselves of various nonbanking investments such as gambling interests.[25]

Government sources had also attacked unfair credit practices throughout the 1960s. Patman, a Texas populist, had ascended to the House Banking Committee chairmanship in the early 1960s. He used the post to draw greater attention to his long-term criticisms of banks' treatment of small business and individual borrowers and of the Federal Reserve for what he saw as an overly restrictive monetary policy that fueled high interest rates. As stagflation set in during 1969, Patman and Rockefeller dueled repeatedly in the *New York Times, U.S. News and World Report,* and the *Congressional Record* over banks' role in setting rates.[26] Patman was not the only source of federal concern about lending. After a seven-year struggle, Congress passed the Consumer Credit Protection Act ("Truth in Lending Act") in 1968, requiring clearer disclosure of interest rates and finance charges on consumer loans and credit.[27] Although the act focused especially on high-interest lenders that targeted poor consumers, critics questioned whether disclosure alone was sufficient to assist low-income borrowers with little financial acumen and few alternative sources of credit. Also in 1968, the Federal Trade Commission issued a blistering report on their probe of installment credit practices in Washington, D.C.[28] State and local governments were active on lending issues throughout the decade.[29] New York City became a hotbed for consumerism. The Department of Consumer Affairs, a key source in *Banks and the Poor,* was the first municipal agency of its kind in country and helped to pass a 1969 ordinance that allowed the city to bring class-action suits against deceptive sellers of all consumer goods.[30]

Under the umbrella of consumerism, civil rights and antipoverty groups targeted unfair lending as well. It is not surprising that the documentary sought out the NAACP Legal Defense and Education Fund, which was bringing numerous suits on behalf of poor consumers, including a New York class action against finance companies for deceptive credit contracts.[31] Similar suits were brought by the new legal services centers for the impoverished—such as the Harlem group featured in *Banks and the Poor*—that were funded through the Johnson administration's War on Poverty.[32] Local consumer and antipoverty groups such as the Philadelphia organization shown in the documentary mounted boycotts of ghetto retailers and banks, started buying cooperatives, and fostered minority-owned businesses to serve their communities.[33]

The documentary's attack on conflicts of interest echoed Patman and the New York Bar Association study. The congressman had attacked Treasury

Banks and the Poor relied on complaints aired against banks by anti-poverty groups such as the Consumers Education and Protection Association, shown protesting outside a Philadelphia bank in the documentary.

Secretary Kennedy for his bank holdings during his confirmation hearings and later spent an hour on the House floor accusing Kennedy of benefiting from rising interest rates and ill-gotten gains through his bank pension.[34] The controversial list of congressional figures linked to banks came from research conducted for the Bar Association study on congressional conflicts of interest, which was funded by the Ford Foundation. The study singled out the banking industry from others it examined as having most clearly compromised politicians' independence.[35] The committee that produced the report was not comprised of upstart Naderites but partners at elite law firms. All eleven committee members had served in government, including Cyrus R. Vance (President Johnson's Secretary of the Army and, later, secretary of state in the Carter administration), Charles A. Horsky (former advisor for National Capital Affairs to the Kennedy and Johnson administrations), and David W. Kendall (former general counsel and assistant secretary at the U.S. Treasury, former special counsel to President Eisenhower, and former vice president of legal affairs at the Chrysler Corporation).[36] In short, the sources and topics treated by the documentary were not outside the realm of congressional debate and mainstream public interest reform.

Framing Banks and Consumers

The ideological frame of *Banks and the Poor* was unadulterated consumerism. The report portrayed the credit problems of the impoverished as stemming from their exploitation by banks and the fraudulent merchants and finance companies that depended on them—what the documentary called "a trilogy of interests against the poor." The problem was not consumer ignorance, the consumer movement, or even a few small rogue contractors and lenders, but a financial system ruled by large banks with little sense of obligation to low-income communities. Consumer advocates repeatedly refuted bankers' claims that they were improving their record of loaning in poor neighborhoods. The report's incorporation and debunking of bank commercials and billboards was of a piece with consumerism's attack on the problem of deceptive advertising. The documentary's picture of unchecked corporate power and congressional regulators as having been captured by powerful lobbying and a web of ties to industry were common causes of abuses cited by the consumer movement. Uncaring, predatory lenders and compromised regulators were the villains. Vulnerable and abused low-income credit seekers were the victims, denied their rights to information (about real rates), to choice (of loans at reasonable rates), and to be heard in government over the voices of the banks.

Banks and the Poor made its case more strongly than most commercial network documentaries of the time through its starkly worded narration and

bitterly ironic contrasts between banks' public relations image and their practices. In addition to the report's discrediting of bank commercials and spokesmen, the documentary's introductory sequence suggested a larger indictment
of banks' historic role in American society. It began with a clip from a Busby
Berkeley chorus line kicking joyfully to "We're in the Money," with its call to
"come lend it, spend it, roll it along!" The narration noted that Americans celebrate money and often turned to banks to borrow it. However, "The banker's
participation in what has been called the free enterprise system has been felt
in both urban and rural acts of survival." Over images of farms and rural banks,
it explained that "the banker has traditionally called himself the friend to the
farmer, although many farmers remember the lack of loans during the great
droughts of the 1930s." Amidst images of factories, the report added, "the
banker has declared himself the friend of the working man, although many
union leaders remember his support of corporations during some of the cru-
elest union-busting of this century." The same dark irony emerged when the
report listed politicians linked to the banks over images of the Capitol and
the patriotic "Battle of Hymn of the Republic," suggesting that the nation's
leaders fought on behalf of financial institutions, not for God and country.

If it exceeded the rhetoric of much consumerist criticism and investigative
reporting, the report's policy frames drew from mainstream, reliable sources:
elected officials and the Bar Association's study. New York Consumer Affairs
commissioner Grant suggested the need for legal reform to give consumers
recourse against finance companies who attempted to collect debts for faulty
merchandise or that were fraudulently induced by home contractors. At the
report's close, it reeled off several proposed reforms, identified as having
been "suggested by critics in this study." Congress could "rework the Federal
Reserve Bank to meet housing and other social priorities," create "a national
development bank as a lender of last resort," and pass a national usury law
to limit interest rates on loans. These proposals all came from Patman.[37] The
report also called for "establishing a code of ethics for Congress," apparently a
reference to the Bar Association's proposal to strengthen existing ethics codes
to minimize conflicts of interest.[38] These reforms were certainly in line with
typical consumerist demands for greater choice in the marketplace and voice
in government. But the documentary's reliance on Patman's policy ideas limited its scope. His development bank would likely have shifted responsibility
to loans in poor neighborhoods from banks to the federal government, much
as the American Bankers' Association president had called for in the report.
Viewers may have been confused by the notion of reforming the Federal
Reserve, the role of which in setting interest rates and banking policy was
not discussed in the report. Legislation requiring banks to make loans to low-

income borrowers in the areas they served seemed like an obvious solution, but it was not within government critics' ken at the time.

Reaction and Impact: Don't Bank on PBS

Patman raised the only support that *Banks and the Poor* garnered from Congress. He entered positive reviews of the program into the *Congressional Record* and commended the report for showing the need for public broadcasting and congressional funding for it.[39] Patman compared the report favorably to commercial networks' coverage of banking for explaining financial complexities to lay people without fear of contradicting bankers' point of view. He introduced into the record letters he had written that year to the private networks asking for more coverage of economic news from more diverse perspectives. Patman attributed these shortcomings in network news to their dependence on bank advertising. This lack of coverage, he complained, "affects attempts in the Congress to legislate on banking issues."[40]

However, within the newly formed Public Broadcasting System, nervous reaction to *Banks and the Poor* began even before the report aired. PBS's board voted to reject it as "journalistically unsound," despite the fact that only two of the board members had viewed it. The report might never have been telecast had not one board member convinced the others that PBS lacked the bureaucratic authority at the time to block the program and pointed out that a favorable review of it in *Life* magazine had already reached the newsstands.[41] Instead, PBS took the unprecedented step of warning its affiliates of the controversial nature of the program. Several affiliates quickly arranged previews for local bankers, who were well represented on public station boards. When the Texas Bankers Association protested the report, some Texas stations canceled it, as did stations in Pittsburgh and Richmond, Virginia.[42] Many stations that ran the documentary scrambled to program "discussions" or "reply time" with local lenders. At the next board meeting of the Corporation for Public Broadcasting (CPB), which was primarily responsible for funding PBS programming, board member and banker Michael Gammino excoriated the report, and others fretted over whether the list of bank-connected congresspeople would trigger the FCC's "personal attack" rule, requiring the network to give the lawmakers time to respond.[43] The controversy led to new PBS guidelines permitting the network to preview all programs and issue alerts to stations about potentially controversial content.[44] PBS vetoed NET's attempt to nominate the documentary for an Emmy.[45]

The documentary helped stir congressional anger against PBS and offered the Nixon administration a pretext to attack the new network, which led to its restructuring. Administration officials were already concerned about the liberal influence of the Ford Foundation, which was the major funder of National Educational Television (NET), then the dominant producer of public affairs programs for PBS stations and the maker of *Banks and Poor.* In 1969, Nixon aide Peter Flanigan told CPB's chairman and director that increased funding for public television was "contingent upon the creation of new program production facilities to replace National Educational Television." After *Banks and the Poor* aired, Flanigan, a former investment banker, mailed a newspaper clipping on the program along with a note to the CPB's director that read, "Herewith another example of NET activity that is clearly inappropriate for a government-supported organization." Flanigan asked how much funding CPB had given to NET that year and had budgeted for the following year. "I am directing this inquiry to you," he added, "in that I think it comes better from you to the board and the management of the corporation than from the White House. Therefore, I'd appreciate you treating this inquiry in that light."[46] The administration devised a plan to restructure public television by cutting CPB's budget, replacing its leadership with new Nixon appointees, opposing long-term funding authorizations that might have insulated programmers from the political pressures of the appropriations process, curtailing the amount of public affairs programs, and decentralizing power over program-

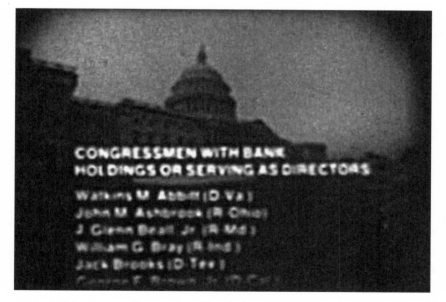

Banks and the Poor sparked a political backlash against PBS, in part because it listed congressional legislators' ties to the banking industry, accompanied by the *The Battle Hymn of the Republic.*

ming by increasing the editorial control and funding of local stations (who were seen as more conservative and less interested in national political programs). On June 30, 1972, Nixon vetoed the annual authorization of CPB's funding. Soon after, the corporation's chairman, president, and director of television all quit, and their replacements carried out the administration's plan. NET's documentary unit disbanded, and the investigative public affairs documentary became almost as rare on public as on commercial television for the rest of the decade.

Banks and the Poor became more of a cause célèbre for reforming PBS than banking. Despite chairing the House Banking Committee, Patman was consistently outnumbered on banking issues by southern Democrats, conservative Republicans, and even northern urbanites, who tended to vote with the large banks. Although interest and mortgage rates were capped on and off during the Nixon administration's experiment with wage and price controls in the early 1970s, limits were soon abandoned. Patman's lifelong attempts to refashion the Federal Reserve as a force for fair allocation of credit to low-income and small business borrowers never succeeded.[47] Congress's next significant laws encouraging bank reinvestment in low-income neighborhoods did not come until the mid-1970s, with the Home Mortgage Disclosure Act of 1975 (requiring banks to disclose demographic and geographic data about their home-loan borrowers) and the Community Reinvestment Act of 1977 (requiring some reinvestment in communities where banks took deposits). Neither law solved the problems of banks' unwillingness to loan directly to the poor, largely because of poor enforcement by federal regulatory agencies.[48] In the 1980s, struggles over fair lending reignited in many cities fueled by community groups, government studies, and yet more investigative reports showing ongoing racial discrimination in mortgage lending.[49]

Producer Morton Silverstein later claimed that *Banks and the Poor* focused "enormous public attention" on congressional conflicts of interest, "which they renounced or resigned," and that Chase Manhattan sold its Resorts International gambling interest.[50] But the bank would have been forced to sell its stake as a result of Patman's bank holding-company legislation, which passed Congress over two months before the documentary premiered. In the wake of scandals throughout the 1960s, Congress indeed became more attentive to its members' direct ties to industry, establishing permanent ethics committees in the House and Senate and adopting formal ethics codes and financial disclosure requirements. All this occurred before the report was begun. The Bar Association study was based on disclosure data that Congress agreed to release beginning in 1969.[51] It is unclear whether the documentary had any impact on growing *observance* of conflict-of-interest rules independent of the bar association report and the ethics committees' efforts. However, it is difficult to argue that conflict-of-interest rules have limited the banking industry's political power in Congress, as exerted through lobbying and campaign donations. Indeed, after Congress allowed the savings and loan industry to enter the risky commercial and real estate loan markets in the early 1980s, with disastrous results, Congress presented the sector with the largest bailout of any industry in American history by decade's end.

Pension Reform: The Broken Promise

NBC's *Pensions: The Broken Promise,* aired September 12, 1972, as part of the *NBC Reports* series. The documentary pointed to the failure of private retirement plans to deliver benefits at a time when Congress was hammering out reforms of the pension system. In response to the broadcast, AIM brought a complaint to the FCC, arguing that the report presented an overly pessimistic picture of pension plans that implied the need for stronger regulation of the industry than was warranted. For the first time, the FCC ruled that a documentary violated the fairness doctrine. The first part of this section examines how *Pensions* grew out of a legislative struggle over retirement funding, closely following Senate liberals' framing of the issue, and how the documentary framed retirement funds as a consumer issue. The next part surveys the regulatory and judicial arena, showing how NBC's attempt to challenge the fairness doctrine revealed splits within the government over broadcast regulation.

Over footage of elderly couples dancing in a community center, narrator Edwin Newman introduced *Pensions* as a story about "ordinary people with the modest hope to finish their working careers with enough money to live in dignity . . . one that is all too often not realized." The first segment focused on the barriers to receiving a pension. Newman appeared in a Department of Labor file room, where he explained that the government's ability to audit pension funds offered "meager protection" for the rights of beneficiaries. In interviews, a woman office worker and male warehouse foreman at A&P supermarkets told of how they lost benefits when they were laid off or when their employer was bought by another company. Ralph Nader and Senate Labor Subcommittee chairman Harrison Williams Jr. (D-N.J.) noted that pension-plan descriptions misled workers by promising them big money in their final years while hiding restrictions in fine print and legal jargon. In Williams's office, Newman studied examples of the "slick brochures" the senator had collected that showed retirees in deck chairs with checks flying about their heads. After Newman archly read a plan description written in dense legalese, Williams said the plans ought to give clear, straightforward accounts of what retirees could expect. At a Labor Subcommittee hearing, several seniors testified that they were forced to retire and then lost pension rights when their Philadelphia baking company declared bankruptcy. Senator Richard Schweiker (R-Pa.) read from their company's pension brochure, noting that it wished employees a "Happy retirement to you when your time comes." Pennsylvania insurance commissioner Herbert Dennenberg summarized the obstacles to getting a pension: "You have to go to work for an employer, you have to stay with him, you have to stay in good health, you have to avoid layoffs, you have to take your money, turn it over to the employer, hope that he invests it safely and soundly. You have to hope that when you're age sixty-five the employer is still around . . . so there's almost a sequence of miracles which you're counting on."

The second segment outlined corporate and union interests in restricting pension eligibility. Two men recently laid off from a Philadelphia machine plant told how they had foregone wage increases in favor of better pensions only to lose them when the plant shut down. Newman explained that employees became more expensive to companies after working long enough and getting old enough to qualify for (or vest in) a pension plan. Newman profiled Allen Sorenson, a manager who "helped to prove that point in a study he did for a large department store chain" and then was fired by the company after twenty-two years of work, just before he was vested. An employee of a Chicago nut company told how he and his colleagues were terminated just before qualifying for pensions and how one fired coworker became "so ill and upset over it that he shot himself." Newman then turned to the Chicago Teamster union locals, each of which had its own pension plan. As somber men loaded boxes on trucks, Teamsters spoke of their need for early retirement because of the physical strain of their work. Union members explained that they lost their pension credits if they switched locals, which many were forced to do when they changed jobs. Teamsters said that their unions had not been entirely honest with them about the lack of pension portability and had turned a deaf ear to their complaints. A cab driver, identified by a supertitle as a Teamster dissident leader, ended the segment by raising the specter of sixty-eight-year-old men forced to keep working because they had lost their pensions. Given the size of modern trucks and their dangerous cargoes, he asserted, "somebody's going to get killed."

The third part of the program explored the impact of lost pensions on the elderly and assessed who was responsible for the situation. Labor leader Victor Gotbaum called the private pension system a "disease of big business . . . a mockery" and blamed its failures for the poverty of the urban elderly. Social workers explained that seniors were financially unprepared for retirement. As a montage showed elders playing checkers, reading newspapers, and sitting stolidly on park benches, voices of retirees testified that "we have made no plans to retire" and that one could not live on social security alone. Newman explained that "retirement is a lot more expensive than it used to be, and the elderly are complaining much more about needing money," in part because seniors no longer lived with their families but tended to settle in warmer retirement communities. An extended sequence focused on an elderly man relating his daily routine, watching every expense, and living a low-cost, "quiet life." Newman summed up by saying that even if the elderly did not plan as well as they might have, they "should not be expected to live in poverty or near poverty or a cut or two higher, lead[ing] a drab, penny-pinching sort of existence."

The final segment briefly related the history of social security and private pensions and examined claims that the pension industry was underregulated. "If there is a pension crisis," Newman said, "it is, at least in part, a crisis of rising expectations," and he noted that baseball players and New York's municipal workers had struck recently for better pensions. The report then looked at the problem of incompetent or dishonest management of larger pension funds and told how union leaders such as Teamster president Jimmy Hoffa (shown leaving a courthouse in handcuffs) had been convicted for mishandling these funds. Justice Department officials told how they had prosecuted pension trustees for embezzlement and kickbacks. Newman explained that banks managed most pension funds and that critics accused the banks of "stick[ing] too much with safe investments in big corporations." At a Bankers Trust investment meeting, a money manager countered by saying that "one of our major concerns is to protect our accounts against risk." Newman then briefly explored the options for regulating the industry. He noted that Ralph Nader wanted "to take the pension funds away from the banks and have the government set up a new set of institutions, responsible only to the pensioners." Others would insure pensions or make them more portable, "but almost everybody agrees that some changes are needed." A National Association of Manufacturers spokesman cautioned against regulation beyond "closing a few remaining loopholes," defending the pension system's record as excellent. A Bank of America executive supported this view by noting that pension plans were set up voluntarily by corporations. Insurance commissioner Dennenberg and labor leader Gotbaum replied that pensions were not a gift from the employer but the employee's money and that they paled in comparison with executive retirement packages. Senator Schweiker called for earlier vesting and for insuring pensions, and the Chicago cab driver demanded congressional action, asking, "how much misery do they want before they actually act upon it?" Newman began his wrap-up with a disclaimer: "This has been a depressing program to work on, but we don't want to give the impression that there are no good private pension plans. There are many good ones, and there are many people for whom the promise has become reality." After summarizing the problems with pensions, Newman said, "These are matters for Congress to consider and, indeed, the Senate Labor Committee is considering them now." He urged those in pension plans to "take a close look" at them and concluded, "the situation, as we've seen it, is deplorable."

Context and Sources: Senate Liberals and Consumer Advocates Target Pensions

Private pension plans, scarce before World War II, grew dramatically in number and size in the postwar years. After Congress enacted wage freezes in the mid-1940s, employers and labor unions began to negotiate more intensely over nonwage benefits. Miners, auto workers, and steel workers led the drive for pension benefits, striking repeatedly and successfully for the establishment of plans, over the terms on which they would be funded, and for the right of unions to comanage them with employers.[52] In the 1950s, the advent of multiemployer plans made coverage available to workers in smaller firms. Private plans boomed between 1950 and 1970 as the number of enrollees almost tripled to 30 million workers, comprising about half of the private-sector workforce.[53]

The expansion of pensions served both union and corporate interests. Just after the war, labor leaders saw pensions as one of the few tangible gains they could present to the rank and file, and one that might increase workers' long-term loyalty to their unions. In addition, union chiefs initially pushed for private pensions in hopes that it would encourage employers to demand offsetting increases in social security benefits (in fact, the emergence of a private source of retirement income probably had the opposite effect).[54] Corporations agreed to found retirement plans in part to attract and retain workers in the tight civilian labor market of the immediate postwar years. Pensions also raised productivity by easing the dismissal of older workers, offering some compensation for mandatory retirement.[55] Just as important, pensions were an effective tax shelter. Sharp increases in corporate and excess-profits tax rates in the 1940s, combined with the tax deductibility of most employer contributions to pension plans, made the funds attractive shelters during high-profit years.[56] Most important, pension funds offered a new source of investment capital, especially since many funds invested heavily in the employer's own stock. As the funds grew in size to become the largest institutional investors in the country by the early 1970s, they helped prop up the stock prices of major American corporations, which were the favored investment vehicles of many pension managers.[57]

By the mid-1960s, the pension system was ripe for reform, however. As pensions became part of collective bargaining agreements, workers understandably saw them less as gifts from employers and more as deferred wages. Yet this understanding was not reflected in union contract terms, which allowed plans to be canceled at employers' discretion. Plan termination and a number of other problems made the likelihood of collecting a pension highly uncertain. Congressional sources estimated that anywhere from 30 percent to 90 percent of those enrolled in plans would not realize a penny from them.[58] The collapse of an auto workers' retirement fund after the closing of a Studebaker plant in Indiana first drew national attention to the issue, which was addressed in a 1965 presidential commission report that called for stricter federal regulation. The report inspired congressional hearings and the introduction of reform legislation by Senator Jacob Javits, a moderate New York Republican, in 1967. The Labor Subcommittee of the Senate Committee on Labor and Public Welfare became a whirlwind of hearings and studies from 1970 onward, and its activities were echoed in investigations by its counterpart House committee in 1971 and by the Treasury and Labor Departments thereafter.[59] Momentum for regulation built further after revelations of mismanagement and corruption in the pension plans of some teamsters, barbers, and mine workers unions.

When *Pensions* won a Peabody Award for broadcast journalism, the awards committee hailed it as "a shining example of constructive and superlative investigative reporting."[60] Indeed, the documentary displayed some of the rhetorical techniques of an increasingly self-conscious television muckraking. Newman first appeared in the Department of Labor record room, establishing a faux credibility as a reporter who seemed to have dug through the files personally and found shocking case studies hidden there. To underscore the point, the camera zoomed in on a file in Newman's hand as he explained how the department received many complaints from retirees, then dissolved to the first examples of workers telling how they lost benefits, as if the camera had gone inside the case file to present its contents. Later, as Newman discussed how banks managed pension funds, he introduced a brief sequence taken from a Bankers Trust investment meeting as "something few outsiders see," touting the program's rare access. What followed was a pension manager's stiff explanation, read from a prepared text, of how the fund was concerned with protecting itself against risk and a thoroughly unspontaneous question-and-answer session with another manager about how chemical stocks would perform in a slow market. (Curiously, none of the program's conservative critics protested this bit of staging.)

However, *Pensions* followed efforts at political reform rather than leading them, coming late to the legislative debate over retirement funds and depending heavily on the Senate Labor Subcommittee's work on the issue, Department of Justice investigations of union mismanagement, and prior media coverage of these government probes. As NBC News president Reuven Frank later admitted to the FCC, the network's interest in pensions originated in "hearings of the Senate Labor Committee into the subject and subsequently written reports in such publications as *Fortune* magazine."[61] NBC was convinced that the subject was worthy of an hour documentary after seeing a 1971 *60 Minutes* story criticizing pension plans.[62]

NBC looked to the federal government investigations for many of its sources and examples. Senators Williams and Schweiker of the Labor Subcommittee appeared as unchallenged experts on pension ills. Most of the disappointed workers who appeared in the documentary had already testified to the Labor Subcommittee before NBC interviewed them, as had representatives of all the business organizations that appeared in *Pensions*.[63] These included the A&P warehouse foreman (who was also profiled in a *New York Times Magazine* article), department store manager Allen Sorenson, and the Philadelphia bakery and machine plant employees. Corruption and other problems in the teamsters' and mine workers' funds had been exposed by union members themselves, who tipped off print reporters, the Justice Department, and the Labor Subcommittee, triggering hearings and indictments from 1969 onward.[64] Charles Ruff and Richard Benveniste, the two Justice Department sources featured in the documentary, had prosecuted the teamster plan managers.

Framing Pension Reform: Following the Senate

Of the numerous interests that were attempting to shape pension reform, NBC most closely followed the Senate Labor Subcommittee in its framing of the problems and solutions of retirement funds. By 1972, when *Pensions* was produced, the congressional push for change was strong enough that unions, employers, and plan managers (mainly large commercial banks and insurance companies) had acquiesced to two broad principles. In view of the union corruption scandals, all accepted that fiduciary standards for investing pension money should be strengthened to prevent self-dealing, increase disclosure of investments to beneficiaries, and offer clearer descriptions of benefits and rules. In addition, all agreed that vesting rules, which determined how quickly employees became eligible for pensions, should be somewhat less restrictive, although there was no consensus on how quickly vesting should occur. Legislation had stalled over several issues, indicating the competing interests that vied for control of some $150 billion in pension funds. Four policy frames emerged, reflecting multiple shades of business and consumerist ideology.

The Nixon administration's plan most closely served the interests of large employers and pension managers. It would have done the least to accelerate vesting schedules, reflecting employers' and managers' desire to keep their pension payouts to a minimum (and some unions' interest in offering higher benefits to a smaller number of long-term workers). This approach encouraged individual employees and the self-employed to create their own retirement accounts. In practice, these forerunners of today's Individual Retirement Accounts (IRAs) would only have been available to upper-income workers who could afford to meet the accounts' minimum annual investment levels. Pension managers liked the plan because they anticipated overseeing the accounts, which promised to bring new investment capital to Wall Street. Like much of the pro-business response to consumerism, the administration's plan suggested that the private pension system was not seriously troubled. The problem of a few rogue funds could be solved by tightening fiduciary standards somewhat. Individual consumers should be encouraged to take responsibility for their own retirement funds by choosing investment vehicles in the open market.

The Senate Labor Subcommittee, under the leadership of Williams and Javits, introduced legislation proposing wider changes. A vesting provision would have allowed employees to qualify for pensions more quickly than in most existing plans. The bill envisioned a portability fund administered by the Secretary of Labor, which all employers would participate in (albeit voluntarily), transferring workers' pension money to the fund when they left their jobs. This proposal would have strengthened funding standards, requiring employers to pump enough money into their pension funds over time to cover all credits, and held employers liable for pension claims even if they terminated their plans. The Williams-Javits plan also aimed to create federal insurance for canceled plans akin to the protection by the Federal Deposit Insurance Corporation (FDIC) of savings accounts in the event of bank failures. The AFL-CIO and American Association of Retired Persons (AARP) supported this approach, with some qualifications. The bill was opposed by the White House, major business groups (the U.S. Chamber of Commerce and the National Association of Manufacturers), plan administrators, and a few unions, who argued that it would increase the costs of administering plans, submit employers and plan managers to inflexible government regulation, and that problems in the pension industry were not widespread enough to warrant this much federal oversight.[65] The Williams-Javits bill reflected a liberal consumerist vision of government correcting market failures and limiting abuses of economic power while leaving control of the pension system in private hands and insuring the pension industry itself against failure.

Consumer advocates, led by Nader's Public Interest Research Group, took a more critical consumerist stance. Although Nader favored some aspects of the Williams-Javits bill (he was the first to propose clearer communication of plan benefits, for example), he argued that the bill was severely flawed. Its vesting proposals were too slow to protect highly mobile workers as well as seasonal and part-time employees. It failed to help the half of the private workforce that was not currently enrolled in a pension plan. It offered nothing to women, who were least likely to accrue enough years of service to qualify for a pension and did not inherit their spouses' pensions when they died. Its portability fund was entirely voluntary and therefore easily ignored by employers.[66] These and other shortcomings inspired Nader's alternative proposal. At its core was a call to create private pension funds independent of union and management control. Unlike the Nixon individual accounts, these would be contributed to by both employees and employers, would be fully funded and federally insured, would pay benefits to surviving family members, and would be regulated by the Securities and Exchange Commission. Pension investors would hold their managers accountable through direct elections and through their ability to switch funds at any time without losing benefits. For those who had already lost their pensions or were not enrolled in a plan, Nader proposed a workers' retirement subsidy funded by a surtax on corporate profits.[67] In short, the Nader plan embodied the classic themes of critical consumer advocacy: democratic shareholder participation and government oversight acting as a check on management power, the benefits of a competitive yet regulated marketplace in pension funds, and some role for government in compensating for inequality and other market shortcomings by providing a subsidy to the elderly poor.

Another perspective, heard faintly in congressional testimony and letters to the editor of major newspapers, advocated abolishing the private pension system in favor of social security. Professor Merton Bernstein was the clearest voice for the public retirement system, arguing in a Senate hearing that it "has never lost a penny to a dishonest trustee, never paid a kickback to a union or management official, never failed to pay off for lack of funding, can readily be made to keep up with increases in the cost of living, pays off to widows and children and other dependents when a worker dies, retires, or becomes disabled."[68] Increasing social security benefits, he maintained, was the cheapest and easiest way to boost retirement income. This view reflected the New Deal vision of public pensions as primarily a social welfare tool and thus as best managed by government.

NBC's documentary construed the problems of pensions as more numerous and serious than did the Nixon administration. The White House reform plan did not address the issues of portability and protecting benefits in the event a plan terminated, both of which were covered in some depth by NBC. In addition, NBC suggested the scope of the problem was larger than admitted by the White House and the interests it represented. No Nixon administration sources appeared in *Pensions,* which is remarkable in itself. Spokesmen from the National Association of Manufacturers and the Bank of America appeared only at the end of the program, briefly touting the private system's achievements. Their comments were edited into a larger sequence in which they were refuted by union president Gotbaum and Pennsylvania pension commissioner Dennenberg. This debate concluded with the Chicago cab driver demanding reform, asking incredulously, "What the hell are they waiting for? . . . How much misery do they want before they actually act upon it?" If Newman began his wrap-up by saying, "we don't want to give the impression that there are no good private pension plans," he ended it by saying, "Our own conclusion about all of this is that it is almost inconceivable that this enormous thing has been allowed to grow up with so little understanding of it and so little protection and such uneven results for those involved. The situation, as we've seen it, is deplorable." Throughout the documentary, sources emphasized the widespread nature of pension difficulties, noting that most enrollees would never see their pension (Dennenberg, Newman), that plans promised more than they delivered (Williams), that the system was a "mockery" and a "national disgrace" (Gotbaum), and that if "its abuses continue to pile up . . . it might collapse of its own weight, and social security will have to take up the slack" (Nader).

Although *Pensions* did not discuss specific solutions in detail, it featured repeated calls for regulation that suggested more dramatic changes were needed than the White House's minimal tinkerings with private plans. The Justice Department's Charles Ruff said that, considering the hundreds of billions at stake in the pension system, the potential for fraud was such that "the federal government ought to take a more active role than it does." Dennenberg compared retirement funds to insurance plans, noting that "we can't even protect the public with full regulation in insurance, but essentially we have a pension system which is precisely an insurance plan and which is almost unregulated." In one of the only moments when a specific solution was presented, Senator Schweiker, of the Labor Subcommittee, called for federally insured pensions and much quicker vesting than the White House wanted, proposing that "once a worker has put in eight years time (on the job), once he's reached a certain age . . . then he doesn't lose it, regardless of what happens to the company."

NBC mostly adhered to the Senate Labor Subcommittee's position. Newman summarized the problems addressed in the documentary as having to do with portability, vesting, funding, insurance, and fiduciary standards—exactly the range of issues that the subcommittee routinely cited in its public pronouncements.[69] "These are matters for Congress to consider," Newman stated, "and, indeed, the Senate Labor Committee is considering them now. They are also matters for those of you who are in pension plans. If you're in one, you might find it useful to take a close look at it." This closing statement suggested that reform efforts were only occurring in the Labor Subcommittee, ignoring hearings, studies, and legislation suggested by the House of Representatives and the White House.

NBC gave a fuller airing to Nader's views than to the White House's but in a carefully circumscribed manner that emphasized his agreement with the Labor Subcommittee. Nader, for example, introduced the notion that plans were written in legal jargon to hide restrictions from workers, which was then taken up by Senator Williams and Newman at greater length. Exploring potential reforms, Newman characterized Nader as rejecting increased reliance on social security (the only mention of this option) and obscured the consumer advocate's criticism of the Williams-Javits bill:

> [N]obody knows what would happen if the [private] system were to be drastically changed—incorporated in social security, for example. Ralph Nader opposes that. Nader wants to take pension funds away from the banks and have the government set up a new set of institutions, responsible only to the pensioners. Other critics would concentrate on insuring pension benefits and making it possible to take pension rights from one job to another. But almost everybody agrees that some changes are needed.

This forced consensus between Nader and the unnamed "other critics" on the Labor Subcommittee cut short any exploration of the shortcomings of the subcommittee's approach and dismissed the idea of expanding social security as beyond the pale of legitimate controversy. Newman's closing remarks suggested that the only role for citizens was to examine their own pension plans, not to take part in running or reforming them.

Why did NBC's producers give consumer advocates as much prominence as they did and yet ignore the White House position? One reason why NBC may have shied away from including Nixon administration officials in the documentary was that it aired in the closing months of the 1972 presidential election, when concerns over presenting equal time on television to the candidates would have been paramount. Had White House sources appeared, Democratic presidential candidate George McGovern may have demanded reply time. Had both sides in the presidential campaign appeared briefly, the White House could have argued that the rest of the documentary so clearly opposed its own position that the administration deserved more time to reply. The safest move in an election season was to pretend that neither Nixon nor McGovern had anything to do with the pension debate. As for consumer advocates' "success," it was due in part to their Washington-friendly tactics discussed above, which conferred a kind of credibility upon them. Moreover, the views Nader espoused had been consecrated previously by some officials. His proposal to create new private pension plans, the only point mentioned in the documentary on which he departed from the Labor Subcommittee, had been entered approvingly in the *Congressional Record* by Senator Philip Hart (D-Mich.) and endorsed by McGovern. Those elements of Nader's plan that NBC presented as realistic alternatives were the ones that cost business the least and preserved the private system. The report ignored Nader's proposed surtax on corporate profits to provide for unpensioned elders.

Perhaps the report's most significant act of framing was to present pensions as a consumer issue rather than a workplace dispute between labor and management. In this, *Pensions* also followed the Senate reformers and consumer advocates as well. Considering pensions as a deceptive consumer product helped remove the issue from the "narrow" demands of labor or management, to which mainstream thought was less sympathetic. This frame also isolated retirement funds from a public welfare calculus that would have required greater attention to providing for the many seniors without pensions by bolstering social security. An unidentified man established the consumerist frame in the opening interviews of the documentary:

> The pension system is essentially a consumer fraud, a shell game, and a hoax. As a matter of fact, when you say it's a consumer fraud, you pay it an undue compliment, because typically you think of consumer frauds in terms of short transactions, the purchase of an automobile, the purchase of a pair of pants. But with the pension system you really have a long-term contract that may run fifty or a hundred years that's designed to guarantee the security of our population. Essentially, you have an insurance contract that doesn't perform.

This strained analogy between the pension, an agreement to defer wages struck between workers and their employers, and an insurance policy, a product bought by individual consumers to mitigate risk, cropped up repeatedly in the documentary. This frame also revealed itself in NBC's extensive attention to the impenetrable pension-plan brochures, treated as shady consumer contracts written in "fine print," and to the trials of the older consumer in sequences focusing on seniors anxiously itemizing their bills. What others framed as an issue of workplace justice or the social safety net NBC presented as an issue of marketplace justice, a story about the abuse of elderly consumers rather than retired workers.

NBC and its major sources found consumerism especially safer to espouse than unionism, judging from how the documentary chose its villains. NBC's focus allowed it to articulate the frustrations of individual workers as consumers, mistreated as much by their unions as by their employers and other plan managers. Certainly a handful of unions that actively comanaged pension plans with employers had participated in restricting eligibility and portability and mismanaging funds. Yet NBC spent a remarkable amount of time "balancing" criticism of management with criticism of union leaders and identified certain problems solely with union pension managers. Justice Department officials spoke of investigating fraud "for the personal benefit of the labor union officials who are charged with administering these funds," not for the benefit of corporate managers. Yet no pension plan was run entirely by union representatives, and the vast majority of the money in pension plans was managed by insurance companies, banks, and investment firms.[70] The report illustrated pensions' lack of portability only by the Chicago teamsters' refusal to let workers transfer pension rights between locals, not by the many corporations that denied workers the right to take benefits with them to a new job. In this sequence, union members were transformed into consumers when a teamster compared building up nontransferable pension credits in two different locals to depositing money in different banks who refused to give it to him when he went to withdraw it. Unions were not shown playing any role in reform efforts despite the fact that the United Auto Workers and the Steelworkers (whose pension plans were financially sound and free of scandal) were among the leading voices for pension reform at the time, testifying repeatedly before the Senate Labor Subcommittee.

The documentary also viewed the labor-management struggle over pensions through the prism of urban poverty issues, establishing the innocence and pathos of elderly victims. As noted in chapter 1, the dominant moral construction of poverty in postwar America absolves the elderly of responsibility for being poor to the extent that they are considered ineligible for work. As Newman put it, accompanied by footage of seniors hunched over on park benches, "[T]hese people played the game. They did what Americans are expected to do: they worked and met their obligations. But at the end of their working lives, they found that they were in trouble." Enter the social workers, the only group in the documentary that had not testified before Congress, and, thus, who were specially sought out by NBC. As in *Hunger in America,* social workers appeared as experts on the conditions of the poor, confirming and authorizing elders' own claims about how their expectations for a secure and happy retirement were dashed by insufficient incomes. Even Victor Gotbaum, the lone union leader interviewed in *Pensions,* was introduced as "one of the few labor leaders who take an interest in retirement problems" and was given more time to describe seniors' poor diets and housing than to attack management for the failures of retirement plans. This framing of a union president as a social worker signaled NBC's interest in the elderly as victims of poverty rather than of exploitation on the job.

However, seniors did not appear as entirely blameless victims, revealing the report's ambivalence about absolving them completely from responsibility. At several points in the report, it was intimated that they really ought to have planned better for their twilight years. In the segment that depicted retirement funds' impact on the elderly, one social worker spoke of how his clients had been cheated by both the pension system and social security, "and they feel very angry at themselves because I think in the back of their mind they know this was going to happen. They knew that when the day came that they would retire, they would be worse off than when they were working. But they're afraid to admit it." Another social worker described his middle-class clients as the most "bitter" and "resentful" because, "our society being what it is, they postpone thinking about old age and its problems, and all of a sudden they find themselves old and poor." Newman amplified this sentiment at the end of the segment: "Now it may be that some of them did not save as much money as they might have. The urge to consume in American life is very strong. Also inflation played its part and maybe they were careless about what the pension plans they were in actually could do. In any case, at the end of their working lives, they feel cheated and cast aside." This image of unprepared or careless seniors coexisted uneasily with evidence that pension plans hid many restrictions in legal jargon or terminated unexpectedly after plant closings and mergers.

Implying that the elderly were irresponsible also ignored the postwar "selling of retirement" in the interests of efficiency, productivity, reduced unemployment, and greater consumption. William Graebner has written most perceptively of how the expansion of old-age benefits coupled with the advent of mandatory retirement expressed the needs of an economy based less on production, which values work, and more on consumption, which prizes leisure. "As this process met with resistance," he explains, "the leading advocates and beneficiaries of retirement—corporations, labor unions, and insurance companies—became increasingly aggressive in marketing retirement as a consumable commodity, ignoring its origins as a device for corporate and bureaucratic efficiency and control."[71] It was no coincidence that in the 1950s, corporations developed programs to adjust reluctant employees to forced retirement, that sociologists and leisure theorists developed new theories of aging that emphasized seniors' "natural" disengagement from work, that social workers increasingly defined the needs of the elderly in terms of social activity outside the job, and that a plethora of magazines premiered that were geared toward the older consumer.[72] These magazines, in particular, helped spread a new vision of the "golden years" as a time to realize unfulfilled wishes in sunbelt retirement communities and on cruise ships. At the same time, elderly organizations such as the AARP developed what Graebner calls a "mythology of individual responsibility," cautioning seniors against becoming a burden on their children, the community, and the economy. The 1961 White House Conference on Aging stated this ideology most bluntly, decreeing that "the individual will assume primary responsibility for self-reliance in old age."[73] Thus when Newman explained the pension crisis as "in part a crisis of rising expectations," when he noted that "the elderly are complaining much more about needing money" and attributed this to the growing cost of retirement as seniors moved away from their families to Florida and California, he blamed the aged for embracing a lifestyle that had been marketed aggressively to them for over twenty years.[74]

In fairness, *Pensions* attempted to do something that is rarely done on television: tackle a major and complex aspect of the larger political economy and how it shaped the lives of retirees. However, it was by no means the kind of investigative reporting that brings new issues or evidence to the attention of policy makers. NBC piggybacked on years of federal reform efforts. The documentary spent little time exploring competing legislation to clean up the private pension system, and narrowed the range of debate over its future to the options put forth within the Senate Labor Subcommittee. Consumer advocates had their say in part because they were preferable to unions and as long as Nader's views could be fit within the sphere of legitimate controversy staked out by the Senate. Seniors mainly appeared as sympathetic victims but also as unrealistically avid consumers who might have saved more, understood their pension plans better, and lowered their expectations for retirement.

Reactions and Impact: Pensions and the Fairness Doctrine

Pensions sparked little public discussion of retirement plans but ended up igniting a major battle over the fairness doctrine. Neither Congress nor the administration made much of the report in public. Senator Schweiker had the documentary's script printed in the *Congressional Record* to support his call to pass the Williams-Javits bill, but he did no more. The White House, which had little to gain on the eve of the 1972 presidential elections by drawing attention to its watered-down version of pension reform, did not openly attack the documentary. Instead, it was AIM that wielded the sword against the program. Although the regulatory and judicial aspects of this case are discussed more fully in chapter 6, it is worth summarizing here how it progressed through the FCC and District of Columbia Circuit Court of Appeals to see how both government bodies divided internally over *Pensions* and the fairness doctrine.

AIM filed a fairness doctrine complaint against the report with the FCC, charging that the program should have balanced coverage of private pension plans' shortcomings with their successes. AIM contended that legislation in the Congress showed that pension reform was a controversial issue of public importance. Even if *Pensions* had not openly endorsed the Williams-Javits bill, the report led viewers to believe that retirement funds were so bad that far-reaching regulation was necessary. Therefore, AIM argued, NBC should be required to offer some airtime for supporters of private plans to reply. AIM also alleged that the documentary inaccurately portrayed the private pension system, giving the impression that failure and fraud were commonplace. Using Department of Labor records, the group argued that many private plans were working well and claimed that more than 5 million retirees were drawing benefits totaling $7 billion per year. AIM said that only about 1 percent of plans terminated annually, affecting roughly one-tenth of 1 percent of employees covered by private plans.[75] (As one commentator noted, one-tenth of 1 percent equaled about 32,000 employees, a substantial number of victims. Furthermore, if five million retirees were splitting $7 billion a year, their average pension was $26.92 per week, far below the poverty line.)[76]

In response to AIM's complaint, NBC flatly refused to provide time for the advocates of private pension plans or even for debate or discussion between proponents of varying perspectives on the issue. Before the FCC, the network only briefly denied the charges of inaccuracy, spending far more time arguing that the doctrine was unworkable and chilled investigative reporting.[77] As CBS had done in its battle with Congress over *The Selling of the Pentagon,* NBC invested little in defending the conclusions of its reporters about the subject of their documentary. Instead, the network put forth a far-fetched, legalistic argument about how the doctrine did not apply to *Pensions* because retirement fund problems were not a controversial issue of public importance and therefore did not require balanced coverage. The network appeared to want to use AIM's complaint as a test case to disable, or even dissolve, the fairness doctrine.

A year after *Pensions* aired, the FCC ruled for the first time that a network documentary violated the doctrine, ordering NBC to provide reply time to the defenders of the pension system.[78] NBC appealed the decision to the District of Columbia Circuit Court. In September 1974, a three-judge panel overturned the commission's ruling, finding that it had misapplied the doctrine and that broadcasters should have more leeway to define whether an issue was controversial, especially if they were engaged in investigative reporting. Although the panel's opinion did not explicitly declare the fairness doctrine unconstitutional, other D.C. Circuit Court justices viewed it as too sweeping a rejection of the doctrine and signaled to the FCC that they would be open to a rehearing before all ten judges of the court. Although a hearing was scheduled at AIM's request, it never occurred, mainly because the FCC had a change of heart. The issue was moot, the commission argued, because Congress had unanimously passed a pension reform bill. In addition, the commission feared that its case was not strong enough to risk judicial toppling of the doctrine. After the circuit court washed its hands of the matter by remanding it to the FCC, the commission rescinded its ruling against *Pensions* in 1975.

Both the FCC and the court of appeals divided over the merits of the case against *Pensions* and the validity of the fairness doctrine. Although the commission attempted to enforce fairness requirements against a network documentary, it quickly retracted the ruling. If the court seemed on the verge of striking down the doctrine in its initial opinion, it too pulled back. Once again, government did not act in a monolithic or clearly threatening manner toward network muckraking in this case. However, as argued in chapter 6, the controversy did seem to weaken enforcement of the fairness doctrine and judicial support for the regulation.

There is little reason to think that *Pensions* influenced retirement fund reform as dramatically. Former CBS News president Fred Friendly claimed: "Although *Pensions* received both an American Bar Association and a Peabody award, the strong remedial action that Congress applied to the problem in the pensions-reform law of 1974 could be considered NBC's most enduring prize."[79] However, the documentary did not bring new problems or solutions to the attention of political leaders. The report did not encourage viewers to involve themselves in reform efforts, instructing them that "these are matters for Congress to decide" and simply advising retirees to examine their own plans. This conclusion was in keeping with the documentary's addressing itself to plan participants as consumers rather than as citizens or workers who might take collective action to improve their retirement security. Nor did the report seem to speed politicians to act. Pension reform stalled for two more years after the documentary aired as the White House dragged its feet on negotiations with the Senate Labor Subcommittee and the Senate Finance

Committee demanded an exhaustive review of the massive legislation's impact on the tax system, which was under its purview.

Nor did the law that finally passed in late summer of 1974, the Employee Retirement Income Security Act (ERISA), address all of the problems raised by the documentary. The act's financial disclosure provisions still permitted plans to conceal information crucial to measuring the performance of their investment managers.[80] Of the three vesting options ERISA offered employers, the most attractive to them was still too slow to protect increasingly mobile workers and part-time employees, and it perpetuated employers' incentive to discriminate against older workers by firing them before they qualified for a full pension. If the act tightened fiduciary standards to protect against fraud and mismanagement, many corporations responded by indemnifying their officers and directors against breaches of the law. Although the Pension and Welfare Benefits Administration, an ERISA creation to protect the security of beneficiaries, was empowered to investigate and prosecute mismanagement, its limited resources allowed it to review less than 1 percent of all plans annually. The act also established the Pension Benefit Guarantee Corporation (PBGC) to insure pensions, but historically, when the corporation has been forced to step in after a termination it has often responded by reducing benefits. By 2005, the PBGC was so underfunded that it threatened to require a multibillion-dollar taxpayer bailout to preserve pensions in the troubled airline and steel industries.[81] For those who are not covered by a pension plan, ERISA created Individual Retirement Accounts, which have failed to benefit most working-class and poor employees who cannot afford to save. The law did not require companies to have pension plans and raised the costs of managing them, which acted as a disincentive to creating new ones. Congress had to return to pensions repeatedly in the following years to address the act's shortcomings, passing laws attempting to encourage small businesses to offer pensions and to increase funding of multiemployer plans. As Merton Bernstein concluded just after the passage of ERISA, "If that's private pension reform, make mine Social Security."[82]

ERISA has made some private retirement funds more secure and available to workers, but it has not fundamentally increased employees' control over pension money. As one observer has written, the act's "greatest significance was its affirmation that, as a matter of public policy, private pensions are expected to play a stronger role in providing income support for the nation's workers in their old age."[83] Yet workers' retirement funds continue to be controlled by private managers whose investment criteria often conflict with the interests of their supposed beneficiaries. In the 1980s, pensions funds pumped billions into leveraged buyouts and mergers that destroyed jobs and into the stocks of corporations that moved operations abroad.[84] The corporate accounting scandals of 2001 revealed that many bankrupt companies' retirement funds were still overinvested in their own stock, which wiped out their employees' pensions. Private fund managers have been reluctant to intervene on behalf of employees' interests in questions of corporate governance and policy through shareholder resolutions and proxy votes. Subscribing to a narrow definition of fiduciary responsibility, pension managers still tend to see beneficiaries as shareholders rather than as jobholders or participants in corporate governance.[85] And despite the raft of problems with individual retirement accounts, the Bush administration moved to partially privatize Social Security funds in 2005.

❋ ❋ ❋

Television investigative reporters were deeply affected by the mainstream political embrace of consumerism and the business-led backlash it attracted. In retrospect, the irony of these two documentaries on consumer issues is that both seem to have had greater impacts on broadcast regulation than financial regulation. The controversy over *Banks and the Poor* helped PBS's foes limit its producers' independence and reduce contentious muckraking on public television. The struggle over *Pensions* helped undermine enforcement of the fairness doctrine by crystallizing media and judicial opposition to the rule's requirements for balancing points of view. These reports' foes, no friends to the consumer movement, successfully turned the fairness and accuracy of television news into consumer issues, perhaps to greater impact than the critiques on issues of the reports themselves.

PART II

REPRESENTATION

4   *Dividing and Distracting the Media*

The impact of investigative reporting on policy and public opinion depends in part on how the rest of the news media react to muckraking stories and any countercharges they provoke. The news media provide the main public forum for subsequent discussion of issues raised by investigative reporters. The media can keep a story alive and build momentum for reform by treating investigative reports as credible, repeating their charges, engaging in further investigation of them, and offering space for like-minded speakers to confirm their analysis of problems and offer policy solutions. Or the news media help kill stories and block change through inattention, refutation, and diversion from the issues raised by muckrakers. Just as investigative reporters frame reality, so the rest of the media frame investigative reporting and its controversies. In these case studies, critics and proponents especially cited print commentary as a resource for attacking and defending reports, the networks' right to muckrake in general, and broadcast regulation. Print coverage of television documentaries has not been studied systematically in the past. Instead, scholars and journalists have tended to cite only the verdicts of television reviewers, who were boosters for the documentary format. Relying on reviewers has offered a deceptively rosy image of how the rest of the media reacted to disputed reports. Little attention has been paid to how network affiliates reacted to investigative reporting despite the fact that the networks depended on these stations to serve as the local outlets for their programs.

In addition to the importance of the media as a public forum, there is another compelling reason to study other news organizations' response to network muckraking. If journalism as a whole became more adversarial to government and business in the 1960s and 1970s, we would expect the rest of the media to have affirmed contentious network documentaries in several ways. First, at a bare minimum, we would expect that other media paid attention to these reports and the controversies they provoked rather than allowing the stories to die on the vine and the pressure on journalists to go unexposed. Second, we would expect that other news organizations reacted affirmatively to the reports. If the media were oppositional, they would have agreed with the political analysis offered in the documentaries. We would expect other journalists to have endorsed television reporters' news gathering and story-telling methods, which were at issue in so many inquiries. We would imagine that the media defended television reporters' First Amendment rights to investigate and take positions on controversial issues. After all, the print media faced many of the same attacks on their rights, especially during the Nixon years, and broadcast affiliates' news operations would have been subject to the same regulatory constraints imposed on the networks that emerged from these government probes. Third, we would expect an adversarial news media to keep attention focused on the issues raised in muckraking reports rather than diverting attention to the procedural claims made against them. As we have seen, attacks on documentaries were, in part, attempts to redirect the public gaze from antipoverty, Cold War, and consumerist struggles to the ethics of television news gathering, editing, and balance. Did media response focus primarily on the charges raised by the documentaries, conferring additional credibility and authority upon them by advancing their stories, or did the media emphasize the charges against television reports, thereby permitting critics to frame the controversies as about broadcast news rather than the issues it covered?

Three documentaries, one from each major issue area that generated controversy, sparked longer controversies and attracted attention from more government agencies than their counterparts, and so were likely to have attracted more media attention as well. *Hunger in America, The Selling of the Pentagon,* and *Pensions* took liberal stands on highly disputed issues, and the media reaction to these can be studied. Affiliates' reaction to these controversies can be assessed by examining broadcasters' actions at industry meetings and in regulatory arenas. Print response can be measured through a content analysis of major newspapers' opinion articles (including editorials, op-eds, columns, and reviews) as well as coverage in the three major newsmagazines.[1] Opinion articles have the advantage of offering the least ambiguous expressions of support or criticism for the documentaries. Furthermore, reviews, especially in prestige papers such as the *New York Times* and *Washington Post,* were influential in the broadcast industry.[2] Like other opinion articles, reviews were less constrained by expectations of objectivity and balance; reviewers did not just evaluate how well documentaries told their stories, but they also editorialized on the issues treated in them. The news magazines, which presented themselves as providing greater depth and analysis than other media, also tended to frame issues more clearly and strongly than did newspaper reporting. Therefore, in this study I considered magazine reports as closer to opinion pieces. In addition, news magazines provide an overview of print coverage because, as Robert Entman notes, they "arguably summarize the dominant news and editorial emphases of the national media in the United States [and] their less frequent deadlines usually allow them to canvass official sources (and other media) more thoroughly, distilling the results in a narrative reflecting the principal themes in the news."[3]

To draw the conclusions offered here, I sampled newspapers and magazines that were regularly accused of being too liberal (*New York Times, Washington Post, Newsweek, Christian Science Monitor*), some that were generally considered conservative (*Chicago Tribune, Wall Street Journal, U.S. News and World Report*), and some that were considered moderate or criticized from both the right and left (*Time, Los Angeles Times*). Here, print outlets are categorized on the ideological spectrum according to their editorial positions on the issues covered in the documentaries under scrutiny. For example, in the case of *Hunger in America,* a paper's position was categorized as liberal or conservative according to whether the editorial nearest in time to the program's air date supported or opposed the documentary's call for increased food aid. It was almost always possible to find editorials written prior to a documentary's appearance, thereby reducing the possibility that the television report influenced the paper's editorial stand. Magazines, which did not carry editorials labeled as such, were omitted from this part of the analysis. The sample overrepresents papers that took liberal positions, as four of the six papers studied consistently took this editorial position, and these papers tended to devote more space to op-eds and television columns (the *New York Times* and *Washington Post* were especially heavily represented throughout). Not included were many smaller dailies and magazines, which tended to be more conservative. Because documentary critics often cited articles from these publications to support their views, especially in the *Congressional Record,* these articles are occasionally discussed here to supplement the content analysis of the major publications.

Media response was coded at three levels: the source, the paragraph, and the article. Source counts indicate which actors were able to insert their views into the debate, but they do not say whether those views were upheld or rejected.[4] Coding paragraphs provides a better gauge of how often opposing views are cited in the course of an argument and therefore made available to readers. Coding at the level of the article reveals the overall position or subject of an opinion piece. Considering coverage only at this level risks overstating an author's commitment to a particular stance or attention to an issue by omitting qualifying arguments and concealing the diversity of positions treated. Yet it acts as a check on the rare article that mostly presents one side of an argument only to attack it through sarcasm, caricature, or terse rebuttal.

Paragraphs coded as supportive of investigative reports included only positive expressions of, or about, claims made by the reports or defenses of the programs of any kind against their critics. Positive statements included those that echoed the networks' resistance to political and regulatory pressure. Conversely, paragraphs critical of the reports included only negative expressions of, or about, the reports' claims or support for the documentaries' critics. Paragraphs were coded as "mixed" when they included at least one example of a positive and a negative assessment of the report or its opponents. Paragraphs that did not explicitly refer to claims about the report were excluded from the analysis. Articles were coded based on whether the total number of paragraphs supporting any one of the three positions exceeded the number of paragraphs supporting the other two positions *combined*. An article was coded as supportive when the number of supportive paragraphs exceeded the combined number of critical and mixed paragraphs. Table 1 shows the statements about each report that most often triggered each coding.

Summary Analysis: Differing Levels of Support

In the aggregate, print response was more likely to support than attack the documentaries' issue frames and their right to criticize their targets, although opinion was by no means uniformly positive (see table 2). For all case studies combined, 57.6 percent of articles supported the documentaries, with the remainder split between articles that opposed them (18.8 percent) and those that mixed favorable and unfavorable coverage (23.5 percent). At the level of the paragraph, support declined somewhat, suggesting that documentary critics were a bit more successful in getting their views into print. Of all paragraphs, 51.9 percent were supportive, 25.4 percent critical, and 22.7 percent mixed. The source counts show a more complex picture, indicating that critics were successful at getting their views in print even if they were not always treated approvingly. Table 3 groups sources cited according to whether they spoke on behalf of or against the programs, or expressed no clear and consistent evaluation of them ("Mixed").[5] I will have more to say later about the kinds of sources permitted to speak; for now, it is enough to observe that across all three case studies, prodocumentary sources held but a slim advantage over antidocumentary sources (368 to 326).

If print commentary voiced support for these investigative reports on the whole, it spoke very differently depending on the type of article (see table 4).

Table 1. Most Common Statements about Reports

Hunger in America	
Supportive	Critical
° Federal food programs do not serve the poor adequately ° Federal food programs serve farmers' needs before those of the poor ° Hunger is widespread ° Malnutrition harms childhood development ° Hunger is unjust, or a national shame	° Federal food programs serve the poor sufficiently, or are too generous ° The poor are hungry because of their own shortcomings (lack of education, laziness, poor dietary choices, etc.) ° The report is inaccurate (hunger is not as widespread or dangerous as CBS claimed; the baby portrayed as dying of hunger died of other causes) ° The report is sensationalistic
Selling of the Pentagon	
Supportive	Critical
° The report is courageous or muckraking ° Pentagon public relations is wasteful ° The military propagandizes American citizens ° Criticisms of the report are unsubstantiated, hypocritical, or politically motivated ° CBS is right to oppose the Congressional contempt citation on First Amendment grounds	° The report misquotes sources or is unfairly edited ° The report's case against the military is inaccurate, biased, or overstated (e.g., some public relations is necessary or benign) ° The Pentagon, Vice President Agnew, or Congress is right to criticize the report
Pensions	
Supportive	Critical
° The report was impressive muckraking ° The pension system has many problems (lack of portability, plan termination, poorly invested, etc.) ° Critics of the report are abusing the fairness doctrine, violating broadcasters' free speech rights	° The report portrays the pension system inaccurately ° NBC overstates pension difficulties, calls for costly regulation ° NBC fails to present a balanced report by including pension defenders

Reviewers were extraordinarily solicitous of broadcast documentaries, generally endorsing their framings of events and praising the networks for engaging in investigative reporting. As one reviewer admitted in 1975, "Too often, TV critics can be found rushing to any TV documentary's script and churning out a column merely by recapitulating the content of the documentary."[6] In addition, television columnists usually completed their stories before documentary opponents launched public rebuttals. Reviews of *Hunger in America*, although scarce, uniformly praised the documentary's treatment of the issue, adopting CBS's framing of "hunger amid plenty" or "the tragic story of poverty."[7] None of these articles linked *Hunger in America* to the hearings

Table 2. Print Response to Reports

	Articles		
	Supportive	Critical	Mixed
Hunger (n=11)	54.5%	27.3%	18.2%
Selling (n=55)	58.2	12.7	29.1
Pensions (n=19)	57.9	31.6	10.5
All Reports (n=85)	57.6	18.8	23.5
	Paragraphs		
	Supportive	Critical	Mixed
Hunger (n=83)	57.8%	22.9%	19.3%
Selling (n=324)	50.3	23.5	26.2
Pensions (n=109)	52.3	33.0	14.7
All Reports (n=516)	51.9	25.4	22.7

Note: Totals may not add up to 100 percent because of rounding. There is no statistically significant difference between levels of support for each report.

Table 3. Sources Cited in Print Response to Reports

	Supportive		Critical		Mixed	
Hunger (n=222)	*Hunger*	34.2%	USDA	27.9%	Health experts	8.6%
	Poverty		Local govt.	4.1	Misc.	3.6
	movement	16.2				
	CBS	3.6	Congress	1.8		
	Totals	54.0		33.8		12.2
Selling (n=360)	CBS	23.9	Congress	22.8	FCC	4.7
	Other media	9.2	Nixon adm.	16.1	Misc.	2.2
	Selling	7.2	Pentagon	8.1	Congress	1.4
	Congress	4.4				
	Totals	44.7		47.0		8.3
Pensions (n=169)	NBC	23.7	FCC	17.2	Misc.	4.2
	Pensions	10.6	AIM	14.8		
	Other media	9.5	Other critics	8.9		
	D.C. circuit	4.7	D.C. circuit	3.5		
	Pension critics	3.0				
	Totals	51.5		44.4		4.2
All Reports (n=751)		49.0		42.5		8.6

Note: Totals may not add up to 100 percent because of rounding.

conducted by the Senate Poverty Subcommittee. Reviews of *The Selling of the Pentagon* were also unanimously favorable. Although a few reviewers briefly mentioned the report's debt to Senator Fulbright, all depicted it as an impressive and exceptional bit of investigative reporting. *Newsweek* praised it as "a landmark of sorts . . . a convincing demonstration that when it comes

Table 4. Print Response to Reports, by Article Type

	Supportive	Critical	Mixed
Reviews (n=60)	83.3%	10.0%	6.7%
Op-Eds/Columns (n=237)	51.5	30.4	18.1
Editorials (n=139)	50.4	25.9	25.9
News Magazines (n=80)	32.6	25.0	42.5
All Reports (n=516)	51.9	25.4	22.7

Note: The unit of analysis is the paragraph. Differences in levels of support between article types are statistically significant (p < .01 at 6 df using one-tailed chi-square test).

to stage-managing the news, no one tries harder or succeeds better than the government itself."[8] The *Washington Post* put it "in the finest tradition of muckraking TV documentary."[9] The *New York Times* wrote that CBS "packed its old-time wallop last night in a brilliant documentary . . . one of the best on TV in a great many years." The review continued, "An institution supposed to be untouchable was roughed up by some hard-nosed digging that not once impinged on national security."[10] Of all journalists, television columnists were most likely to perpetuate the myth of broadcast muckraking as an independent and aggressive force confronting "Washington," ignoring its dependence on government sources.[11]

Op-eds, columns, and editorials displayed a greater range of opinion about the disputed reports. These articles usually appeared after the documentaries were accused of misrepresenting their subjects and sometimes acted as a vehicle for new charges and countercharges. The majority of this kind of coverage sided with the networks, but, as explored below, there were important differences between conservative and liberal papers' opinion pages. Magazines tended to treat the documentary controversies evenhandedly, balancing support and criticism, and playing their role as summarizers of the range of views in the news.

The volume of reaction on the opinion pages and in magazines was lower than one might expect considering the centrality of welfare policy, the war, and pension reform to public debate at the time, not to mention the free-speech issues raised by the investigations of broadcast reporting. This was especially true of commentary on *Hunger in America,* which comprised just eleven articles over a one-year period. Vigorous efforts to reform food aid continued after the report aired. In December 1968, the prominent liberal group Americans for Democratic Action denounced Congressman Whitten's probe into the report as "a gross abuse of both Congressional and executive authority and a dangerous threat to the right of free expression," urging the media to be particularly concerned about the threat Congress posed to their First Amendment rights.[12] Indeed, given the swirl of government investigative activity around *Hunger in America,* one might expect the country's leading papers and newsmagazines to have carried some defense of CBS's ability to take a government agency to task. Yet the print media sounded no call to arms on behalf of the documentary nor of broadcast investigative journalism in general. In particular, there was little response by the editorial and op-ed writers of the major daily papers. *Pensions* also drew little commentary—just nineteen articles over a three-year period in which Congress continued to debate pension reform legislation and the fairness doctrine case wound its way through FCC and court hearings that offered many news pegs. The *Selling of the Pentagon* controversy, which lasted just five months, sparked far greater media reaction, largely because of the high stakes House vote on whether to hold CBS's Frank Stanton in contempt.

In short, print coverage overall tended to support the documentaries more than it opposed them. However, the print media did not cry out as one to celebrate or defend broadcast reporting. Sources hostile to the documentaries appeared almost as often as supporters. With the exception of *The Selling of the Pentagon,* the documentary struggles were not featured often in opinion coverage, and initial reviews were more positive than subsequent coverage.

Liberal versus Conservative, Network versus Affiliate

Perhaps the worst-kept secret in television at the time was affiliate stations' growing discomfort with network news coverage, particularly of the Vietnam War, student militancy, civil rights, and police brutality.[13] Local broadcasters tended to be both more conservative and less willing to risk profits by carrying prime-time news programming, particularly if it were likely to stir controversy in their home markets. CBS News had spurred conflicts with affiliates since Edward R. Murrow's reports on Senator Joseph McCarthy in the 1950s.[14] In 1961, CBS News president Richard Salant argued to affiliates that "the price of avoiding angry letters is blandness; the price of blandness, in this field at least, is public indifference; and we cannot afford those prices either."[15] Nonetheless, CBS previewed its documentaries to local stations via closed circuit to give affiliates a chance to preempt them, a system that Fred Friendly, Salant's temporary successor, admitted "tempered our broadcasts . . . I found myself subconsciously applying a new kind of conformity to our documentaries."[16] Also in 1961, NBC News executives had to defend the *NBC White Paper* series against stations' objections to its "editorial comments" and "slanting" of reports.[17] Ten years later, thirty CBS stations still refused to carry the *CBS Reports* documentary series, and local station delegates attacked NBC News at their annual meeting for alleged liberal slant.[18]

In the print media, liberal publications were much more likely than conservative ones to devote space to these reports but only somewhat more likely to praise and defend the documentaries (a difference that was not statistically significant). Opinion paragraphs in papers that editorialized similarly to the documentaries were 56.5 percent positive, while those in more conservative papers were 50.0 percent supportive (see table 5). As argued below, this unity of support came more from shared concerns about journalistic freedom than from conservative endorsements of the documentaries' analysis of food aid, military PR, or pension reform. However, table 5 also suggests that liberal papers paid far more attention to the documentary disputes than did conservative ones, contributing 352 of all 426 paragraphs coded. This is true despite the oversampling of liberal print media: liberal outlets devoted an average of 88 paragraphs to the controversies, while conservative outlets spent an average of just under 25 paragraphs.

Hunger in America

However, support did divide rather cleanly among liberal and conservative print media in coverage of *Hunger in America*. Papers were categorized as liberal if they called for expanding food aid and/or criticized the USDA for favoring the interests of farmers over the poor. Some 81.8 percent of paragraphs in liberal papers backed *Hunger in America*, while 52.0 percent of coverage in conservative papers did likewise. The split emerged even in the different kinds of praise that reviewers offered. Jack Gould of the *New York*

Table 5. Print Response to Reports, By Editorial Position

	Supportive	Critical	Mixed
Hunger			
Liberal (n=33)	81.8%	0.0%	18.2%
Conservative (n=25)	52.0	28.0	20.0
Selling			
Liberal (n=220)	55.9	23.2	20.9
Conservative (n=48)	47.9	29.2	22.9
Pensions			
Liberal (n=99)	49.5	35.4	15.2
Conservative (n=1)	100.0	0.0	0.0
All Reports			
Liberal (n=352)	56.5	24.4	19.0
Conservative (n=74)	50.0	28.4	21.6
Total (n=426)	55.4	25.1	19.5

Note: Totals may not add up to 100 percent because of rounding. Differences in levels of support between liberal and conservative media were statistically significant only in the case of *Hunger* (p < .01 at 2 df using a one-tailed chi-square test).

Times commended the program, if not CBS, for having "successfully pricked the conscience of the viewing citizen, especially when seen in conjunction with a companion spot announcement glamorously proclaiming the consumer as 'king.'"[19] In a second review published after *Hunger in America* was attacked and rebroadcast, Gould offered an extended defense of the program, casting it as an example of television muckraking at its best: "The power of television to rock the social status quo with rare constructive force," he gushed, "has been brilliantly demonstrated." Gould used the controversy to urge the networks to do more such investigative journalism, "to get mad on occasion and make a sustained fight for what it knows is right." Indeed, for Gould, the documentary showed that the for-profit networks were still legitimate and necessary because of their substantial resources and creative talents: "The case illustrates why even granting all the imperfections of a medium economically rooted in the mores of Madison Avenue, commercial TV continues to have a viability not to be denied."[20] Clay Gowran, of the conservative *Chicago Tribune,* took a different tack. He praised *Hunger in America* as "the kind of reporting television can do better than magazines or newspapers, because it can put the living, moving, hurting human evidence of its findings before the audience, to tell without necessity for words its own story." But Gowran's conclusion read against the grain of the documentary's argument. "There is another side to the picture," he wrote, "and CBS touched upon it." He noted that "almost every family shown was enormous," cited the San Antonio county commissioner's argument that poor fathers wouldn't work, and ended by frowning on America's willingness to feed the poor abroad before feeding its own. In short, the liberal Gould praised *Hunger in America* as an example of the prestigious investigative documentaries that legitimated network television and still contributed greatly toward excusing its unfortunate commercialism. By contrast, Gowran commended the documentary for its immediacy but only by reframing it somewhat as including criticism of the poor and international food aid.

The ideological split was even clearer on newspapers' opinion pages.[21] The *Christian Science Monitor,* which called for additional food aid, carried an op-ed column that intertwined excerpts from the documentary with criticism of food stamps as unaffordable, and of the USDA as catering to agribusiness rather than feeding the poor.[22] By contrast, a *Chicago Tribune* editorial dismissed the CBS report as inaccurate, discussing at length Secretary Freeman's claims that one of the Alabama families shown in *Hunger in America* would have been able to buy food stamps more cheaply than they said, given their stated income.[23] The problem of hunger, the *Tribune* concluded, "is more likely to be remedied by careful consideration of facts, rather than through careless appeals to emotions." Some papers that had editorialized on the left and right sides of the food issue mixed support and criticism. The "liberal" *Washington Post* referred to *Hunger in America* in an editorial entitled "Poverty—and Progress," which speculated that hunger "may not, upon investigation, prove to be very widespread" but that the government ought to try to eliminate it nonetheless.[24] The *Wall Street Journal* mentioned the documentary briefly in an editorial that attacked international food aid, domestic farm subsidies, and welfare as wasteful and ineffective.[25] "The Columbia Broadcasting System and others may, as Mr. Freeman believes, overstate the prevalence of hunger in the U.S.," the *Journal* wrote. "To the extent that hunger exists, at any rate, it is clearly not the fault of inefficient agriculture. . . . It can more reasonably be blamed on the curious mix of Federal farm and welfare policies."[26]

The Selling of the Pentagon

Network-affiliate friction was most intense over *The Selling of the Pentagon.* The report ignited CBS stations, with a little prodding from the network's foes in the White House. At a March 1971 meeting of CBS's advisory board of affiliates, network executives faced angry local station owners who thought *The Selling of the Pentagon* should have given more time to military spokesmen to defend the Pentagon.[27] A Charlotte, North Carolina, affiliate offered an entire hour of prime time to the administration and to Congressman Hébert because it believed the documentary's foes were not given adequate time to respond after the network rebroadcast *The Selling of the Pentagon.* At the National Association of Broadcasters convention in March, a CBS affiliate attempted to organize a mass exodus of stations from the network.[28] As of mid-April, only 5 of 204 CBS affiliates had sent messages of support to the network for refusing to honor the House subpoena.[29] Even CBS chairman William Paley had reservations about the editing of the documentary, and later faulted network president Frank Stanton for spending too much time and money defending it.[30]

Print reactions to *The Selling of the Pentagon* appear less closely linked to papers' editorial positions than in the case of *Hunger in America,* with 55.9 percent of coverage in liberal papers supporting the documentary and 47.9 percent in conservative outlets. In this case, liberal papers were defined as those that editorially attacked military news management or the credibility of Pentagon and Nixon administration claims to be ending the Vietnam War swiftly. Conservative papers were defined as defending the Defense Department and administration on these issues. However, these totals mask the initial divisions among the media along liberal-conservative lines. It was only after the House subpoenaed CBS's outtakes and notes that journalists perceived a common threat to their interests, and support solidified behind CBS on

First Amendment grounds. Throughout the conflict, many columnists and editorialists treated the accusations of unfair editing against the documentary as legitimate and important. As a result, the media themselves displayed anxieties about the quality of television news that undermined any broad defense of the program or of television's free-speech rights. A *Christian Science Monitor* editorial was typical of many opinion pieces in liberal papers in that it blamed CBS for "inaccurate reporting and unfair editing" while resisting "any inclination of government to move into an editorial office of any kind no matter what mistakes may have been committed."[31] The *Chicago Tribune* put it more bluntly in an editorial that grudgingly supported the House vote excusing CBS even as it characterized the program as "an abomination of innuendo and juggled film sequences."[32]

The Selling of the Pentagon probably garnered as much praise and defense as it did because the major papers linked the affair to the larger Nixon administration attacks on the news media and because military credibility was at a low ebb after two years of expanding the Vietnam War amid promises to curb U.S. involvement. Of the major papers included here, all but the conservative *Chicago Tribune* and *Wall Street Journal* were chafing at the White House campaign against the media during this period, and they were regularly criticizing the administration's handling of the war (although this criticism was of a mainly technical nature). The *New York Times* and *Washington Post* were particularly sensitive to administration efforts to manage war coverage, and these two papers were by far the biggest contributors of opinion pieces to the study, with a combined twenty-seven opinion pieces comprising 49.0 percent of all articles (data not shown in tables).

Many smaller and more conservative publications not included in the sample assailed *The Selling of the Pentagon* more fully, deriding both the editing and the politics of the CBS documentary. These articles were cited widely by CBS's congressional critics and entered into the *Congressional Record.* The *Detroit News,* for example, found Agnew "restrained, indeed charitable, last week when he charged CBS with distorting facts and making propaganda in its recent so-called documentary on the Pentagon."[33] The *Arizona Republic* called *The Selling of the Pentagon* a "hatchet job" in which "scenes were spliced, edited, and chopped beyond recognition in order to make the worst possible case against the 'military establishment.'" The paper attacked all network documentaries as "set[ting] out to present a liberal point of view."[34] Although admitting the Pentagon should "re-examine some of its informational programs," the *San Diego Union* told its readers that "what CBS intended to be an indictment of armed forces public relations emerges more as an indictment of its own standards."[35] The *Omaha World-Herald* called the broadcast

"The Smearing of the Pentagon."[36] But the strongest attack came in *Barron's National and Financial Weekly,* in a front-page editorial that rehashed ten years of allegations against CBS News documentaries, drawing mainly on two sources: Staggers's subcommittee and Accuracy in Media. *Barron's* concluded that CBS "had forfeited its access to the nation's airwaves" and that "the time has come to turn it off."[37]

These political divisions were thrown into relief by an Agnew appearance in St. Louis in March 1971 where he blasted *The Selling of the Pentagon.* The White House ensured that press credentials to cover Agnew's news conference would be distributed by the conservative *St. Louis Globe-Democrat.* The *Globe-Democrat* denied passes to their more liberal rivals at the *St. Louis Post-Dispatch,* who protested. In the end, the chosen reporters sat around a table with Agnew, while the uncredentialed journalists were shunted off to sit around the walls of the room and forbidden by Agnew's staff to pose any questions. The following day, the *Globe-Democrat* reported that the press conference was "a no-holds barred meeting with newsmen. No restrictions were imposed by Agnew on what type of questions could be asked."[38]

It was only after CBS president Stanton faced the contempt citation that the media as a whole—print and television, liberal and conservative—recognized a common threat to their interests and mobilized their resources against it. The National Association of Broadcasters passed a resolution in support of CBS, as did the American Society of Newspaper Editors, the Association of American Publishers, the Newspaper Guild, and the National Academy of Arts and Sciences. The Peabody Award committee hastened to honor *The Selling of the Pentagon* before the House vote. The report won an Emmy for best documentary and many other journalism prizes. CBS mounted its lobbying campaign, including soliciting letters of support from journalism schools and professors and pressure from some CBS affiliates on members of the House.

Pensions

Print commentary also divided over *Pensions* and broadcast regulation, although not between supporters and detractors but between supporters and ignorers. In this case, liberal papers were defined as those that endorsed the Williams-Javits plan and conservative papers as those that expressed reservations about the bill, citing the overall soundness of the private pension system or the costs of regulation. Liberal outlets, while primarily supporting *Pensions,* offered a less clear defense of this report than they had for the prior documentaries, with 49.5 percent of coverage positive and 35.4 percent negative. Conservative papers' opinion pages ignored the story, devoting just one paragraph to it (thus the 100 percent positive reading is misleading). The lower level of liberal support for *Pensions* was mainly due to splits over the value of the fairness doctrine. In discussing the controversy, *Los Angeles Times* editorial writers and *New York Times* columnist Tom Wicker repeatedly opposed the FCC's ruling against the documentary as government intervention in journalistic decision making, while *New York Times* television critic John J. O'Connor wrote several columns affirming the need for broadcast fairness. In this case, print journalists reflected larger divisions over the fairness doctrine that crossed the bounds of traditional political ideologies (as discussed more fully in chapter 5). For their part, conservative papers may have avoided the story since it offered no clear position for them to take. Had they sided with the FCC against a liberal network documentary, they would have had to endorse government intervention in the broadcast industry. Had they sided with NBC, they would have been offering aid and comfort to a report that implied the need for stricter regulation of the pension industry.

Even local stations were not entirely supportive of NBC's attempt to use *Pensions* as a test case against the fairness doctrine. Shortly after the report aired, the National Broadcast Editorial Association, representing station editorialists, organized a committee on freedom of information. The committee's first task was to report on the NBC case, and it reached a split verdict. A "majority report" found that "responsible journalism should place shocking disclosures properly within the context of what is 'working right,'" and that *Pensions* "with undue zeal had subordinated balance to program impact." Yet, it continued, "we believe . . . that for such delicate questions of documentary program content to be evaluated by the FCC would indeed drastically inhibit broadcasting exercise of gutsy journalism." Among the two authors of this less-than-ringing proclamation on behalf of *Pensions* was a representative of NBC's owned-and-operated Chicago station, WMAQ. A "minority report," penned by another local broadcaster, was even more critical of NBC's refusal to honor the fairness doctrine, arguing, "The broadcaster, more than any other single part of the communications complex, must think of himself as a conduit for increasing the understanding of controversial issues."[39]

In short, the media did not present a united front to documentary critics. Ideological differences over welfare, the military, and television regulation helped shape coverage of the reports—more so than the content analysis sometimes reveals. Even within broadcasting, affiliates shied away from divisive programming and assailed the network news departments as too far left. Rather than revealing widespread liberalism and adversarialism, print and local station responses demonstrated substantial resistance to network news's criticism of government and business, and broadcasters' First Amendment interests.

Driven to Distraction

Who was most successful at setting the terms of these public disputes, and did news coverage present these battles as over policy issues (food aid, the military, and retirement funds) or over First Amendment issues? Did the print media primarily defend the documentaries because of how they framed their subject matter or because of other considerations? To answer these questions, print response was coded for whether it focused on charges made by a documentary or charges made against it by its critics, regardless of whether these accusations were treated positively or negatively. Coverage emphasized accusations made by the documentaries when it included only statements about the subject matter in the reports. Coverage focused on charges against reports when it included only statements about the criticisms of the documentaries without discussing what the reports covered.

Table 6 shows that documentary critics were increasingly successful at

Table 6. Focus on Charges by and against Reports in Print Response

	By Report	Against Report	Mixed
Hunger			
Reviews (n=36)	94.4%	0.0%	5.6%
Editorials (n=15)	60.0	26.7	13.3
Op-Eds/Columns (n=6)	100.0	0.0	0.0
News Magazines (n=27)	66.7	25.9	7.4
Total (n=84)	79.8	13.1	7.1
Selling			
Reviews (n=30)	86.7	10.0	3.3
Editorials (n=107)	10.3	81.3	8.4
Op-Eds/Columns (n=142)	47.2	45.1	7.7
News Magazines (n=42)	4.8	81.0	14.3
Total (n=321)	33.0	58.6	8.4
Pensions			
Editorials (n=13)	30.8	38.5	30.8
Op-Eds/Columns (n=87)	18.4	57.5	24.1
News Magazines (n=9)	11.1	55.6	33.3
Total (n=109)	19.3	55.0	25.7
All Reports			
Reviews (n=66)	90.9	4.5	4.5
Editorials (n=135)	17.8	71.1	11.1
Op-Eds/Columns (n=235)	37.9	48.5	13.6
News Magazines (n=78)	26.9	59.0	14.1
Total (n=514)	37.7	50.4	11.9

Note: The unit of analysis is the paragraph. Totals may not add up to 100 percent because of rounding. Differences in levels of support between article types were statistically significant for *Hunger* (p < .05 at 6 df), *Selling* (p < .01 at 6 df), and all reports combined (p < .05 at 6 df), using one-tailed chi-square tests.

shifting print attention from the reports' subjects to the charges against them. Of all paragraphs, 50.4 percent focused on accusations against the documentaries while 37.7 percent emphasized the allegations made by them. Reviews, which usually appeared before documentary critics raised objections, almost always stuck to the documentary's concerns. All other articles tended to focus most on the charges against the reports. There was no significant difference between liberal and conservative papers in this regard.

Coverage of *Hunger in America* kept the focus on the documentary's complaints about the USDA. Those who attempted to debunk the network's criticism of federal food programs in print did so mainly by offering their own framings of the hunger issue rather than redirecting public attention to issues of news staging or sensationalism. Whether coverage favored or opposed the report's charges about the scope and causes of hunger, 79.8 percent of all paragraphs were about those charges. Just 13.1 percent of paragraphs mentioned solely the accusations of staging, inaccuracy, or sensationalism, revealing no other information about the subject matter of the documentary. Congressman Gonzalez's numerous soliloquies on staging given from the House floor and Congressman Whitten's investigation of CBS inspired no commentary in the major papers. If CBS detractors succeeded in creating some doubts about the accuracy of *Hunger in America* in the media, they were unable to divert attention from the hunger issue. In part, this was because an organized constituency of antihunger forces continued to press the USDA, especially the Poor People's Campaigners and the Citizen's Board. As shown in table 3, this was the only case in which social movement sources were cited during controversies over reports. Most important, Senate forces continued to hold hearings, introduce legislation, and lobby the White House for greater food aid.

Coverage of *The Selling of the Pentagon* was very different. Whether editorial and op-ed writers defended CBS, they did not primarily debate the virtues of military propaganda but whether documentary editing could be trusted and whether television journalists should be subject to congressional subpoena. Only the reviews, written before the attacks on *The Selling of the Pentagon* began, gave full play to the accusations against the Pentagon. Of all paragraphs, 33.0 percent focused mainly on the issues CBS raised about military publicity, while 58.6 percent grappled mostly with the claims that the documentary misquoted sources and was unfairly edited, or commented on whether the congressional subpoena was legal and the White House criticism was proper. The Pentagon, Agnew, and Congressmen Hébert and Staggers successfully deflected attention from the military to the media.

Why was *The Selling of the Pentagon* less successful than *Hunger in America* at keeping media attention focused on its investigative target? First, the Pentagon's public relations arsenal made the Agriculture Department's look like a pitchfork in comparison. The Defense Department brought greater resources to bear on its battle with CBS, particularly in the hometown media. Second, there was no organized constituency for reducing the Pentagon's public relations budget that could win the ear of Congress the way that the War on Poverty groups had done. The mainstream antiwar movement had not made propaganda a priority, and the New Left was untouchable for almost everyone on Capitol Hill. Third, and perhaps most important, there was no vocal congressional leadership on the issue. Senator Fulbright was curiously silent in the last months before the contempt vote, and there was no comparable figure in the House who was willing to keep the heat on the Pentagon. Finally, CBS shares some of the blame for the ease with which the Defense Department wriggled free from further scrutiny. The network responded to criticism with a legal and a lobbying strategy of rallying the media around the First Amendment by focusing on reporters' privilege issues. CBS also could have fought back by releasing more information its documentarians had gathered on the Pentagon. Producer Peter Davis would have much preferred this option, which might have inspired congressional inquiries into military public relations rather than news editing.[40]

Print discussion of *Pensions* also focused more on the charges raised against the report (55.0 percent) than by it (19.3 percent). It is remarkable that NBC's account of pension problems was widely ignored since pension legislation was pending for two years after the network aired its story and reform enjoyed broad congressional support. NBC and print journalists were most responsible for converting the struggle over *Pensions* into a referendum on the fairness doctrine. *New York Times* television columnist John J. O'Connor scored NBC for shifting the battle over retirement funds off the airwaves and into the courts by refusing to engage pension critics in on-air debate. "In the end," he wrote, "the subject of pensions became secondary to NBC's campaign against the Fairness Doctrine. Information and debate were sacrificed to corporate crusading."[41] Alas, O'Connor was also responsible for concentrating on the media freedom aspects of the case, writing several columns that were more concerned with defending FCC regulations than exploring NBC's and AIM's views on pension reform.

In these case studies, the print media increasingly aided sources that distracted public attention from the documentary's subjects. Often, it was because print commentary followed journalistic custom by letting government sources shape the news agenda. Just as the controversial reports were indexed to official opinion, so were the reactions to them. In addition, the networks themselves increasingly refused to continue fighting for their documentaries' political analyses, instead using the controversies to argue for less government oversight on news. *Hunger in America* provides the exception. Glancing back at table 3, one can see that print response mainly cited the documentary itself and movement forces that informed its analysis (the Poor People's Campaign and Citizen's Board) to defend the report. The agency that *Hunger in America* held responsible for food aid problems, the USDA, was most often featured criticizing the documentary. This choice of sources on both sides kept coverage focused on the charges related to welfare policy and allowed advocates of increasing aid to add to CBS's reporting. Yet, starting with *The Selling of the Pentagon,* print reaction cited the report itself less in its own defense, turning instead to network sources (who were generally defending themselves in regulatory arenas) and other media sources rebutting attacks on news ethics. The most prominent critics were not the Defense Department but congressional investigators and White House sources (mainly via Vice President Agnew's criticisms of CBS's journalistic practices). Similarly, most of the support for *Pensions* came from NBC sources, the circuit court of appeals majority that found for the network in its fairness doctrine challenge, and other media sources taking on the doctrine. The few pension critics cited all appeared in one article.[42] Here, subsequent attention to pensions, which was minimal, depended on a few comments by the report's antagonists, such as AIM and some of NBC's other critics. The main critical voices raised—the FCC, the court minority, and some media defenders of the fairness doctrine—focused on broadcast regulation, not pensions.

❉   ❉   ❉

There was no uniform "liberal" or "adversarial" reaction to these investigative reports among the media. The publications sampled here did speak more favorably than unfavorably of the documentaries' treatment of issues and their right to criticize government and business. Yet their response was characterized less by unanimity than by differences between article types and ideology. Reviewers were much more likely than other commentators to celebrate these reports, often perpetuating a mythical image of them as muckraking done wholly independently of government sources. Reviewers were most likely to present investigative reports as legitimating network television and offering evidence against government regulation of news. However, conservative papers tended to be less supportive than liberal ones, mostly because conservative media attacked the documentaries' conclusions and somewhat because these media were less likely to champion network freedom from government oversight. Many affiliates clashed with the networks, branding documentaries as excessively liberal or as controversial ratings losers. All print media focused more on First Amendment concerns raised by charges against the reports than on the issues raised by the documentaries. Despite frequent appeals to the importance of muckraking, broadcasters, print commentators, and the networks themselves helped blunt the impact these documentaries might have had in the political arena by allowing the issues they raised to be pushed out of the headlines in favor of disputes over television news techniques and regulation.

The Ethics of Representation

By the time *The Selling of the Pentagon* came under fire in 1971, attacks on investigative documentaries had assumed regular enough patterns that former CBS News president Fred Friendly compiled a mock five-step "demolition manual" for use by the aggrieved. It involved enlisting sympathetic federal politicians to decry a report, planting editorials in industry trade papers and approaching columnists in the mainstream press, organizing letter-writing campaigns to the Congress and the FCC, raising questions about television's production techniques to distract from its charges, and organizing pressure on the documentary's sponsor (a less effective effort since the early 1960s, he admitted, given the move to multiple sponsorship).[1] Indeed, as we have seen, investigative reporting's critics used many of these techniques. However, Friendly's attack kit implied that journalism's critics acted solely to defend their political and economic interests. To be sure, many campaigns against these reports' accuracy and ethics were a way of pursuing politics by other means. Many couched political and economic struggles in technical terms, as disputes over the means of depicting issues rather than over the issues themselves. Yet these factors do not fully explain why investigative reports drew such intense criticism in the 1960s and 1970s.

Many politicians' and journalists' reactions to these conflicts over reports were not simply functions of their political and economic interests. Populist Democrat Henry Gonzalez (D-Texas), who advocated expanding welfare payments, joined his conservative Texan colleagues in attacking *Hunger in America*. Some representatives who advocated immediate retreat from Vietnam and rarely praised the military still voted for the contempt citation against Frank Stanton during the *Selling of the Pentagon* brouhaha, and some who supported the war did not. Representative John E. Moss (D-Calif.), a hero to journalists for authoring the federal Freedom of Information Act, joined eight other House members in concurring with Representative Staggers's criticisms of *Project Nassau* and calling for direct regulation of the networks to ensure that they did not engage in criminal activity in pursuit of news.[2] So did Robert O. Tiernan (D-R.I.), the only House Commerce Committee member who praised *The Selling of the Pentagon* for exposing military propaganda. The *New York Times* carried extensive criticism of NBC's attempt to sink the fairness doctrine despite its editorial support for pension reform and ownership interests in broadcasting.

These reactions suggest additional reasons why the documentary provoked intense strife, despite politicians' and broadcasters' high hopes in the early 1960s that the format would serve their needs and solve television's problems. This chapter shows how officials, journalists, and broadcast executives genuinely struggled with how reporters should portray truth as they developed the tools of television journalism. By examining more deeply how politicians and journalists reacted, we can see how their growing concerns over television's representation of reality exerted their own force in these controversies. Once again, these struggles divided media and government internally, rather than simply setting them against each other as adversaries. This discussion shows how documentary critics' concerns sprang in part from conflicts over how to represent national and local interests, between the culture of print and of television, and between the demands of objectivity and the attractions of muckraking. In the end, conflicts over the ethics of representation, while not reducible to politics, were more likely to arise in the contentious political atmosphere of the late 1960s and early 1970s. This helps explain why certain issues were likely to spark representational disputes. As consensus assumptions that underpinned American poverty, consumer, and foreign policy dissolved, so too did widely shared ways of depicting them.

The Local in the National

Certainly, there were practical reasons for politicians and business organizations to direct greater scrutiny toward network documentaries than other news formats. The investigative report was a rare and prestigious event on the television schedule, and it was announced well in advance through print advertisements and promotional spots touting the networks' public-service programming. Even if the prime-time documentary never drew the same ratings as entertainment shows, it was still seen by more Americans than any comparable print report. The documentary was a discrete segment in the flow of television and therefore easier to monitor and summarize than following the evening news programs every day in an era before home video recorders. In short, the documentary was a rare bird whose flight pattern was announced

well beforehand and who rose and fell in an hour's time; if it failed to soar as
high as its competitors, it was still widely viewed, and, like most endangered
species, it had a way of drawing hunters from the bushes.

Joshua Meyrowitz writes, "A great part of the social significance of television . . . may lie less in what is *on* television than in the very existence of television as a shared arena."[3] The networks' ability to create a national news forum
was not fully realized until the early 1960s, when 90 percent of households
possessed television sets and news and public affairs programming expanded
in length, format, and amount.[4] Political and business leaders especially felt
the effects of the Washington scene's new visibility and the networks' ability
to bring local issues and figures to national prominence. Whether people paid
close attention to television news, whether they believed it or not, it had the
potential to reach them all simultaneously. As Meyrowitz notes, "knowledge
of people's access to information is itself a significant piece of social information."[5] Many political and business leaders treated the medium with an oracu-
lar power it did not possess at all times, in all circumstances, in part because
television's reach encouraged them to believe that because the whole world
might be watching, it in fact was.

Television news and documentary had a peculiar relationship to the local
that became an ongoing source of friction. On the one hand, network news
focused almost entirely on Washington doings because they were cheaper to
cover and because affiliates expected the networks to offer coverage of national
politics first and foremost (of course, stations also complained about the networks' tendency to interpret affairs from a parochial New York–Washington
perspective). On the other hand, the networks, especially in their documentaries, needed to travel further afield for local stories that could be assembled
into a package of national significance in the interests of achieving some geographic balance and appearing to cover the whole country. Thus the networks
knit local stories into national "trend" stories, sometimes forcibly.[6] Tied to a
national audience and national advertisers, the networks were less beholden
to local elites than newspapers and other broadcasters. Local boosterism and
political wounds therefore spurred some of the charges against documentaries.
Like the muckraking magazines that arose at the turn of the twentieth century,
television exposés' turn toward federal officials for their framing of social
problems conflicted with local papers' provincialism and greater indebtedness
to local power holders.[7]

Reports on poverty especially provoked outrage against documentaries
by state and local officials, spurring accusations of unfairly generalizing from
worst-case examples and presenting locales in their worst light. In *Harvest of
Shame,* Murrow took pains to emphasize at the outset that "this is a national

story" about migrant labor. In response, Senator Holland defended Florida's farmers, and the *Palm Beach Post* published a series of articles touting local farmers' and towns' efforts to improve migrant conditions. Politicians' discomfort with the networks' national gaze, at least when it looked askance at their own constituents' interests, was evident in a remarkable exchange between Senator Frank J. Lausche of Ohio and Murrow at the latter's confirmation hearings for the leadership of the United States Information Agency. Lausche, noting that constituents who wrote him believed the program reflected conditions in Ohio, asked Murrow whether he had investigated migrants in Ohio. Murrow said he had not. Lausche asked whether "your picture [was] directed at the nation as a whole?" Murrow said it was. Lausche asked incredulously, "How could you direct it at Ohio if you made no study of Ohio?"[8] Of course, requiring network muckrakers to investigate an issue in every state would have rendered national reporting impossible. The senator's remark only made sense against a background of local media covering local issues for local audiences, a background that politicians could assume more easily in the era before television.

Defenders of Newburgh, New York, also portrayed network journalists as ignorant and troublesome outsiders. Albert Wasserman, who produced *Battle of Newburgh,* later explained that when he grew interested in making a report on welfare, Newburgh "gave us a very good focus for doing a specific story involving specific people, but yet with nationwide implications."[9] In the report, Chet Huntley characterized Newburgh town manager Joseph Mitchell as "a national figure, carrying his war against welfare far beyond the tiny boundaries of his city." In response, Mitchell complained not only that NBC broke a promise to portray his views fairly but also that it ignored Newburgh's beautiful neighborhoods, portraying the entire town as a slum. Network executives and the FCC brushed aside these complaints more easily than the local media or the district's congresswoman, which both sided with Mitchell.[10]

Spiro Agnew's attack on the "eastern establishment" networks was shared by many affiliates and some liberal Democrats who asserted local and regional rights to self-definition on the national stage. Among Congressman Gonzalez's objections to *Hunger in America* was that it misleadingly offered up County Commissioner A. J. Ploch's pitiless views of San Antonio's poor as representative of an uncaring local government.[11] On the House floor, Gonzalez accused "the barons of Manhattan" of "sell[ing] the public trinkets in the place of truth."[12] If Gonzalez engaged in some trinket pushing himself when he minimized the scope of hunger in his district, he pointed to one of the more significant and least discussed biases of the television documentary: its need to nationalize local struggles for its audience.

Documentarians did not simply gravitate toward Senate sources for the inspiration of many reports because they were liberal and accessible. Federal politicians framed issues from a national perspective. Even when local figures had their say in network investigative reports, it was usually because they spoke in generalizing terms about social problems. Newburgh's Mitchell presented himself as a "symbol of unrest . . . of the people throughout the nation over welfare policies."[13] San Antonio's Ploch did not speak about the roots of hunger in San Antonio but about how hunger would always be with us because of the irresponsibility of the poor, now and forever, here and elsewhere. Nor did CBS's report on hunger frame the problem as having significant local causes in the legacy of slavery in the South, or the conquest of Texas, or the taking of the Southwest from the Navajo. National problems suggested national solutions, such as the expansion of federal food programs. It was not just network liberalism that favored federal fixes or network conservatism that avoided serious discussion of historic oppression, but a need to address a national audience.[14]

A Print Culture Encounters Television

Television images possessed new dangers for jurists, politicians, and journalists reared in an age of print, yet they struggled to understand the medium in terms of the culture of the word. Like live coverage of social protest, investigative reporting had a way of crystallizing political and media anxieties about the relatively new medium of television news. Documentary critics accorded these programs a rare power to move the public to action despite the fact that few reports ever solicited it from their audiences. Documentary disputes sparked debates between print and television journalists over the ethics of reporting and the competing authority of reporters and sources. These debates raged even within broadcast journalism itself.

Regulating Video by the Book

Documentary accusers often disparaged television news as inherently flawed by the audiovisual properties of the medium and therefore in need of stricter control than print journalism. Calling on Congress to license the networks, rather than regulating their programming indirectly through their owned-and-operated stations, Representative Gonzalez warned his House colleagues, "The combination of film and sound has always been a powerful one; it produces great drama, elicits strong emotions, sets loose fervid thought."[15] Gonzalez and others were themselves remarkably responsive to television's visual powers. All of CBS's foes spent a great deal of energy attacking *Hunger in America* for misrepresenting the San Antonio baby's cause of death as malnutrition, in what Gonzalez called "one of the most shocking scenes ever presented on television."[16] Curiously, neither Gonzalez nor any subsequent critic of the documentary (including Spiro Agnew and AIM) paid much attention to another error alleged against CBS in Congressman Whitten's report. After showing its interview with a pregnant Alabama woman, CBS told viewers that her baby later died at birth from malnutrition. According to Whitten's FBI investigators, the woman's child was stillborn because of prolonged labor (indeed, they claimed the baby was too big, necessitating a cesarean delivery). The error involving the San Antonio infant's death was remembered because the child was shown on the program being resuscitated, but the mistake concerning the unvisualized Alabama child was quickly forgotten.

Despite their professed concerns about the abuse of images and sound tracks, it is remarkable how much political and media critics judged television documentaries according to a naive model of print journalism. Without much knowledge of how film and video were produced and assembled, and lacking a language to speak of how audiovisual texts made meaning, regulators focused most of their attention on how the documentaries treated words, asking whether their sequences and meanings were faithfully reproduced. For example, many editing choices in *The Selling of the Pentagon* that contributed to the unflattering portrait of the Pentagon were not investigated. Utterly ignored were questions about how editing constructed meaning by connecting images and sounds. This is not simply a question of staging events for the cameras, which were the basis of many investigations. Instead, it concerns how television editing creates new meanings and does so in a far more complex manner than critics recognized.

Consider the sequence in *The Selling of the Pentagon* that showed children imitating hand-to-hand combat displays, which ended with images of one boy leaping on another, who began to "cry." That his "wails" were dubbed over the scene to enhance its pathos is obvious from watching the documentary. A literalist like Congressman Staggers might have made much of it. But this kind of manipulation was missed or ignored, probably because House investigators and editorialists based their conclusions on written transcripts rather than on viewing the documentary itself, although the Pentagon had quickly made it available to Staggers. CBS's critics also never appreciated how editing constructed meanings from the interaction of shots. Colonel John McNeil arguing that the United States could not pull out of Vietnam after having put a half million troops there because "we placed the national interest at stake when we did that" was followed by a cut to a close-up of a warning light blinking "Nuclear Attack on the U.S." at a Pentagon shopping mall exhibit. This was a blunt example of what film theorist and director Sergei Eisenstein called "intellectual montage," or the collision of two ideas that produces a third.[17] In this case, an argument for defending the abstract principle of American honor abroad was followed by the terrifying prospect of nuclear annihilation, suggesting that one might lead to the other. We certainly need not mourn the fact that CBS's critics failed to seize on these moments to discredit the documentary. The point is that they did not because to do so would have required considering not just whether television news treated the words of powerful sources responsibly, but how it made meaning differently from print.

So dominant was the notion that words defined social reality that regulators often judged whether documentaries had violated canons of truth and fairness with less reference to the programs themselves than to transcripts and to print reporting about them. In the most heavily litigated fairness doctrine case involving a documentary, sparked by NBC's *Pensions,* neither the complainant (AIM), nor the FCC, nor the District of Columbia Court of Appeals justices ever appear to have watched the film itself.[18] The case turned primarily on two questions: whether the report addressed a controversial subject of public importance and whether it covered the narrow issue of problems in a few pension plans or had attacked the pension system as a whole. Under the fairness doctrine, one of the main indicators of whether an issue was a public controversy was the amount of prior print coverage of the subject. In addition, NBC successfully argued to the court of appeals that *Pensions* had not addressed the overall retirement system by presenting a stack of print reviewers' commentaries on the program as evidence of what the report was about. Thus, the majority ruling not only depended on the print media to help decide whether pensions were important and controversial but also seems to have relied more heavily on the reviews than on the documentary to define the main issue of the report.[19]

Cultural Competition between Print and Broadcast Journalists

It is a rhetorical commonplace in American politics to link one's opponent with the emotional, the irrational, and the self-interested and to paint oneself as thoughtful, reasoning, and concerned with the public good. In many of these controversies it was not just the reports' political enemies who deployed these techniques but also many print journalists, even when they were expressing some support for television's First Amendment claims. A Portland *Oregonian* editorial that appeared during the *Selling of the Pentagon* dispute was typical of many opinion pieces that pointed to the junior medium's shortcomings: "The electronic media is understandably more sensitive than the print newsmen, as it operates at sufferance of the government, and has not been in the news business long enough to develop the thick skins of newspapers, that have grown up under a constant bombardment of criticism, both fair and unfair, but protected by the First Amendment. Further, television news has come out of the traditions of show business. It judges news by whether it has filmed it or not, and then it must look for the most exciting and entertaining film clips for its nightly show that must compete for audience ratings or go under."[20]

The Selling of the Pentagon showed, according to the *Oregonian*, that television was a lesser news outlet than print, not simply because of its vulnerability to regulation but because it was immature, show-business oriented, and ratings driven. Like many publications, the *Oregonian* implied that its own coverage was above influence by petty motives such as attracting readers, pleasing advertisers, generating profits, and avoiding offense against the powerful. Print commentary such as this often drew on the unexamined and long-standing cultural distinction between media based primarily on the word (as inherently complex, subtle, cognitive) and on the image (as inescapably simplistic, dramatic, affective).[21] At a time when polls claimed that television had become the primary news source for most Americans, a point remarked on by many editorialists in the documentary debates, print commentators also seemed driven by anxious attempts to maintain a higher rung on American journalism's cultural register, if not on its economic ladder.

A debate in the *Washington Post* and *Time* magazine over editing interviews, also inspired by *The Selling of the Pentagon*, exemplified representational rivalries between print and television journalists. This *guerre de plume* revealed how their differences could not be reduced to economic ties and political commitments, and could be exploited by forces hostile to the free-speech claims of both media. The conflict also showed that when print patricians had words with video muckrakers, the credibility of both suffered. A month after the initial broadcast, the *Post* praised *The Selling of the Pentagon* for exposing military practices but agreed that "some of the criticism of the documentary—in terms of production techniques and occasional inaccuracies—is valid." It added that "the line between reporting and staging events in this kind of television program is a fine one and also one that is too easily crossed." CBS had crossed it when editing its interview with Assistant Secretary of Defense Henkin, according to the *Post*. The *Post* argued that failing to preserve the original sequence of remarks, indicate cuts, "and/or give the subject of the interview an opportunity to see and approve his revised or altered remarks does in fact result in a material distortion of the record."[22]

Television news executives responded swiftly. CBS News chief Richard Salant retorted that the *Post* did not question the rights of their own editors and reporters to condense subjects' statements and therefore should not question CBS employees' rights to do the same. Salant continued, *"But most astonishing of all you propose that we should give the subject of the interview an opportunity to see and approve his revised remarks . . .* this strikes at the very core of independent and free journalism. To grant a subject such a right of review is to remove the basic journalistic function of editing from the hands of the journalist and place it—in the case of the documentary in question—in the hands of the Pentagon" (emphasis in original).[23] The *Post*, in a reply the same day, argued, "We were and are objecting to the fact that *specifically, in relation to question-and-answer sequences,* two sets of standards *already* exist . . . and that what [Salant] and others in television appear to regard as simple 'editing' seems to us to take an excess of unacknowledged liberties with the direct quotations of the principals involved" (emphasis in original). The *Post* condemned "the practice of printing highly rearranged material in a Q-and-A sequence as if it were verbatim text, without indicating to the reader that changes had been made and/or without giving the subject an opportunity to approve revisions in the original exchange . . . TV can and does simulate an impression of actuality in the way it conveys such rearranged material."[24] The exchange over print and television editing continued as former CBS News president Fred Friendly and NBC News president Reuven Frank wrote to support Salant's views.[25] Even WTOP-TV, owned by the *Post*, rebuked the paper for "lapsing . . . into a technical, one-upsmanship debate with CBS over editing techniques."[26]

In an editorial that borrowed its title, "The Art of 'Cut and Paste,'" from Vice President Agnew's attacks on television news, *Time* offered qualified support to the *Post*, rejecting its call for a right of review but restating the distinction between the media. Print readers and editors, it said, "understand that what is printed is a comprehensible reordering of reality; written stories normally can and do make that clear . . . By its immediacy, TV creates the illusion of verisimilitude."[27] *Time* recommended alerting viewers to television's condensing techniques by superimposing a warning, such as "edited excerpts," over interviews such as Henkin's.

In the abstract, both publications were right to request more sensitive editing of question-and-answer sessions. Anyone who has seen their remarks rearranged in the media might sympathize. However, the *Post* and *Time* were hypocritical in asserting that the problem existed in television alone since print journalists are not above taking remarks out of sequence, out of context, and sometimes even out of thin air, either to fit their particular frames or to "clean up" the fractured logic and syntax of powerful sources.[28] Nor do they always indicate that changes have been made to those remarks. In fact, print journalists rarely even include the questions they ask their subjects in interviews, questions that solicit some kinds of answers and not others. And if television "can and does simulate an impression of actuality" in reporting highly edited remarks, so does the printed word.[29] More hypocritical, however, was the *Post*'s suggestion that subjects of television interviews should be given a right of review, a right no print journalist would grant, as Salant and Frank pointed out.

The implication that television was more irresponsible than print at reporting interviews and more likely to influence its audience served CBS's foes in Congress. The positions taken by the *Post* and *Time* meshed nicely with House attempts to undermine the credibility of *The Selling of the Pentagon*, divert attention from its criticisms, divide the media, and create fear of the networks as more powerful than Congress and the Defense Department. CBS's detractors repeatedly cited the editorials from the *Post*, *Time*, and *Barron's* (which recommended banning CBS from the airwaves) and entered them into the *Congressional Record*.[30] Irony of ironies, after Congressman Staggers moved to subpoena the documentary's outtakes, the *Post* complained that its editorial remarks were taken out of context: "[W]e think the program made a substantial contribution in airing an aspect of the Pentagon that sorely needs airing but thought some of the editing techniques used were open to serious question, mostly because they exposed the show to needless attack. It is remarkable how both defenders and critics of the program have seized on that second point and ignored the first."[31] The *Post* later muted its doubts about the network's editing practices and attacked the constitutionality of Staggers's subpoena (it may have helped that in the meantime one of the colonels shown on the program had named WTOP, which showed *The Selling of the Pentagon*, in a $6 million libel lawsuit against the network).[32]

Time got its comeuppance too. At the end of its editorial, it suggested that taking remarks out of sequence contradicted policy at all the networks. David Buksbaum, an ABC News producer, was quoted as saying, "when we edit, it never gets out of sequence. And if someone would edit out of sequence, the guy ought to be fired."[33] Soon after, Buksbaum wrote to the magazine's letters to editor department, protesting, "I was quoted as saying 'When we edit, we never take quotes out of sequence so as to change their context. And if anybody did it, he ought to be fired.' I think the essential word is *context*. It should be obvious from all of this that quotes, whether in print or film, demand loving editorial care to keep their context correct—especially quotes about quotes."[34] Everyone, it seemed, was in danger of being misquoted in the news, even those who made it. *Time* apologized, noting that "our correspondent did not hear you correctly,"[35] but did not print Buksbaum's letter.

This print criticism stemmed more from professional and cultural combat between journalists than from their organizations' political leanings or market interests. In their coverage, neither the *Post* nor *Time* defended military public relations, and the Washington paper's own station editorialized against it. Both publications were more concerned with affirming their place in a cultural hierarchy of journalism. When the *Post* responded to Salant's attack on the paper for dividing the media, it concluded, "We agree with Mr. Salant's premise that we are all in the same dinghy. That is why we are so concerned that neither end should sink."[36] This implication that television threatened to drag down all of the news media in the public's estimation was echoed by the *Time* editor's disparagement of television imagery. Although acknowledging that print shared a common need to select and synthesize the news, *Time* wrote, "But pictures lend themselves less readily to this process than words—which is one reason why print journalism is capable of subtlety and depth that can almost never be achieved on TV. It is also why editing TV news requires a special kind of vigilance."[37] Here and elsewhere, *Time* repeated widespread beliefs about the distinctions between audiovisual media and print. The word, print commentators asserted, was not only more complex, rational, and independent of market pressures but had a greater purchase on the real. Yet when *Time* misquoted and protected its credibility by concealing it from its readers and when the *Post* covered itself by complaining about how its call for ceding a right of reply to television interviewees was "taken out of context," print journalists showed that mendacity and the slipperiness of meaning threatened to undermine both media.

The Word in Television Newsrooms

In many ways, the print debate over *The Selling of the Pentagon* reflected struggles *within* network news departments over the primacy of the image or the word and the editing of interviews with elite sources. Michael Curtin has argued that the documentary was "the product of two competing notions of professionalism, one journalistic, the other filmic. In fact, this competition sometimes fueled heated confrontations between network news correspondents who were steeped in the mores of American journalism and documentary producers, many of whom were trained as film makers."[38] During the early years of network documentary, Curtin finds a noticeable shift from emphasizing "talking head" shots of expert commentators and sources to a new appreciation of narrative visual conventions such as setting, character, plot, and affect. As producers trained in film techniques took greater creative control, some reporters disputed the increased editing of their sources' comments, as when CBS correspondent David Schoenbrun attacked executive producer Fred Friendly for "tak[ing] interviews with the most famous men and chop[ping] them up at will, without consulting the reporter or the man interviewed."[39] Producers' authority to edit and recontextualize elite voices also emerged in David Rockefeller's resentment of *Banks and the Poor* for intercutting his remarks with Congressman Patman's to construct a debate between them over Chase Manhattan Bank's lending practices.[40]

The war of words and images continued throughout the period. On-air reporters, increasingly promoted by the networks as celebrity figures in their own right, found that emphasis on words served their interests. Correspondents often deployed printed government reports as authoritative props to support their editorial positions in investigative reports. In the conclusion to *Harvest of Shame,* Murrow brandished the presidential commission's report on migrants as he summarized its recommendations for improving their lives. Huntley held up the New York State Board of Welfare report criticizing Newburgh's reforms before reading a long passage from it. Edwin Newman proffered Department of Labor files on pension complaints to substantiate NBC's concern about the issue before the camera zoomed in, appearing to go inside the files to present its first case of victimization.

Producers who wanted to explore the audiovisual potential of television and assert their authority over shaping documentary texts frequently expressed frustration at the demands of reporters. In 1968, Arthur Barron, a sociologist turned CBS documentarian, groused about what he saw as the growing dominance of the "word people" over the network documentary. "We should try more to be novelists and poets of film rather than such damn good reporters," he argued. "I want to make people weep and cry."[41] He attributed the supremacy of the narration to network executives' backgrounds in print journalism and executives' and regulators' tendency to define public-service programming as "hard news" reporting on social issues.[42] Producer Daniel Klugherz mourned how omnipresent correspondents frustrated the documentary's ability to observe and portray events in montages, to think in pictures and natural sound.[43] Reuven Frank, who produced *The Tunnel* and then alternated as a documentary executive producer and NBC News president, regretted that anchors, managers, and lawyers who "think a television program is the same as its transcript" took control of the news at expense of its imagery. Television, he maintained, was "best as a narrative medium, worst as an expository medium," but because it had to report all the news, including events that lent themselves less well to storytelling, "Photojournalism on television had become a possibility forever lost."[44]

This struggle over the dominance of narration or audiovisual interpretation stemmed from competing claims to authority by print versus television journalists, by reporters versus elite sources, and by television correspondents and executives versus producers. Investigations into controversial reports unearthed these divisions and may have exacerbated them but did not solve them.

The Myth of Objectivity and the Myth of Muckraking

Any attempt to contrast objective and investigative reporting must confront a myriad competing definitions of both. Too many attempt to portray these types of journalism as mutually exclusive. For example, Investigative Reporters and Editors (IRE), the national organization for muckrakers, has defined this kind of reporting in part through its ability to reveal matters that others have tried to keep secret.[45] But there are few stories worth telling that do not involve publicizing information that some parties would prefer kept out of the public eye to serve their interests, whether this involves a corporation's falling stock price or a politician's gaffe. In addition, some investigative reports involve analyzing and finding unrecognized patterns in large masses of public data, such as campaign finance records or tax law, not prying loose information from reluctant sources that are attempting to hide it. This information, like most facts revealed by muckraking, is not entirely unknown. Part of IRE's definition of investigative journalism is that it must result from the reporter's initiative and work rather than from others' investigations or the simple airing of leaks.[46] However, as the case studies in this book show repeatedly, this distinction is untenable because investigative journalists often draw on the work of official and social movement sources when selecting stories and gathering news.

To overcome these definitional difficulties, objective and investigative reporting are better understood as journalistic genres. The concept of genre, most fully developed by literary and film theorists, offers a more flexible and accurate way of thinking than exclusive definitions. A genre, writes Barry Dornfeld, is a "complex of stylistic and formal features historically and conventionally grouped together, employed in both production and reception" of texts.[47] Thus genres are widely used schemes for classifying texts that shape how their makers create them and their audiences interpret them. Once a producer knows that she is working on an investigative piece, certain methods for gathering and telling news become more relevant than others. Despite growing concerns about the blurring of information and entertainment in news, contemporary viewers attempting to interpret *60 Minutes* as, say, situation comedy are likely to be confused or disappointed. Why has the crisis not been resolved by the end of the program? Genres "are not discrete systems, consisting of a fixed number of listable items," notes Christine Gledhill.[48] Elements and examples of genres frequently overlap, whether between action films and thrillers or investigative reports and other types of journalism. However, as Daniel Chandler maintains, if "particular features which are characteristic of a genre are not normally unique to it . . . it is their relative prominence, combination and functions which are distinctive."[49]

In this light, objective and investigative journalism can be construed as genres that differ in four main ways. First, as a set of *news-gathering techniques,* each delineates a legitimate means of acquiring facts. For objective journalism, facts are accumulated principally through witnessing events first-hand or confirming them by the testimony of multiple witnesses, by interviewing sources, and drawing on a material record (texts of speeches, statistics, a police report, and so on). Muckraking, while often drawing on similar methods, sanctions broader notions of research and investigation than beat reporting or the mere airing of leaks from confidential sources. These methods may include confrontational interviews, observations based on concealing the journalist's presence or identity (undercover reporting, hidden cameras or microphones, and so forth), the assembly and analysis of larger bodies of information (such as studies of mortgage loan patterns by race and neighborhood), and arranging tests or "stings" to demonstrate some harm that people or products may cause the public. Although muckrakers frequently rely on the investigative work of others, these journalists enjoy more power to select stories and sources than beat reporters, who tend to be more reactive and to rely more on the traditional news gathering means of interviews, press conferences, and publicity releases.

Second, each type of journalism offers typical *ways of framing stories.* In objective reporting, journalists must appear to efface their own interpretation of facts (attributing opinions to sources, using the third-person address and the passive voice) and seem to balance competing versions of the truth. Investigative reporting involves a more analytical bent than the primarily descriptive and reactive work of beat reporting.[50] Muckraking features more overt assertions of truth, mediation between the claims of opposing social actors, and definition of problems that require reforming (although, as we have seen, reporters rarely recommend specific solutions). Investigative journalism more openly distinguishes between villains and victims, asserting its own moral authority. These reports are not structured according to a mathematical balance of competing points of view but as indictments. Television muckraking in particular often mimics legal argument through a format consisting of opening remarks, the presentation of evidence and witnesses, and a summation. This kind of news, in the words of one investigative journalist, purports to offer an "orderly and systematic presentation of evidence, both testimonial and material, to a judge or jury."[51] Hostile witnesses are interviewed to offer some semblance of "balance" but mainly so that muckrakers can dismantle and refute their evidence. This journalism depends not only upon description and citation, as does objectivity, but relies more on demonstration and dramatization of representative examples, relating the felt experience of those who are affected by social problems. As several scholars of journalism have noted, the objective and investigative texts often prioritize two different functions of news.[52] Objectivity draws more of its authority from an informational mode, which stresses its affiliation with the sciences as a neutral vehicle for the presentation of data. Muckraking, at least on television, leans more toward a storytelling or dramatic approach, one that is not simply concerned with transmitting information about the world but with conveying what it is like to live in it and with making sense of social life through narrative.

Third, each type of news constructs a different *social role for journalists*. Objective journalists claim to be impartial observers, reporting on a reality that is external to their beliefs and news-gathering methods, and presenting themselves as independent from government, politicians, parties, and interest groups. Muckrakers, while publicly avoiding the appearance of partisan or political affiliation, are freer to confront and denounce problems and to show how they violate common moral and social values. Muckrakers often fashion themselves as detectives, prosecutors, social critics, and moral watchdogs.[53] Most often, they present themselves as protecting citizens and consumers from abuses of power by political, economic, and social institutions.

Finally, the two journalisms address themselves to different *ideal audiences*. By striving to present audiences with a balanced treatment of competing interpretations of events, objective reporting constructs a rational audience that is responsible for weighing the truth of matters. Investigative reporting goes further, aiming to inspire in its audience moral outrage at injustice, a call to solidarity with its victims, and perhaps action to reform wrongdoing.[54] This is not to say that this kind of news can be distinguished by its actual effects on viewers. We have seen that many political and journalistic critics did not accept reports' framing of events and that much investigative reporting fails to spark a response from audiences or policy makers. In addition, whether audiences see investigative reporting differently from other news is an open question not yet explored in the research on muckraking. However, after many years of watching investigative reporting on television, today's viewers likely recognize it as a distinct kind of news and bring a characteristic set of criteria to bear in interpreting it. If audiences do not always agree with investigative reporters' conclusions, viewers likely evaluate muckraking according to certain questions that they do not ask as often of other kinds of news. Is the journalist's indictment of wrongdoing convincing? Is the wrongdoing significant? Are the victims innocent and sympathetic? Are the villains powerful and guilty enough to deserve comeuppance at journalists' hands?

Network reports reflected both the objective and muckraking traditions in part by mixing two narrative modes of documentary: the expository and the interactive.[55] The dominant form of address was expository, an essayistic approach that emphasized persuasion by an omniscient narrator whose voice seemed to exercise ultimate authority in the world of the report. This mode, inherited from Hollywood newsreels and radio documentaries, subordinates interviewees and visuals to the film's argument. The logic of the editing is to preserve rhetorical continuity of the report's argument over unities of space and time. *Pensions,* for example, was highly essayistic. The report relied heavily on Edwin Newman's narration to frame problems and stitch together talking-head interviews of expert sources to advance an argument about the short-comings of retirement funds and the challenges of growing old. This mode presents a number of advantages to reporters. It affords succinctness—an initial statement followed by a string of sound bites can quickly introduce a complex issue such as pension vesting. It allows reports to address new issues through widely shared frames—pensions as consumer fraud, the elderly as vulnerable victims, unions and corporations as bureaucratic, greedy villains. It supports generalizing, in this case about the problems of the pension system as a whole rather than any local or contingent difficulties explored. And it helps to establish clear causation of events, such as one pension critic's list of successive "miracles" that had to take place for one to collect a pension. The expository approach clads muckraking arguments in the armor of thoroughly documented facts and commonsense interpretations, offering "the impression of objectivity and of well-substantiated judgment."[56]

Within this larger essayistic approach, documentarians embedded elements of an interactive mode that shared greater narrative authority with outside sources. *Hunger in America,* with its four guest narrators, made greatest use of this mode, although all of the documentaries contained some element of it. This second approach stresses the testimony of social actors, such as the hunger reformers and the poor, and demonstrates how they experienced deprivation and injustice through vignettes that depicted scrounging for meals at home, negotiating the welfare system in government offices, and battling malnutrition in hospitals. Interactive segments focused on the situated, local knowledge of the poor and social workers, deployed as witnesses in a larger argument about the failures of food programs. Editing maintained the logical continuity between the viewpoints of the impoverished, the guest narrators, and Charles Kuralt's overarching narration. Interactive sequences offered representative examples of a single problem drawn from diverse locales. These moments also propped up Kuralt's and the guest storytellers' authority, grounding it in the views and experiences of "the people." The local, emotional, experiential voices of these sources could be separated from, yet support, the rational and universalizing claims of narrators.

The Uncertain Embrace of Muckraking

Although the conventions of objectivity remained dominant in television reporting of the 1960s and early 1970s, they were increasingly questioned. Embarrassment at having uncritically reprinted McCarthyist accusations in the 1950s spurred many in the media to criticize objectivity as preventing reporters from pursuing more skeptical, responsible reporting on government. Academics and participants in the new social movements pointed to how the balanced style and subservience to government sources made journalists complicit with official views (especially in Vietnam War reporting), rejecting reporters' high-minded claims to neutrality as deceptive and delusional. Some journalists themselves embraced these views. As Morton Silverstein, who produced *Banks and the Poor* before going on to do investigative work on the commercial side for WCBS-TV and NBC, said, "I think there is often only one side to a story, despite the aphorisms to the contrary. There is only one side to the truth. There is only one truth . . . Thus, there are no two sides to economic repression, or to social injustice."[57] This critique also drew strength from the larger attack on claims of expert neutrality across the professions, in psychiatry and medicine, law, education, and social work.[58] As objective journalism appeared less desirable—or possible—network news departments gingerly explored investigative reporting. As time passed, television journalists began to assert their authority to interpret politics and social life more forcefully, and they and their managers attempted to reconcile the attractions of muckraking with the need to appear above the political struggle. This raised a host of representational dilemmas.

Each type of journalism held its own appeal for the networks in the 1960s. Objective reporting helped shield journalists and news organizations from political and regulatory attacks for bias and inaccuracy. Muckraking offered prestige value in the eyes of television's cultural critics and some regulators, and allowed networks to claim they were good corporate citizens providing a public service by helping to address social problems. Investigative documentaries also helped to satisfy television journalists' aspirations to match their print colleagues' authority in the social and political arenas.[59] Nonetheless, news departments remained ambivalent about their commitments to both types of journalism. Which horn of their dilemma they clung to often depended on whom they were addressing.

Network news executives were more likely to employ the rhetoric of objectivity than documentarians, especially in their official operating standards or in regulatory arenas when they were under scrutiny. In these moments, executives tended to invoke an older, more positivist version of objectivity that suggested journalists simply mirrored reality rather than filtering and interpreting it. Executives did so to assure their critics and the public that the networks could be trusted not to stage or slant the news. The 1963 version of the CBS News operating standards, for example, flatly declared, "there will be *no* re-creation, *no* staging, *no* production technique which would give the viewer an impression of any fact other than the actual fact, no matter how minor or seemingly inconsequential. The only way there can be certainty is not to let the bars down at all. Anything which gives the viewer an impression of time, place, event, or person other than the actual fact as it is being recorded and broadcast cannot be tolerated."[60] Yet as Bill Leonard, the CBS vice president who oversaw documentaries for much of this period, later admitted of these standards, "occasionally some of them [were] as honored with a wink as with an observance."[61] Peter Davis, who produced *The Selling of the Pentagon*, recalls that the rules against editing interviews out of sequence were never followed: "they were violated as soon as they were written . . . they were silly rules, and nobody ever paid any attention to them."[62]

Claims about fairness also tended to be qualified when made outside the earshot of regulators. NBC's Reuven Frank contended, "Pictures are like words—they are not facts—they are symbols. Whatever is selected will create a point of view . . . The question is not one of objectivity—but responsibility. Objectivity is a screen we hide behind . . . 'Fairness' is not an objective criterion. It is subjective. 'Fairness' is not equal by the stopwatch."[63] At the same time, news executives deployed notions of balance and fairness to discipline producers when they strayed too far from the sphere of legitimate controversy or seemed to advance their personal views too obviously. Those higher on the corporate hierarchy were most concerned with the appearance of balance.[64] Leonard characterized CBS News president Richard Salant as "generally more uncomfortable than I with talented offbeat documentary producers who might be longer on imagination than they were on objective journalism," mentioning *Hunger in America* producer Martin Carr as an example. But Leonard, who as a producer angered political apologists for the Dominican Republic with his critical portrait of Trujillo in the early 1960s, also spoke disparagingly as an executive of "a few producers, certain that they knew most if not all the routes toward the creation of a better world, [who] tended to load their documentary dice in the direction of those they perceived as the good guys . . . Salant and I, and [executive producers Burton] Benjamin and [Robert] Chandler too, spent many a long hour trying to make sure that every devil got his due at air time."[65] By the late 1960s, news executives, and even network president Frank Stanton, closely scrutinized any report that appeared controversial. At NBC, Reuven Frank distinguished between documentarians and "filmmakers" who sought to express their point of view, saying that he reacted to the latter "as Hermann Goring said he did to the word *culture.*" Despite his appreciation for narrative and visual reportage, Frank asserted that "the rules of information are good old rules, not to be trifled with." He derided those who sought outlets for "'expressing themselves,' or . . . 'making a statement,' which really means exerting a sort of power over those who watch . . . they smudge the line between what exists and what they have arranged."[66]

The novelty of investigative reporting on television was one source of network ambivalence over how expectations of objectivity should apply to muckraking. Genres such as investigative reporting are not static but susceptible to innovation and reordering of techniques and elements. Although Edward R. Murrow and Fred Friendly's *See It Now* series in the 1950s offered some examples of investigative reporting, documentarians mainly reinvented the genre for television in the 1960s. During transitional periods such as this, unstable genres offer less clear prescriptions for journalists and less familiar expectations for viewers. Thus conflicts between producers, correspondents, and executives were not surprising when the aims and rules of this kind of reporting were less fixed. Similarly, at a time when sources and viewers were not yet trained by precedent to expect contentious and editorially pointed reporting, they were bound to be shocked when they brought the same interpretive assumptions to documentaries that they did to beat reporting. In this sense, the controversies over investigative reports can be seen in part as resulting from genre confusion among all involved.

A Clash of Myths

However, the investigative report often failed to convince elites of its ability to embrace objectivity and exposé reporting. One reason is that the older myth of objectivity still had great currency, structuring expectations about what was proper journalism. Of course, the kind of objectivity called for by a Spiro Agnew or a Harley Staggers never existed. This was not simply because the commercial media's political-economic biases meant that they were not neutral about the value of a market economy, or because they needed to limit the range of opinion to elite positions, or because their news-gathering routines favored government sources' ability to frame the news. This simple version of objectivity was impossible because it refused even to acknowledge that facts are never just found but must be selected, produced, and arranged according to some set of procedures that tell us where to look, what is significant, and how to make sense of it all. If documentary critics tended to measure reports against a mythic version of objectivity, the networks often defended their work by appealing to an equally mythic tale about how investigative reporting was really contiguous with objectivity and how the technical "demands" of television news necessitated controversial journalistic practices.

Consider how the networks and their critics butted heads over frequent allegations of staging, which were raised in relation to almost every controversial report. Congressman Staggers stated the problem in the following terms:

> Today, we know that techniques of electronic manipulation have been developed which facilitate the presentation of artificially created scenes as objectively observed facts. The visual capture of an event by a camera implies the elimination of that editorial process so obviously a part of the process of recording events in the printed medium. The viewer reasonably expects that the visual recording of an event is a means of preserving for history's sake that event as it occurred. When such is not the case, the viewer should be told.[67]

This view distinguished sharply between the authenticity of passively witnessing spontaneous events and any arranging or directing of them by television journalists. Even relatively innocuous techniques thus appeared as dangerous acts of deception. The House subcommittee reproached *The Selling of the Pentagon* not only for distorting the meaning of Assistant Secretary of Defense Henkin's words but for the common practice of shooting reverse shots of journalists after they finished an interview, to be used later for covering edits in a source's responses. It attacked the report not just for supposedly mixing Colonel McNeil's views with the Laotian prime minister whom he cited, but for changing the sequence of his remarks (which had no effect on their meaning). Concerns about the raw authenticity of events extended beyond defending political interests. ABC questioned whether National Geographic filmmakers were overly directive with their animal subjects and demanded that they include a disclaimer in a documentary that warned, "This program is based on real events and real people. Some scenes have necessarily been planned for our cameras."[68]

Staggers and others often drew questionable parallels between news staging and the quiz-show scandals of the late 1950s, which had been probed by the same subcommittee under the leadership of Staggers's predecessor. Staggers defended his hearings by arguing that communications law prohibited false and misleading advertising and quiz programs, and that news should not be more protected, "given the technical ability of the medium to deceive, and the economic incentive to boost ratings."[69] Subcommittee members often referred to staging as "rigging," the same term used to describe how the game shows were fixed. These parallels also cast doubt on any payments made by journalists to people involved in a news story, which critics presented as de facto staging and deception. Congressman Gonzalez, for example, noted that the producers of *Hunger in America* had made small compensations to food aid recipients for missing work when they were interviewed. "If it was payment for services," he charged, "CBS was reporting the lines of performers, and misrepresenting the performances as spontaneous news."[70] Comparisons between the game shows and documentary practices were not entirely spurious since ratings considerations may have influenced some reports to make outsized and shocking claims. Certainly, the producers of the aborted *Project Nassau* and *The Tunnel* made payments to news sources that enabled them to engage in activities they might not have afforded to otherwise, and without disclosure to audiences. Yet innocuous practices such as shooting reversals, asking sources to repeat an insignificant act such as parking a car or walking into one's home for the cameras, or paying a few dollars to a field hand who missed work to appear in a report were hardly comparable to the intense scripting of who would win on the quiz shows. Whatever the motives of news sources were, they could not be reduced to competing for cash and prizes. The Berlin students aimed to dig a tunnel and rescue friends and family, and they would have done so had they gotten money from another source than NBC. Regardless of what moved journalists to accentuate the pathos of victims, it was something more than selling detergent to audiences. These sequences were part of larger explorations of public affairs.

For their part, investigative journalists countered charges of staging and checkbook journalism by recasting and mystifying them as merely technical solutions to the practical problems of television journalism. Payments to sources were for "film rights" to secure long-term access to a person or place, or "consulting fees" to experts, both of which were required by the extensive investigations that documentaries involved.[71] Journalists defended themselves against staging accusations by maintaining that the medium itself required significant planning and directing of subjects. Bill Leonard argued that "as every seasoned producer, correspondent and editor knows . . . it is impossible simply from a practical point of view to film or tape an extensive story without a certain amount of what could technically be construed as staging."[72] It would be nonsensical to wait in the bushes for several days for someone to enter and reenter their home to get footage of this event from several angles, he maintained, so it was fine to ask them to do it several times for the cameras. Similarly, a CBS sound man for *Project Nassau* told the subcommittee that he thought it was acceptable that the documentary's producer asked a weapons smuggler to repeat his arrival at a safe house several times and that the producer arranged for a group of commandos to hold a training sequence for the cameras, whereas it would have been wrong for a hard news reporter to do so. Unlike daily reporting, he explained, documentaries were less about what happened at a given moment in time and more concerned with "what is going on, what does happen."[73] A CBS cameraman defended the reenactments as necessary "for continuity purposes."[74]

Although most of these acts of staging did not misrepresent "what does happen," network muckrakers justified them in a way that occluded their own commitment to presenting dramatized vignettes according to traditional fiction film techniques. In this respect, network news critics who equated documentaries with Hollywood productions were right.[75] There would have been no need to reenact or stage events had documentarians not based their credibility on offering the illusion of realism as defined by conventional filmmaking. By the late 1960s, this style had become second nature, an unexamined set of beliefs about what constituted reality in television documentary. Yet only a few years prior, news managers had to teach these techniques actively to journalists and standardize them through news department memoranda.[76] Journalists had to learn to introduce viewers to scenes through the use of an establishing shot, a medium shot, and a close-up, how to match the eyelines of interviewees and interviewers in a shot/reverse shot format to make them appear to be sharing the same physical space, to cover edits with cutaways to avoid jump cuts, and other conventions for creating the look and feel of continuity. Perhaps most important, television journalists learned to prize representing the direct experience of their subjects in an unbroken narrative, thereby giving viewers a sense of unmediated access to events as they occurred. This kind of continuity drove Reuven Frank to have his tunnelers reenact their initial surveying of the Berlin Wall, making drawings for project, and breaking ground for the tunnel, all of which occurred before NBC learned of the project.[77] (The report disclosed that these scenes were reenactments.) But later journalists would have been less vulnerable to some staging charges had they not been concerned with continuity. In *Project Nassau,* for example, the arrival of the car and the military training could have been described through the narration. This is not to argue that documentarians ought to have abandoned these techniques, only that they were unable to acknowledge them as choices, and that their critics' attacks were often based on questioning whether these methods were necessary.

Documentarians and their critics also envisioned different roles for journalists and whether they should be impartial and detached from social struggle. For Spiro Agnew, the great power of the networks meant that their journalists ought to be scrupulously neutral. He warned, "A raised eyebrow, an inflection of the voice, a caustic remark dropped in the middle of the broadcast can raise doubts in a million minds about the veracity of a public official or the wisdom of a government policy."[78] When Staggers and others drew comparisons between documentaries and the quiz shows, they implied that journalists ought not to "rig" the outcomes of the political debates they presented. "Slanted documentary films are fully as unethical as rigged quiz shows," cried Senator Spessard Holland about *Harvest of Shame.* "Perhaps they are more dangerous to a free society, since they present a false picture as a basis for shaping public opinion and the laws resulting therefrom."[79] Muckraking's foes consistently appealed to a vision of journalists as chroniclers of a knowable world and stenographers to others' views of it. Often, critics' appeals to objectivity were rhetorical attempts to pull reporting to the right, placing a documentary's analysis outside the sphere of legitimate controversy, but they resonated with many because of the widespread attraction of the ideal of neutrality.

As they came under attack, documentarians developed a new rationale for departing from balance in the text. Increasingly, they rooted their public claims to authority in an inductive professionalism, justifying their conclusions as having been arrived at after exhaustive research. Reuven Frank defended *Pensions* from fairness complaints by saying it

> was put together by a group of reporters and editors who had no stake in how it came out, except to tell people more than they might already know about something of interest to them, in a manner which would hold their interest until the tale was told . . . The reply, if there were to be one, would necessarily be by someone who had a position to promote, one identifiable in advance. Then his credentials would be presented as journalistically equal to those of the reporters and editors who did the program and his argument of his belief on a level with what they worked hard to find out.[80]

This peculiar logic fused older notions of journalistic detachment with the new claim that reporters should be able to express conclusions without reply by others, who were inevitably biased in advance. As long as reporters did not begin from a definite position, it was fine to arrive at one. Never mind that many documentaries originated in government hearings designed to support disputed legislation. Never mind that having no point of view in advance was an impossible task because journalists would have no way of deciding what to investigate and what to ignore. By the 1970s, an objectivity of motive now justified muckraking.

Much resistance to fairness requirements involved an assertion of professional authority. As Frank's defense of *Pensions* suggested, the problem for news organizations with allowing critics to respond to reports was not that they were wrong but that doing so would challenge journalists' credentials.

"The *Pensions* program was not a discussion; it was a job of reporting," Frank wrote. "Having it subject to reply as though it were one side of a discussion damages journalism."[81] Indeed, offering a response would have challenged the ability of investigative journalists to appear as independent investigators, above partisan debate, yet with a right to arrive at conclusions (even if vague) on matters of public policy. This was precisely the image that producers such as Albert Wasserman, who made *Battle of Newburgh,* aimed to cultivate:

> A television documentary cannot seem to be saying to the audience, this is the way I feel and I want you to feel the same way. A television documentary must seem to be much more dispassionate. The film maker . . . and the correspondent who reports it should not seem to have come in with a preconceived attitude. Whatever the thrust of the story is, it should emerge from the substance of the film. There can be an emotional process, but it should be in the journalistic text of the story itself, rather than in what the audience would perceive as the orientation of the people who made the film.[82]

For Wasserman and others, what was important was that reports not *seem* to violate expectations of fairness. Inductive professionalism offered a way for journalists to explain how they could arrive at authoritative conclusions without appearing to have any "orientation" at the start.

As documentarians grew less enamored of objectivity in the 1960s while their managers still needed to uphold this ideal publicly, the figure of the independent and authoritative journalist who transcended partisanship in pursuit of the public interest and moving stories held great appeal. Yet the persistence of beliefs in objectivity acted as a brake on journalistic commentary, especially when regulators asserted traditional demands that the news present the facts and scrupulously balance competing interpretations of them. News critics put forth a positivist critique of deception while news organizations disavowed responsibility for choosing their techniques of representing reality. As a result, both parties failed to appreciate how conflict emerged from broadcast journalism's representational commitments.

Objectivity, Interpretive Community, and Political Dissensus

I have argued that representational conflicts over the investigative documentary were not simply a cover for competing political agendas, yet they were related to the larger political context. Indeed, we must draw these connections to understand why an older and simpler notion of objectivity seemed not only less desirable but less achievable in the 1960s. For a news report, or any statement, to appear self-evidently factual and ideologically neutral depends upon the existence of an interpretive community with shared techniques and rules for reading texts, a common belief about what texts are worth reading, and agreement about the goals of the enterprise.[83] Literary critic Stanley Fish first suggested the notion of an interpretive community to account for how readers arrived at common interpretations of literature.[84] Barbie Zelizer has maintained that journalists themselves form one such community, through their informal talk, professional meetings, trade reviews, and memoirs, and she argues that this community has helped collectively legitimate reporters' authority to interpret historical events.[85]

Investigative documentarians helped form one such community within journalistic circles. Although they relied on congressional sources to frame their reports, muckrakers validated new investigative techniques for television (such as the hidden camera), unconventional sources (especially the testimony of academic experts, social reformers, and popular voices, however carefully chosen), and new goals for broadcast journalism (such as defining social problems and soliciting public outrage at them). However, like Fish's original theory of separate groups with their own rules for reading, Zelizer's notion of a reportorial community does not account for differences within journalism over the meaning of texts and over the legitimate categories, conventions, or strategies of reading itself. As we have seen in the response to controversial documentaries, there was significant disagreement within the media over the truth, legitimacy, and techniques of network muckraking. Like most communities, journalistic circles were conflicted, which helps explain why documentary critics found support among the media.

Furthermore, the partial rejection of objectivity by television journalists and of the objectivity of their reports by critics needs to be understood not just at the level of a professional community but in relation to challenges to a larger political consensus. Representational disputes over truth and fairness, while not reducible to political conflict, were inseparable from it. Daniel Hallin takes this broader view, explaining how doubts about journalistic neutrality emerged from the collapse of postwar political consensus and the decentralization of party leadership. Greater divisions, most significantly among the economic and political elites whose voices carry more weight in the media, and the weakening grip of the major parties over politicians and the public encouraged a more overtly interpretive style of reporting to fill the vacuum in public discourse.[86] Hallin argues that, while postwar American politics were not always characterized by agreement, Cold War foreign policy and New Deal domestic policy marked off a relatively large set of assumptions as ideologically "neutral" and underwrote greater confidence in political leadership than exists today. To this idea I would add that the tremendous economic growth of the postwar period generated greater confidence in, or at least acquiescence to, corporate power. There was a widespread belief that business delivered the goods, in the form of jobs, rising wages and benefits, and startling new products (including television itself). Television contributed to that belief in no small part, warning of political and material deprivation suffered behind the Iron Curtain and acting as a vast national sales medium.

As agreement broke down in the 1960s over these basic features of the political landscape, it was no coincidence that the most disputed network reports were ones that examined the legacy of the New Deal's welfare system, Cold War foreign policy, and business and consumerism. We have seen that these issues divided both parties, particularly the Democrats, whose dominance of the Congress and White House made them favored sources for network reporters. The sphere of legitimate controversy broadened, and television documentarians stepped in to the widening circle with their cameras and a mandate to muckrake. What Bill Nichols has written about recent perceptions of the blurring line between fiction and nonfiction can be applied to the disintegrating boundary between fact and opinion in the 1960s. He observes that an impression that the stable representational categories that govern public discourse are disintegrating arises "[w]hen a single idea about the nature of reality, a common set of shared values and collective purpose, does not prevail . . . These blurrings of what used to be effective distinctions may be not simply logical confusions but the arena within which major political, or ideological, contestation occurs."[87]

The way political dissensus triggered representational conflicts, and vice versa, may have been clearest in the case of *The Selling of the Pentagon*. One of the attractions of foreign policy issues for network documentarians in the early 1960s was that the superpower division of the world seemed to be uncontroversial ground on the home front. Documentarians did not risk offending a powerful audience segment or advertising interest by challenging communism abroad. But by the early 1970s, support for aggressive anticommunism slackened as the war bogged down in Southeast Asia, and leaders such as Senator Fulbright questioned the role of the military-industrial complex. Investigative reporters staked out a somewhat larger interpretive role for themselves, at least within the news text, as the military's credibility waned. The ensuing struggle encapsulated the slow collapse of shared routines for citing powerful sources—military, congressional, and media—and concealing public relations strategies.

The *Selling of the Pentagon* debates also showed journalistic and political elites' inability to define staged or slanted news using the terms and techniques inherited from print and objective reporting. If some government and media critics attacked CBS using the language of "bias," implying that the news could be fully accurate and impartial if only it were reported faithfully by good souls, the documentary and ensuing conflicts offered insights into the news as constructed discourse. In the documentary, powerful sources such as the Pentagon were shown managing news events and concealing information. Daniel Henkin and Roger Mudd fought over who was more responsible for staging their interview, not whether it was staged. Quotes, condensed and torn from their contexts, acquired unintended significances, not only in the Henkin interview but also when the *Washington Post* claimed its editorials were cited by politicians arguing that the First Amendment had only limited application to television and when *Time* misdeployed David Buksbaum's editing credo against CBS. All were at pains to correct the record. The news was defended by *Time* not as truth but as a "comprehensible reordering of reality," and the magazine characterized television as offering the "illusion of verisimilitude"—hardly the most confident claims about the news media's ability to capture reality.

As the normally symbiotic relationship between news organizations and politicians broke down, journalists pointed to how Congress misquoted sources and massaged the political record. The *Congressional Record,* an important source for journalists, was unmasked by a *Post* editorial that pointed out how politicians regularly revised the actual remarks they made on the House floor before they were set in print. The paper condemned congressional hypocrisy for applying more stringent editing standards to CBS's documentaries than to the *Record,* which the *Post* called "that most altered, revised, rearranged, cut-and-pasted version of 'reality' that exists among public documents."[88] Others revealed that many in Congress, including Staggers, provided "interviews" to their home-district radio stations by recording statements and then mailing them along with a script listing suggested questions.[89] Charge and countercharge revealed the news to attentive watchers as a reality constantly negotiated, mainly among elites, who spoke of journalism and the political record in less transparent terms than usual, engaging in unintended acts of mutual deconstruction.

✿ ✿ ✿

In an era when television journalism was still inventing itself, conflicts among journalists, their employers, and their powerful political sources over the rules of representation were inevitable. The political upheavals of the time helped to provoke discontent with television journalism by contracting the space of consensus in which journalists might operate free from criticism. However, political self-interest did not completely dictate the controversies or the stances that protagonists took toward them. National and local forces clashed, as did those who would have imposed the norms of print journalism on television, and supporters of muckraking and objective news. And the battle lines ran straight through journalism and government's own houses, not just between them.

PART III

REGULATION

6 The Politics of Regulation

In the 1960s and 1970s, the investigative documentary became a crucial battleground in struggles over regulating television news content as old and new actors in the policy process challenged the networks.[1] Yet the FCC consistently protected broadcasting against its critics, as did some within Congress and the judiciary. If previous chapters have shown how television muckrakers were by no means hostile to government in the abstract, this chapter demonstrates that government was not uniformly adversarial to the media.

Controversial investigative reports' most profound influence on government was not on welfare, consumer, or foreign policy, but on broadcast regulation of news's fairness and accuracy. In chapter 3, we saw that *Banks and the Poor* gave PBS's critics an example of all that they thought was wrong about news in public broadcasting, which they used to restrict the adventurous and liberal NET's influence and diminish investigative reporting on the public network. Here we will concentrate on the regulatory impact on commercial network reporting. Documentary controversies helped and hurt the cause of television muckraking, but in the end, government did little additional regulating of news. The networks' reaction to these struggles helped to weaken content regulations on news. By the mid-1970s, Congress and the FCC, the traditional overseers of broadcast news, retreated from direct attempts to enforce fairness and counter deception and instead encouraged the development of competing services and technologies to lessen network dominance over news programming.

The regulatory apparatus engaged in symbolic regulation of news distortion and unfairness by a variety of means: the FCC's fairness doctrine and its lesser-known rules against news distortion, as well as congressional, judicial, and White House activity. After explaining the theory of symbolic regulation, I briefly canvass the origins of the fairness and distortion policies, then show how they were not enforced vigorously against investigative reports. The chapter concludes by accounting for the demise of congressional attention to television news practices and the Nixon administration's alternate means of reining in the power of network reporting.

Symbolic Regulation, Fairness, and Distortion

In American broadcast history, most content-based broadcast regulations ultimately derive from licensees' primary formal obligation to serve the "public interest, convenience and necessity."[2] Yet, as Murray Edelman's theory of symbolic regulation maintains, laws and policies that purport to protect the public interest can be repealed in effect by administrative neglect, industry recalcitrance, congressional and executive branch pressure, and budget starvation. However, Edelman argues, "the laws as symbols must stand because they satisfy interests that are very strong indeed: interests that politicians fear will be expressed actively if a large number of voters are led to believe that their shield against a threat has been removed."[3] If regulators repeatedly fail to apply rules in ways that challenge the industry, that failure must be managed carefully in policy discourse. FCC decisions often "give the rhetoric to one side and the decision to the other,"[4] affirming abstractions such as the "public interest" in vague and hortatory language that assures all involved that citizens' needs have been duly considered in decision making and that broadcasters must serve them before clearing the licensee of wrongdoing or applying a regulatory tap on the wrist. If the symbolic aspects of policy making are rarely acknowledged openly, they play no small part in legitimizing the process.

Similarly, Thomas Streeter has noted how the FCC's long-term inclination to protect broadcasters' claims to the spectrum against competition and enlarge their First Amendment rights at the expense of public accountability must be cast in the discourse of neutral principles and technical expertise to establish rhetorical distance from industry influence.[5] Indeed, when the commission has failed to do so, its critics in the judiciary and even in its own house have sometimes decried the symbolic nature of its oversight.[6] If FCC policy decisions are to be accepted by the regulators and the regulated, they must appear disinterested. Policy talk, like news, relies on a myth of expert objectivity. This is not to say that all broadcast regulators have been engaged in a conscious conspiracy against the public. As Streeter argues, the discursive rules of the policy community themselves come to exert influence over what options can be put forth as "practical" and "realistic," militating against overt commitments to political-economic interests, actors, and ideologies as the basis for rule making.[7] This discursive need to transcend particular interests can occasionally open up space for aberrant decisions that challenge industry prerogatives. Once the for-profit, commercially supported, government-licensed nature of the system is taken as a given, commitments to the public interest and regulatory disinterest sometimes limit what the industry can win from the regulators. In addition, even symbolic regulations may exert some small checks on industry by presenting the threat of government intervention, as the fairness doctrine sometimes did by giving broadcasting's critics some leverage to negotiate informally for response time.[8]

The theory of symbolic regulation would apply when regulators preserve and maintain the appearance of applying a rule that purports to protect the public interest yet avoid enforcing the rule in such a way as to challenge the industry practices it was meant to address. Disconfirming evidence of symbolic politics would demonstrate consistent enforcement of the rule or its abolition, as in the partial repeal of the fairness doctrine in 1987. If these two policies were indeed symbolic, we would expect to see some investigative activity by the commission in such cases but few findings against broadcasters, light penalties, and a lack of fit between the pattern of enforcement and the policy's stated goals.

Development of the Fairness Doctrine and News Distortion Rules

The fairness doctrine originated in horse trading between Congress and the industry as they settled on the outlines of commercial network broadcasting in the late 1920s. The 1927 Radio Act's equal time provision stipulated that broadcasters must offer equal access to the airwaves to competing political candidates (although it allowed stations to deny time to all of them).[9] The provision reflected a compromise between congressional calls for broader and guaranteed rights of access to radio for candidates and the public, and network demands for editorial control. Equal time and some public interest expectations were small prices to pay for broadcasters' exclusive and lucrative licenses to use the public airwaves, especially because the offer of equal time to the political class short-circuited demands for greater public, educational, and labor access.[10]

The FCC created the fairness doctrine in 1949 in response to ongoing concerns about broadcasters' ability to ignore public affairs and to exclude varying perspectives on them, and mounting demands by broadcast owners to editorialize on the air. The doctrine prescribed two obligations: (1) that broadcasters had "an affirmative responsibility to provide a reasonable amount of time for the presentation . . . of programs devoted to the discussion and consideration of public issues," and (2) that "licensees have an affirmative duty generally to encourage and implement the broadcast of all sides of controversial public issues . . . over and above their obligation to make available upon demand opportunities for the expression of opposing views."[11] A majority of broadcasters supported the doctrine's advent, in part because the FCC simultaneously dropped its eight-year-long ban on editorial commentaries by broadcast owners.[12]

The doctrine was rarely enforced until 1963, when the Kennedy-era FCC switched from considering fairness complaints only when stations' licenses were being renewed to enforcing the doctrine on a case-by-case basis.[13] The commission argued that the public would gain by receiving a quicker response while disputed issues were still of public importance. Yet the change was not wholly intended as an extension of regulatory authority, as the commission made clear that the new arrangement would also protect broadcasters, who could remedy complaints quickly or seek legal relief, lessening the chances of losing their licenses.[14] In practice, the ruling inserted the FCC and the courts as a buffer between the networks and their critics on Capitol Hill and in the White House, who had occasionally brought fairness complaints and demanded response time.[15]

Additional administrative and court decisions expanded and affirmed the doctrine, leading to a swift rise in fairness complaints by the late 1960s. In the 1963 case of *Cullman Broadcasting Co.*, the commission ruled that if a licensee sold airtime to the proponents of one side of a controversial issue, it could not exclude advocates of opposing views solely because they could not afford to buy airtime. The Cullman corollary, which applied mainly to ballot referenda, did not require the provision of free response time in all cases but only those instances when the inability to pay for access would leave the public uninformed.[16] Two court decisions also made the doctrine more available to the public. In the first, the United Church of Christ successfully sued the FCC to establish that citizen groups had legal standing to take part in the licensing process.[17] For the first time, public participation was permitted in license renewal hearings, where fairness complaints were often part of challenges to stations' programming practices. In the second case, the Supreme Court upheld the doctrine itself as constitutional and affirmed its spectrum scarcity rationale in the landmark 1969 *Red Lion Broadcasting* ruling.[18] The Court focused mainly on the doctrine's personal attack rule, which required stations to notify and offer reply time to individuals or groups whose honesty, integrity, or character were attacked during discussions of controversial public issues on the air. Critics from across the ideological spectrum pressed more fairness doctrine complaints, which mushroomed from 1,689 in 1969 to 2,800 in 1972.[19]

The FCC's prohibition against willful distortion of news also dates to 1949. At that time, the FCC expressed its concern for deceptive news in broad terms, stating, "The basis for any fair consideration of public issues, and particularly those of a controversial nature, is the presentation of news and information concerning the basic facts of the controversy in as complete and impartial a manner as possible. A licensee would be abusing his position as public trustee of these important means of mass communications were he to withhold from expression over his facilities relevant news or facts concerning a controversy or to slant or distort the presentation of such news."[20] Thus the commission initially justified its need to regulate in this area as ensuring the conditions for freewheeling coverage of public affairs and the contribution it could make to citizen self-governance. Indeed, the commission wrote that "the very reason for our allocation of so much scarce spectrum space to broadcasting [was] our realization of the valuable contribution it can make to an informed electorate."[21] However, it was not until a series of decisions from 1969 to 1973, most involving disputed investigative reports, that the commission began to formalize its definition of distortion in response to congressional pressure. This policy eventually prohibited deliberate staging, slanting, and falsifying of news, as well as promotion or suppression of news to serve broadcast owners' ideological or business interests rather than the public interest.

Keeping in mind the power of symbolic politics, we can still appreciate how the new arrangements of the 1960s threatened to depart from the long-established course of broadcast regulation. At this time, television especially became an object of political struggle in an expanded field of competing interests. The administrative and judicial decisions of the era often responded to pressures to expand the policy community. For a brief period, broadcast regulation was not merely negotiated among the commission, Congress, the industry, and the White House, but the courts and citizen groups played a somewhat larger role than they had in the past.[22] Mainly liberal broadcast reformers used their newly won access to contest license renewals, to require stations to ascertain community needs for programming, to push for the employment of women and racial minorities in the industry, to criticize the impact of violence and advertising on children, to demand public access to cable television, and to develop public broadcasting as an alternative. Broadcast reformers' gains were small, but it took substantial industry efforts to hold them off in the late 1960s and early 1970s.[23]

The commission issued its first significant rulings on documentary fairness and deception on the same day in 1962. One concerned CBS's 1961 *Biography of a Bookie Joint,* a report that focused on a Boston store that fronted for illegal bookmaking, apparently with the support of city police. In the program, Massachusetts state representative Harrison Chadwick suggested that some fellow lawmakers were cozy with the bookies, representing them in court and taking campaign contributions from them. The speaker of the state House of Representatives complained to the FCC, charging that CBS unfairly picked out Boston for criticism of gambling, distorted the activities of the alleged bookmakers and police, and knew or should have known that Chadwick's allegations about legislators were false. The FCC dismissed the complaint, noting that narrator Walter Cronkite clearly stated that gambling was a national problem and that there was no distortion because the bookmakers were eventually indicted. As for Chadwick's claims, the FCC maintained that he explicitly distinguished in the report between "a wholesale condemnation of legislators, and the fact that a relatively few are actively involved" in bookmaking. The commission noted that if Chadwick were lying, there was no evidence that CBS knew it, and the network could not be expected to confirm independently every source's testimony, "particularly where a participant is a person holding a high elective office and possessing experience reasonably qualifying him to be considered an expert on the subject under discussion."[24] The commission also appeared to be swayed by the brevity of CBS's attention to the issue, noting that Chadwick's accusation made up three lines of a twenty-seven-page script.

The second ruling concerned *The Battle of Newburgh*. Town manager Joseph Mitchell's complaint alleged that the program was biased against his welfare reform efforts, that it omitted many positive aspects about the city, and that NBC paid the head of a poor family to lie about why he had been denied welfare. The FCC rejected the notion that NBC was obligated to include additional material about the sunnier side of Newburgh, saying that in judging accuracy it must "limit its consideration to the program material actually broadcast." It also refused to find that NBC's source had been untruthful on the program, citing the man's testimony that city officials coerced him into saying he had lied to NBC and adding that the man's remarks in the report "remain substantially uncontroverted." The commission reminded Mitchell that the fairness doctrine required NBC to provide *"reasonable opportunity* for the discussion of opposing views," not strictly equal time, and Mitchell's views were featured in "substantial portions of the program" (emphasis in original). Although this was true, the ruling went on to make the more dubious assertion that "Nowhere . . . is there any evidence of an effort by NBC to present a documentary which would deliberately favor one side over the other."[25] This ignored the report's consistently critical stance toward Mitchell's welfare reform plan.

These cases presaged a number of issues central to later disputes. First, the commission treated the fairness aspects of the complaints as significant enough that they needed to be addressed separately from the license renewals of the networks' owned-and-operated stations. Since the rulings came a year before the commission changed its policy to evaluate all fairness complaints on a case-by-case basis, it may well be that these documentary disputes played a role in the switch. Second, the commission relied on its own authority to determine the main issues and subissues of news reports when it interpreted Cronkite's remarks as evidence that *Bookie Joint,* despite being set entirely in Boston, was about the *national* problem of illegal gambling and corruption, and when it ruled that Chadwick's accusations were only a small part of the documentary's case. Third, the FCC had few qualms about determining the truth of events portrayed in the documentaries, citing the indictments of the Boston bookmakers as evidence that they were indeed guilty and deciding that the Newburgh man had not lied. Finally, the commission displayed an early sign of its later deference to the claims of investigative reporting, stating in the *Bookie* decision, "in the production of documentary programs, licensees must, of necessity, be permitted great latitude in the selection and presentation of program material."[26] Some have claimed that these rulings were a double-edged sword for the networks. The FCC cleared them for impartiality and applauded them for taking on controversial subjects, signaling its support for investigative documentaries. Yet the commission, it is said, also set itself up as the judge of journalistic neutrality and truth telling.[27] However, the FCC would increasingly pull back from overtly deciding issues of truth and balance in later rulings, especially when doing so would have caused it to rule against broadcasters.

The News Distortion Rules as Symbolic

The commission began to formalize its news distortion rules in 1969 in response to three complaints, all forwarded to it by Congress, about *Hunger in America* and coverage of the Democratic National Convention in Chicago. The FCC declared the gravity of the offense by calling distortion "a most heinous act against the public interest—indeed, there is no act more harmful to the public's ability to handle its affairs. In all cases where we may appropriately do so, we shall act to protect the public interest in this important respect." However, in this decision the FCC also raised its countervailing commitment to broadcasters' freedom of speech and pledged not to chill it: "But in this democracy, no Government agency can authenticate the news, or should try to do so. We will therefore eschew the censor's role, including efforts to establish news distortion in situations where Government intervention would constitute a worse danger than the possible rigging itself." Thus, in cautioning that it would not be "the national arbiter of the truth,"[28] the FCC also bid to maintain its discursive neutrality. The FCC said it would not investigate charges that involved "filming of conduct engaged in because of the knowledge that the cameras are there," such as occurred in press conferences or demonstrations, since these activities were not directly under journalists' control. Nor would the commission investigate "scenes in a documentary which obviously involve such 'staging' as camera direction, lights, action instructions, etc." Instead, the FCC would limit its concern to cases in which "a licensee has staged or culpably distorted the presentation of a news event," where staging consisted of "a purportedly significant 'event' which did not in fact occur but rather is 'acted out' at the behest of news personnel."[29]

Over the next four years, the commission would flesh out its approach to news distortion in several other precedent-setting cases involving investigative reporting, all of which were spurred by House Commerce Committee Investigations Subcommittee probes. In the end, the FCC crafted a definition of distortion that made it highly unlikely that it would ever find a licensee guilty. When it could have found so, the commission sought other reasons to avoid applying its own rules. Instead, it called on the networks to regulate themselves, despite mounting evidence of their failure to do so.

The commission's definition of staging allowed it to absolve a journalist who had instigated lawbreaking for a report on marijuana use produced by CBS's Chicago affiliate, WBBM-TV. The report, entitled *Pot Party at a University*, explored arguments for and against the legalization of marijuana (mainly the latter), but, as its title suggested, its centerpiece was the spectacle of Northwestern University students smoking pot in a campus apartment. Based on testimony from the students, who were quickly identified from the report by university officials despite WBBM's promise to conceal their identities fully, the House subcommittee charged that the reporter, a recent Northwestern graduate, organized the party and enticed the students to commit a crime for the cameras.[30] The commission agreed in its decision that "the party was held at the instigation and behest of WBBM-TV's representative" after the reporter repeatedly pressed the students to do so for his story. The FCC took WBBM to task for misleading viewers by claiming on the air to have been "invited" to the gathering, rather than organizing it, and for inducing the students to break the law. Nonetheless, the affair was "authentic" since it involved real college students, smoking real pot, in a campus apartment where other such soirees had been held previously by the same participants. The FCC found therefore that "it cannot be deemed a flagrantly staged event."[31]

The ruling called for self-regulation but offered little incentive for WBBM and CBS to engage in it. The FCC blamed CBS for lacking written policies to guide its station managers on investigative reporting techniques and for conducting an inadequate inquiry into the incident (WBBM quickly destroyed outtakes from the report, and CBS stonewalled throughout the inquiry, refusing to admit that its journalist arranged the party). Yet the commission declined to penalize the station or the network, noting that investigative journalists had often covered unfolding crimes without alerting authorities and that they had been "commended, not condemned, for these efforts to hold a mirror before the public."[32] Indeed, there are many instances in which coverage of extralegal activities can inform the public, but by deploying the passive cliché of holding a mirror up to society, the FCC reasoned away its own finding that WBBM actively initiated the party. The commission ignored further evidence that the reporter instructed his student contact on what kind of people to invite ("clean-cut people, no beatniks") and helped subsidize the affair by promising to buy marijuana from the students afterwards.

In a decision released several months later, the FCC declined to fault CBS for its *Hunger in America* documentary, raising new barriers to claims of staging and slanting (or deliberate inaccuracy) to make one's case. The ruling rejected Congressman Henry Gonzalez's complaint that CBS overstated the prevalence of malnutrition in San Antonio. CBS argued successfully that it had taken its estimate from authoritative sources, including a state senator and county commissioner. The FCC also dismissed Gonzalez's charge that CBS misrepresented a San Antonio baby's cause of death as starvation whereas the child had succumbed to complications arising from premature birth. CBS producers maintained that a nurse told them that the infant shown was malnourished, which the nurse later denied. FCC investigators found no evidence that the baby died of malnutrition, but "CBS had reasonable basis for assuming a very high prevalence of malnutrition in the nursery and pediatric wards."[33] The question, then, was whether CBS was "recklessly indifferent to the truth" by not doing more to confirm the reasons for the infant's death. The FCC concluded that because CBS employees claimed they were told the cause of death by a hospital official, it was inappropriate for the commission to hold hearings on whether the network was being truthful without "extrinsic evidence" that CBS had sought deliberately to stage or slant the news.[34]

This ruling established that the commission would no longer investigate conflicting statistical evidence such as the number of hungry nor would it inquire into "a dispute as to the truth of the event (i.e., a claim that the true facts of the incident are different from those presented)" without extrinsic evidence of deception. This kind of evidence might include testimony that "a newsman had been given a bribe, or had offered one to procure some action or statement"; material such as "an outtake or written memorandum" that clearly showed intentional deception; or testimony from reporters that they were instructed by the owner, manager, or news director of a station to invent or distort a news item.[35] Without such evidence, the FCC would not "enter the quagmire of investigating the credibility of the newsman and the interviewed party," matters that were best left to the licensee to investigate.[36] Most important for broadcasters, the ruling stipulated that, absent extrinsic evidence, the FCC would no longer delay license renewals while such complaints were pending as it had done in both the *Hunger in America* and *Pot Party* cases.

Whether CBS producers were being truthful or not (and at least one FCC official doubted it), the ruling placed great faith in the self-regulatory abilities of the media.[37] In a footnote, the ruling cautioned, "The licensee's investigation of substantial complaints referred to it must be a thorough, conscientious one, resulting in remedial action where appropriate . . . efforts to cover up wrongdoing by his news staff would raise the most serious questions as to the fitness of the licensee."[38] Yet the commission's WBBM ruling, which was prepared at the same time as the *Hunger in America* ruling but inexplicably released a few months earlier, took no action against CBS for what the commission charitably described as its "inadequate investigation." Instead, after commending CBS for "undertaking this documentary on one of the tragic problems of today," the FCC praised a San Antonio journalist for investigating CBS and showing that it had erred in identifying the child's death as from malnutrition. This reporter's criticisms, the commission stated, "served the public interest," adding, "it is vital that the media be subject to scrutiny by critics, and there is, we think, no better way than for news competitors to be constantly checking on each other. The beneficiary of such criticism is clearly the American people."[39] Thus the FCC held up a few articles in a small city newspaper as effective counterweights to a national network documentary. These articles generated almost no attention in the major press despite Congressman Gonzalez's repeatedly citing them on the House floor.

After calling for extrinsic evidence, the commission then ignored its presence. In its ruling on *The Selling of the Pentagon,* the FCC found that it could not intervene since it was lacking such evidence, although the commission had been given a transcript and recording of Roger Mudd's interview with Assistant Secretary of Defense Daniel Z. Henkin. This evidence showed that CBS had rearranged Henkin's remarks to make him look more evasive by taking the answer to one question and appending it to his response to another. Whether the commission ought to have punished CBS for this small bit of fudging or not, it had "an out-take or memorandum" showing that Henkin's interview was deceptively edited, which was the kind of evidence the FCC said would prompt an investigation in its *Hunger in America* decision.[40] Indeed, the commission admitted that "CBS has failed to address the question raised as to splicing answers to a variety of questions as a way of creating a new 'answer' to a single question. The very use of a 'Question and Answer' format would seem to encourage the viewer to believe that a particular answer follows from the question preceding."[41] Again, CBS refused to admit error. Network president Frank Stanton claimed that the interview was "fairly edited," and CBS News president Richard Salant attested that it had been put together "in accordance with customary journalistic practice."[42] Yet the commission did no more than urge the network to engage in "good-faith, earnest self-examination" in such instances.[43] In its reply to the House report on *Project Nassau,* the FCC declined to comment on whether CBS journalists' payments to the coup plotters to enact a training exercise and to lease a boat for the invasion fit the definition of extrinsic evidence of staging as including situations in which "a newsman had been given a bribe, or had offered one to procure some action or statement."[44] Instead, it dismissed the complaint largely because the report never aired and thus did not pose a threat of deceiving the public, and pointed to CBS's revised policy guidelines for reporting as effective self-regulation.[45]

The House subcommittee's last investigation, in 1972, sparked strong language by the FCC but no action. The House probe focused on staging, simulations, and reenactments in a number of network evening news and local station reports.[46] Staggers forwarded the hearings transcripts and asked the FCC to clarify its staging policy with reference to his latest examples of deception. The commission replied over a year later, rehashing its prior distortion decisions. The ruling declined to fault NBC for *Say Goodbye,* a 1971 documentary on endangered species in which animal handlers tranquilizing a polar bear were misrepresented as hunting and killing it. The commission explained that the documentary was produced by an independent filmmaker, and there was no evidence that NBC knew the scene was staged. However, the ruling censured CBS and admonished ABC for "failure to make complete investigation into certain incidents" of deception that the subcommittee had brought to light. CBS got the stronger reprimand in this ruling because, as the decision delicately put it, the network "discovered facts only after the FCC confronted it with evidence contrary to its original statements."[47] Despite more evidence that the networks would not investigate themselves, the commission declared that because it had no evidence that management knew the reports had been massaged or because they were produced by outside filmmakers, no penalties would be assessed.

FCC policy on news distortion traveled some distance in these years. In the early 1960s, the commission had no reluctance ruling that the indictments of Boston bookies were proof that CBS accurately portrayed them as criminals or that a Newburgh man had indeed been coerced into saying he was ineligible for welfare. By the end of the decade, the commission refused to be the "national arbiter of the truth" in such matters. Yet this apparent transcendence of contending political and industry interests was itself deceptive. The FCC never stopped judging the truth of conflicting evidence. It simply chose to accept almost all claims at face value, regardless of their merits, and to use the presence of conflicting evidence as a justification for affirming the industry's free-speech rights and shielding it from congressional charges of misrepresentation. The FCC's switch accorded greater authority to the news organizations to arrange and portray events, to edit interviews, and to discipline journalists themselves. At the same time, the commission retained an overt commitment in its rulings on distortion, consistently affirming that the public interest was better served by giving the networks broad latitude to instigate, investigate, and represent events than by furthering network critics' ability to punish misrepresentation. In some of these cases, especially *Pot Party at a University* and *The Selling of the Pentagon,* the FCC gave the language of its decisions to network critics, yet it always gave the ruling to the networks.

The commission's faith in self-regulation was misplaced. The most tangible result of the FCC's entreaties, the extensive revisions to CBS's news guidelines in 1971, were often violated by the network's journalists. News president Richard Salant's files are stuffed with memos attempting to enforce them, but many CBS reporters and executives have said they ignored the rules routinely.[48] However, network executives responded to FCC and congressional investigations by exerting more organizational constraints over their producers. The greater editorial and creative freedom of the early 1960s gave way to more intense executive oversight of reports in later years. New layers of managers inserted themselves between the news divisions and network presidents and owners. Documentaries received more rigorous initial screenings and vetting before airtime by the late 1960s and early 1970s as political and representational attacks mounted against them.[49] The networks treated this process as an in-house means of reining in potentially troublesome journalists as they stonewalled in public when asked to admit error. Self-regulation may have worked for network interests but not always for producers or outside groups.

Symbolic regulations such as the FCC's distortion rules extend a deceptive promise to the public—ironically, in this case, that the FCC would act as a bulwark against deceptive news. As the FCC's chief of Complaints and Compliance at the time wrote some years later, "Time after time, after denouncing news rigging or slanting as the most 'heinous' sin of all, the commission has found some reason for doing nothing."[50] One need not argue that it would have been better for coverage of public affairs had the FCC brought severe sanctions against the networks in these cases. Honest investigative reporting may have grown even scarcer. Yet some of these complaints, regardless of the motives of those who brought them, raised legitimate concerns about the accountability of television journalists to their subjects and to the public, and about the integrity of broadcast reporting. Because the FCC's distortion policy raised such formidable barriers to complainants, it would later fail to protect journalists themselves when they brought complaints against their employers for instructing them to distort news reports to serve management's ideological or business interests.[51]

Fairness: Controversy, Issues, and Subissues, and Who Defines Them

Perhaps no broadcast regulation has been as hotly debated—yet had so little impact on the industry—as the fairness doctrine. The doctrine served more as a shield against public complaints than a sword of justice for the public or a sword of Damocles over broadcasters. No station ever lost its license for violating the doctrine.[52] It did not require broadcasters to provide equal time for replies except to political candidates. It did not require opposing views to be included in the same program or even the same series in which the offending report aired. It did not require broadcasters to offer time to the complainant, merely to any reasonable representative of the complainant's views. Making a successful complaint was extremely difficult. Complainants had to notify broadcasters of their displeasure first. Only after they received an unsatisfactory response could complainants contact the FCC. At this time, the aggrieved would have to specify the station or network that carried the offending broadcast, prove that it was about a controversial issue, that the issue was of public importance, and that the broadcaster had not presented contrasting views on the issue in the program or elsewhere on their overall schedule. The FCC rejected most complaints for failing to demonstrate that the broadcaster had not presented opposing views at some other time.[53] This was hard for complainants to disprove because broadcasters were not required to release any information on the matter (except for notification of personal attacks). In the early and mid-1970s, the FCC's staff and travel resources allowed it to look into less than 5 percent of cases it deemed worthy of a field investigation.[54]

Unsurprisingly, few complaints were successful. Most were actually informal phone calls to the commission that were never referred to stations.[55]

In fiscal years 1973 and 1974, the commission received 4,300 complaints, including politicians demanding equal time and people seeking to respond to personal attacks and broadcast editorials. Over 97 percent of the complaints were rejected for failing to meet the doctrine's requirements. Of 138 grievances forwarded to stations seeking an explanation, 19 were eventually resolved against the licensee (or .4 percent of all complaints).[56] Another study of fairness rulings from fiscal years 1973 to 1976 found that complainants had about a 1 in 1,000 chance of winning.[57] A 1972 Radio and Television News Directors Association survey of its members asked them to list their main problems. The fairness doctrine and personal attack rule were the lowest ranked of the answers provided (getting a big enough budget from management was first). Only 5 percent of respondents ranked fairness and equal time as major problems.[58] Nonetheless, the doctrine offered some small leverage to those who sought access from broadcasters. A handful of savvy complainants used the existence of the rule to negotiate informally for airtime, especially in response to paid political advertisements by monied interests on ballot measures and referenda.[59]

From 1962, when the FCC began applying the fairness doctrine on a case-by-case basis, to 1987, when the doctrine was repealed, the commission found just one investigative documentary in violation of the rule. This was *Pensions*. In this case, the FCC grappled with three major issues raised by the doctrine: what constituted a controversial subject, what was the main issue of a report, and who should define it. Although the FCC's decision against NBC was atypical, the issues it addressed were at the heart of many fairness complaints. The case history shows that the commission and the courts were deeply ambivalent about enforcing the doctrine, rather than posing a monolithic government threat to free speech. It also offers a glimpse into the poverty of the larger debate over investigative reporting and fairness within the policy apparatus. NBC deployed the myth of muckraking in an attempt to disable or dissolve the doctrine and undermined its own documentary in the process. In return, the network's opponents affirmed the equally mythic ideal of objectivity and network control over government. In the end, the regulatory system coughed up a familiar result, bringing no sanctions against NBC but the legal costs of battling fairness requirements. The doctrine was weakened, however, and the opportunity for greater public debate over the pension system on NBC was lost.

Recall that the case followed a tortuous course through the administrative and judicial system at a time of great uncertainty in the government and media over the fairness doctrine. After the FCC found against the documentary and ordered NBC to provide some opportunity for defenders of the private pension system to reply, NBC appealed the decision to the District of Columbia Circuit Court, where a three-judge panel overturned the commission's decision. The full court then moved to reconsider the ruling, but the FCC lost its resolve to pursue the case, and the court remanded it to the commission. The FCC rescinded its decision in 1975.

In its petition to the FCC, AIM argued that the documentary wrongly depicted the private pension system as rife with failure and fraud. Mustering evidence (however weak) that many plans worked well, AIM charged that the program should have balanced coverage of retirement funds' shortcomings with their successes. The group noted that the congressional struggle over pension legislation showed that it was a controversial issue of public importance, and if NBC had not explicitly advocated the Williams-Javits bill as the best solution, its report suggested retirement funds were so bad that such far-reaching regulation was necessary. Therefore, AIM argued, NBC should be required to offer airtime for supporters of private plans to reply. In response, NBC flatly refused to provide time for the advocates of private pension plans or even for debate or discussion between proponents of varying perspectives on the issue. Before the FCC, the network only briefly denied the charges of inaccuracy (given the commission's rules on distortion, NBC did not have much to fear) yet argued extensively that the doctrine was unworkable and chilled exposé reporting.[60]

The network put forth a far-fetched argument about how the doctrine did not apply to *Pensions* because retirement fund problems were not a controversial issue of public importance and therefore did not require balanced coverage. First, NBC argued that the issue was not of widespread significance because there was little public dialogue about pensions, despite extensive prior media coverage and the ongoing debate in Congress. Second, NBC claimed that pension reform was not controversial because all groups testifying before Congress agreed that some reform was necessary. NBC's lawyers furthered this line of reasoning later in court when they pointed out that Congress ultimately voted unanimously to enact the Employee Retirement Income Security Act (ERISA). The appeals court panel agreed, finding that if some specific reform proposals were controversial, they were neither the subject of the documentary nor endorsed by it. This conclusion ignored that viewers' support for competing legislation might well hinge on how the performance of the pension system was portrayed, that NBC focused almost entirely on its faults, that it concluded that congressional action was needed, and that it raised a number of problems with the pension system that were not addressed in the Nixon administration's reform plan.[61]

Next, NBC claimed that its documentary "dealt not with the 'overall performance' of the private pension system, but rather with some problems with some pension plans."[62] Since it was not an indictment of the entire system, NBC claimed, the documentary did not address the larger controversial public issue of pension reform. In addition, the network interpreted the commission's regulations as stating, "The questions of what issue has been the basic subject matter of a program and whether it is a controversial one are matters on which broadcasters' judgments must be upheld unless clearly unreasonable or in bad faith."[63] In short, NBC claimed that the main subject of the report and whether that subject was publicly disputed were up to the network to decide. NBC said that it would face "administrative chaos" if the commission decided that the program was about the larger and controversial issue of pension reform, that it was unbalanced, and that AIM deserved reply time, since "some AIM-of-the-left might well file a fairness complaint" in response to AIM's views.[64] Other potential fairness complaints about the program might center on how each company and union referred to in the report treated their workers, when rights should vest to employees, and so forth. To avoid this nightmare, NBC must be given "the broadest leeway to determine what subjects to consider and what subjects have been considered."[65] The appeals court panel agreed, finding that NBC was reasonable in arguing that the "dominant thrust of the program was an exposé of the abuses that appeared in the private pension industry, and not a general report on the state of the industry."[66]

This was a remarkable assertion of authority on NBC's part. As AIM pointed out, allowing NBC or other licensees to define the subject matter of programs would simply allow them to define away all fairness doctrine complaints in the future as pertaining to subissues rather than the main subject of a report. In this case, NBC and the appeals court strained credulity when they asserted the program was about a handful of abuses, ignoring its numerous and pervasive generalizations about the pension system as a whole.[67] As one commentator wrote later, "The court seemed to enter an Alice-in-Wonderland world in its analysis of explicit comments made on the overall performance of private pension plans."[68] In addition, NBC's nightmare scenario of endless fairness claims being made upon it was obviated by existing FCC policy.[69] And, although NBC trumpeted its editorial freedom to engage in investigative reporting, its legal strategy ultimately denigrated its own documentary. "The value of investigative reporting is to raise matters of substantial public interest," wrote the FCC. "It is difficult to see why a network would devote its time and effort to a program with no broad impact or value, and we cannot agree that NBC has done so here."[70] Appeals court justice David Bazelon, a critic of the fairness doctrine who nevertheless attacked the panel's majority ruling, wondered "what the professional journalists who prepared the 'Pensions' program think about NBC's litigation position in this case that their program was not really controversial. My own thought is that NBC had by its litigation position done more to attack and undercut the 'Pensions' program than anything AIM could have done through the FCC."[71]

Finally, NBC claimed that the FCC threatened its editorial freedom to engage in muckraking, thereby chilling debate. "If there is a hierarchy within the speech protected by the First Amendment," NBC claimed, "investigative journalism is surely at its apex."[72] Judge Harold Leventhal, writing for the appeals court majority, expressed similar views:

> Investigative reporting has a distinctive role of uncovering and exposing abuses. It would be undermined if a government agency were free to review the editorial judgments involved in the selection of theme and materials, to over-rule the licensee's editorial "judgment as to what was presented," though not unreasonable, to conclude that in the agency's view the exposé had a broader message in fact than that discerned by the licensee and therefore, under the balancing obligation [of the fairness doctrine], required an additional and offsetting program.[73]

Numerous journalists and scholars celebrated the decision as a victory for the networks' right to muckrake.[74] In doing so, they perpetuated the myth of investigative reporting as a wholly independent journalistic endeavor, created ex nihilo. However, this documentary, like so many others, was the product of close attention to a Senate subcommittee's work, so the hand of government was in it from the beginning. NBC "uncovered" nothing; it *amplified* criticisms already circulating in the print media and policy community in a way that only network television could do at the time.

Leventhal and others vastly overstated the fairness doctrine's intrusion in the editorial process, depicting the FCC's tepid regulations as near Orwellian. The FCC had not censured NBC for its report but merely required the network to offer some reply time for further discussion of the issue that included defenders of the existing retirement system. The commission took great pains to make it clear to NBC from the beginning that it did not have to air an hour documentary on happy pensioners, that no precisely equal amount of time had to be provided (a few minutes on the *Today* show had sufficed in the past). Nor did the network have to air opposing views in any particular format, and it could choose the spokespeople for those views as long as their choice was reasonable.[75] These were modest requirements that need not have curbed speech but might have enlarged the public discussion of pensions somewhat.

Unfortunately, the doctrine's defenders in this case relied on the pinched and naive vision of good journalism as always adhering to the precepts of objectivity. AIM denounced the documentary as an example of "advocacy journalism," whose practitioners scandalously favored "taking sides and rigging your story in order to influence public opinion," adding that "most responsible journalists reject this concept of 'good' journalism."[76] Judge Edward Tamm, who dissented from the court's majority decision, embraced AIM's narrow views, charging that NBC's position

> means that a telecaster's presentation under the label of investigative reporting of a few factual bones covered with the corpulent flesh of opinion and comment fulfills the obligation of the network to give a fair picture to the public and to assist the public in knowing the facts essential to a determination of basic policies. The majority opinion fails to recognize that as a practical matter there is no real distinction between this type of so-called investigative reporting and propaganda. The investigative reporter, regardless of his initial motivation, too often reaches a point where objectivity disappears and he becomes an ardent advocate for a particular position or viewpoint.[77]

Tamm cast the networks as Big Brother, asking rhetorically, "Is it an exaggeration to say that the telecasting industry constitutes a power system comparable if not superior to government itself but basically free of the restraints imposed on government power?" Indeed it was, given network investigative reporters' dependence on government sources and unwillingness to stray too far from their frames.

The panel did not explicitly strike down the fairness doctrine as unconstitutional, but several of its colleagues on the full circuit court were alarmed at such a broad rejection of it. They notified the FCC that they would be open to a rehearing before all ten judges of the court and vacated Leventhal's opinion. Although an appeals hearing was scheduled at AIM's request, it never happened. In the interim, the FCC decided to abandon the case, claiming that the issue was moot once Congress enacted ERISA. The FCC seemed unwilling to risk losing the doctrine on the merits of the *Pensions* case. A disgusted Judge Bazelon remarked, "I certainly hope we have not yet reached the stage where a majority of Congressmen can by their votes determine that an issue is no longer 'controversial.'"[78] Yet in the end, as in the beginning, congressional action played the major role in determining whether pension reform was a matter of public significance. After the court dispensed with the case, the commission rescinded its ruling against *Pensions* in mid-1975. The commission never dared to find another documentary unfair.

Some have argued that the protracted wrangling over the *Pensions* case best exemplifies how the fairness doctrine had become too complex to administer, that it wasted broadcasters' resources on needless litigation, and that it impelled government to intrude on journalistic decision making.[79] The fairness doctrine only became "unworkable" in the *Pensions* case because NBC denied that its report had addressed the larger issue it obviously had and caviled about what constituted a controversial issue, what made it of public significance, and how one should distinguish between the main issues and subissues of the documentary. Obviously, had NBC not engaged in this sophistry, it would not have had to pay legal fees. Here, as in most fairness complaints, the notion that the FCC poked its nose into "journalist's" editorial decisions is a partial truth. Network management, not documentarians, had final say over these reports. More important, mandating reply time did not involve censorship or even disapproval of what *Pensions* had to say, only that opposing views should be included in some token measure elsewhere on NBC's schedule at some point. The doctrine appeared byzantine and intrusive only because NBC's lawyers made it look so in an attempt to overthrow it.

Why did the FCC break with tradition and hold that a network documentary had violated the fairness doctrine? For one, NBC flouted the doctrine so aggressively that it would have been difficult to maintain the appearance that it still applied to news without challenging the network. Had NBC won, any broadcaster might simply have brushed off fairness complaints by refusing to acknowledge that it concerned the main issue of a report. Even so, the commission was typically ambivalent about ruling against the industry. The FCC's two most liberal members, Nicholas Johnson and H. Rex Lee, were absent for the decision. Even Nixon-appointed chairman Dean Burch later said that he told his colleagues on the day he signed the ruling, "This is the worst piece of crap we've ever put our hands on." Yet he claims to have voted for it "because we had turned down so many foolish AIM complaints in the past," which is an odd rationale, to say the least.[80]

Perhaps more important than the merits of the case, the commission must have been mindful of the growing and bipartisan congressional criticism of its inaction. The Staggers subcommittee and others regularly implied the FCC was a pawn of the networks. As the House subcommittee forwarded numerous complaints without success, it began stating its purposes not only as investigating news but also the FCC's policies. Staggers was not alone in his crusade against the CBS documentaries, finding strong support from the members of his subcommittee in all but his last inquiry. Representatives William Springer (R-Ill.) and J. J. Pickle (D-Texas) participated enthusiastically in most of the documentary hearings. John Moss (D-Calif.) and John Dingell (D-Mich.) chaired hearings in the *Pot Party* investigation. Moss, who won media accolades for authoring the Freedom of Information Act, was particularly critical of the networks and disgusted with the commission. In reference to *Hunger in America,* Moss wrote to the FCC chairman at the time asking him "not to seek a means of avoiding findings of fact in this instance which actually expose CBS to responsibility for its actions . . . There should be no whitewashing as occurred in *Pot Party* . . . It is time the Commission acts in the public interest and not try to stretch the First Amendment into a cloak large enough to cover all wrongdoing and misrepresentation a licensee might desire to present as 'news' or 'documentaries.'"[81] These congressmen and many others on the Commerce Committee urged the FCC to consider CBS's conduct in the *Project Nassau* case when the network's stations came up for renewal, and called for congressional legislation to regulate the networks.[82]

Regulatory Dissensus and Resolution

Struggles over fairness and news distortion revealed that a political consensus over broadcast regulation was dissolving. The fairness doctrine became "un-workable" for the same reason most regulations do: the leaders of the regulated industry—CBS and NBC—no longer saw an advantage in complying with it. The industry responded to White House and congressional forces who in the past had usually been satisfied with securing their own access to the airwaves but who now briefly threatened more direct oversight of news content. The FCC, which previously had dependably shielded the networks from most fairness and distortion complaints, now appeared to be less effective in doing so as the agency's political overseers and a bevy of organized citizens' groups pressured it to expand and enforce its authority. But, in the end, Congress and the FCC signaled that they would no longer intervene directly in disputes about the content of television news.

Congress Staggered

As we have seen, Congress spoke out more extensively in this period for many reasons. Lawmakers responded to the rising cries of local interests against how they were portrayed in the new national medium. Congressional figures also performed constituent service for the industries they represented, who were increasingly attentive to how they were portrayed on the national screen. In addition, many lawmakers feared the growing power of network television to frame national politics, especially when those frames ran contrary to their own. Federal policy makers' long-standing concerns over their own access to the airwaves surfaced in most of these disputes and was explicitly stated by many in the House debate over *The Selling of the Pentagon*. If Congress remained wary of alienating the custodians of the cathode ray, they were still most beholden to local broadcasters rather than the networks, because politicians' home state and district stations were more likely to shape their images to the voters on an everyday basis. It is no coincidence that the leading congressional voice against investigative reporting, Harley Staggers, had no television station in his district. The House Commerce Investigations Subcommittee's numerous probes also reflected its members' particular discomfort with television's means of representing issues and its potential for deception. Finally, these investigations were inspired by growing congressional ire at the FCC's protective crouch around the industry. The Staggers subcommittee often stated its purposes as not only investigating news but also the FCC's inaction. Toward the end of this period, the commission itself became more scrutinized and criticized for its solicitous approach to the industry in a number of executive branch and congressional studies.[83]

Many lawmakers introduced bills to oversee the networks and their news departments more stringently in response to the documentary probes, attempting to effect directly what the FCC would not. Staggers's proposed legislation would have required broadcasters to retain all used and unused film and tape for six months in case of challenges to their reports, made it a crime to falsify news broadcasts, and made investigative news gathering and reporting that involved violation of the law a threat to license renewal.[84] Others would have banned rearranging the remarks of interviewees and required television journalists to provide sources with unedited transcripts of their interviews.[85] Still others devised bills to label reenacted material, guarantee a right of reply to broadcast news, prohibit staging, and ban the use of reverse camera angles to mask edits in interviews.[86] Representative Gonzalez would have licensed the networks directly rather than through their owned-and-operated stations.[87]

In the end, however, Congress seemed to be practicing the old symbolic politics of making a great deal of noise about protecting the public without resolving to intervene. Staggers developed just one bill from his six years of hearings into news practices. Neither this bill nor any of the others that would have regulated television news more strictly ever made it to a floor vote. The Staggers subcommittee's probes were focused on relatively narrow issues and lone examples of news distortion rather than on larger problems with network commercialism and exclusion of other voices, or broader policy questions about the FCC's relationship to the industry. The House vote against Staggers in the *Selling of the Pentagon* controversy began his undoing. Soon after, when the Commerce Committee agreed to limit members to one subcommittee post apiece, the most senior members of the Investigations Subcommittee deserted Staggers for other positions.[88] His 1972 hearings into news deception drew few of his colleagues; one was attended only by Staggers himself. "Harley just dreams of bringing CBS to its knees," observed one colleague, "but that will never happen." Congressional opposition to further confrontations with the networks led Staggers to mute his opposition thereafter. Two years later he was deposed from his Commerce Committee chairmanship. As one scholar of the committee maintained, broadcast news regulation was a low-salience issue for the public and a high-conflict issue with a powerful interest group—broadcasters.[89]

Rolling Back the Fairness Doctrine

Once the FCC made it clear that it was not likely to find against broadcasters in distortion cases, the industry turned its attention to the fairness doctrine. The *Pensions* case was part of a larger campaign against the doctrine launched by CBS, NBC, the National Association of Broadcasters, and the Radio and Television News Directors Association.[90] Thus, the FCC's fears of risking the doctrine in the courts were well founded by 1974. By that time, the Senate Subcommittee on Communications had held hearings on whether to repeal it, Senator William Proxmire introduced legislation to do so, and the FCC itself reviewed the doctrine extensively. As the Nixon administration's strong-arm tactics for managing the news came to light and Watergate unfolded, the networks became more assertive about their editorial rights.

The industry quickly attached its campaign against fairness requirements to broadcasters' bigger concerns: repeal of the doctrine's extension to advertising and increased licensing security. Having ruled in 1967 that cigarette commercials were subject to the doctrine, the FCC inadvertently opened up advertising to requests for balance.[91] In the early 1970s, it was still scrambling in the courts to keep antismoking, environmental, and other groups from establishing that speech oriented toward promoting a product could also be considered controversial commentary on public issues.[92] That would have disturbed the commercial basis of broadcasting much more significantly than requirements to balance news programs. Many groups demanded free reply time to advertisements. If they were successful, they would have threatened the value of television as an advertising medium. Who would want to advertise knowing that public interest groups could demand reply time to debunk the advertising claims? Network calls for abandoning news regulation also extended to demands for longer licensing periods to further insulate broadcasters from "political pressure." Nixon confidante Bebe Rebozo suspiciously showed up to compete for the licenses of two *Washington Post* stations when the paper was the main outlet for Watergate coverage, but the bulk of renewal challenges at the time were brought by liberal and African American reform groups to secure more local programming and diverse staffing. At hearings on government and the media before Senator Sam Ervin's Constitutional Rights Subcommittee in the fall of 1971, CBS's Frank Stanton and Walter Cronkite offered a one-two punch, with Stanton calling for repeal of the fairness doctrine while his anchorman asked for the abolition of *all* licensing of broadcast stations. NBC produced correspondent Bill Monroe to demand the same. As the industry had done in the 1930s, after establishing its rights to the spectrum, it held up its news departments as the basis for "delicensing," demanding protection of their rights to the spectrum in perpetuity.[93] The 1970s version of this argument had a new twist, emphasizing how government chilled investigative reporting on controversial subjects.

However, the doctrine survived, at least on a pro forma basis, until much of it was repealed in 1987. It still enjoyed bipartisan political support from the White House and many in Congress, particularly representatives from smaller districts where a lone broadcaster would have exercised great power over representing politics without the doctrine. Citizens' groups on the right and left joined together to protect their small access to the airwaves.[94] And many in the media supported the regulation, including ABC as well as some local affiliates who saw it as a bulwark against network liberalism.[95]

Resolving Conservative Contradictions

Serious contradictions marred conservative efforts to rein in broadcast investigative reporting in these years. When right-wing commentators attacked coverage of poverty and foreign policy, they chided journalists in part for not properly respecting the authority of official sources and appealed to the FCC to impose fairness. Yet when conservatives assailed muckraking reporting on business, they complained that the media wanted to increase government authority over private corporations—and appealed to the government to impose fairness on the broadcast industry. Thus, conservative critics portrayed the media as both antigovernment and yet proregulation. And these critics argued for less government regulation of business but greater oversight of the commercial news media. The right's goals of deregulating industry and managing the news were at loggerheads.

These contradictions were fought out within the Nixon administration, which began the long resolution of conservatives' tactical dilemma in relation to the media. The answer was to emphasize aggressive news management through unofficial channels while courting more favorable coverage by extending broadcasters' license terms and absolving the industry of public-service requirements to cover unprofitable news and public affairs. Clay Whitehead, director of Nixon's Office of Telecommunications Policy, laid out the deal in a 1973 speech remembered more for his attacks on "ideological plugola" by the network news departments than for his generous offers to extend license terms from three years to five, make challenges to license renewals more difficult, and ban the FCC from demanding minimum amounts of public-service programming.[96] All of these proposals and more would be enacted by the Reagan-era FCC. At the same time, the Nixon administration began fostering broadcasting's competitors in cable and other technologies, laying the groundwork for the eventual dilution of network power.

Whitehead would also have proposed abolishing the fairness doctrine, but he lost a debate with administration opponents such as Charles Colson, who wanted to retain it as a check on the "liberal" media. Colson watched Whitehead's public pronouncements on the doctrine carefully, repeatedly intervening to stop Whitehead from calling for its overthrow.[97] Whitehead occasionally failed to toe the White House line and called for the end of the doctrine in a 1972 speech, saying that, "Big Brother himself could not have conceived a more disarming 'newsspeak' name for a system of government program control than the Fairness Doctrine." Two months later, Whitehead said the rule should be maintained and that compliance with it ought to be a requirement for license renewal.[98] Thereafter, the administration presented itself in public as neutral on repealing the doctrine but privately resisted it.

Meanwhile, the administration assisted in developing nominally private surrogates to move news coverage rightward. The administration fostered new conservative think tanks, such as the American Enterprise Institute, to provide policy ideas and expert sources in the news that seemed to be independent from government.[99] The White House also helped develop AIM as its chosen instrument for criticizing perceived liberal bias in the news. AIM's ties to government and industry, including conservative media leaders, were discussed in chapter 3. Both AIM and the administration denied any connections, but the media watchdogs had less than an arm's-length relationship to the White House.[100] Administration records opened decades later indicate that the White House helped expand the group's funding and coordinated many attacks on media bias with AIM. Although information about AIM's early contributors is unavailable, in later years no fewer than seven Nixon administration officials donated money to the group, directly or through their foundations.[101] We know now that at least some of them worked closely with AIM while they held office.

Many of AIM's early complaints and campaigns against media bias pursued specific White House news-management goals. AIM spent most of its time defending the Vietnam War, filing three of its first six fairness doctrine complaints against news specials that attacked Nixon's continuation and expansion of the war.[102] Nixon aide Charles Colson became aware of the group in part through its public attack on *The Selling of the Pentagon*. The group raised numerous objections to PBS programs as too liberal and filed a legal brief asking the FCC to enforce a section of the Public Broadcasting Act that required all PBS programming to observe the dictates of objectivity and balance.[103] This assisted the administration's own efforts to reduce the influence of NET programs and to cut PBS's public affairs coverage in general, which were at issue in the *Banks and the Poor* controversy. In a 1971 memo outlining White House attempts to undermine public broadcasting, Colson noted, "We got Accuracy in Media to file fairness complaints with the FCC concerning recent PBS programs. These complaints were cited in such publications as *Time* and *Broadcasting,* among others."[104]

If these issues generated broad support among conservatives, other AIM complaints were remarkably focused on protecting the administration from accusations of scandal. The group was especially solicitous of the Treasury Department, attacking obscure news items alleging department favoritism toward specific corporations. AIM worked to discredit reports that the department had acceded to pressure by International Telephone and Telegraph (ITT) to deny foreign aid to Ecuador in 1971 and 1972 as punishment for nationalizing ITT property.[105] Departing from its primary mission of assailing the major media, AIM attacked a tabloid story that alleged that large amounts of gold were missing from Fort Knox because the Federal Reserve had secretly sold it to Chase Manhattan's David Rockefeller (Treasury Secretary William Simon led reporters and congresspeople to Fort Knox to offer firsthand evidence that no bullion was missing).[106] And AIM strenuously denied a single columnist's assertion that the Precision Valve Company, owned by Nixon campaign contributor Robert Abplanalp, received special treatment from the Justice Department in an antitrust case.[107] None of these stories was sustained front-page news.

Throughout 1971, Charles Colson repeatedly urged fellow presidential aide and investment banker Peter Flanigan to help AIM expand its activities. In January, Colson observed that AIM's staff "really perform yeoman services for us and are gaining in stature and effectiveness" and asked Flanigan to help "recruit top names" for the group's board.[108] In May, he wrote Flanigan "a reminder with respect to your recruiting this weekend of top level business people for the Accuracy-In-Media operation," suggesting that he enlist large advertisers to the cause.[109] In July, Colson asked whether "we ever pursued further . . . the funding of accuracy-in-media?"[110] Flanigan described the situation to the president in a long memo written later that year: "You may be interested in a project aimed at forcing accuracy in news and other public service television broadcasting. This project, the subject of several discussions between administration supporters and Chuck Colson and me, relies on a mechanism under which private non-governmental pressures can be brought to bear on the three networks . . . What is needed is a greatly expanded and effective effort of this type." "Pete: Excellent!" replied Nixon. "Follow up."[111] Colson also noted in a memo that conservative philanthropist Richard Mellon Scaife had installed a professional fundraiser at AIM, "and the money is beginning to roll in." Colson added that the group would make use of the newly created television news archive at Vanderbilt University, also funded by Scaife, as "the basic research tool" for making the case for media unfairness.[112]

Colson increasingly directed his staff to forward examples of offending coverage to AIM to use as the basis of its complaints. In July, Colson's staff arranged for an AIM-sponsored speech at the National Press Club by Edith Efron, where the *TV Guide* columnist promoted her book about how media coverage of the 1968 presidential campaign discriminated against Nixon.[113] AIM organized another Press Club speech by James Keogh, formerly a White House aide and once executive editor of *Time*. Keogh drew on his book about the media's alleged hostility to the Nixon administration and attacked reports that ITT's large campaign contributions had swayed the White House to drop an antitrust suit against it.[114] Colson later wrote that Keogh had "worked a deal with AIM which means that we will have a very good outlet for media attacks."[115] One of AIM's earliest successes came in 1972 when it convinced ABC to air five corrections to a documentary entitled *Arms and Security: How Much Is Enough?*[116] Shortly after, when Colson's ire was piqued by a news report on Nixon opponent George McGovern's defense proposals, Colson urged his staff to "go after this hard—AIM, an official protest to FCC, a paid AIM ad; squeeze them like we did with ABC on their defense program."[117] If AIM did not make much of this McGovern item, it seemed more responsive to another complaint Colson told his staff to pass along. This was prompted by an unusually long *CBS Evening News* segment on the McGovern campaign on a night when the president's activities drew little coverage. AIM's subsequent study of campaign reporting attacked CBS for anti-Nixon bias and used the report as a major example.[118]

Given the White House's attention to AIM, it is unlikely that the group chose *Pensions* as a target entirely independent of administration influence. In a memo on the White House's campaign to counter alleged media bias to chief of staff H. R. Haldeman, written several months before AIM filed its complaint against *Pensions,* Colson reported, "We intend to use AIM to bring fairness complaints before the FCC as in the past, but on an expanded scale."[119] The media gadflies later said they were alerted to NBC's documentary by "businessmen, business organizations and actuaries."[120] Yet Flanigan spearheaded the administration's effort to minimize pension reform as chair of the president's Committee on Pension Plan Reform Legislation, which brought together representatives from the Departments of Labor, Treasury, and Commerce. The Commerce Department, which opposed all but the most minimal pension reforms, was headed by Maurice H. Stans, whose foundation subsequently supported AIM. Another future AIM funder, William E. Simon, was then deputy secretary of the Treasury Department, which also advocated minimal change. The department appointed a Teamster fund administrator to its advisory council on the issue. The Teamsters, who endorsed Nixon's presidential campaign in 1972, were unflatteringly portrayed by NBC and opposed the Williams-Javits pension bill. In addition to his media monitoring activities, Colson was also the White House liaison to labor, and he was credited with winning the union's endorsement.[121] AIM used Teamster connections to raise funds for its investigations.[122] Given that the administration figures closest to AIM were the ones most involved in the pension issue, that the White House was directing numerous media complaints through the group at the time, and that representatives of a union that NBC portrayed as part of the problem had footholds both in the administration and AIM, it would be surprising if AIM arrived at the decision to attack NBC on its own. If the "watchdog media" were less than independent from the Senate pension reformers, the "media watchdogs" were less than distant from the White House.[123]

* * *

Despite the Nixon administration's campaign against the news media, government did not present a unified threat to investigative reporting on television in the 1960s and early 1970s. Where network muckraking was concerned, the FCC engaged in symbolic enforcement of fairness and distortion rules, and the judiciary questioned the commission's single finding of unfairness, against NBC. Congress made halfhearted efforts, none successful, to legislate in the wake of the Commerce Committee investigations of broadcast news. The Nixon White House, broadcasters' most threatening critic, was split between those who would have used the state primarily to serve the media's economic ends and those who would have used it mainly to advance policy goals by enforcing replies to hostile reporting. By 1975, a brief period in which regulators closely scrutinized network news and documentaries came to an end. Congress had fallen silent on the issue, and the Nixon administration had fallen entirely. The FCC had signaled that it would not discipline the networks for news distortion. And, if the *Pensions* case set no legal precedent, it sent a clear message that the doctrine was in trouble on the circuit court of appeals and that the commission was unlikely to press another fairness complaint against anything that looked like investigative reporting.

The Nixon administration planted the seeds of a new conservative media

strategy. Through structural regulation, it courted broadcasters' business in-
stincts by offering greater license security, yet it began to break the networks'
power by promoting competing technologies such as cable television. Through
content deregulation, the White House wooed broadcasters by promising
reductions in public-service programming requirements while sending mixed
signals about retaining the fairness doctrine. This strategy, pursued aggressively
in the Reagan administration, allowed conservatives to present themselves as
champions of the First Amendment by removing requirements for public input
on licensing (thus excluding the mainly liberal reformers of the early 1970s)
and by killing the fairness doctrine (thereby allowing broadcasters to carry
mostly right-wing talk shows and commentary). The conservative strategy,
devised in part as a response to documentary controversies, shaped the future
of broadcast regulation far more powerfully than all the of the era's attacks on
investigative reporting combined.

The Privatization of Regulation

Despite the many investigations of investigative reporting, the regulatory regime of the 1960s and early 1970s provided rich soil for the growth of television muckraking. Regulators' demands for public-service programming helped prompt the networks and local stations to plow resources into substantive reporting, including in-depth documentaries. Regulatory protection of networks and licensees from greater competition within broadcast markets and from competing technologies such as cable television ensured that broadcasters had the resources to spend on expensive and risky news programming while taking home record profits. When critics attacked the fairness and accuracy of muckraking, FCC rulings helped shelter broadcasters from the storm.

What has been the legacy of these struggles over investigative reporting? Since the 1970s, the White House, Congress, and the FCC have all but abandoned attempts to regulate the content of broadcast news and investigative reporting. The Reagan administration largely carried out the regulatory strategy first envisioned in the Nixon years, all but guaranteeing renewals of station licenses and rescinding content regulations on news almost completely while weakening network news power by promoting competing technologies that dilute its reach. The Reagan FCC almost immediately declared its opposition to the fairness doctrine, stopped enforcing it, and repealed most of the doctrine in 1987.[1] Although still on the books, the news distortion rules have likewise been orphaned by the agency that created them.[2] The "deregulation" of television news has become a free-speech feather in conservatism's cap, allowing some of the same forces that attacked investigative documentaries in the past to present themselves as the true friends of unfettered journalism. For broadcasting's critics, the death of fairness requirements is but one part of a larger corporate capture of the First Amendment.

Without executive and legislative branch constraints, has television muckraking become more free? Does it serve the public better? These questions presuppose another: who regulates investigative reporting on television today? Proponents of the current arrangements would likely say that no one does. After all, television news has been "deregulated." Yet regulation is not a light switch that can be turned on and off, but a balloon—squeeze it at one end and its force is displaced elsewhere. As legal realists point out, government always acts to regulate and balance the speech rights of private actors by creating and enforcing rights of property, tort, and contract.[3] Even the most "laissez-faire communications policies merely assign the regulation of broadcasting to non-state powers," writes Onora O'Neill.[4] Government regulation is not an "intervention" in natural, preexisting markets but constitutes them by defining individual rights and the rules of the game, at no small public expense. The state continues to be involved in the market in broadcasting through spectrum licensing, awarding and enforcing exclusive editorial control over the public airwaves to private broadcasters while excluding others who would like to speak. Government also continues to regulate through the judiciary, which has taken up much of the state's oversight of news practices since the 1970s through civil litigation. Tort law, as Martin Shapiro notes, is "also public law, an integral part of the regime of government regulation of private enterprise."[5] Thus, television news is regulated today by markets for broadcasting and for tort claims.

The Courts and Torts

Over the past thirty years, the courts have played a larger role in regulating news media conduct, first through libel litigation and then through a range of news-gathering torts. These suits have raised greater costs to the media of defending themselves and have been far more intrusive in scrutinizing journalists' methods than FCC regulations were. The new regulatory regime has not freed investigative reporters and may well have exerted greater chilling effects.

In the 1980s, the number of defamation cases brought against media organizations rose dramatically, as did the size of damages awarded. Resolved libel cases brought against the media grew 550 percent (from fourteen to seventy-seven cases) between 1975 and 1982. The media became the main target of libel allegations as well, rising from 68 percent of all defendants in defamation cases in 1975 to 94 percent in 1983.[6] In constant dollars, libel awards from 1980 to 1986 increased more than 400 percent over awards in the entire decade that ended in 1964, the year the Supreme Court rewrote modern libel law in *New York Times Co. v. Sullivan* in an attempt to offer greater protection to media speech about public issues.[7] Before 1980, only one libel judgment against a media organization topped $1 million, but by 1985 roughly one-third exceeded that figure. Although appeals judges reversed about two-thirds of jury judgments against the media, the increased complexity of a libel defense meant that the "winners" were incurring significant legal costs, lost staff time, and rising libel insurance premiums. Broadcast investigative reports were particularly likely to spark libel claims (by the mid-1980s, 60 *Minutes* had been sued over 150 times).[8]

The growth in libel lawsuits against broadcast news was due in part to the lack of enforcement of the fairness doctrine and distortion rules. Elite targets of media reports began to sense that appealing to the FCC was a waste of time. In 1983, the conservative Media Institute warned corporate figures seeking to counter negative media coverage that fairness doctrine complaints were increasingly fruitless, but, "in the future, judicial remedies may offer more hope for the plaintiff."[9] If the FCC was no longer a realistic avenue for pursuing grievances against reporting, the courts appeared to be. Some scholars have found that judges and juries increasingly used the libel tort in the 1980s not simply to compensate victims for harm to their reputations but also to try to regulate media practices by setting journalistic standards of conduct and deterring irresponsibility by assessing large punitive damages.[10]

These were the aims of conservative supporters of General William Westmoreland, who sued CBS in the most publicized libel trial of the 1980s. Westmoreland objected to *The Uncounted Enemy: A Vietnam Deception,* a 1982 documentary that drew on military sources to accuse him, of understating enemy troop strength in order to make America's war in Vietnam appear more successful than it was. The goals of the conservative foundations, Mobil Oil, and AIM—all of which bankrolled the general's legal expenses and public relations efforts—ranged from killing CBS's documentary series to rewriting libel law in favor of plaintiffs and against the media.[11] Westmoreland's attorneys sued for the staggering sum of $120 million, a figure that seemed chosen to chill and punish the networks for their coverage of the war rather than simply compensate the general for damages to his reputation. Westmoreland's central countercharges were eerily similar to those raised against CBS's 1971 report, *The Selling of the Pentagon.* The general claimed that CBS had selectively edited his interview to make him seem to admit guilt, omitted his denials of understating enemy troops, and misedited interviews with other sources to make them seem to be accusing the general in stronger terms. Because libel law provides for extensive discovery of journalists' state of mind when preparing their reports, CBS was compelled to release its outtakes and notes, the same materials that the network successfully refused to give Congress in

1971. Demonstrating its own irrelevance, the FCC did not rule on the case until after the trial concluded, when it dismissed a complaint against CBS for unfairness and distortion. Although Westmoreland dropped the case during trial, CBS paid legal costs in the millions and lost its libel insurance soon after the case was filed. Libel insurance premiums doubled in 1984 and again in 1985 for the other networks.[12]

By the 1990s, personal libel suits had become a less attractive means for all but the wealthiest or most powerful targets of exposé journalism, for several reasons. The complexity of libel law raised legal costs for plaintiffs as well as defendants. In addition, although legal costs—or the threat of them—remained a useful cudgel with which to punish reporters, media defendants as a whole enjoyed a high success rate in defamation cases. A study of 614 defamation suits brought between 1982 and 1988 found that, although the media only won about a quarter of jury trials, they won more than four-fifths of all cases brought against them, the vast majority decided by summary judgment, motions to dismiss, or on appeals.[13] According to another study, only about 10 percent of plaintiffs classified as public figures won libel suits.[14] In 1986, in *Anderson v. Liberty Lobby,* the Supreme Court acted to curb the spread of defamation suits by facilitating their quick dismissal. The Court gave its imprimatur to lower courts granting summary judgment for defendants in cases involving public figures when plaintiffs failed to demonstrate in pretrial the potential to prove knowing or reckless falsehood on the part of the media.[15]

The tightening of personal libel law prompted new strategies for countering investigative reports. The libel-related law of business disparagement, which protects a party's economic interests rather than reputation, posed new threats to investigative reporting. Thirteen states passed agricultural disparagement statutes, or "veggie libel" laws, to protect food producers against unsubstantiated criticism of their products. Many states acted in response to the Washington State apple industry's failed disparagement suit against a 1989 60 *Minutes* report that accused growers of putting consumers at risk by spraying a carcinogenic chemical, Alar, on apples.[16] Texas cattle ranchers brought the most celebrated case of this type when they sued Oprah Winfrey and a guest on her talk show for their comments about mad cow disease and the health risks of eating beef. Although Winfrey won the first round of the case in U.S. district court, the judge failed to rule on the constitutionality of Texas's agricultural disparagement act, and the ranchers appealed. Winfrey spent anywhere from $500,000 to $2 million defending the case according to press estimates.[17]

Investigative reporting's critics also began to bring suits that focused not on stories' fairness or accuracy, but on the methods used to produce news, such as the use of hidden cameras and undercover reporting. Muckraking targets brought a rash of suits claiming damages as a result of the news-gathering process, rather than from the impact of publishing negative information about a plaintiff's reputation or business. Suits for fraud, trespass, breach of duty, tortious interference with contractual relationships, intrusion, intentional infliction of emotional distress, and illegal surveillance were brought in part to curb undercover reporting and hidden cameras and to uncover reporters' confidential sources.[18] These suits allowed many public figure plaintiffs to avoid the formidable burden, required under libel law, of proving that journalists acted with knowing or reckless disregard for the truth.[19] In response, First Amendment scholars roundly criticized these cases for bypassing the constitutional protections that the *Sullivan* court established to encourage robust media coverage of public affairs, and they called for establishing a public interest defense in news-gathering cases.[20] As with libel, plaintiffs did not appear to be very successful in winning judgments, especially on appeal, but they inflicted large litigation costs and sometimes won retractions of critical reports. As Michael Richards found, even when news organizations defeated these suits, "judges sometimes chide[d] plaintiffs' attorneys for failing to raise all possible claims such as fraud or trespass or breach of contract, that might have succeeded."[21]

The highest-profile suit of this kind, brought against a 1992 ABC *Primetime Live* report that alleged unsafe food handling and unfair labor practices by the supermarket chain Food Lion, ended up as a mixed bag for investigative reporting. Food Lion's core complaints that survived pretrial accused ABC journalists, who had gone undercover with hidden cameras to work in the chain's stores, of committing fraud on their job applications, trespassing on company property, and breach of loyalty to Food Lion as their employer.[22] By emphasizing these private offenses against the company and its property, Food Lion never had to address in court whether ABC's claims that the market threatened its consumers' safety and exploited its workers were true or false. The jurors never saw the *Primetime Live* segment, which might have turned their attention to the public interest value of the story, but Food Lion was able to convince the trial court that it should be able to see ABC's outtakes, and it obtained all forty-five hours of footage shot in its stores. The jury found against ABC, awarding just $1,402 in compensatory damages, which are meant to cover actual harm to the plaintiff, but assessing $5.5 million in punitive damages. Posttrial interviews indicated that jurors did so to deter ABC and others from using intrusive and deceptive investigative methods—as a form of regulation of media conduct rather than as an award to Food Lion for actual harm suffered. As one juror explained, "We were just really trying to just send a message across: if you're going to do it, just do it legally."[23]

Although the Fourth Circuit Court of Appeals eventually reversed the large monetary judgments seven years after the report aired, the case did not represent a ringing victory either for the media's First Amendment claims or for the public stake in investigative reporting. The appeals court rejected the fraud claim and threw out the multimillion-dollar punitive damages on grounds that Food Lion had attempted to use the news-gathering torts to make an "end-run around First Amendment strictures" set out in libel law.[24] However, the court upheld the jury's finding that ABC's reporters breached their duty to be loyal to Food Lion by seeking to videotape and expose unsanitary practices while working there, and trespassed by taping in nonpublic areas of the stores.

Litigation Public Relations

Public relations campaigns have become inextricable parts of corporate legal strategies to discredit reporting, distract attention from targets' own culpability, inflict costs of litigation on broadcasters, and influence potential jurors. Corporate counsel in high-stakes cases increasingly make use of public relations experts, who exert growing influence over plotting legal strategies as well.[25] Together, they have developed the new fields of "litigation public relations" and of "risk communication," which includes training corporate executives to handle the media and manage public opinion in crises.[26] Investigative reporters must increasingly contend with opponents whose ability to influence the public and policy makers through the media not only matches but dwarfs their own.

The power of litigation public relations to silence critical reporting by turning attention to journalistic methods is evident from General Motors' response to a 1992 *Dateline NBC* report. The story claimed some GM pickup trucks with external, "sidesaddle" gas tanks were prone to explode in accidents. NBC cited estimates that as many as three hundred deaths had been attributed to the fuel tank design, and that about 5 million of the vehicles were still on the road. The report presented what it called an "unscientific" test crash in which a GM truck exploded into flames after being hit from the side. The morning before NBC's report aired, internal GM documents were leaked that suggested company officials were concerned about the tank design as early as 1978 and that its engineers had warned in 1983 that the vehicles would be safer if the tanks were moved inside the truck frame. In a follow-up story, NBC reported that over one hundred lawsuits had been filed against GM and most of them had been settled out of court. One lawyer estimated that the company had paid around $20 million to settle seven such suits in Texas.[27]

In response, GM launched a public relations effort that included a libel suit against NBC, charging that the network rigged its test by attaching toy rockets as incendiary devices to the truck's gas tank. After defending the report for six weeks, NBC admitted to using the rockets, made an on-air apology to GM, paid the company an estimated $2 million settlement, later fired three producers who contributed to the segment, and accepted the resignation of its news president. Other news organizations and journalists excoriated NBC for staging the explosion, and some of them expressed sympathy to GM for being "victimized" by the report.[28] Yet after NBC's apology, an outside law firm hired by the network to investigate the test crash concluded that a broken headlamp, not the toy rockets, ignited gasoline that spilled from the truck's tank after the collision punched a hole in the tank and dislodged its gas cap. The Institute for Safety Analysis, which acted as a consultant to the report's producers, found that "the fire was caused by one of the car's headlamps, not by the igniters," and the law firm agreed that "to our untrained eyes the videotape does appear to support the consultants' reports."[29] Two years later, the U.S. Department of Transportation found that the trucks were indeed prone to fires in side collisions and blamed GM for 150 deaths caused by them.[30] One need not defend NBC's use of the rockets without disclosing so to its viewers to appreciate that its journalists may have correctly reported the cause of the fire and produced an otherwise unchallenged story on a significant threat to the public.

Nonetheless, GM successfully diverted media attention from the question of its trucks' safety, doing so more through public relations than through the libel suit, which it had little chance of winning. To prevail in court, GM would have to have proved not only that NBC reporters knew the report was staged but that it conveyed a falsehood about trucks that juries had previously found to be dangerous (later confirmed by the Transportation Department) and that the report damaged GM's reputation more than it already had been by years of lawsuits against it.[31] Instead, GM prevailed through the news media itself. Although the company began sending letters to NBC complaining about the report soon after it aired, GM did not file suit until several months passed, on the day after the company lost a $105.2 million verdict against the parents of a Georgia boy who was killed when his truck caught fire. Deflecting attention from the verdict, GM announced its suit against NBC at a press conference beamed via satellite to media worldwide, making it one of the top stories on all the major U.S. networks' evening newscasts. NBC settled the following day, before it was even served legal papers, in an attempt to repair its own image and avoid further legal fees.

Impacts of Judicial Regulation

It may be argued that face-offs between private plaintiffs in court offer a better means of resolving conflicts over news than allowing the more "politicized" FCC and Congress to intervene. We have seen that leading voices in the media bridled at the allegedly intrusive, costly, and potentially chilling effects of content regulations on news. However, the FCC's investigations now look like mild pat downs compared to the prolonged and expensive strip searches to which media defendants are subjected in the courts.

Tort suits are far more costly and intrusive on journalistic decision making than Congressional or FCC investigations ever were. This is especially true since the Supreme Court ruled in 1979, in *Herbert v. Lando,* that media defendants in libel cases do not enjoy a First Amendment privilege to avoid the normal discovery process.[32] The *Herbert* court reasoned that since public figures who bring libel suits must prove that journalists exercised reckless or knowing disregard for the truth, plaintiffs had to be able to probe reporters' state of mind at the time they prepared the disputed report. The *Herbert* case itself lasted over twelve years, during which time CBS producer Barry Lando was deposed twenty-eight times and the network spent over $4 million in legal fees.[33] In the years since, plaintiffs have delved more deeply into broadcast editorial judgments than the FCC ever did, gaining greater access to reporters' notes, outtakes, discussions with sources and editors, estimation of sources' credibility, and failure to consult evidence contradictory to the thrust of their reports.[34] News-gathering claims can justify many of the same tactics used extensively by Food Lion.

In contrast, neither the fairness doctrine nor the news distortion policy offered complainants any right of discovery, and the FCC did not subpoena reporters' notes or outtakes. Whereas the news distortion rules explicitly urged each broadcaster to develop and enforce its own journalistic standards and guidelines, tort cases involve the courts in both activities more deeply than before. This creates an uncertain situation for journalists, who must contend with a welter of different state tort laws and piecemeal applications of them by different trial and appeals courts. Ironically, close reviews of journalists' practices in defamation cases have deterred some media organizations from developing their own written policies for fear that they might be used as legal standards against which their conduct might be judged in court.[35] Tort claims also exact much higher costs than FCC investigations of fairness and distortion complaints, which were brief, involved little discovery, and did not result in fines. If courts tend to overturn large damage awards eventually, these complex and interminable cases have inflicted multimillion-dollar litigation costs, which in turn jack up libel insurance rates. Even when licensees lost a fairness or distortion claim, complainants were responsible for their own legal fees.

As with any counterfactual situation, it is not easy to compare the relative self-censorship inspired under the past and present regulatory regimes. However, as the previous chapter indicated, few news directors feared the fairness doctrine's impact on them, and the light enforcement of the doctrine and distortion policy offered little cause for trembling in the newsroom. Evidence of the impact of recent litigation raises concerns, however. For example, a study involving over 150 interviews with media lawyers and editors at the height of the libel wave in the mid-1980s uncovered numerous instances in which news organizations declined to publish material for fear of a defamation suit, especially if the organization had been sued previously.[36] A 1983 survey of investigative reporters found that 65 percent agreed that "stories are not being covered that ought to be covered, because of recent libel judgments."[37] Network evening news time devoted to the tobacco industry dropped by more than 75 percent in the second half of 1994 after Philip Morris brought a libel suit against ABC for a story criticizing the industry for manipulating the amount of nicotine in cigarettes to keep smokers hooked.[38] ABC later aired an apology for the report. Even before ABC capitulated, the suit discouraged the network from airing reports based on leaked papers from tobacco giant Brown and Williamson, which suggested it too manipulated nicotine levels. "[I]n an action that stunned those in the business," wrote investigative reporter Philip Hilts, "the papers were confiscated from news staff. They were ordered to erase their computer notes about the papers."[39] In addition, ABC killed a documentary in production for its *Turning Point* newsmagazine on the day Philip Morris filed suit. This report showed former surgeon general C. Everett Koop relating his disgust at a Reagan administration memo promising the tobacco companies no regulatory trouble during the Reagan presidency and at how administration trade representatives threatened tariffs to open Asian markets to U.S. cigarettes. This insight into government protection and advocacy of the industry never aired.[40] On the same day that it was revealed that CBS suppressed a report on Brown and Williamson, the network's owned-and-operated Los Angeles station refused to air a commercial criticizing the tobacco industry.[41]

At least one investigative team felt the chilling effect of the veggie libel laws and the initial trial victory for Food Lion. In 1997, WTVT, a Florida affiliate of the Fox network, prepared a heavily promoted four-part investigative series about rBGH, a growth hormone used to increase milk production by cows. The series would have alleged improper safety testing of rBGH before it was released in the market, the spread of disease among some herds injected with the hormone, and suspected cancer risks of drinking rBGH-treated milk. Monsanto, which makes rBGH, sent threatening letters that accused the reporters of making defamatory statements in their report and alluded to the large damages against ABC won by Food Lion. Heavy pressure ensued from the Florida dairy industry, where a state agricultural disparagement law was in effect. Fox management scrutinized and rewrote the story, delaying its air date six times, before firing the reporters for refusing to produce what the journalists said was an inaccurate and dishonest version of the story. Eventually an abbreviated, tamer version of the story ran, prepared by a different reporter. "A lot of people now are more fearful of doing investigative journalism since Food Lion . . . which is why we have so many lawyers involved," the station's news director later commented. "We have to be careful and prudent."[42]

To summarize, the switch in forums from the FCC to the judiciary disadvantages journalists' First Amendment rights and the public right to know by increasing regulatory costs and uncertainty. In the courts, "policy" emerges from a patchwork of jurisdictions and cases. The current regime places the defense of reporters' and the public's rights more firmly in the hands of private media corporations, whose profit-maximizing interests do not always coincide with a vigorous defense of a story's right to air. Muckraking's censors are less likely to be government investigators than tort lawyers or their employers' own corporate counsel.

Market Regulation

As public-service regulations waned from the 1970s onward, broadcast news has shifted from a money-losing proposition aired to serve licensees' public interest obligations to a profit center in its own right. Investigative reporting played an important role in this shift. CBS's 60 Minutes investigative newsmagazine first demonstrated that a prime-time news show could make money.[43] Its ratings success all but doomed the documentary on commercial television by the mid-1980s as all the networks moved to the newsmagazine format. Similarly, broadcasters found that their local news could turn a profit and help secure an audience flow for their evening programming.[44] Muckraking reports provided one strategy for differentiating local newscasts from their competitors. As the growth of cable and satellite television, VCRs, and the Internet fragmented television audiences from the 1980s onward, the networks aired more newsmagazines in prime time because they were cheaper to produce than situation comedies and hour dramas. As a result, there appears to be more investigative reporting on network and local television than ever before, but it is doubtful that such reporting serves the public any better.

Market regulation of muckraking undermines investigative reporters' ability to cover public affairs. Between 1968 and 1975, stories on politics and economics were the main topics of both network documentaries and television newsmagazines.[45] By the fall of 1997, however, a study of four network newsmagazines found that over half of all stories focused on lifestyle, human interest, and celebrity news. Just 8 percent of reports were about politics, economics, social welfare, and education.[46] Veteran 60 Minutes reporter Mike Wallace has complained that the networks are doing "damned little" investigative work of substance and that their newsmagazines are "much softer than they used to be."[47] A similar 1998 study of local news by the Project for Excellence in Journalism found a drop in all forms of original, or "enterprise," reporting, including muckraking.[48] Because investigative reporting must compete for ratings with fictional and tabloid television programs, such as *Entertainment Tonight* or *Inside Edition*, it must increasingly focus on the same topics. By 1997, there was little difference in story selection between the tabloid programs and the network newsmagazines, according to one television monitoring company. The runaway story of the year for both was Princess Diana's death.[49]

Television muckrakers make do with fewer resources than in the past. The documentary format of the 1960s offered journalists longer deadlines. Producers might have up to a year to research and produce a single report.[50] At the newsmagazines, producers work on multiple projects at once, each of which may warrant no more than a few months work.[51] In the mid-1960s, the networks spent around $150,000 to $170,000 for an hour documentary.[52] Adjusted for inflation, this is roughly 13 to 24 percent more than the price tag for an hour episode of a network newsmagazine in the early 1990s.[53] Compared with documentaries, even less of the newsmagazine budget goes into newsgathering costs and more to pay the rising salaries of star correspondents like Wallace, who leave most of the investigative work to their producers.[54]

Under market regulation, today's muckrakers must fill a larger news hole with more and briefer stories, compete with tabloid-style reality programming, and produce a profitable product. These pressures push journalists to use material that might not have been aired in the past, especially if expensive techniques such as hidden-camera reporting are employed, because the news division must justify its investment.[55] Often, trivial reports on perennial consumer rip-offs such as auto-body shops billing for unnecessary repairs or minor insurance scams must be made to appear as earth-shattering revelations. As Howard Good has commented, "It is the investigative style that matters most in journalism today, not the subject or outcome of an investigation."[56] He offers the example of a television newsmagazine report that deployed hidden-camera footage and other techniques of investigative reporting to probe whether brunettes or blondes get hit on more in singles bars. Briefer reports make it even more unlikely than in the 1960s that a program will cover social problems broadly and deeply. Muckraking stories now must narrow their focus ever more tightly in the search for individual villains. Vietnam becomes the deception of a lone general rather than of a larger selling operation by the military. Consumer and labor reporting focus less on a broad category of products and labor practices, such as pensions, and more on the abuses of a lone supermarket chain or the dangers of a single truck.

Profit pressures increasingly undermine the ethics of investigative reporters themselves, breaking their bonds of trust with the public. Important stories are marred by employing unnecessarily deceptive techniques to grab public attention with dramatic pictures, such as NBC's staged test of GM trucks. Increasingly, local television investigative reports are outsourced entirely to news suppliers, who provide canned reports that stations present as their own work by having their reporters record voice-overs and insert themselves asking interview questions. The source of the reporting is not credited, reducing local station "investigative reporters" to little more than professional plagiarists. The stations that air these reports without attribution routinely violate the Radio-Television News Directors Association Code of Ethics, which states that journalists should "clearly disclose the origin of information and label all material provided by outsiders."[57]

Diminished resources and the twenty-four hour news cycle have driven network television journalists to rely even more deeply on government sources for investigative stories of national significance. Sometimes, this partnership can serve the public interest in holding powerful institutions accountable to public opinion. For example, revelations of American troops torturing prisoners at Iraq's Abu Ghraib prison in 2004 by CBS's *60 Minutes* (as well as the *New Yorker* magazine and the *Washington Post*) were largely driven by information and photographs leaked from military investigations, from military personnel attempting to protect themselves from perceived scapegoating for abusing prisoners, and perhaps from Pentagon sources disgruntled by the war.[58] For more than a year before the story broke human rights organizations such as the International Committee of the Red Cross, Amnesty International, and Human Rights Watch had pointed to a pattern of mistreatment of terrorism suspects, but it took the release of images of torture to *60 Minutes* to focus American media attention on the charges. However, television's need to produce muckraking on the cheap also puts journalists in greater danger of being used by government sources for their own ends, especially on block-buster stories where media competition is high. For example, most "inves-tigative" reporting on the President Clinton–Monica Lewinsky adultery and perjury scandal in 1998 and 1999 consisted of relaying leaks from independent prosecutor Kenneth Starr's probe and counter-leaks from the White House. Because both sides released a mix of truths, partial truths, speculations and falsehoods, the public was not well-served by the breathless and sometimes inaccurate reporting.[59]

Although the FCC's news distortion rules still ban suppression of news in the private interest of media owners or advertisers, market censorship of investigative reporting is rampant. In a recent survey, over 40 percent of broad-cast investigative reporters admitted that advertisers had recently succeeded in influencing a news report.[60] New threats arise from the swallowing up of the broadcast networks, and more local stations, by conglomerate owners. As today's broadcast news departments become smaller parts of larger corpora-tions, they are expected to make their synergistic contributions to cross-pro-moting the parent company's other holdings and avoid damaging them with unfavorable news coverage. A 2000 survey of three hundred journalists and news executives found that 41 percent reported that they avoid newsworthy stories or soften their tone to protect the financial interests of their parent companies.[61]

Corporate cost-benefit analyses and the threat of litigation have weakened news organizations' resolve to defend their reports. In the 1960s and 1970s, the networks repeatedly stood up to the FCC, refusing to admit guilt or retract stories. As we have seen, they did so to avoid public accountability for some-times dubious news practices but also defended reports against political and economic powers whose oxen were gored by the reporting. Today, the networks sometimes seem too ready to sacrifice truthful reporting on the horns of parent company interests in avoiding litigation. After NBC's complete capitulation in 1992 to GM, in 1995 ABC said it was mistaken in claiming that tobacco producers added nicotine to cigarettes, apologizing to two cigarette companies and to their viewers, and paying Philip Morris's legal fees of $15 million in exchange for the tobacco giant's dismissing a libel suit against the network. In the same year, the head of the Food and Drug Administration confirmed the charge of nicotine manipulation in extensive testimony to Congress.[62] Observers attributed ABC's apology to its pending acquisition by Disney, which might have been less enthusiastic about buying a network that faced a $10 billion defamation suit.[63] Also in 1995, CBS withheld a report in which a former Brown and Williamson tobacco executive alleged that his company had committed perjury and neglected to make less dangerous and addictive products. CBS executives pulled the story, citing fears of a lawsuit for inciting the executive to break a confidentiality agreement with his former employer. This novel claim for "tortious interference" had rarely been applied to media law and had not been used successfully in the past.[64] Others pointed to CBS's interest in avoiding litigation at a time when Westinghouse was purchasing the network. Westinghouse was courting Brown and Williamson because CBS's largest shareholder, Loews Corporation, was acquiring six brands from the tobacco company.[65] In a recent book, half a dozen broadcast muckrakers tell of additional cases in which their employers censored or retracted substantiated reports on government malfeasance to avoid running afoul of powerful defense, intelligence, or law enforcement sources.[66]

The emergence of individual Internet journals, or blogs, as a forum for fact-checking and criticizing reporting has been hailed as democratizing media regulation.[67] Bloggers' ability to bring collective individual scrutiny to bear on the claims of investigative reporting can have the salutary effect of acting as a counterweight to corporate and government actors' powers to do the same. Yet early signs suggest that the bloggers who attract the most readers are comparable to talk radio hosts: not always accurate, intensely partisan, and intimately entwined with journalistic and political elites. Blogs provide fertile new ground for public relations companies' established techniques for generating the illusion of spontaneous grassroots resistance to investigative reports. This kind of "astroturfing" can be easily concealed behind the anonymous nicknames of those who post to blogs and other Internet discussion sites. Blogs may simply extend traditional public relations backlashes against muckraking techniques to a new medium rather than represent a democratic flowering of journalism's accountability to the disempowered.

An ill-fated story aired by *60 Minutes II* during the heat of the 2004 presidential campaign illustrates many of the dangers of market regulation of news—the commercial pressures it places on journalists as well as the way they are regulated via counterspeech and media companies' self-regulation.[68] Two months before the election, CBS's Dan Rather narrated a story accusing President George W. Bush of failing to fulfill his Vietnam-era service in the Texas Air National Guard and alleging that his superior was pressured from above to give Bush positive evaluations of his service. The report was based on four memos provided to CBS by a former guard member that purportedly were written by Bush's commanding officer, who had since died. Conservative bloggers, many of them fed information by Republican public relations professionals to create the impression of a grassroots rebellion, immediately questioned the authenticity of the memos. CBS strongly defended the story for several weeks, then admitted that the source who provided the memos had lied to CBS about their origins and that the network's producer had ignored warnings made before the story aired by hired experts that they could not authenticate the documents. The network appointed independent investigators who issued a lengthy public report detailing the failures of judgment involved, and CBS dismissed the story's producer and three news executives. Separately, Dan Rather announced his retirement from his post as *CBS Evening News* anchor. The network was widely condemned in the press.

Once again, competitive pressure and reduced resources meant a network rushed to air a report based on unnecessarily weak evidence. Once again, the report's critics engaged in a well-funded and well-organized campaign to discredit the way CBS gathered its evidence, this time using the blogosphere to fan the fires against the network. Once again, substantive evidence that the story may well have been true was swept aside both by network leadership and by a press distracted by charges of faked memos. If the documents may have been faked—and the independent investigation noted that it could not say with certainty that they were or were not—several sources testified in the story and afterward that the substance of the memos was true. The former lieutenant governor of Texas admitted in the story that he had recommended that Bush receive preferential treatment to get into the guard in order to avoid serving in Vietnam. The typist for Bush's former commanding officer later said that although she doubted the memos' authenticity, they accurately described the officer's views of Bush. Nonetheless, subsequent media coverage focused overwhelmingly on whether the memos were real rather than the larger question of whether the story was true. Many journalists relied uncritically on bloggers' unsupported claims to dismiss the entire story as a fabrication, rather than simply to cast doubt on the memos' authenticity.[69] Once again, a network caved in to well-organized pressure, not only refusing to pursue further the story of Bush's service but even shelving another *60 Minutes* report critical of Bush's decision to go to war in Iraq.[70]

Privatizing Regulation

Changes in broadcast regulation since the 1960s are better understood as a shift to privatized regulation rather than deregulation. Judicial and market oversight of muckraking continue to act as severe constraints on investigative reporters' ability to serve the public as watchdogs on power. In practice, we have moved from the largely symbolic politics of FCC regulation in the name of the public interest to a privatized politics governed by the market for news and the market for disciplining it through the legal system or the court of public opinion. This new regime has enacted three kinds of privatization.

First, it has privatized the regulatory criteria used to judge news. In the old regulatory arenas, television's critics had to frame their faultfinding with reference to how reporting harmed the public interest. To bring a successful fairness doctrine complaint required showing that the public's need for diverse points of view in the news had not been met. To win a news distortion case, one had to show that the public was deceived about a matter of importance. In the courts, however, plaintiffs generally need to prove that the media have violated private rights of property, privacy, and contract. Tort suits throw the regulatory spotlight off of questions about the fairness or accuracy of reports and their impact on audiences. In libel cases, much attention is focused on journalists' state of mind when preparing their stories and alleged harms to the plaintiff. In news-gathering suits, courts primarily consider injuries that arise from journalists' techniques of seeking information while the report and its relationship to the public are largely irrelevant. Admittedly, these cases address the public interest in checking media irresponsibility and intrusion, but the courts do not always balance these interests consistently against the public stake in learning about abuses of power. The corporate and political figures that tend to bring these suits do so to deflect attention from journalists' embarrassing findings and to encourage juries and public opinion to condemn muckraking without considering the fruits of its methods. GM, the tobacco companies, and others have forced journalists to mute, muddy, or retract valuable criticism of life-threatening corporate behavior. We need not embrace a simple utilitarianism to recognize that the value of information to the public needs to be weighed against harms caused by investigative reporting.

Second, the new arrangements privatize participation in regulation. When market-driven news draws inevitable barbs for its unnecessarily rushed and invasive hunt for dramatic footage, the power to regulate it now resides more fully with wealthy individuals and organizations than with a more diverse public. The complexity of libel law, the exotic nature of news-gathering torts, and the difficulty of waging effective litigation public relations mean that all are costly. Thus these responses to muckraking are generally a privilege of the moneyed or those subsidized by them. If FCC regulations were complex and frustrating for citizens, local politicians, and public interest groups, at least they could bring complaints relatively cheaply. In the late 1970s and early 1980s, approximately three-quarters of libel plaintiffs in the courts were government, business, or professional figures.[71] By contrast, these figures brought only 28 percent of news distortion complaints to the FCC between 1969 and 1999, while citizens and citizen groups brought 52 percent, by far the most of any type of complainants.[72] Comparable data on fairness doctrine complainants is not available in the literature, but citizen groups on the right and left objected strenuously to the repeal of the doctrine in the 1980s because it gave them some ability to negotiate for response time to one-sided news and some political advertising. Today, the ability to pursue justice against the media has become a commodity more shaped by private actors' power in the market. The traditional argument that the best remedy for irresponsible speech is more speech falls flat when the only effective means of circulating such counterspeech are not available to the vast majority.

Third, it is broadcast market regulation that most privatizes muckraking by casting aside coverage of politics and public life in favor of lifestyle and entertainment coverage. The public interest in news is rearticulated in market terms as whatever news organizations can produce cheaply enough to garner the largest or most lucrative audiences and whatever voices must be included or excluded to do so. Market regulation robs investigative reporters of the resources they need to do their jobs and do them responsibly. It dissuades muckrakers from stories that threaten their parent companies' interests. When reports come under fire, journalists' ability to defend them are increasingly at the mercy of their self-interested employers. Increasingly, local television muckraking is provided by firms that see their primary role not as informing citizens but in acting as "a business-to-business content service, providing content for local stations for their use with their talent," in the words of one news supplier.[73]

❈   ❈   ❈

The privatized regime fails the most important goals of the First Amendment: that free speech should foster citizen deliberation for self-government and that it should do so under conditions of viewpoint diversity and political equality. Today's regime has not only failed to free journalists but has undermined broadcast journalism's claims to First Amendment protection. Profit-minded newscasters fail to cover public affairs, and, thus, to serve the highest end of free speech. Journalists work under conditions of vast inequality, becoming less accountable to public complaints yet still deeply vulnerable to the ire of corporate and political Goliaths, parent company conflicts of interest, and advertiser censorship. FCC and congressional retreats from regulation seem to legitimate greater government intrusion into journalistic practices by the judiciary because the courts act on behalf of private plaintiffs. Yet many juries appear to see the news as any other sales pitch dressed in free-speech garb, and broadcasters are largely responsible. In the 1980s, they went to war for "deregulation" behind an FCC chairman who famously argued that "television is just another appliance. It's a toaster with pictures."[74] The more that news looks and sounds like any other form of commercial speech or corporate cross-promotion, the less it merits enhanced First Amendment privileges.[75] Toasters do not need freedom of speech.

8   *Media, State, and Investigative Reporting*

In the early 1960s, the rising television documentary was buoyed by widespread elite support from political leaders, regulators, cultural critics, network executives, and journalists. By the mid-1970s, that consensus had fractured. What do the growing elite conflicts over the documentary at this time tell us about theories of media-state relations, the construction and impact of investigative reporting, and the media's role in society? This chapter draws conclusions about claims of media adversarialism toward government, about how muckraking is assembled and how its critics attempt to subvert its legitimacy, and about critical theory of the news media and democracy.

Media Adversarialism and Indexing

Theories of growing media adversarialism toward the state in the 1960s cannot explain network investigative reporting or the contentious response to it. This notion, put forth by many journalists and their critics alike, ignores that muckrakers themselves were highly dependent on government sources. As a result, the most controversial documentaries studied in this book reflected intragovernmental struggles over poverty, Cold War, and consumer policy. Elites were newly divided over these issues at a time when the bonds of party discipline had weakened, engendering greater expression of dissent within government itself. Claims of an oppositional media fail to explain why reporters relied on federal politicians' frames in these reports, ignoring or filtering the claims of social movement actors through mainstream policy perspectives. Investigative reports also turned to federal policy makers to alleviate the problems raised in reports. The notion of media adversarialism ignores print journalists' and network affiliates' substantial criticisms of television muckraking as deceptive or unfair. Broadcasters who claim that government became more antipathetic to the media are hard pressed to account for why the FCC and the judicial system often supported their free-speech rights against congressional and White House attacks.

Nor did growing frustration with investigative reports arise simply from network news' liberalism. Certainly the documentaries that drew fire favored liberal positions. But the reports considered here, if indicative of the kind that conservatives attacked, were not representative of all network documentaries. Most long-format reports avoided the controversial subjects of the era. Indeed, few documentaries touched on controversial subjects, much less investigated them. Of all documentaries aired between 1948 and 1975, 37 percent dealt with issues such as the Vietnam War, civil rights, criminal justice, and foreign policy.[1] According to an ABC study, of the 164 documentaries produced by the three networks from 1963 to 1966, less than 10 percent grappled with "U.S. social conflicts and problems."[2] By the late 1960s, print reviewers praised muckraking efforts as rare exceptions to the rule. Nor was the documentary representative of all television news, which was more tied to the dictates of objectivity. Nor was television news representative of all television, most of which was fictional programming that did not touch on troubling social issues, but aimed at creating an upbeat milieu for the insertion of commercials. Nor can television stand in for the media in general, judging from the vociferous opposition to these documentaries in some print publications.

If the investigative documentaries that sparked criticism were liberal, they reflected and reinforced the ascendance of liberal ideas in government and the networks' tendency to nationalize the news. Looking back from the vantage point of the late 1970s, CBS executive producer Perry Wolff recalled the documentarians of the 1960s as "the voices of embattled liberalism," adding, "I don't think they see themselves this way now, and I certainly don't." After Watergate and the growth of the public sector, he noted, "right now the enemy seems to be the government," and he attested to a new skepticism about appeals for government solutions to social problems in the documentaries of the time.[3] In addition, documentarians' frequent calls for federal intervention reflected the economic needs of the networks and the professional aspirations of journalists to address a nationwide audience by depicting social ills as national issues that required solutions at that level. Television journalists were not simply eastern establishment liberals; they had to represent the country by appearing to transcend local and regional complexities. To that end, Washington sources were the easiest and safest people to consult.

Indexing theory, which posits that the range of policy debate in news is set by government elites, helps explain how these reports framed social problems. Across these cases of investigative reporting, the news media consistently mainstreamed social movement actors' frames by passing them through a filter of official sanction. Those portions of movement frames that officials did not adopt did not make it into investigative reports. This was the case for ideological frames that exceeded policy elites' thinking, such as the NAACP's attributing Newburgh's welfare reform to a backlash against black political organizing and the New Left's analysis of the Vietnam War as imperialist. It was true of policy frames as well, such as Ralph Nader's call for democratizing pension plan governance and the Poor People's Campaign's call for increasing the participation of the poor in running antipoverty programs and growing their own food. Journalists took pains to show government approval even of nonmovement actors such as the Haitian and Cuban coup planners and the Berlin tunnelers.

Yet what influences political leaders' frames? This has been an unexplored black box for indexing studies, which tend to assume government opinion is an independent variable and thus do not examine interactions between government and interest groups. Social movements and interest groups surely had some influence on policy makers' understanding of issues. Antipoverty groups worked closely with the Senate Labor Committee before *Hunger in America* aired, supplying testimony and sources in federal hearings. The AFL-CIO was organizing in the fields and giving input on congressional and executive branch policy proposals on farm labor before *Harvest of Shame.* Attorneys from the NAACP, Legal Services, and the New York Bar Association challenged credit practices and political conflicts of interest, helping to define the policy arena prior to *Banks and the Poor.* This does not cast doubt on the fact that the media calibrated interest group expressions of dissent to official positions, but it suggests that government figures did not form their views in a vacuum.

Rethinking the Mobilization Model

The mobilization model of investigative reporting states that journalists independently uncover social problems, moving the public to demand change, who in turn induce politicians to deliver reform. This simplistic model cannot account for the dynamics of television muckraking in the 1960s and early 1970s. This mythic vision of investigative reporting conceals too much about the origins of network reports in prior government studies, commissions, and hearings. Network documentarians most often engaged in coalitional journalism with federal politicians, especially in the Senate, relying on their analyses of welfare, foreign policy, and consumer issues. Although public response to the reports cannot be reliably reconstructed, there are strong reasons to doubt that the documentaries significantly affected the process or content of policy making. Most issues covered in reports were the subject of extensive prior media coverage and policy attention. Some reports did not call for specific policy action, and when they did, the steps advocated seemed to be influenced by what was considered realistic to achieve within mainstream policy circles. These reports publicized social problems and a narrow range of solutions, but it is difficult to believe that this was enough to spur public opinion single-handedly. For their part, politicians did not all fall in line behind the reports; many of them launched angry rebuttals and punitive investigations into documentaries. Often, these attacks successfully distracted subsequent coverage of the reports from paying further attention to the issues raised by them. When lawmakers did tend to social injustices explored in documentaries, their responsiveness could not be traced easily to the reports but emerged from long campaigns by organized forces such as the antihunger groups or pension reformers. Subsequent reforms were sometimes enacted long after reports aired and were minimal and symbolic, failing to address many problems raised by these reports.

These findings both confirm and suggest revisions to the most comprehensive and best substantiated model of investigative reporting's origins and impact that is offered in *The Journalism of Outrage,* by David Protess and his colleagues.[4] I adapt the authors' model (see figure 1), adding the role of indexing as well as the dynamics of hostile reactions to reports and media response that we have seen in prior chapters. The mobilization/demobilization model

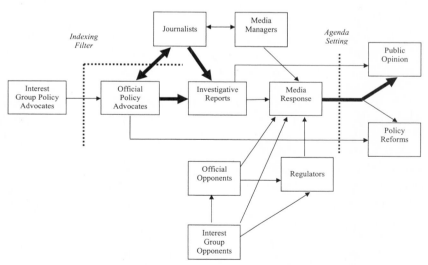

Figure 1. Mobilization/Demobilization Model of Investigative Reporting

lays out schematically how investigative reporting attempts to mobilize support for policy reform and how its critics aim to demobilize support. In shaping reports, the crucial interaction (indicated by bolder arrows) is between official policy advocates and journalists. The controversial documentaries examined in this book were largely reports of federal government investigations. Interest groups' policy frames generally must pass through a filter of government sources on whom journalists often rely to select frames. Media managers and lawyers then work closely with journalists to vet reports—for accuracy and fairness in the period of the study, and increasingly for libel and other potential legal claims thereafter.

A more complex process shapes the impact of investigative reports on policy and public opinion. Interest-group opponents of reports' policy frames advance their views through multiple channels. Some groups, such as the agribusiness interests that attacked *Harvest of Shame,* provide information rebutting the reports to congressional figures. Hostile officials and interest groups both attempt to influence media response to reports. These forces tried to shape coverage on the offending network by demanding reply time in the fairness doctrine era or trying to win on-air apologies after offending reports, as General Motors did from NBC. As *The Journalism of Outrage* found, journalists' need to defend a story publicly shaped the nature of follow-up coverage in several instances.[5] When *The Selling of the Pentagon* was attacked, CBS scheduled a debate between Pentagon representatives, friendly politicians, and official critics, both to fulfill fairness obligations and to confer official legitimacy on the report's conclusions. Many local public television stations scheduled discussions with local bankers in response to *Banks and the Poor.* The ways in which official and interest-group foes of muckraking also attempt to shape media response by other news organizations becomes clearer in this study. Opponents aimed both to discredit investigative reports' characterization of problems and to distract attention from those problems by shifting debate to media ethics questions. Both officials and interest groups appealed to regulators—the FCC in the past, the courts more recently—in hopes that decisions in their favor might shape ongoing coverage.

Response by the rest of the media, Protess and his colleagues found, may be influenced by newsmaker reaction, market competition, and the potential to develop new angles on the story.[6] Newsmaker reaction to events provided grist for follow-up coverage in these cases but largely because all the reports were attacked strenuously by federal officials. As a result, much subsequent coverage focused on First Amendment issues rather than on the subjects of reports, a distinction to which future studies of investigative reports should pay more attention.[7] Certainly, competition played a role in reaction to investigative documentaries, but it was not simply economic in nature as *The Journalism of Outrage* suggests. Ideological rivalry between liberal and conservative media (including network affiliates) shaped the amount of journalistic sympathy with documentaries. So too did a cultural competition between print and television reporters over who represented reality more accurately and fairly.

Because media response was such an important forum for investigative reporting's critics and defenders in these instances, its impact on policy change is featured more prominently in this model than in prior thinking about the subject. It has long been recognized that the news media play an agenda-setting role in society, not always telling audiences what to think about issues but telling the public quite effectively what issues are high on the list of things to think about.[8] Supporters and opponents of these reports all attempted to influence media response, as best exemplified in the prolonged debate over *The Selling of the Pentagon,* both on CBS and in the pages of *Time,* the *Washington Post,* and other print outlets. It is likely that the majority of the public and many officials, who never saw the controversial reports themselves, depended on subsequent debate in the media to form opinions about the documentaries. Opponents' attempts to shift attention toward staging and unfairness helped to limit the ability of friendly forces to use these reports as a resource for advancing their policy goals. These strategies were largely disseminated through the media because of its agenda-setting role.

Investigative Reporting and Hegemony

These struggles over investigative reporting can be placed within a larger account of the media's role in democracy. It is not the classical liberal theory of the news media, however, which presents watchdogging on government as one of the media's major functions in democracy, for we have seen that media and government purposes were too closely intertwined in these reports. Rather, it is the theory of hegemony. Although this approach to understanding the news media has been criticized often, sometimes for good reason, a chastened version of it is indispensable for grasping the muckraking conflicts of the 1960s and 1970s.

Italian political theorist Antonio Gramsci defined hegemony as the process by which a society's dominant classes and groups propagate values that reinforce their control of politics and the economy.[9] Through ideology, ruling groups attempt to portray their own interests as the interests of all and legitimate their control over the state. It is by these ideational means, rather than through the coercive force of the state, that rule is most often maintained. This power is most effectively exercised not through the ability to commit overt inculcation and censorship but "also and especially [by] the ability to *define* the parameters of legitimate discussion and debate over alternative beliefs, values and world views," as David Sallach puts it.[10]

The economic specialization and social diversity of contemporary capitalist democracies means that neither elites nor subordinate groups march in lockstep on all issues. Elites often differ substantively over policy strategies, and subordinate groups rarely accept hegemonic claims fully and regularly. In such a society, ideology takes on an especially important role as a cohesive force for ensuring the consent of the subordinated. The institutions of civil society, including the news media, are prime sites for the creation and distribution of hegemonic ideas as well as any resistance to them. However, as Todd Gitlin has written, if ideology provides the social glue under liberal capitalism, "the relative autonomy of the different sectors legitimates the system as a whole."[11] The news media, therefore, cannot play a role in securing consent without appearing independent of other elite interests—hence the widespread acceptance of the occupational ideal of objectivity and toleration of journalists' claims to be watchdogs on power.

Part of the appeal of the theory of hegemony is its ability to overcome classical Marxism's untenable claim that the economic base of society dictates its political, civil, and cultural institutions and beliefs. As Raymond Williams has suggested, we can only speak of economic "determination" if determination means "setting bounds" or "setting limits" rather than "to cause."[12] Indeed, controversial investigative reports often offended the owners of capital by pointing out inequalities of wealth and abuses of power, such as the injustices of welfare programs, labor conditions that served large farm owners better than the poor, or the exploitation of workers and consumers by their banks and retirement fund managers. Yet documentaries were generally reticent when it came to supporting policy frames that questioned the private control of capital in more thoroughgoing ways. None of these reports included demands that government redistribute subsidies from agribusiness to sharecroppers, that the poor should not only exercise control over welfare administration but own the means to feed themselves, or that social security might do a better job of supporting the aged than private funds. All of these demands circulated among the reports' sources or in policy discourse of the time. Similarly, demands for increased regulation of network news had their limits. If the Nixon administration helped end government protection of broadcasting against its competitors in cable and satellite television and many officials supported content regulations of news, none of them challenged private ownership of communications. Demands to enforce the fairness doctrine and distortion rules did not undermine the basic First Amendment rights of the industry to control most of its programming, and the regulatory apparatus rarely permitted even these small demands to be heard.

The most convincing applications of hegemony take full stock of the notion that consent can be structured without consensus. The consent of the subordinate is a "complex mental state . . . mixing approbation and apathy, resistance and resignation," notes T. J. Jackson Lears.[13] Certainly, hegemonic discourse involves bolstering support for the market and the liberal state by marginalizing discussion of viable alternatives and lowering expectations for ameliorating inequality and social turmoil created by the economy. However, just as often it is not agreement with ruling ideas that keeps the subjected in their places, "but rather a *lack* of consensus in the crucial area where concrete experiences and vague populism might be translated into radical politics," as Michael Mann puts it.[14] The structure of the investigative documentary was symptomatic of such barriers to challenging the state and market. As noted, it tended to exclude policy options that removed significant power over capital from private hands. It incorporated popular frustration through the voices of the poor, the sick, and the elderly but generally limited them to testifying about their experience rather than encouraging them to speak within a larger political framework or to appear as political actors in their own right. It took cues from liberal politicians and social workers when they obscured the causes of hunger in the "cycle of poverty" or cautioned that the elderly had not shown personal responsibility for saving for their golden years, ignoring the postwar restructuring of retirement as an age of consumption. It was often unable to discuss or propose concrete solutions to social problems. If citizens took any political action in response to documentaries, it was not because reports encouraged them to act, as most pointed to the federal government as the legitimate reformer.

Gramscian theory does not reduce the ruling forces of a society solely to a static capitalist class but allows us to speak of a shifting coalition of interests that share a political solidarity at a given point in time. These historical blocs may be bound as much by ideological ties as by shared economic interests, and they are subject to change. To be sure, such ruling coalitions must include the leading industries, but they also include subordinate groups across class lines. Similarly, controversial documentaries, and the groups whose views they best represented, were not simply class-interested. Rather, the list of forces on both sides of these controversies suggests that these conflicts were in part between a declining liberal coalition and an ascending bloc that would come to power in the Reagan years under the banner of the New Right.[15] Antipoverty reports mainly expressed the views of northern Democrats and their constituencies (urban dwellers, blacks, liberals). These documentaries were attacked by Dixiecrats and farm state Republicans, by their supporters in the USDA, by southern whites, and by large farmers. *The Selling of the Pentagon* followed moderate antiwar groups that drew support from many sectors of society and was opposed by equally diverse supporters of the military-industrial complex in Congress, the Pentagon, and the White House. *Pensions* relied on a coalition of Democrats and moderate Republicans, along with consumer groups and most unions. AIM's attack on it represented the interests of major business organizations, pension fund managers, and the Teamsters. *Banks and the Poor,* opposed by banking interests, embraced critiques of credit and political ethics advanced by rural populists, urban civil rights and antipoverty forces, and liberal officials and lawyers concerned with government conflicts of interest.

Hegemony: Open and Closed

Theorists of the media that rely explicitly or implicitly on the notion of hegemony have taken a broad continuum of positions, stretching from more open versions of domination to more closed ones. My evaluation of these conflicts over investigative reporting conflicts challenges both extremes.

At the open end of the spectrum, some cultural studies scholars set up a rather simple and unified dominant ideology of the capitalist state and then find substantive acts of opposition in almost every departure from it by audiences or social movements. In this view, assertions of social or cultural diversity are assumed to be challenges to the ideas propping up the powers that be. "Social change," claims John Fiske, "can only be motivated by a sense of social difference."[16] Because the investigative reporting cases studied here sparked such controversy, they would seem to confirm this open version of hegemony. But this view still assumes a monolithic dominant ideology that cannot be squared with the conflict among political elites or journalists evident in muckraking struggles. It locates resistance mainly in public opinion, which did not appear to play a major role in the controversies, and in the views of social movements, which journalists tailored to official bodies. And it mistakes declarations of difference as the source of challenges to hegemony, rather than recognition of common interests among subordinate groups and organizing on behalf of them. The fact that such groups do so rarely indicates that hegemony works not simply by instilling consensus, but by fostering inconsistent and fragmented belief systems and by blocking citizens from linking expressions of dissent to effective public action.[17] I have argued that the investigative documentary did just this.

At the closed end of the spectrum, some political economists see a similarly unitary dominant ideology but admit of few opportunities for social movements or journalists to disrupt the smooth flow of hegemonic ideas from the news media and the capitalist state. Edward Herman and Noam Chomsky, for example, propose what they call a propaganda model of the way news builds consent by filtering information through the media's commercial biases, reliance on official sources, organized news critics (who are all assumed to be right wing), and anticommunist ideology. Many of these factors indeed shape investigative reporting. However, despite occasional disclaimers, Herman and Chomsky tend to take an instrumental view of the media as a tool of the state and capital. The term "propaganda" implies a conscious and concerted effort to spread common messages, which fails to account for official and journalistic contentiousness over investigative reports. The documentaries studied here attacked rather than endorsing the views of agribusiness, banks, and money managers, as well as the Department of Agriculture and the Pentagon.

Another difficulty with the closed version of hegemony is its tendency to present the media in functionalist terms, as always serving the demands or needs of a larger capitalist system.[18] For example, Todd Gitlin, in his otherwise nuanced treatment of the media and the New Left, concludes that the media place movements in "a fundamental, an inescapable dilemma" between rejecting the rules of mainstream political discourse, and thus being portrayed as irrelevant or dangerous, and observing its conventions, and thus being assimilated. "This is the condition of movements in all the institutions of liberal capitalism," he continues. By excluding and taming dissent, "the media reinforce one of the central rhythms of American political history. Opposition movements emerge but their radical identities weaken."[19] To be sure, these investigative reports mainstreamed movement policy ideas by emphasizing those that could be shown to have official imprimatur. But this does not mean that official frames were entirely unaffected by movement groups. Functionalist accounts of hegemony often assume the only substantive change is systemic and that all else is mere compromise that only ends up strengthening "the system." This view tends to dichotomize potentially dialectical relationships between revolutionary and reformist movements, radicals and pragmatists, resistant and dominant ideologies, transforming the political-economic structure and trying to change a policy.[20] From this perspective, radicals are marginalized in the media, reformists are co-opted, and there is little ground in between. However, as William Gamson and Gadi Wolfsfeld note, "it is a major achievement of some movements that they succeed in moving issues from the uncontested to the contested realm."[21] The radical wing of a movement accomplishes something when it helps legitimate moderates, even if it fails to get the credit in the media, government, or public opinion.

The restrictive version of hegemony presents other difficulties as well. It has trouble explaining the eruption of substantive policy conflicts within media, economic, and political elites, such as arose in many of the cases in this book. The media are unique among industries in that they not only form a dissemination point for dominant ideologies but also are the main forum for elites to debate, share information, and struggle over tactics and values. The interests of other corporations may not always square with the economic goals of the networks, who depend on maintaining some credibility with audiences as independent observers and commentators. Likewise, closed views have difficulty accounting for investigative reporting as a genre, which often attracts audiences by featuring the harms caused by market and political powers. All news, but especially muckraking, creates conflicts between the media's role in legitimating dominant ideas, the industry's interests in maximizing profits, and journalists' honoring of professional codes of detachment or revealing social problems.[22]

In this light, we can see how real conflicts arose over television's investigative reporting in the 1960s and 1970s, and the complex interests at play in these disputes. The creation of documentary units at the networks sprang from a relatively broad elite consensus among corporate leaders, cultural critics, network executives, and Kennedy New Frontiersmen. They hoped that documentaries would instruct Americans about the need for an internationalist foreign policy and the rest of the world about the virtues of American television, culture, and economic influence. Documentary, for them, would offer a public-service dividend in exchange for the private control of television and remove the stigma of commercialism from the medium. Yet the justification for documentary also included invigorating democracy by offering citizens greater analysis of social issues and problems. Broadcast journalists took that mandate seriously, using the documentary to assert their own authority to interpret public affairs.

What emerged was a format that had greater potential for social critique than other television news genres at the time, even if it was rarely realized in practice. Networks' needs to present the documentary as above commercial imperatives and journalists' demands for independence from outside pressures helped insulate documentary units somewhat within larger media corporations, endowed them with the resources to conduct longer-term investigations, and guaranteed their access to large prime-time audiences. Under these conditions, some documentarians revived an older credo of journalistic muckraking that yielded consequences unforeseen by the rest of the "documentary coalition" of the early 1960s. Reporters developed a flexible ideology that fused objectivity and exposé reporting, and both elements justified including

nonelite voices and experiences in their reports. A format that was supposed
to serve common elite interests at the start of the decade soon raised conflicts
as journalists responded to the increasing disintegration of the political system. Social movements critical of economic injustice and government power
gained some footing in Congress. Journalists turned to some of these activists
and their congressional sponsors with relatively sympathetic eyes. As elites
themselves divided over Cold War, welfare, and consumer politics, attacks on
the credibility of government and corporate actors mounted, and journalists
stepped in to assume greater authority over the news text if not the political
agenda.

Many moved to rein in this unintended creation, and they did so for multiple and sometimes conflicting reasons. Conservative politicians and business
organizations tried to discredit individual reports to defend their powers. They
were joined by elements of the media that opposed the dominant liberalism
of the time but who also pursued economic objectives (such as affiliates'
resistance to programming that was controversial or drew poor ratings) and
cultural ones (such as print journalists' attempts to maintain their authority).
The defense of an older notion of objectivity and calls for powerful networks
to observe fairness requirements cut across all the institutions involved in
documentary disputes. The networks themselves limited muckraking for political and economic reasons. Executives disciplined documentarians who
pushed their frames beyond the sphere of legitimate controversy or appeared
to be expressing personal beliefs too overtly through careful censorship of
their reports or by farming out "problem" employees. Commercial dictates,
political liabilities, and declining public-service requirements encouraged the
networks to produce fewer investigative documentaries.

The legacy of these struggles is a different and disturbing kind of regulatory regime over television journalism. If the networks successfully warded
off direct content regulations over news, they did not escape other forms of
regulation. Beginning in the Nixon years, the networks paid for their increasing freedom from FCC and congressional oversight of journalism with a loss
of bulwarks against competing services and greater vulnerability to judicial
scrutiny. Investigative journalists were not successful at gaining more power
over their reports: they wriggled free of the fairness doctrine and news distortion policies only to face increased market pressures and corporate censorship.
Today, television's watchdogs are more vulnerable to owners, advertisers, and
well-heeled plaintiffs and less accountable to the public interest or citizen
complaints than in the past.

Despite muckrakers' reluctance to advocate collective action in response
to the social problems they unearth, investigative reporters' only hope may

be to enlist organized political support for their ability to contribute to democracy—the kind of support that allowed regulators to help sow the seeds
of the investigative documentaries of the 1960s. Contemporary regulations
should focus on nurturing the independence of journalistic institutions and
nonprofit organizations that often serve as sources of investigative reporting. Our aim should be to provide these institutions with the financial and
regulatory insulation that will allow them to produce investigative journalism
with greater freedom from economic and government pressures. Without
romanticizing a "golden age" of muckraking on television in the 1960s, we
can draw a lesson from the time: creating the conditions for robust watchdog
reporting on the state and corporations requires more government intervention in media markets, not less. There are many viable policy ideas that
would bolster investigative reporting on what is still the most important and
influential medium for news. Efforts to reduce the market and political pressures that restrict and dilute investigative journalism must begin by cultivating
noncommercial sources of funding and channels of distribution. Muckraking
on television would benefit most from dramatically increasing investment in
public broadcasting, guaranteeing its funding over the long term to reduce
its vulnerability to congressional and executive branch pressure and restructuring its governance to make it more accountable to a broader strata of
Americans. Advertising could be taxed to subsidize nonprofit media including
independent organizations that now produce some of the most professional
and influential investigative reporting available, such as the Center for Public
Integrity in Washington, D.C., and the Center for Investigative Reporting in
San Francisco. As the transition to digital television offers broadcasters more
channels, each station should be required to set aside daily commercial-free
news time funded by a percentage of the station's revenues.[23]

❋ ❋ ❋

This book has shown that although government forces are often investigative
reporters' targets and tormentors, officials and jurists are also often reporters'
best sources, collaborators, defenders, and regulatory champions. Investigative
journalism will not survive without sustaining the web of relationships with
government that ensures that this most important kind of news for democracy
is funded, distributed, and protected from extinction at the hands of media
owners, advertisers, corporate targets, and government itself.

NOTES

INTRODUCTION

1. On classical liberal theory, see James Curran, "Mass Media and Democracy: A Reappraisal," in *Mass Media and Society,* ed. James Curran and Michael Gurevitch (London: Edward Arnold, 1991), 82–117. A current example of liberal theory's elevation of investigative reporting may be found in Stephen Holmes, "Liberal Constraints on Private Power? Reflections on the Origins and Rationale of Access Regulation," in *Mass Media and Democracy,* ed. Judith Lichtenberg (New York: Cambridge University Press, 1990), 51.

2. Fred Friendly, *Due to Circumstances Beyond Our Control . . .* (New York: Vintage Books, 1967), 3–99.

3. Erik Barnouw, *Tube of Plenty: The Evolution of American Television* (New York: Oxford University Press, 1975), 247; Burton Benjamin, "The Documentary: An Endangered Species," Freedom Forum Occasional Paper, 1987; Friendly, *Due to Circumstances,* 99–113.

4. Mary Ann Watson, "The Golden Age of American Television Documentary," *Television Quarterly* 23 (1988): 135–36.

5. James L. Baughman, "The Strange Birth of 'CBS Reports' Revisited," *Historical Journal of Film, Radio, and Television* 2 (1982): 28–38.

6. Michael Curtin, *Redeeming the Wasteland: Television Documentary and Cold War Politics* (New Brunswick, N.J.: Rutgers University Press, 1995), 1–16.

7. House Committee on Interstate and Foreign Commerce, Special Subcommittee on Investigations, *Network News Documentary Practices—CBS "Project Nassau," Hearings,* 91st Cong., 2nd sess., 1970, 5.

8. I used three sources to identify investigations of reports, reviewing the secondary literature on television history and regulation mentioned in this chapter, the index to the *Congressional Record* for 1960–1975 (under the term television and its subheadings, as well CBS, NBC, and ABC), and all fairness doctrine and news distortion cases mentioned in the index to the *Federal Communications Commission Record* during this period.

9. Leonard Downie, *The New Muckrakers* (Washington, D.C.: New Republic Books, 1976); Curtis D. MacDougall, *Interpretative Reporting* (New York: MacMillan, 1977); Clark R. Mollenhoff, *Investigative Reporting* (New York: MacMillan, 1981); Paul N.

Williams, *Investigative Reporting and Editing* (Englewood Cliffs, N.J.: Prentice-Hall, 1978); David Anderson and Peter Benjaminson, *Investigative Reporting* (Bloomington: University of Indiana Press, 1976); Rosemary Armao, "The History of Investigative Reporting," in *The Big Chill: Investigative Reporting in the Current Media Environment*, ed. Marilyn Greenwald and Joseph Bernt (Ames: Iowa State University Press, 2000), 35–50.

10. The two television reports are in Judith and William Serrin, *Muckraking!: The Journalism That Changed America* (New York: New Press, 2002). No television stories appear in Bruce Shapiro, *Shaking the Foundations: 200 Years of Investigative Journalism in America* (New York: Thunder's Mouth Press/Nation Books, 2003).

11. Raymond L. Carroll, "Economic Influences on Commercial Network Television Documentary Scheduling," *Journal of Broadcasting* 23 (1979): 415.

12. Early examples of investigative teams established at metropolitan papers include those at *Newsday* in 1967, the *Chicago Tribune* in 1968, and the *Boston Globe* in 1970. Michael Schudson, *Discovering the News* (New York: Basic Books, 1978), 189–90.

13. Carroll, "Economic Influences," 415.

14. Perry Wolff, "Is Television Capable of Sustaining Higher Forms of Life?" Speech presented at University of Chicago, Chicago, Ill., 1972, Perry Wolff Papers, MSS 830, box 1, SHSW.

15. These government inquiries rate only brief mentions in the major histories of television, such as Barnouw, *Tube of Plenty;* Christopher Sterling and John Kittross, *Stay Tuned: A Concise History of American Broadcasting,* 2nd ed. (Belmont, Calif.: Wadsworth, 1990). The probes are ignored almost entirely by those few documentary historians who examine television's contribution to the genre, such as Erik Barnouw, *Documentary: A History of the Non-Fiction Film* (New York: Oxford University Press, 1983); Jack C. Ellis, *The Documentary Idea: A Critical History of English-Language Documentary Film and Video* (Englewood Cliffs, N.J.: Prentice Hall, 1989); Richard M. Barsam, *Non-Fiction Film: A Critical History* (Bloomington: Indiana University Press, 1992).

16. Accounts of *See It Now* include Friendly, *Due to Circumstances;* Alexander Kendrick, *Prime Time: The Life of Edward R. Murrow* (Boston: Little, Brown and Co., 1969); A. M. Sperber, *Murrow: His Life and Times* (New York: Freundlich Books, 1986); Joseph E. Persico, *Edward R. Murrow: An American Original* (New York: McGraw-Hill, 1988); Thomas Rosteck, *See It Now Confronts McCarthyism: Television Documentary and the Politics of Representation* (Tuscaloosa: University of Alabama Press, 1994). Analyses of the rise of television newsmagazines include Axel Madsen, *60 Minutes: The Power and the Politics of America's Most Popular TV News Show* (New York: Dodd, Mead, 1984); Don Hewitt, *Minute by Minute* (New York: Random House, 1985); Richard Campbell, *60 Minutes and the News: A Mythology for Middle America* (Urbana: University of Illinois Press, 1991).

17. A. William Bluem, *Documentary in American Television: Form, Function, Method* (New York: Hastings House, 1965); Stephen Mamber, *Cinema Verité in America: Studies in Uncontrolled Documentary* (Cambridge, Mass.: MIT Press, 1974); Robert C. Allen and Douglas Gomery, *Film History: Theory and Practice* (New York: Alfred A. Knopf, 1985).

18. Carroll, "Economic Influences," 411–25; Charles M. Hammond Jr., *The Image Decade: Television Documentary, 1965–75* (New York: Hastings House, 1981); Watson,

"Golden Age," 135–36; Mary Ann Watson, *The Expanding Vista: American Television in the Kennedy Years* (New York: Oxford University Press, 1990).

19. Ernest F. Martin Jr., "The 'Hunger in America' Controversy," *Journal of Broadcasting* 16 (1972): 185–94; Michael D. Murray, *The Political Performers: CBS Broadcasts in the Public Interest* (Westport, Conn.: Praeger, 1994); F. Leslie Smith, "CBS Reports: The Selling of the Pentagon," in *Mass News: Practices, Controversies, and Alternatives*, ed. David J. Leroy and Christopher H. Sterling (Englewood Cliffs, N.J.: Prentice-Hall, 1973), 200–210; Richard J. Schaefer, "Reconsidering *Harvest of Shame*: The Limitations of a Broadcast Journalism Landmark," *Journalism History* 19 (1994): 121–32.

20. Fred W. Friendly, *The Good Guys, the Bad Guys, and the First Amendment* (New York: Random House, 1975); Marilyn Lashner, *The Chilling Effect in TV News* (New York: Praeger, 1984); Lucas A. Powe Jr., *American Broadcasting and the First Amendment* (Berkeley: University of California Press, 1987); Hugh Carter Donahue, *The Battle to Control Broadcast News* (Cambridge, Mass.: MIT Press, 1989); Thomas G. Krattenmaker and Lucas A. Powe Jr., *Regulating Broadcast Programming* (Cambridge, Mass.: MIT Press and Washington, D.C.: AEI Press, 1994); Corydon B. Dunham, *Fighting for the First Amendment: Stanton of CBS vs. Congress and the Nixon White House* (Westport, Conn.: Praeger, 1997). For a counterexample, see William Ray, *FCC: The Ups and Downs of Radio-TV Regulation* (Ames: Iowa State University Press, 1990).

21. Peter B. Clark, "The Opinion Machine: Intellectuals, the Mass Media, and American Democracy," in *Mass Media and American Democracy*, ed. Harry M. Clor (Chicago: Rand McNally, 1974); Samuel J. Huntington, "The United States," in *The Crisis of Democracy*, ed. Michel J. Crozier, Samuel J. Huntington, and Joji Watanuki (New York: New York University Press, 1975), 98–100; Michael J. Robinson, "American Political Legitimacy in an Age of Electronic Journalism," in *Television as a Social Force*, ed. Douglass Cater and Richard Adler (New York: Praeger, 1975), 97–140; Stanley Rothman, "The Mass Media in Post-Industrial Society," in *The Third Century*, ed. Seymour Martin Lipset (Chicago: University of Chicago Press, 1979), 345–88.

22. The phrase is from Daniel P. Moynihan, "The Presidency and the Press," *Commentary* (March 1971): 41–52.

23. Spiro Agnew, "Speech before Midwest Regional Republican Committee Meeting, Des Moines, Iowa, 13 November 1969," reprinted in *Killing the Messenger: 100 Years of Media Criticism*, ed. Tom Goldstein (New York: Columbia University Press, 1989), 67, 69.

24. See sources cited in note 21 and Michael J. Robinson, "Public Affairs Television and the Growth of Political Malaise: The Case of 'The Selling of the Pentagon,'" *American Political Science Review* 70 (June 1976): 409–32.

25. Daniel Bell, *The Coming of Post-Industrial Society* (New York: Basic Books, 1976).

26. Irving Kristol, "Business and the New Class," *Wall Street Journal*, 19 May 1975, 8.

27. In 1968, 70 percent of Americans polled agreed that business struck a fair balance between profits and the public interest, while only 15 percent said so in 1977. In the same time period, the number of Americans expressing a great deal of confidence in the leaders of large corporations fell from 55 percent to 15 percent. By the late 1970s,

polls assessing people's level of confidence in American institutions placed business last. See David L. Paletz and Robert M. Entman, *Media Power Politics* (New York: Free Press, 1981), 133; Nancy Needham Wardell, "The Corporation," *Daedalus* 107 (1978): 101.

28. W. Lee Burge, "Fair Information Practices: Some Imperatives for the Media and Business," in *Business and the Media,* ed. Craig E. Aronoff (Santa Monica, Calif.: Goodyear Publishing, 1979), 175.

29. Cited in Robert F. Hurleigh, "The Social Responsibility of the Media in Reporting on Corporate Social Responsibility," in *Business and the Media,* ed. Craig E. Aronoff (Santa Monica, Calif.: Goodyear Publishing, 1979), 201–2.

30. Martin Linsky, *Impact: How the Press Affects Federal Policymaking* (New York: W. W. Norton, 1986), 45.

31. Tom Wicker, *On Press* (New York: Viking Press, 1978), 259.

32. Daniel Schorr, *Clearing the Air* (Boston: Houghton Mifflin, 1977), viii.

33. David L. Protess et al., *The Journalism of Outrage: Investigative Reporting and Agenda-Building in America* (New York: Guilford Press, 1991), 276.

34. Examples of recent books decrying media liberalism include former CBS reporter Bernard Goldberg's *Bias: A CBS Insider Exposes How the Media Distort the News* (Waterville, Maine: Thorndike Press, 2002); and William McGowan, *Coloring the News: How Crusading for Diversity Has Corrupted American Journalism* (San Francisco: Encounter Press, 2001).

35. Larry J. Sabato, *Feeding Frenzy: How Attack Journalism Has Transformed American Politics* (New York: Free Press, 1991); Adam Gopnik, "Read All about It," *New Yorker,* 12 December 1994, 84–102.

36. David Croteau and William Hoynes, *By Invitation Only: How the Media Limit Political Debate* (Monroe, Maine: Common Courage Press, 1994), 7.

37. S. Robert Lichter, Stanley Rothman, and Linda Lichter, *The Media Elite* (Bethesda, Md.: Adler and Adler, 1986).

38. A more recent survey of Washington, D.C., reporters found similarly that journalists were more liberal than the public on social issues but more conservative on economic issues. See David Croteau, "Examining the 'Liberal Media' Claim: Journalists' Views on Politics, Economic Policy, and Media Coverage," *Extra!* (June 1998) http://www.fair.org/reports/journalist-survey.html.

39. Edward J. Epstein, *News from Nowhere* (New York: Random House, 1973), xiv; Mark Fishman, *Manufacturing the News* (Austin: University of Texas Press, 1980), 51–52; Gaye Tuchman, *Making News* (New York: Free Press, 1978), 66, 87; Herbert Gans, *Deciding What's News* (New York: Pantheon, 1979), 116; Stephen Hess, *The Washington Reporters* (Washington, D.C.: Brookings Institution, 1981), 115; Leon V. Sigal, *Reporters and Officials* (Lexington, Mass.: D. C. Heath, 1973).

40. Glasgow University Media Group, *Bad News* (London: Routledge and Kegan Paul, 1976); John Downing, *The Media Machine* (London: Pluto Press, 1980); Michael Parenti, *Inventing Reality* (New York: St. Martin's Press, 1986); Charlotte Ryan, *Prime Time Activism: Media Strategies for Grassroots Organizing* (Boston: South End Press, 1991).

41. Paletz and Entman, *Media Power Politics,* 134–37; Curtis D. MacDougall, "Business's Friend, the Media," in *Business and the Media,* ed. Craig E. Aronoff (Santa Monica, Calif.: Goodyear Publishing, 1979), 44–54.

42. Daniel Hallin, *The "Uncensored War": The Media and Vietnam* (Berkeley: University of California Press, 1986).

43. W. Lance Bennett, "Towards a Theory of Press-State Relations," *Journal of Communication* 40 (1990): 103–25; W. Lance Bennett, "An Introduction to Journalism Norms and Representations of Politics," *Political Communication* 13 (1996): 373–84; W. Lance Bennett, "Cracking the News Code: Some Rules That Journalists Live By," in *Do the Media Govern?*, ed. Shanto Iyengar and Richard Reeves (Thousand Oaks, Calif.: Sage, 1997), 18–28.

44. On muckraking as moral discourse, see James S. Ettema and Theodore L. Glasser, *Custodians of Conscience: Investigative Journalism and Public Virtue* (New York: Columbia University Press, 1998).

45. Reuven Frank, *Out of Thin Air: The Brief Wonderful Life of Network News* (New York: Simon and Schuster, 1991), 171. Among the television networks, ABC was exceptional during this time, which helps account for why none of its documentaries drew the kind of extended investigations as NBC, CBS, and PBS reports. In the 1960s, ABC was economically weaker than its commercial rivals, and its news executives tended to be more conservative than their colleagues at the other networks (Eisenhower press secretary James Hagerty took the helm of the news division in the early 1960s, and ABC was known later as the "Nixon network"). Thus, for most of the decade, it avoided investigative reporting, opting instead for the cinema verité profiles of Robert Drew Associates, cultural and historical compilation films, and nature documentaries. The network did not turn to more aggressive documentary investigations until the mid-1970s. See Hammond, *The Image Decade*, 133–34, 143–45. In addition, of all the networks, ABC presold the highest proportion of documentaries to sponsors in the 1960s, which allowed for more advertiser influence (Epstein, *News from Nowhere*, 128–29).

46. Scott L. Althaus, Jill A. Edy, Robert M. Entman, and Patricia Phalen, "Revising the Indexing Hypothesis: Officials, Media, and the Libya Crisis," *Political Communication* 13 (1996): 407–21; John Zaller and Dennis Chiu, "Government's Little Helper: U.S. Press Coverage of Foreign Policy Crises, 1946–1999," in *Decisionmaking in a Glass House: Mass Media, Public Opinion, and American and European Foreign Policy in the Twenty-first Century*, ed. Brigitte L. Nacos, Robert Y. Shapiro, and Pierangelo Isernia (Lanham, Md.: Rowman and Littlefield, 2000), 61–84.

47. Zaller and Chiu, "Government's Little Helper," 82.

48. Protess et al., *Journalism of Outrage*, 12.

49. For example, Av Westin, who produced documentaries for CBS, ABC, and public broadcasting, claimed the investigative documentary's impact stemmed from the fact that "the viewer is 'investing' so much time in staying tuned. . . . Once involved, the viewer is more easily stirred to anger or to 'doing something.' . . . There is a tacit plea by us for audience involvement and follow-up action in each of those broadcasts" (Westin, *Newswatch: How TV Decides the News* [New York: Simon and Schuster, 1982], 201). For examples of scholars who embrace claims that investigative reporting mobilizes the public, see Carl Jensen, *Stories That Changed America: Muckrakers of the Twentieth Century* (New York: Seven Stories Press, 2000), 21–22; Serrin and Serrin, *Muckraking!*, 388.

50. Protess et al., *Journalism of Outrage*; Gladys Engel Lang and Kurt Lang, *The Battle for Public Opinion* (New York: Columbia University Press, 1983); Michael

Schudson, *Watergate in America: How We Remember, Forget, and Reconstruct the Past* (New York: Basic Books, 1992); Silvio Waisbord, *Watchdog Journalism in South America: News, Accountability, and Democracy* (New York: Columbia University Press, 2000).

51. Protess et al., *Journalism of Outrage,* 246.

52. Robert Entman, "Framing: Toward Clarification of a Fractured Paradigm," *Journal of Communication* 43 (1993): 52.

CHAPTER 1: INVESTIGATING POVERTY AND WELFARE

1. See, for example, Edward Bliss Jr., *Now the News: The Story of Broadcast Journalism* (New York: Columbia University Press, 1991), 391–92, 395–96; A. William Bluem, *Documentary in American Television: Form, Function, Method* (New York: Hastings House, 1965), 104, 117; William B. Leonard, *In the Storm of the Eye: A Lifetime at CBS* (New York: G. P. Putnam's Sons, 1987), 159–61; Robert Miraldi, *Muckraking and Objectivity: Journalism's Colliding Traditions* (New York: Greenwood Press, 1990), 97; William J. Small, *To Kill a Messenger: Television News and the Real World* (New York: Hastings House, 1974), 39.

2. The following discussion of farm labor history is indebted to Nick Kotz, *Let Them Eat Promises: The Politics of Hunger in America* (Englewood Cliffs, N.J.: Prentice-Hall, 1969); Ardith Maney, *Still Hungry After All These Years* (Westport, Conn.: Greenwood Press, 1989); Patrick H. Mooney and Theo J. Majka, *Farmers' and Farmworkers' Movements: Social Protest in American Agriculture* (New York: Twayne Publishers, 1995).

3. One indicator of *Harvest of Shame*'s stature in American broadcasting is the number of follow-up reports that have been produced in the years since it was aired. In 1970, NBC made *Migrant,* produced by Martin Carr, who also produced *Hunger in America.* Minute Maid and its parent Coca-Cola attacked the report for its unflattering portrayal of labor conditions on the company's farms, and Coca-Cola pulled its advertising from NBC during the quarter following the documentary. See Frank, *Out of Thin Air,* 320. The documentary was further enshrined by television journalists as a cornerstone of network muckraking by a 1980 NBC update, *Migrant: An NBC White Paper,* and a 1990 PBS *Frontline* sequel, *New Harvest, Old Shame.*

4. *Harvest of Shame* echoed *Crisis of Abundance,* a 1956 Murrow report for *See It Now* that criticized Eisenhower administration farm policy for driving small farmers out of business. Agriculture Secretary Ezra Taft Benson demanded response time and was given it. Senators Hubert Humphrey and Clinton P. Anderson then called for response time as well. See A. M. Sperber, *Murrow: His Life and Times* (New York: Freundlich Books, 1986), 492.

5. Joan London and Henry Anderson, *So Shall Ye Reap* (New York: Thomas Y. Crowell Co., 1970), 77.

6. Miraldi, *Muckraking and Objectivity,* 84.

7. My discussion of the administration's policy draws on Henry P. Guzda, "James P. Mitchell: Social Conscience of the Cabinet," *Monthly Labor Review* 115, no. 2 (1991): 23–29; remarks of Senator Harrison Williams Jr., *Congressional Record,* 16 February 1961, 2212.

8. Presidential Committee on Migratory Labor, *Report to the President on Domestic Migratory Farm Labor* (Washington, D.C.: U.S. Government Printing Office, 1960). The report's recommendations are also summarized in *Congressional Record,* 16 February 1961, 2221–22.

9. The bills are described in *Congressional Record,* 16 February 1961, 2222.

10. See Mooney and Majka, *Farmers' and Farm Workers' Movements,* 153. Among the groups represented in these coalitions were the National Council of Churches, the National Board of the Young Women's Christian Association, the Bishops' Committee for Migrant Workers, the AFL-CIO, and the National Child Labor Committee.

11. J. Craig Jenkins, *The Politics of Insurgency: The Farm Worker Movement in the 1960s* (New York: Columbia University Press, 1985), 114.

12. Sam Mase, "Criticism of CBS for Migrant Labor Film Is Justified, Says Sponsor of Show," *Tampa Tribune* (undated), reprinted in *Congressional Record,* 6 February 1961, 1756.

13. *Congressional Record,* 30 March 1961, A2283–84. For the rest of the series, see 11 April 1961, A2396–97, A2399; 12 April 1961, A2427, A2429, A2431; 13 April 1961, A2464, A2466, A2480; 18 April 1961, A2563–64, A2568, A2576, A2633–34, A2645–46; 25 April 1961, A2805–6; 26 April 1961, A2817–18. Representative Robert H. Michel of Illinois was the first to attack the report. See *Congressional Record,* 2 February 1961, 1686–87. Three House members from New York later entered criticisms into the record. See *Congressional Record,* 16 January 1961, A238–39 (by Representative Jessica M. Weis); 24 March 1961, A2107 (by Representative Steven B. Derounian); 17 April 1961, A2553–54 (by Representative Carleton J. King).

14. *Congressional Record,* 16 February 1961, 2221. For the Farm Bureau's similar reasoning, see *Congressional Record,* 16 February 1961, 2218.

15. For Senator Holland's and the Farm Bureau's criticisms of the documentary, see *Congressional Record,* 2 February 1961, 1686–89; 6 February 1961, 1756–58.

16. In the *Congressional Record,* Holland's claims appear on 6 February 1961, 1757; CBS's refusal of equal time appears on 6 February 1961, 1758; CBS's reply to Holland's charges is on 16 February 1961, 2218–22.

17. *Congressional Record,* 22 March 1961, 4533; see 4532–33 for the administration's response to the BBC controversy.

18. On Holland's role in pressuring Murrow, see Joseph E. Persico, *Edward R. Murrow: An American Original* (New York: McGraw-Hill, 1988), 473. On Murrow's dealings with his Senate opponents, see Sperber, *Murrow,* 628–32.

19. For press criticism of Murrow, see, for example, "TV-Radio: This—Is Murrow?" *Newsweek,* 3 April 1961, 82; "The Harvester," *Time,* 31 March 1961, 30. On Murrow's regrets, see Sperber, *Murrow,* 630–31.

20. *Congressional Record,* 28 March 1961, 5012.

21. *Congressional Record,* 24 March 1961, 4764.

22. Ibid., 4762.

23. For claims that the documentary led to legislative change, see Protess et al., *Journalism of Outrage,* 47.

24. Philip L. Martin and David A. Martin, *The Endless Quest: Helping America's Farm Workers* (Boulder, Colo.: Westview Press, 1994), 22. Congress appropriated additional funding for migrant health care in 1962, for job training in 1964, and for education in 1966.

25. London and Anderson, *So Shall Ye Reap,* 77.

26. *Congressional Record,* 23 January 1961, 1145.

27. *Congressional Record,* 16 February 1961, 2213.

28. Lisa Levenstein, "From Innocent Children to Unwanted Migrants and Unwed Moms: Two Chapters in the Public Discourse on Welfare in the United States, 1960–1961," *Journal of Women's History* 11, no. 4 (2000): 17. For a summary of Mitchell's plan to curb welfare, see "An Address by the City Manager of the City of Newburgh, N.Y., Joseph McDowell Mitchell," reprinted in *Congressional Record,* 11 September 1962, 19120–23, 19120.

29. On political support and opposition for Mitchell, see Joseph P. Ritz, *The Despised Poor: Newburgh's War on Welfare* (Boston: Beacon Press, 1966), 34–38, 85–86, 110, 125, 150–57.

30. See, for example, Eve Edstrom, "Newburgh Is a Mirror Reflecting Us All," *Washington Post,* 6 August 1961, E1.

31. Ritz, *Despised Poor,* 125.

32. Ibid., 54.

33. On movement and religious organizations' responses, see Levenstein, "From Innocent Children," 21; Ritz, *Despised Poor,* 54, 59–60. On Catholic Charities' involvement, see "NBC Comments on Mr. Mitchell's Objections," reprinted in *Congressional Record,* 11 September 1962, 19117.

34. See letter to the membership from Howard B. Hollenbeck, National Association of Social Workers, 1 February 1962; National Association of Social Workers, "Will the Newburgh Plan Work in Your City?" undated pamphlet; both in *"Battle of Newburgh* Project, 1961–1962" folder, series 2, box 1, Muriel and Ralph Pumphrey Papers, Washington University in St. Louis Library, St. Louis, Missouri.

35. Ritz, *Despised Poor,* xi. On Newburgh's place in the history of poverty discourse in the 1960s, see Martin Gilens, *Why Americans Hate Welfare: Race, Media, and the Politics of Antipoverty Policy* (Chicago: University of Chicago Press, 1999), 115; Thomas Kaplan, "New Deal to New Frontier: From Security to Opportunity in the American Welfare State" (Madison: University of Wisconsin–Madison Institute for Research on Poverty, October 1994), 25–28. On the initial, uncritical media coverage of Newburgh and editorial support for Mitchell, see Ritz, *Despised Poor,* 41, 55–57.

36. "Statement by City Manager Joseph McD. Mitchell, Clarifying City's Position on NBC White Paper No. 9, 'The Battle of Newburgh'—January 29, 1962," in *Congressional Record,* 11 September 1962, 19123–24.

37. The letters are reprinted in *Congressional Record,* 11 September 1962, 19111–27; 20 September 1962, 20233–34. Representative Katherine St. George, who represented Newburgh and surrounding areas, also spoke on behalf of Mitchell. See *Congressional Record,* 31 January 1962, A747.

38. *Letter to Mr. Joseph McD. Mitchell, In re Complaint under Fairness Doctrine Requirements,* 40 FCC 526 (1962).

39. Letter from Thomas Curtis to Newton Minow, reprinted in *Congressional Record,* 20 September 1962, 20234.

40. On public opinion toward Mitchell in Newburgh, see Ritz, *Despised Poor,* 169–72. On Kennedy administration policy, see James T. Patterson, *America's Struggle against Poverty in the Twentieth Century,* 2nd ed. (Cambridge, Mass.: Harvard University

Press, 2000), 123–27; Edward D. Berkowitz, *America's Welfare State: From Roosevelt to Reagan* (Baltimore: Johns Hopkins University Press, 1991), 106–11.

41. This controversial phrase, vaguely defined in legislation, was interpreted in three main ways. Civil rights and antipoverty groups tended to construe participation as a means to organize the poor into a political force to act as a counterweight to the power of large welfare bureaucracies. Social welfare professionals saw participation more as individual therapy, as a way to change the behavior of the poor by giving them a psychological stake in reforming themselves. Welfare administrators tended to interpret participation as a way of taking advantage of the poor's "expertise" about their own conditions in the name of increasing the efficiency of programs. David Zarefsky, *President Johnson's War on Poverty: Rhetoric and History* (Tuscaloosa: University of Alabama Press, 1986), 45–48.

42. On the divisions discussed in this paragraph, see S. M. Miller and Pamela Roby, "The War on Poverty Reconsidered," in *Poverty: Views from the Left*, ed. Jeremy Larner and Irving Howe (New York: William Morrow and Co., 1968), 68–82; Jill Quadagno, *The Color of Welfare: How Racism Undermined the War on Poverty* (Oxford: Oxford University Press, 1994), 10–13.

43. Howard Thorkelson, "Federal Food Programs and Hunger," in *Poverty: Views from the Left*, ed. Jeremy Larner and Irving Howe (New York: William Morrow and Co., 1968), 184–95.

44. Randall Ripley, "Legislative Bargaining and the Food Stamp Act of 1964," in *Congress and Urban Problems*, ed. Fredric N. Cleaveland (Washington, D.C.: Brookings Institution, 1964), 279–310.

45. Kotz, *Let Them Eat Promises*, 44.

46. Maney, *Still Hungry*, 3.

47. The committee's official name was the Subcommittee on Employment, Manpower, and Poverty of the Committee on Labor and Public Welfare.

48. The Citizens Board membership reflected the CCAP's, but also included a number of administrators, medical school professors, and law school faculty drawn from black colleges and Ivy League universities.

49. Hunger coverage appeared in the *Boston Globe, Washington Post, Washington Star, Christian Science Monitor, New York Post, New York Times, Des Moines Register, St. Petersburg (Fla.) Times, Charlotte Observer, Raleigh News and Observer, Look, Good Housekeeping, Time,* and *Newsweek*. See reprints in Senate Committee on Labor and Public Welfare, Subcommittee on Employment, Manpower, and Poverty, *Hunger and Malnutrition in America*, 90th Cong., 1st sess., 1967, 259–91; Senate Committee on Labor and Public Welfare, Subcommittee on Employment, Manpower, and Poverty, *Hunger and Malnutrition in the United States: Hearings before the Senate Subcommittee on Employment, Manpower, and Poverty*, 90th Cong., 2nd sess., 1968, 297–345. PBL's documentary *Hunger American Style* aired 25 February 1968, three months before *Hunger in America*. For a transcript, see Senate Committee on Labor and Public Welfare, *Hunger and Malnutrition in the United States*, 337–45.

50. Kotz, *Let Them Eat Promises*, 135–45.

51. This account of Freeman's tenure at the USDA is indebted to Maney, *Still Hungry*, 54, 66–67; Kotz, *Let Them Eat Promises*, 56, 77–78.

52. Marian Wright, who had testified to the Senate Poverty Subcommittee at its

Jackson, Mississippi, hearing in April 1967, served as the Poor People's Campaign's chief liaison to the federal government. She worked closely with Senator Robert Kennedy's aide, Peter Edelman, and Poverty Subcommittee counsel Bill Smith and negotiated with USDA officials (Kotz, *Let Them Eat Promises*, 154–55).

53. In the winter of 1965–1966, thirty-five blacks occupied an abandoned Greenville, Mississippi, Air Force base and distributed leaflets saying they were hungry and jobless. They were evicted by federal troops. The event triggered the creation of a Federal Interdepartmental Committee on Nutrition, which pumped some additional food stamp funding into the state. Secretary Freeman had largely ignored the recommendations of his own Advisory Committee on Civil Rights, appointed in 1965 after President Johnson and the U.S. Commission on Civil Rights chided the USDA for discrimination in its programs and hiring practices. The advisory committee asked Freeman to liberalize the food stamp and commodity programs, start federal food aid programs himself where local officials wouldn't, and keep segregationist politics out of the school lunch program. The advisory committee asked Freeman to gather data it could use to make a public case for these changes but got no response. Freeman acknowledged criticisms of unfair administration of programs in the South in private memos to his own staff, who investigated these charges, but did little to enforce changes. Memos circulated within the USDA beginning in 1965 show that Freeman knew of the growing employment crisis in the South for black tenant farmers and that the food stamp program's minimum purchase requirement excluded many of them who had no cash income (Kotz, *Let Them Eat Promises*, 11, 60–61; Maney, *Still Hungry*, 71, 73–80).

54. Michael D. Murray, *The Political Performers: CBS Broadcasts in the Public Interest* (Westport, Conn.: Praeger, 1994), 77–90.

55. Maney, *Still Hungry*, 94.

56. Citizens Board of Inquiry into Hunger and Malnutrition in the United States, *Hunger, U.S.A.* (Washington, D.C.: New Community Press, 1968), 18–19.

57. Robert Coles and Harry Huge, "FBI on the Trail of the Hunger-Mongers," *New Republic*, 21 December 1968, 11–13.

58. Citizens Board, *Hunger, U.S.A,* 21.

59. Leonard, *In the Storm,* 160.

60. The transcript appears in *Congressional Record,* 29 May 1968, 15567; 9 July 1968, 20392. The SCLC's Reverend Ralph Abernathy, in testimony to the Senate Poverty Subcommittee, portrayed the dying baby in *Hunger in America* as signifying how urgently food aid was needed. See "Statement of Ralph Abernathy," in Senate Committee on Labor and Public Welfare, *Hunger and Malnutrition in the United States,* 69.

61. Letter from Orville Freeman to Frank Stanton and letter from Orville Freeman to Carl Perkins, reprinted in *Congressional Record,* 3 June 1968, 15818–23. Freeman wrote to Perkins to answer a request from Perkins's House Education and Labor Committee for information about the program.

62. Kotz, *Let Them Eat Promises,* 47.

63. Letter from Orville Freeman to Carl Perkins, reprinted in *Congressional Record,* 3 June 1968, 15818–19.

64. Letter from Orville Freeman to Frank Stanton, reprinted in *Congressional Record,* 3 June 1968, 15818. In private, Freeman was far less supportive of the Poor People's Campaign, as when he wrote to President Johnson on June 28, "At least, I

find many people who write or come to me and say thank goodness you are standing firm and not letting this ragtail, bobtailed group of so-called 'Poor People' push you around" (Kotz, *Let Them Eat Promises,* 183).

65. Ibid., 182.

66. All quotes in this paragraph are from Ernest F. Martin Jr., "The 'Hunger in America' Controversy," *Journal of Broadcasting* 16 (1972): 189.

67. Freeman considered requesting an FCC ruling, and he sought the USDA general counsel's legal opinion on the matter. He was advised that a ruling "could take six months or more," i.e., after the 1968 elections, by which time the issue could be considered moot for the outgoing secretary (Edward M. Shulman, USDA general counsel, to John Obert, assistant to the secretary, 31 May 1968, Farm Program 8-1-1 [2 of 2], box 4814, general correspondence, ROSA, College Park, Md.).

68. Robert C. Maynard and George Lardner Jr., "FBI Used in Probe of Hunger Surveys," *Washington Post,* 8 December 1968, A1.

69. See House Committee on Appropriations, Subcommittee on Agricultural Appropriations, *Department of Agriculture Appropriations for 1970; Hearings before a Subcommittee of the Committee on Appropriations,* part 5, *Consumer and Marketing Service,* 91st Cong., 1st sess., 1969, 52.

70. Jean M. White, "Priest Says FBI Agents Harass Poor," *Washington Post,* 10 December 1968, A4. Several "government employees" who were questioned said the agents encouraged them to discredit the hunger reports. See Maynard and Lardner, "FBI Used," A1, A13.

71. House Committee on Appropriations, *Department of Agriculture Appropriations for 1970,* 74.

72. *Congressional Record,* 2 May 1968, 11501–3.

73. W. R. Poage (D-Texas), chair of the House Committee on Agriculture, touted San Antonio's efforts against hunger and defended the city's exposition as creating jobs for the poor (*Congressional Record,* 3 June 1968, 15839–40). O. C. Fisher (D-Texas) assailed *Hunger in America* as part of a wider attack on the "poverty cult," claimed that jobs were available in San Antonio if people wanted them, and called for tightening welfare eligibility standards (*Congressional Record,* 11 June 1968, 16785–86). Robert H. Michel (R-Ill.) and E. C. Gathings (R-Ark.) cited a *Chicago Tribune* editorial questioning the CBS report and defending Secretary Freeman (*Congressional Record,* 26 June 1968, 18995; 27 June 1968, 19173).

74. For Gonzalez's attacks in the House, see *Congressional Record* 22 July 1968, 22738–39; 31 July 1968, 24432; 12 September 1968, 26625; 23 September 1968, 27811–12; 5 February 1969, 2935–36; 27 May 1969, 14100–14101; 27 May 1969, 14389–40; 2 June 1969, 14420–21; 5 June 1969, 14984; 9 June 1969, 15069–15070; 21 October 1969, 30877.

75. "Hunger Pains," *Newsweek,* 10 June 1968, 100.

76. Leonard, *In the Storm,* 161.

77. "San Antonio's Hungry Get Pudding Shipment," *New York Times,* 8 August 1968, 4.

78. Cited in Martin, "'Hunger in America' Controversy," 188.

79. Leonard, *In the Storm,* 160.

80. See CBS News Washington bureau chief William J. Small's *To Kill a Messenger,* 39; untitled article, *The Sign,* August 1968, reprinted in *Congressional Record,* 12

September 1968, 26626; Jack Gould, "Hunger Is Not for Quibbling," *New York Times,* 23 June 1968, sec. 2, 19.

81. On the token nature of reform in 1968 and the more substantial changes made thereafter, see Kotz, *Let Them Eat Promises,* 22, 190–91; and Maney, *Still Hungry,* 110–27. Kotz summarizes the political shifts that pushed Congress and the Nixon White House to approve more aid. Under a Republican president, liberal Democrats could sharpen their attacks on the executive branch without alienating fellow party members (205). An institutionalized source of this pressure was created in the new Senate Select Committee on Nutrition and Human Needs, led by Democratic presidential candidate George McGovern. Republican governors of states with large urban constituencies began to cooperate with food aid advocates (216–17). Congressional and White House support for farm subsidies slackened somewhat since Nixon owed less to southern Democrats than Johnson did, and urban liberal senators continued to increase their committee powers in Congress (206). Southern Democrats realized that if they wanted to preserve high farm subsidies, they would have to agree to more food aid.

82. Robert Sherrill, "The Happy Ending (Maybe) of 'The Selling of the Pentagon,'" *New York Times Magazine,* 16 May 1971, 78, 80.

83. Spiro Agnew, untitled speech to Middlesex Club, Boston, Mass., 18 March 1971, series 3, subseries 7, box 5; Spiro T. Agnew Papers; Special Collections, UMCP.

84. "Hunger in America," *AIM Report,* September 1974, 4–5.

85. Max Weber's concept of ideal types is central to sociological thought. Gerth and Mills define the ideal type as "the construction of certain elements of reality into a logically precise conception." Ideal types are more "logically controlled and unambiguous conceptions" than the sometimes shifting, contradictory ideas deployed by social agents embedded in actual historical moments. The advantage of ideal types is that they allow us to offer clearer comparisons and contrasts between competing political discourses considered in their "purest" forms. See H. H. Gerth and C. Wright Mills, *From Max Weber: Essays in Sociology* (New York: Oxford University Press, 1958), 59–60.

86. "Excerpts from 'Hunger Study' by the House Committee on Agriculture, W. R. Poage, of Tex., as chairman," reprinted in Senate Committee on Labor and Public Welfare, Subcommittee on Employment, Manpower, and Poverty, *Hunger in America: Chronology and Selected Background Materials,* 90th Cong., 2nd sess., 1968, 160. For similar themes on poverty, see also Albert O. Hirschman, *The Rhetoric of Reaction: Perversity, Futility, Jeopardy* (Cambridge, Mass.: Belknap Press, 1991).

87. Kotz, *Let Them Eat Promises,* 21.

88. Frances Fox Piven and Richard A. Cloward, *Regulating the Poor: The Functions of Public Welfare,* 2nd ed. (New York: Vintage Books, 1993), xvii.

89. Kotz, *Let Them Eat Promises,* 25.

90. See Thorkelson, "Federal Food Programs," 187; Citizens Board, *Hunger, U.S.A,* 54.

91. Citizens Board, *Hunger, U.S.A,* 77, 78.

92. This is largely because the groups on the left that were most active in the national political debate over hunger at this time included some of the original framers of the War on Poverty, mainstream trade unionists, as well as the least radical elements of

the civil rights movement (the Southern Christian Leadership Conference and the National Association for the Advancement of Colored People).

93. Citizens Board, *Hunger, U.S.A,* 85–87.

94. *Washington Post,* "Poor List 49 Demands," 13 June 1968, reprinted in Senate Committee on Labor and Public Welfare, *Hunger and Malnutrition in the United States,* 197–200.

95. The PBL documentary focused in part on hunger conditions among the farm workers at a plantation owned by Mississippi senator James Eastland (D-Miss.), portrayed as one of the biggest recipients of farm subsidies in the state.

96. Zarefsky, *President Johnson's War on Poverty,* 40–41. Although appropriated by conservative and centrist critics of the War on Poverty, the theory of a self-perpetuating "culture of poverty" originated in liberal thought, with Oscar Lewis, *Five Families: Mexican Case Studies in the Culture of Poverty* (New York: Basic Books, 1959) and Michael Harrington, *The Other America: Poverty in the United States* (New York: MacMillan, 1962).

97. Paul Jacobs, "America's Schizophrenic View of the Poor," in *Poverty: Views from the Left,* ed. Jeremy Larner and Irving Howe (New York: William Morrow and Co., 1968), 39–57.

98. Piven and Cloward, *Regulating the Poor,* 277–78.

99. See "June 9, 1967. U.S. Department of Agriculture Memorandum: Review of Domestic Food Programs—Background and Recommendations," in Senate Committee on Labor and Public Welfare, *Hunger in America,* 34–39.

100. See Richard J. Schaefer, "Reconsidering *Harvest of Shame:* The Limitations of a Broadcast Journalism Landmark," *Journalism History* 19 (1994): 121, 127.

101. Brian Winston, "The Tradition of the Victim in Griersonian Documentary," in *New Challenges for Documentary,* ed. Alan Rosenthal (Berkeley: University of California Press, 1988), 274. In addition, Winston notes that this approach has tended to provoke yet ignore ethical questions about whether the poor and powerless truly give "informed consent" for documentarians to use their images, about the filmmaker's role in encouraging subjects to take risks for the sake of the documentary, and about when the filmmaker should intervene to help subjects.

102. Michael Curtin, *Redeeming the Wasteland: Television Documentary and Cold War Politics* (New Brunswick, N.J.: Rutgers University Press, 1995), 121–27, 138–47.

103. On investigative journalists' role as mediators, see Campbell, *60 Minutes and the News,* 113–36.

104. Kuralt introduced the guest narrators as follows: Dr. Granger, "the Loudon County Medical Officer, knows and treats many of the tenant families"; Dr. Van Duzen "has practiced among the Navajo Indians for the past fourteen years"; Dr. Wheeler was introduced as one of the "prominent doctors" the Field Foundation had sent to investigate hunger in Mississippi, and as one "who has lived and practiced in the South all his life"; Father Ruiz was introduced as a priest "who lives and works with the poorest of San Antonio's Mexican-Americans" and "a missionary among his own people."

105. All quotes from the programs in this book are from direct viewing by the author.

106. Nancy Fraser, *Unruly Practices: Power, Discourse, and Gender in Contemporary Social Theory* (Minneapolis: University of Minnesota Press, 1989), 154–55.

107. According to the report on *Hunger in America* compiled by the House Agricultural Appropriations Committee, the assistant probation officer later claimed that the girl was retarded and was placed in a foster home at the time of the CBS interview but "had been brought to the juvenile court hearing room specifically to be displayed on the program" (House Committee on Appropriations, *Department of Agriculture Appropriations for 1970*, 57). It is important to note, however, that this report aimed to discredit CBS, and that it paraphrased the probation officer rather than quoting her directly.

108. Joel F. Handler and Yeheskel Hasenfeld, *The Moral Construction of Poverty* (Newbury Park, Calif.: Sage, 1991), 7.

109. See Quadagno, *Color of Welfare;* Gilens, *Why Americans Hate Welfare.*

110. Fraser, *Unruly Practices,* 144–60.

111. Gilens's findings are based primarily on newsmagazine coverage. However, he found the same dynamic in examining national evening television news stories that aired in 1968. See Gilens, *Why Americans Hate Welfare,* 102–32.

112. See Schaefer, "Reconsidering *Harvest of Shame*," 127.

CHAPTER 2: INVESTIGATING THE COLD WAR

1. *Congressional Record,* 5 June 1961, 9497–98.

2. Friendly, *Due to Circumstances,* 133.

3. Joseph S. Tulchin, "The Promise of Progress: U.S. Relations with Latin America during the Administration of Lyndon B. Johnson," in *Lyndon Johnson Confronts the World: American Foreign Policy, 1963–1968,* ed. Warren I. Cohen and Nancy Bernkopf Tucker (Cambridge: Cambridge University Press, 1994), 235.

4. Friendly, *Due to Circumstances,* 133–34.

5. Edward Jay Epstein, *Between Fact and Fiction: The Problem of Journalism* (New York: Vintage, 1975), 213–14.

6. Peter Wyden, *Wall: The Inside Story of Divided Berlin* (New York: Simon and Schuster, 1989), 290–91.

7. Ibid., 291. This account of the origins of the tunnel draws also on Robert E. Kintner, *Broadcasting and the News* (New York: Harper and Row, 1965), 36–38; and Frank, *Out of Thin Air,* 192–212.

8. Kintner, *Broadcasting and the News,* 36; Wyden, *Wall,* 290–91.

9. This account of the administration's public policy draws on Frank Costigliola, "The Pursuit of Atlantic Community: Nuclear Arms, Dollars, and Berlin," in *Kennedy's Quest for Victory: American Foreign Policy, 1961–1963,* ed. Thomas G. Paterson (New York: Oxford University Press, 1989), 24–56; Thomas Alan Schwartz, "Victories and Defeats in the Long Twilight Struggle: The United States and Western Europe in the 1960s," in *The Diplomacy of the Crucial Decade: American Foreign Relations during the 1960s,* ed. Diane B. Kunz (New York: Columbia University Press, 1994), 115–48; Thomas W. Zeiler, *Dean Rusk: Defending the American Mission Abroad* (Wilmington, Del.: SR Books, 2000), 45–49.

10. Schwartz, "Victories and Defeats," 124.

11. Costigliola, "The Pursuit of Atlantic Community," 41.

12. Ibid., 41.

13. Josephine Brain, "Dealing with De Gaulle," in Mark J. White, *Kennedy: The New Frontier Revisited* (New York: New York University Press, 1998), 169.

14. Georg Schild, "The Berlin Crisis," in Mark J. White, *Kennedy: The New Frontier Revisited* (New York: New York University Press, 1998), 122.

15. Nancy E. Bernhard, *U.S. Television News and Cold War Propaganda, 1947–1960* (Cambridge: Cambridge University Press, 1999), 122–25.

16. Frank, *Out of Thin Air,* 197–98.

17. Ibid., 194.

18. Ibid., 201, 204.

19. Kintner, *Broadcasting and the News,* 35, 37.

20. Wyden, *Wall,* 293; Frank, *Out of Thin Air,* 203.

21. Frank, *Out of Thin Air,* 203.

22. Kintner, *Broadcasting and the News,* 38.

23. Frank, *Out of Thin Air,* 209–12.

24. Montague Kern, Patricia W. Levering, and Ralph B. Levering, *The Kennedy Crises: The Press, the Presidency, and Foreign Policy* (Chapel Hill: University of North Carolina Press, 1983), 107–11, 140.

25. Lawrence Freedman, *Kennedy's Wars: Berlin, Cuba, Laos, and Vietnam* (New York: Oxford University Press, 2000), 173, 189–90.

26. The following account draws on House Committee on Interstate and Foreign Commerce, Special Subcommittee on Investigations, *Network News Documentary Practices—CBS "Project Nassau," Hearings,* 91st Cong., 2nd sess., 1970; F. Leslie Smith, "The Selling of the First Amendment: An Analysis of Congressional Investigations of Four CBS Television Documentary Projects" (Ph.D. diss., Florida State University, 1972), 146–205; Leonard, *In the Storm,* 156–58.

27. The description of the report here is based on House Committee on Interstate and Foreign Commerce, *Network News Documentary Practices,* 45–57.

28. Paul Farmer, *The Uses of Haiti* (Monroe, Maine: Common Courage Press, 1994), 109.

29. Warren Hinckle and William W. Turner, *The Fish Is Red: The Story of the Secret War against Castro* (New York: Harper and Row, 1981), 249, 238.

30. George Thayer, *The War Business: The International Trade in Armaments* (New York: Simon and Schuster, 1969), 154.

31. House Committee on Interstate and Foreign Commerce, *Network News Documentary Practices,* 37–39. In response to my Freedom of Information Act requests, the CIA denied access on grounds of national security, and the State Department and Customs Bureau denied having any relevant records.

32. Hinckle and Turner, *The Fish Is Red,* 258.

33. House Committee on Interstate and Foreign Commerce, *Network News Documentary Practices,* 67–73.

34. Ibid., 9–10.

35. Ibid., 84.

36. Hinckle and Turner, *The Fish Is Red,* 258.

37. House Committee on Interstate and Foreign Commerce, *Network News Documentary Practices,* 6.

38. Ibid., 74–84.

39. Ibid., 82.

40. Ibid., 151.

41. The discussion of CBS's reply and all quotes in this paragraph are taken from Richard S. Salant to Harley O. Staggers, 8 May 1970, in Richard S. Salant Papers, New Canaan Public Library, New Canaan, Conn.

42. The discussion in this paragraph is based on "Response to Congressman Staggers on CBS 'Project Nassau,'" FCC press release, 21 January 1972, obtained from the FCC.

43. Frank, *Out of Thin Air,* 202.

44. See, for example, William J. Small, *Political Power and the Press* (New York: W. W. Norton, 1972), 311–72; Smith, "CBS Reports: The Selling of the Pentagon," 200–210; William E. Porter, *Assault on the Media: The Nixon Years* (Ann Arbor: University of Michigan Press, 1976), 114–26; Hammond, *The Image Decade,* 175–85; Garth S. Jowett, "The Selling of the Pentagon: Television Confronts the First Amendment," in *American History, American Television,* ed. John E. O'Connor (New York: Frederick Ungar, 1983), 256–78.

45. On foreign policy leaders' opposition to the war, see Louise T. Brown, *War and Aftermath in Vietnam* (London: Routledge, 1991), 64, 111. On corporate opposition to the war for generating inflation and undermining confidence in American goods abroad, see Thomas R. Dye, *Who's Running America,* 4th ed. (Englewood Cliffs, N.J.: Prentice-Hall, 1986), 254–55.

46. The hawkish frame is drawn from Peter Braestrup, *Big Story: How the American Press and Television Reported and Interpreted the Crisis of Tet 1968 in Vietnam and Washington,* abridged ed. (Novato, Calif.: Presidio, 1994), 465–507; Peter B. Clark, *The Opinion Machine: Intellectuals, the Mass Media, and American Government* (Chicago: Rand McNally, 1974); Guenter Lewy, *America in Vietnam* (New York: Oxford University Press, 1978); and Claudia Springer, "Military Propaganda: Defense Department Films from World War II and Vietnam," in *The Vietnam War and American Culture,* ed. John Carlos Rowe and Rick Berg (New York: Columbia University Press, 1991), 95–114.

47. I draw the radical frame from Gabriel Kolko, *Anatomy of a War: Vietnam, the United States, and the Modern Historical Experience* (New York: Pantheon, 1985); and Mary Susannah Robins, ed., *Against the War: Writings by Activists* (Syracuse, N.Y.: Syracuse University Press, 1999).

48. The mainstream frame is discussed in William C. Berman, *William Fulbright and the Vietnam War: The Dissent of a Political Realist* (Kent, Ohio: Kent State University Press, 1988); Todd Gitlin, *The Whole World Is Watching* (Berkeley: University of California Press, 1980), 274; and Hallin, *The "Uncensored War,"* 183, 201–4, 207.

49. Berman, *William Fulbright,* 85.

50. Gitlin, *The Whole World Is Watching,* 205–17; Hallin, *The "Uncensored War,"* 163–80; Epstein, *Between Fact and Fiction,* 210–32.

51. In the early 1970s, Pentagon journalists continued to define "enterprise reporting" as seeking information from congressional sources to supplement Defense Department press releases, underscoring the importance of House and Senate dissent. See Juergen Arthur Heise, *Minimum Disclosure: How the Pentagon Manipulates the News* (New York: W. W. Norton and Co., 1979), 176.

52. Gitlin, *The Whole World Is Watching,* 274.

53. Hallin, *The "Uncensored War,"* 183, 201–4, 207.

54. Robert M. Entman and David L. Paletz, "The War in Southeast Asia: Tunnel Vision on Television," in *Television Coverage of International Affairs,* ed. William Adams (Norwood, N.J.: Ablex, 1982), 183.

55. Thomas M. McNulty, "Vietnam Specials: Policy and Content," *Journal of Communication* 25 (1975): 177–85.

56. Jongsoo Lee, "Network Television Documentaries about the Vietnam War: CBS Documentaries from 1964 to 1984 in a Changing Historical Context" (Ph.D. diss., University of Minnesota, 1994), 274–77. The exceptional reports included *Morley Safer's Vietnam* (CBS, 1967), which described the war as a stalemate at the same time General William Westmoreland was promising that victory was in sight. Safer explored some of the war's uglier aspects, showing the movement of body bags through the Than San Nhut airport and interviews with laughing fighter pilots, who described killing North Vietnamese as comparable to target practice on wooden dummies: "You just thumb off a couple pair of rockets—like they weren't people at all." A two-part report, *The POWs: Pawns of War* (CBS, 1971) examined the suffering of American prisoners of war, giving families of POWs and congressional critics ample time to express mistrust of the Vietnamization policy (Lee, "Network Television Doumentaries," 275).

57. Adam Yarmolinsky, *The Military Establishment* (New York: Harper and Row, 1971).

58. Peter Davis, phone interview with author, 19 May 1995.

59. The analysis in this paragraph is indebted to Jimmie N. Rogers and Theodore Clevenger Jr., "'The Selling of the Pentagon': Was CBS the Fulbright Propaganda Machine?" *Quarterly Journal of Speech* 57 (1971): 266–73.

60. Ironically, Secretary of Defense Robert McNamara had enacted the ban not because he feared military personnel propagandized the public but in an attempt to centralize control over releasing information. Congressional opponents objected that the policy precluded military personnel from testifying before them and muzzled public dissent within the services. See Heise, *Minimum Disclosure,* 97–98.

61. Braestrup, *Big Story,* 475–76.

62. J. William Fulbright, *The Pentagon Propaganda Machine* (New York: Liveright, 1970), 151.

63. Ibid., 14–15, 38, 82–83, 130, 133, 138, 147, 150.

64. Ibid., 13–16, 141–42.

65. Ibid., 144.

66. Davis, phone interview.

67. CBS did not mention the cost of television advertising for military recruiting, which had netted the network over $1.2 million in the prior year (Robert Sherrill, "The Happy Ending (Maybe) of the 'The Selling of the Pentagon,'" *New York Times Magazine,* 16 May 1971, 26). The report did not discuss CBS president Frank Stanton's friendship with President Johnson and his occasional expression of the president's displeasure with CBS News coverage to the news division (Gitlin, *The Whole World Is Watching,* 276). Stanton was also chairman of the board of trustees of the Rand Corporation, one of the largest military think tanks at the time, and sat on the United States Information Agency's advisory board. One of the propaganda films shown in *The Selling of the Pentagon* was produced by CBS Films, which was not noted (Small, *Political Power,* 316–17). The report did not mention that its executive producer,

Perry Wolff, had collaborated with the Air Force to produce *Air Power,* one of the longest-running documentary series of the 1950s (this was CBS's answer to the NBC-Navy series, *Victory at Sea*). The documentary did not discuss widespread media cooperation with the Central Intelligence Agency at least until the early 1960s. News organizations, including CBS, allowed CIA agents to monitor incoming reports from overseas correspondents before they were broadcast, provided outtakes and blowups of news film from political protests, and allowed returning foreign correspondents to debrief with the CIA. Several previous CBS employees had likely been on the CIA payroll, although the network denied knowledge of this (Robert B. Sims, *The Pentagon Reporters* [Washington, D.C.: National Defense University Press, 1983], 110–12). Sims, former deputy chief of information for the Navy, notes that many previous CBS documentaries were "considered balanced and objective by the Pentagon" (112). Writing in the early 1980s, he suggests that ill will generated by *Selling* still lingered in the Defense Department.

68. Fulbright, *Pentagon Propaganda Machine,* 151.

69. Producer Peter Davis went on to direct *Hearts and Minds,* one of the most powerful documentaries critical of the American war in Vietnam, which included experiences of the war from the other side. It is telling that he had to leave the network system to make the independent film.

70. Hallin, *The "Uncensored War,"* 190.

71. See, for example, Marilyn Lashner, *The Chilling Effect in TV News* (New York: Praeger, 1984).

72. Lashner, *The Chilling Effect,* and Porter, *Assault on the Media,* provide the best summaries.

73. Although CBS chairman William S. Paley contributed money to the Nixon campaign in 1968, Paley favored the East Coast Rockefeller wing of the party; subsequently, Nixon denied Paley a coveted ambassadorship to London (Sally Bedell-Smith, *In All His Glory: The Life of William S. Paley, the Legendary Tycoon and His Brilliant Circle* [New York: Simon and Schuster, 1990], 471–79). At a May 1971 dinner of the White House Correspondents Association, Nixon joked, "The vice-president has three television sets in his bedroom. The first is turned to ABC. The second is turned to NBC. The third one he has standing in the corner" (Small, *Political Power,* 332). Nixon aide Charles Colson saw CBS as most supportive of congressional Democrats' calls for a right of response to televised presidential addresses, a right the administration opposed. In April 1971, Nixon aide John Ehrlichman tried to persuade CBS to remove Dan Rather from his post as White House correspondent, calling him a "hatchet man" (Porter, *Assault on the Media,* 72, 112).

74. Martin Mayer, "Freedom of the Press Can Be a Matter of Self-Interested Definition," *Harper's,* December 1971, 40–53.

75. Martin Mayer, *About Television* (New York: Harper and Row, 1972), 256.

76. Undated letter from Daniel Z. Henkin to CBS affiliates. Obtained by the author through a Freedom of Information Act request.

77. Fred Powledge, *The Engineering of Restraint: The Nixon Administration and the Press* (Washington, D.C.: Public Affairs Press/American Civil Liberties Union, 1971), 25.

78. Jerry Friedheim to Jeb Magruder, 24 February 1971, EX FG 13, 1 April 1971–30 April 1971; box 2; WHCF, SF, NPM.

79. House Committee on Interstate and Foreign Commerce, Special Subcommittee on Investigations, *Hearings: Subpoenaed Material Re Certain TV News Documentary Programs,* 92nd Cong., 2nd sess., 1971, 57.

80. David Wise, *The Politics of Lying* (New York: Random House, 1973), 211.

81. The original transcript of the interviews can be found in House Committee on Interstate and Foreign Commerce, Special Subcommittee on Investigations, *Proceeding against Frank Stanton and the Columbia Broadcasting System,* 92nd Cong., 2nd sess., 1971, 130–33.

82. House Committee on Interstate and Foreign Commerce, *Hearings,* 12.

83. Colonel McNeil's edited comments were as follows, with slashes separating out-of-sequence sentences and underlining denoting the two Phouma quotes: "Well, now we're coming to the heart of the problem—Vietnam. / Now the Chinese have clearly and repeatedly stated that their land [Laos] is next on their list after Vietnam. / If South Vietnam becomes communist it will be difficult for Laos to exist. / The same goes for Cambodia, and all the other countries of Southeast Asia. / I think if the communists were to win in South Vietnam, the record in the North—what happened in Tet of '68—makes it clear there would be a bloodbath in store for a lot of the population of the South. / The United States is still going to remain an Asian power."

84. The minority report of the House Commerce Committee agreed the editing was true to McNeil's statements as well. House Committee on Interstate and Foreign Commerce, *Proceeding against Frank Stanton,* 206–41.

85. Congressman William Springer (R-Ill.), for example, repeatedly cited a recent speech by British journalist Malcolm Muggeridge excoriating television for covering demonstrations that "bearded academics and lib-females" staged for the cameras. "Does this give you some idea of what we are talking about in this investigation?" Springer asked (House Committee on Interstate and Foreign Commerce, *Hearings,* 50). Since CBS was not accused of staging any scenes in this report, and no demonstrations were shown, Springer's query was obviously related to the program's political content. Indeed, if representatives such as Springer were truly concerned in the abstract about news staging and its potential to mislead citizens, they would have investigated the Pentagon as well, given CBS's revelations of South Vietnamese patrols staged for CBS by Defense Department officials.

86. "CBS Legal Opinion," reprinted in House Committee on Interstate and Foreign Commerce, *Proceeding against Frank Stanton,* 26.

87. Steve Knoll, "Gov't Grab of TV News 'Notes,'" *Variety,* 20 May 1968, 1, 40; Steve Knoll, "CBS and NBC Ducked Confrontation with Gov't and Broke Own Policies in Yielding Out-Takes sans Subpoenas," *Variety,* 11 December 1968, 37; Morry Roth, "Chicago's Universal Subpoena," *Variety,* 19 November 1969, 31.

88. Small, *Political Power,* 323.

89. Spiro Agnew, untitled speech to Middlesex Club, Boston, Mass., 18 March 1971, series 3, subseries 7, box 5, Spiro T. Agnew Papers, Special Collections, UMCP.

90. Cited in Lester A. Sobel, *Media Controversies* (New York: Facts on File, 1981), 155.

91. Henry Kissinger to Melvin Laird, 13 March 1971. Obtained by the author through a Freedom of Information Act request.

92. Herbert G. Klein, *Making It Perfectly Clear* (Garden City, N.Y.: Doubleday and Co., 1980), 210.

93. Cited in Sobel, *Media Controversies*, 42.

94. News Summary, April 1971, Annotated News Summaries, April 1971, box 33, POF, NPM.

95. John Scali to President Nixon, 19 May 1971, box 14, WHSF, SMOF, Ron Ziegler, NPM.

96. Mort Allin to H. R. Haldeman, 25 February 1971, Chronological Files, January 1971–December 1971, box 1, WHSF, SMOF, Patrick J. Buchanan, NPM.

97. Charles Colson to Ron Ziegler, 16 March 1971, [CF] PR 16-1, Broadcasts-Telecasts (1971–74), box 54, WHSF, Central Files, Confidential Files, NPM.

98. Charles Colson to George Bell, 16 March 1971, Chronological Files, March 1971, box 128, WHSF, SMOF, Charles Colson, NPM (hereafter referred to as "Colson files").

99. Charles Colson to Van Shumway, 29 April 1971, FCC, box 64, Colson files.

100. "Broadcast License: CBS Has Forfeited Access to the Nation's Airwaves," *Barron's National and Financial Weekly*, 29 March 1971, cited in *Congressional Record*, 30 March 1971, 8616–18.

101. Charles Colson to President Nixon, 2 April 1971, Misc. Staff Memos, box 14, Colson files.

102. *Congressional Record*, 16 February 1972, 1232–36.

103. Reed Irvine, "The Selling of 'The Selling of the Pentagon,'" *National Review* 23 (1971): 857–58.

104. Henry Geller, general counsel to FCC, oral history conducted by James L. Baughman, Oral History Research Office, Columbia University, 30 June 1981, 57; Ray, *FCC*, 9–11.

105. Nicholas Johnson, "A Defense of TV vs. White House," *Washington Post*, 28 March 1971, B1, B4.

106. Joseph C. Spear, *Presidents and the Press* (Cambridge, Mass.: MIT Press, 1984), 160.

107. Jerry Landauer, "House Panel Chairman Promises Full Battle against CBS if It Defies Subpoena on Film," *Wall Street Journal*, 18 June 1971, 30.

108. *In Re Complaint Concerning the CBS Program "The Selling of the Pentagon,"* 30 FCC 2d 150 (1971).

109. Reprinted in *Congressional Record*, 12 July 1971, 6953. William J. Small, head of the network's Washington bureau, correspondent Daniel Schorr, and other CBS employees protested the new regulations as caving in to government power (Small, *Political Power*, 358). A year after the controversy, Stanton admitted in a speech to the National Association of Broadcasters that the new standards grew out of a "study" of *The Selling of the Pentagon* (Frank Stanton, "National Association of Broadcasters, Remarks of Frank Stanton," 11 April 1972, in Columbia Broadcasting System, box 336, Emmanuel Celler Papers, Manuscript Division, LOC).

110. Small, *Political Power*, 312. The three were Representative Michael J. Harrington (D-Mass.), Senator William Proxmire (D-Wis.), and Senator Thomas Eagleton (D-Mo.).

111. Opinion of Representative Robert O. Tiernan, in House Committee on Interstate and Foreign Commerce, *Proceeding against Frank Stanton*, 255–62.

112. See Schorr, *Clearing the Air*, 47–49; David Halberstam, *The Powers That Be* (New York: Knopf, 1979), 656.

113. Henry Cashen to Charles Colson, 9 July 1971, CBS, box 46, Colson files.

114. Charles Colson to H. R. Haldeman, 20 July 1971, CBS, box 46, Colson files.

115. Charles Colson to H. R. Haldeman, 22 July 1971, Meetings/Phone Conversations with President, box 15, Colson files. In this memo, Colson noted that the *CBS Evening News* featured Nixon's China initiative more heavily and favorably than other networks and that CBS had not missed an administration news event since the vote. CBS was the only network to show up at an administration press conference on the Veterans Administration's drug program and Jobs for Veterans program. "There was no news in the press conference," Colson noted, "it was a pure 'puff' job. Cronkite's report was a pure 'puff' job. Neither of the other networks carried it and it was not really that much of a news story." Yet Colson also pointed to a report on a possible personnel shake-up at CBS, claiming that he was certain that CBS News president Richard Salant would be replaced, which did not happen.

116. See especially Corydon B. Dunham, *Fighting for the First Amendment: Stanton of CBS vs. Congress and the Nixon White House* (Wesport, Conn.: Praeger, 1997). The author was NBC's general counsel during the *Pensions* case in which the network challenged the fairness doctrine, discussed in chapter 6.

117. Colson concluded his account of the July 1971 meeting with Stanton by saying: "I don't expect great things. Anything we will gain will be a plus" (Charles Colson to H. R. Haldeman, 20 July 1971, CBS, box 46, Colson files). After the 1972 election, Colson told Stanton that in revenge for the network's Watergate reporting, "We will bring you to your knees in Wall Street and Madison Avenue. . . . We'll break your network" (Spear, *Presidents and the Press*, 150).

118. Charles Colson to H. R. Haldeman, 14 July 1971, Meetings/Phone Conversations with President, box 15, Colson files.

119. See Mayer, "Freedom of the Press," 40–53.

120. Examples of the many letters CBS gathered from broadcasters and broadcast organizations expressing these fears to Congress can be found in Columbia Broadcasting System, box 336, Emmanuel Celler Papers, Manuscript Division, LOC.

121. Small, *Political Power*, 367–68.

122. Robert Sherrill, "C.B.S. and Congress: The Shelling of the Pentagon," *New York Times*, 18 July 1971, sec. 4, 3.

123. The CBS legal opinion is reprinted in House Committee on Interstate and Foreign Commerce, *Hearings*, 361–66; the minority report is reprinted in House Committee on Interstate and Foreign Commerce, *Proceeding against Frank Stanton*, 206–41; the House debate is in the *Congressional Record*, 13 July 1971, 24720–54.

124. In fact, the minority report found that the "physical and technical limitations of the medium and the questionable practices of the past may force Congress at some future date to formulate a more effective national policy in this area" (House Committee on Interstate and Foreign Commerce, *Proceeding against Frank Stanton*, 237).

125. *Congressional Record*, 13 July 1971, 24748.

126. Ibid., 24727. See also the remarks of Joe Waggoner Jr. (D-La.), 24922–23.

127. Ibid., 24733–36, 24748–49.

128. Representative Gilbert Gude to Secretary of Defense Melvin R. Laird, 1 March 1971; Representative Glenn M. Anderson to Melvin R. Laird, 24 April 1971. Obtained by the author through Freedom of Information Act requests.

129. "Pentagon's Civilian Tour Cost $80,000," *Chicago Tribune*, 12 July 1971, sec. 1, 16.

130. Heise, *Minimum Disclosure*, 54.

131. Jeff Blyskal and Marie Blyskal, *PR: How the Public Relations Industry Writes the News* (New York: Morrow, 1985), 9.

132. Small, *Political Power,* 386.

133. Heise, *Minimum Disclosure,* 85.

134. *Branzburg v. Hayes,* 408 U.S. 665 (1972). However, in the years since, lower courts and state legislatures have established a qualified First Amendment privilege to withhold notes, outtakes, and other materials in some circumstances.

135. "Statement by William J. Small," reprinted in *Congressional Record,* 2 July 1971, 24617–18.

136. Alliane Horne Willis, "An Analysis of the Controversy Surrounding 'The Selling of the Pentagon,'" (Ph.D. diss., Emory University, 1987), 149.

137. Davis, phone interview.

138. Sanford J. Ungar, *The Papers and the Papers* (New York: E. P. Dutton and Co., 1972), 129. Of course, another possible reason why CBS avoided the Pentagon Papers is that Stanton was chairman of the board of the Rand Corporation, the military think tank where Ellsberg had violated national security protocol by copying the secret documents. Rand officials feared they would be indicted along with Ellsberg after he was identified as the source of the papers. Stanton, in a meeting with Colson around the time of the contempt hearings, attempted to shift the blame from Rand to the FBI, which had dropped an investigation of Ellsberg back in 1969. Stanton, who took part in the discussions at CBS about whether or not to accept the papers, must have feared that if the network took them, it would give the administration more reason to retaliate against him as CBS president and Rand chairman.

CHAPTER 3: INVESTIGATING BUSINESS AND CONSUMERISM

1. Ronald Inglehart and Scott Flanigan, "Value Change in Industrial Societies," *American Political Science Review* 81 (1987): 1289–1319; Samuel P. Hays, *Beauty, Truth, and Permanence: Environmental Politics in the U.S.* (New York: Columbia University Press, 1987); Robert Paehlke, *Environmentalism and the Future of Progressive Politics* (New Haven: Yale University Press, 1989).

2. Mark V. Nadel, *The Politics of Consumer Protection* (New York: Bobbs-Merrill, 1971), 37–40.

3. Ibid., 31–44.

4. Ibid., 163.

5. *Report of the National Commission on Civil Disorders* (New York: Bantam Books, 1968), 274–77.

6. David L. Rados, "Product Liability: Tougher Ground Rules," in *Consumerism: Viewpoints from Business, Government, and the Public Interest,* ed. Ralph M. Gaedeke and Warren W. Etcheson (San Francisco: Canfield Press, 1972), 259–71.

7. Michael Pertschuk, *Revolt against Regulation: The Rise and Pause of the Consumer Movement* (Berkeley: University of California Press, 1982), 52, 84.

8. The classic study of how poor consumers pay more in relative and absolute terms for credit and merchandise is David Caplowitz, *The Poor Pay More: Consumer Practices of Low Income Families* (New York: Free Press, 1963).

9. Nadel, *Politics of Consumer Protection,* 198.

10. Pertschuk, *Revolt against Regulation*, 33–34. See also 30, 35–36, where Pertschuk attests to the general picture of consumer advocates and the media offered here.

11. The account of expanded government regulation in this paragraph draws on Richard B. DuBoff, *Accumulation and Power: An Economic History of the United States* (Armonk, N.Y.: M. E. Sharpe, 1989), 107; Michael Schudson, *The Power of News* (Cambridge, Mass.: Harvard University Press, 1995), 183–85; Paletz and Entman, *Media Power Politics*, 133–34.

12. The discussion in this paragraph is indebted to Peter Dreier, "Capitalists vs. the Media: An Analysis of an Ideological Mobilization among Business Leaders," *Media, Culture, and Society* 4 (1982): 111–32; and Mark Green, "How Business Sways the Media," in *Business and the Media*, ed. Craig E. Aronoff (Santa Monica, Calif.: Goodyear Publishing, 1979), 55–60. On the rise of right-wing think-tank sources as news sources, see Lawrence C. Soley, *The News Shapers: The Sources Who Explain the News* (Westport, Conn.: Praeger, 1992), 47–64.

13. Schudson, *Power of News*, 183.

14. Robert P. Keim, "Economic Understanding: A Challenge to the Media," in *Business and the Media*, ed. Craig E. Aronoff (Santa Monica, Calif.: Goodyear Publishing, 1979), 71.

15. Louis Wolf, "Accuracy in Media Rewrites News and History," *Covert Action Information Bulletin* (Spring 1984): 25–26. Information on AIM's contributors, officers, and advisors from Wolf; House Committee on Banking, Currency, and Housing, Subcommittee on Domestic Monetary Policy, *Audit of the Federal Reserve*, 94th Cong., 1st sess., 1975; Daniel Epstein, "The Aims of AIM: A Critical Look at One of the Press Critics," *American Society of Newspaper Editors Bulletin* (March 1974), reprinted in Congress, *Audit*, 36–42; Bob Kasen, Institute for American Democracy memo, reprinted in Congress, *Audit*, 58–62.

16. AIM officers and directors included Executive Secretary Abraham Kalish, a former writer with the United States Information Agency and a retired teacher of military communications at the Defense Intelligence School; Murray Baron, AIM's president after 1976, who was also a trustee of the anticommunist human rights group Freedom House, a member the CIA-funded Citizens Committee for a Free Cuba and Citizens Committee for Peace with Freedom in Vietnam, and member of the Committee of One Million (a major defense lobby); and Bernard Yoh, AIM cofounder and communications director after 1974, an advisor in counterinsurgency techniques to South Vietnamese president Ngo Dinh Diem, and lecturer at the Air War College at Alabama on counterinsurgency and psychological warfare. Advisory board members included Elbridge Durbrow, who had been a State Department official and ambassador to Vietnam from 1957 to 1961; Frank Newton Trager, a former National War College professor and head of the National Strategy Information Center, which performed classified research for the Pentagon and CIA; Admiral Thomas H. Moorer, retired, former Chief of Naval Operations and Joint Chiefs of Staff chairman during the Nixon years; Marine Corps General Lewis W. Walt, retired, who appeared in *The Selling of the Pentagon* as a leading speaker on behalf of the Vietnam War effort; and Rear Admiral William Chamberlain Mott, retired, former special assistant to the Joint Chiefs of Staff chairman.

17. Friendly, *Due to Circumstances*, 132–34; Albin Krebs, "A.M.A. Asks Study on Documentary," *New York Times*, 4 May 1973, 75.

18. This picture of consumerist ideology is a composite drawn from Philip G. Schrag, "Consumer Rights," in *Consumerism: Search for the Public Interest,* 2nd ed., ed. David S. Aaker and George S. Day (New York: Free Press, 1974), 361–74; Ralph Nader, "The Great American Gyp," *New York Review of Books* (21 November 1968): 27–34; and Lucy Black Creighton, *Pretenders to the Throne: The Consumer Movement in the United States* (Lexington, Mass.: Lexington Books, 1976), 66–67.

19. National Commission on Product Safety, "Perspective on Product Safety," in *Consumerism: Viewpoints from Business, Government, and the Public Interest,* ed. Ralph M. Gaedeke and Warren W. Etcheson (San Francisco: Canfield Press, 1972), 119.

20. *Consumer Advisory Council, First Report,* Executive Office of the President (Washington, D.C.: U.S. Government Printing Office, 1963), 5–8.

21. This composite sketch of business's ideology is based on Creighton, *Pretenders to the Throne,* 83–95; Ralph K. Winter, *The Consumer Advocate versus the Consumer* (Washington, D.C.: American Enterprise Institute, 1972), 1–16; Frank E. McLaughlin, "Problems Encountered by the President's Committee on Consumer Interests," in *Consumerism: Viewpoints from Business, Government, and the Public Interest,* ed. Ralph M. Gaedeke and Warren W. Etcheson (San Francisco: Canfield Press, 1972), 220–26; Ralph M. Gaedeke, "What Business, Government, and Consumer Spokesmen Think about Consumerism," in *Consumerism: Viewpoints from Business, Government, and the Public Interest,* ed. Ralph M. Gaedeke and Warren W. Etcheson (San Francisco: Canfield Press, 1972), 97; and Chamber of Commerce of the United States, "Business-Consumer Relations," in *Consumerism: Viewpoints from Business, Government, and the Public Interest,* ed. Ralph M. Gaedeke and Warren W. Etcheson (San Francisco: Canfield Press, 1972), 348–51.

22. See Daniel Bell, *The Coming of Post-Industrial Society* (New York: Basic Books, 1976).

23. Irving Kristol, "Business and the New Class," *Wall Street Journal,* 19 May 1975, 8.

24. Christopher Elias, *The Dollar Barons* (New York: MacMillan Publishing Co., 1973), 94–96.

25. Nancy Beck Young, *Wright Patman: Populism, Liberalism, and the American Dream* (Dallas: Southern Methodist University Press, 2000), 248–49.

26. Young, *Wright Patman,* 375, n. 29.

27. Homer Kripke, "Gesture and Reality in Consumer Credit Reform," *New York University Law Review* 44 (1969): 1–13, 51–52.

28. Federal Trade Commission, *Economic Report on Installment Credit and Retail Sales Practices of District of Columbia Retailers* (Washington, D.C.: U.S. Government Printing Office, 1968), ix–xvi, 1–24.

29. Creighton, *Pretenders to the Throne,* 45–49; Jonathan Kwitny, "The Money-Lenders," in *Hot War on the Consumer,* ed. David Sanford (New York: Pitman Publishing Co.), 141–45.

30. Schrag, "Consumer Rights," 370–71.

31. Ronald G. Shafer, "Bills to Let Customers Join to Sue Companies Are Mulled by Congress," in *Consumerism: The Eternal Triangle,* ed. Barbara B. Murray (Pacific Palisades, Calif.: Goodyear Publishing Co.), 376; *Report of the ABA Commission to*

Study the Federal Trade Commission (Washington, D.C.: Bureau of National Affairs, 1969), 54–55.

32. Nader, "Great American Gyp," 51.

33. Frederick D. Sturdivant, "Better Deal for Ghetto Shoppers," in *Consumerism: Search for the Public Interest*, ed. David S. Aaker and George S. Day (New York: Free Press, 1971), 403.

34. Young, *Wright Patman*, 249–50.

35. James C. Kirby Jr., *Congress and the Public Trust* (New York: Atheneum, 1970), 59.

36. Ibid., v–vi.

37. Young, *Wright Patman*, 251, 267–68.

38. Kirby, *Congress and the Public Trust*, 233–42.

39. *Congressional Record*, 19 December 1970, 42653–60.

40. *Congressional Record*, 16 November 1970, 37426; for Patman's letters to the networks, see 3724–26.

41. James Day, *The Vanishing Vision: The Inside Story of Public Television* (Berkeley: University of California Press, 1995), 178–79.

42. Jack Gould, "TV Stations Alerted on Bank Program," *New York Times,* 9 November 1970, 82; Day, *Vanishing Vision*, 179.

43. John Witherspoon and Roselle Kovitz, *The History of Public Broadcasting* (Washington, D.C.: Current, 1987), 41.

44. Ralph Engelman, *Public Radio and Television in America: A Political History* (Thousand Oaks, Calif.: Sage, 1996), 168.

45. James Ledbetter, *Made Possible By . . . : The Death of Public Broadcasting in the United States* (New York: Verso), 68.

46. Witherspoon and Kovitz, *History of Public Broadcasting*, 39, 40.

47. Young, *Wright Patman*, 221, 262–66, 267.

48. Calvin Bradford and Gale Cincotta, "The Legacy, the Promise, and the Unfinished Agenda," in *From Redlining to Reinvestment*, ed. Gregory D. Squires (Philadelphia: Temple University Press, 1992), 251–52.

49. Gregory D. Squires, "Community Reinvestment: An Emerging Social Movement," in *From Redlining to Reinvestment*, ed. Gregory D. Squires (Philadelphia: Temple University Press, 1992), 9.

50. Interview with Morton Silverstein in Alan Rosenthal, *The Documentary Conscience: A Casebook in Filmmaking* (Berkeley: University of California Press, 1980), 103.

51. Kirby, *Congress and the Public Trust*, xxi.

52. Merton C. Bernstein, *The Future of Private Pensions* (New York: Free Press of Glencoe, 1964), 10.

53. William C. Greenough and Francis P. King, *Pension Plans and Public Policy* (New York: Columbia University Press, 1976), 109.

54. Ralph Nader and Kate Blackwell, *You and Your Pension* (New York: Grossman Publishers, 1973), 16.

55. William Graebner, *A History of Retirement: The Meaning and Function of an American Institution, 1885–1978* (New Haven: Yale University Press, 1980), 217–18.

56. Greenough and King, *Pension Plans*, 43.

57. Graebner, *History of Retirement*, 220–21.

58. Senator Richard Schweiker, using what he called a "conservative estimate," estimated the proportion of people who expected pensions but would not receive them to be at least 30 percent to 50 percent in the *Congressional Record*, 3 October 1972, 33323. Senator Javits offered the 90 percent estimate in several hearings, cited in Nader and Blackwell, *You and Your Pension*, 4.

59. Peter Henle and Raymond Schmitt, "Pension Reform: The Long, Hard Road to Enactment," *Monthly Labor Review*, November 1974, 3–12.

60. Cited in Ben Bagdikian, "Pensions: The FCC's Dangerous Decision against NBC," *Columbia Journalism Review*, March–April 1974, 16.

61. Cited in *Accuracy in Media, Inc.*, 44 FCC 2d 1027, 1028 (1973).

62. Friendly, *Good Guys*, 143.

63. See Senate Committee on Labor and Human Resources, Subcommittee on Labor, *Hearings: Private Welfare and Pension Plan Study, 1971*, parts 1 and 2, 92nd Cong., 1st sess., 1971; Senate Committee on Labor and Human Resources, Subcommittee on Labor, *Hearings: Private Welfare and Pension Plan Study, 1972*, part 2, 92nd Cong., 2nd sess., 1972; Senate Committee on Labor and Human Resources, Subcommittee on Labor, *Hearings: Retirement Income Security for Employees Act, 1972*, part 2, 92nd Cong., 2nd sess., 1972.

64. Senate Committee on Labor and Human Resources, Subcommittee on Labor, *Hearings: Private Welfare and Pension Plan Legislation*, 91st Cong., 2nd sess., 1970; Senate Committee on Labor and Human Resources, Subcommittee on Labor, *Hearings: United Mine Workers Election*, 91st Cong., 2nd sess., 1970; Committee on Labor and Human Resources, Subcommittee on Labor, *Hearings: United Mine Workers Welfare and Retirement Fund*, 91st Cong., 2nd sess., 1970. Press investigations of the Teamsters included an *Oakland Tribune* series by Jeff Morgan and Gene Ayres in September 1969 and a July 1970 Associated Press series by Dick Barnes. A June 1971 *60 Minutes* segment had treated pension plans critically as had many other print reports in the years leading up to NBC's broadcast.

65. Charles Culhane, "Labor Report: Industry, Labor Push Conflicting Approaches to Pension Legislation as Congress Nears Action," *National Journal* (9 September 1972): 1423–25. Arguments against the bill are in American Enterprise Institute, *The Williams-Javits Pension Reform Proposal* (Washington, D.C.: AEI, 1973). Union leaders who opposed this plan were mainly those that exercised more control over managing plans and did not want to relinquish it, most notably the Teamsters and Mine Workers, whose plans were under investigation for corruption.

66. Nader and Blackwell, *You and Your Pension*, 117–20.

67. "Remarks by Ralph Nader before the Sixth Annual Conference on Employee Benefits," New York City, 24 May 1972, reprinted in Nader and Blackwell, *You and Your Pension*, 158–68.

68. Cited in ibid., 122–23.

69. For example, a typical press release issued by Senator Williams's office summed up the deficiencies of pensions as "related to inadequate or nonexistent vesting; underfunding; lack of portability provisions; lack of reinsurance of unfunded liabilities to protect employees in the event of plan termination; lack of uniform fiduciary requirements; and poor communication among employees and plan administrators." The issue

of "poor communication" referred to the opaque plan brochures, also addressed in the NBC documentary (press release, office of Harrison A. Williams Jr., 20 March 1972, folder 72-55, box 1180, Harrison A. Williams Jr. Papers, Rutgers University).

70. Nader and Blackwell, *You and Your Pension*, 75–76.

71. Graebner, *History of Retirement*, 215.

72. Ibid., 215–41.

73. Cited in ibid., 235.

74. Newman was not alone in questioning the costs of retirement. Graebner argues that as economic growth slowed in the 1970s, the institution of retirement built in the postwar years became too expensive to maintain. Thus, by the end of the decade, mandatory retirement was reconsidered at several levels of government, and the growth of public pensions and social security slowed. Graebner maintains that challenges to forced retirement were spurred less by elderly organizations fighting to free seniors from forced unemployment and more by corporate and government needs to cut benefits (Graebner, *History of Retirement*, 242–62). Similarly, the senior lobby played little role in pension reform. Judging from the slim participation in congressional hearings of groups such as the AARP, other interests (unions, employers, plan managers and investment advisors) shaped the debate far more powerfully.

75. *Accuracy in Media, Inc.*, 44 FCC 2d 958 (1973).

76. Bagdikian, "Pensions," 20.

77. *Accuracy in Media, Inc.*, 44 FCC 2d 958 (1973).

78. The account of the case in this paragraph draws on Friendly, *Good Guys*, 142–66.

79. Ibid., 150.

80. The critique of ERISA in this paragraph draws on James A. Kujaca, *The Trillion Dollar Promise: An Inside Look at Corporate Pension Money, How It's Managed, and for Whose Benefit* (Chicago: Richard D. Irwin, 1996), 21–22, 31.

81. Steve Johnson, "Why the Government's Pension Insurance System Could Dump Billions of Dollars of Debt into the Laps of Taxpayers," *San Jose Mercury News*, 23 January 2005, F1.

82. Greenough and King, *Pension Plans*, 55.

83. Ibid., x.

84. William M. O'Barr and John M. Conley, *Fortune and Folly: The Wealth and Power of Institutional Investing* (Homewood, Ill.: Business One Irwin, 1992), 161.

85. Ibid., 194–201.

CHAPTER 4: DIVIDING AND DISTRACTING THE MEDIA

1. Letters to the editor were excluded because the research questions posed were about how the print media, not the public, responded to television controversies. In each case study, newsmagazine articles were identified using the *Reader's Guide to Periodical Literature* (New York: H. W. Wilson and Co., 1968–1975). For *Hunger in America*, articles in the *New York Times, Christian Science Monitor, Los Angeles Times*, and *Wall Street Journal* were identified using the indexes to each paper for the full two-year period of 1968 and 1969. The *Chicago Tribune* and *Washington Post* were not indexed at this time, and so their television, editorial, and op-ed pages were examined during the periods when coverage of *Hunger in America* was most likely,

judging from coverage in indexed papers: 21 May to 1 August 1968 (initial airing and countercharges); 7–16 December 1968 (story breaks that FBI investigators are looking into the documentary); 20–31 May 1969 (release of the Whitten subcommittee report; documentary wins Emmy and Peabody awards); 12–24 October 1969 (FCC complaint dismissed). Based on the lack of coverage in all indexed papers outside of these dates, I am reasonably confident that there was no coverage of the controversy during these intervals in the unindexed papers. For *The Selling of the Pentagon,* print sources were surveyed from 22 February (the day before the report aired) to 23 July 1971 (ten days after the House killed the contempt citation against Frank Stanton) using the same methods as for *Hunger in America.* For *Pensions,* all articles were identified using the newspapers' indexes, starting in 1972 (when the report aired) and ending in 1975 (when the FCC dropped the fairness doctrine complaint against it).

2. NBC's Reuven Frank recalls that network executives read closely the verdicts of reviewers, especially those by Jack Gould of the *New York Times,* because executives assumed prestige press reviews were influential with elites (Frank, *Out of Thin Air,* 78, 92).

3. Robert M. Entman, "Framing U.S. Coverage of International News: Contrasts in Narratives of the KAL and Iran Air Incidents," *Journal of Communication* 41 (Autumn 1991): 8–9.

4. The unit of analysis for source citations was the sentence. Sources were considered cited when they were quoted directly or when their views were paraphrased and attributed. Excluded were clearly rhetorical attributions of opinion, such as "CBS news people say they know better than the public." Composite sources represent the citations to all individuals affiliated with an organization. For example, "CBS" includes all the citations to a producer, executive, or other employee of the network as well as statements attributed to the network as an organization ("CBS claims the documentary is accurate.")

5. When sources from the same institution took opposing points of view, they were sorted into mutually exclusive categories. For example, in the case of *The Selling of the Pentagon,* congressional sources were split into those who spoke favorably and unfavorably about the report, and those who did not express a clear view either way ("other.")

6. John J. O'Connor, "Why Broadcasters Oppose the Fairness Doctrine," *New York Times,* 22 June 1975, 27.

7. The first quote is from Jack Gould, "TV: Hunger Amid Plenty," *New York Times,* 22 May 1968, 95; the second quote is from Clay Gowran, "TV Today: CBS Show Reports Tragic Story of Poverty," *Chicago Tribune,* 22 May 1968, sec. 2, 19.

8. "The Media: Unmasking the Pentagon," *Newsweek,* 8 March 1971, 74.

9. William C. Woods, "The Selling of the Pentagon," *Washington Post,* 26 February 1971, B1.

10. Jack Gould, "TV: CBS Explores Pentagon Propaganda Costs," *New York Times,* 24 February 1971, 83.

11. *Pensions* was not reviewed in the major papers, probably because it appeared during the opening weeks of the fall television season when TV columnists were preoccupied with reviewing new series.

12. Robert C. Maynard, "ADA Assails Probe of Hunger Reports," *Washington Post,* 9 December 1968, A2.

13. F. Leslie Smith, "The Selling of the First Amendment: An Analysis of Congressional Investigations of Four CBS Television Documentary Projects," (Ph.D. diss., Florida State University, 1972), 20. Many affiliates declined to carry network news specials on Vietnam (Erik Barnouw, *The Image Empire* [New York: Oxford University Press, 1970], 280). On stations' opposition to civil rights coverage, see Mary Ann Watson, "The Golden Age of American Television Documentary," *Television Quarterly* 23 (Summer 1988): 67. On affiliates' dislike of controversial programming, see Fred Powledge, *The Engineering of Restraint: The Nixon Administration and the Press* (Washington, D.C.: Public Affairs Press/American Civil Liberties Union, 1971), 34.

14. Hugh Carter Donahue, *The Battle to Control Broadcast News* (Cambridge, Mass.: MIT Press, 1989), 112.

15. A. William Bluem, *Documentary in American Television: Form, Function, Method* (New York: Hastings House, 1965), 105.

16. Friendly, *Due to Circumstances*, 135.

17. "Minutes of Meeting of NBC-TV Board of Delegates," 6 February 1961, folder 4, box 7, MSS 86AF, Harry Ray Bannister Papers, SHSW.

18. Robert Sherrill, "The Happy Ending," 90.

19. Jack Gould, "Hunger Amid Plenty," *New York Times*, 22 May 1968, 95.

20. Jack Gould, "Hunger Is Not for Quibbling," *New York Times*, 23 June 1968, sec. 2, 19.

21. The spectacle of a Democratic USDA secretary finding his best friends in the conservative media was noted by Freeman assistant John Obert in a memo to Freeman: "These days we're getting 90 percent of the heat from liberal writers and liberal publications and 90 percent of our support from conservative quarters." If Obert overstated the case somewhat, he was not too far off (John Obert to Orville Freeman, 13 June 1968, Farm Program 8-1-1 [2 of 2], box 4814, general correspondence, ROSA).

22. Richard L. Strout, "No Corn, No Nuthin'," *Christian Science Monitor*, 31 May 1968, 20.

23. "Facts vs. Emotions in Hunger," *Chicago Tribune*, 25 June 1968, 14.

24. "Poverty—and Progress," *Washington Post*, 25 May 1968, A10.

25. "Mr. Freeman's Formula," *Wall Street Journal*, 14 June 1968, 18.

26. Although newsmagazine coverage was not included in this portion of the analysis, it too divided along ideological lines. *Newsweek* briefly mentioned the secretary of agriculture's criticisms yet found, "When it came down to specific charges, Freeman's list of alleged inaccuracies was more picky than pithy." The more conservative, business-oriented *U.S. News and World Report* gave greater space to Freeman's charges in three articles on the hunger debates. See "Hunger Pains," *Newsweek*, 10 June 1968, 100; "'Poor' vs. Freeman—How Many Hungry?" *U.S. News and World Report*, 3 June 1968, 22, 24; "Hunger in U.S.—More Controversy," *U.S. News and World Report*, 10 June 1968, 16; "More on Hunger in U.S.," *U.S. News and World Report*, 17 June 1968, 46–48.

27. Rowland Evans and Robert Novak, "Stations versus CBS," reprinted in *Congressional Record*, 9642–43.

28. Alliane Horne Willis, "An Analysis of the Controversy Surrounding 'The Selling of the Pentagon'" (Ph.D. diss., Emory University, 1987), 125.

29. Jack Gould, "Talk among TV Sponsors Hints at Spring of Political Tensions," *New York Times*, 19 April 1971, 75.

30. Sally Bedell-Smith, *In All His Glory: The Life of William S. Paley, the Legendary Tycoon and His Brilliant Circle* (New York: Simon and Schuster, 1990), 476.

31. ". . . but like us all CBS makes mistakes," *Christian Science Monitor,* 14 July 1971, 14.

32. "CBS Gets a Pass," *Chicago Tribune,* 13 July 1971, 20.

33. "What Agnew Sees on CBS: TV's Credibility Gap," *Detroit News,* reprinted in *Congressional Record,* 6 April 1971, 9894–95.

34. Cited in Lester A. Sobel, *Media Controversies* (New York: Facts on File, 1981), 36.

35. "The Selling of Integrity: CBS Broadcast Distorts Facts," *San Diego Union,* 26 March 1971, reprinted in *Congressional Record,* 15 April 1971, 10479.

36. Cited in Small, *Political Power,* 349.

37. "Broadcast License: CBS Has Forfeited Access to the Nation's Airwaves," *Barron's National and Financial Weekly,* 29 March 1971, reprinted in *Congressional Record,* 30 March 1971, 8616–18. Other editorials and columns attacking CBS and/or supporting the Staggers investigation may be found in *Congressional Record,* 1971, 8570–71, 9894–95, 10477–80, 11667, 28615–16.

38. Joseph C. Spear, *Presidents and the Press* (Cambridge, Mass.: MIT Press, 1984), 119–20.

39. John J. O'Connor, "All's Fair in Love and War, Maybe, but Not in TV Reporting," *New York Times,* 16 September 1973, 19.

40. Davis, phone interview. A memo from Davis to Salant, later leaked, gave an idea of what else the network might have disseminated. It told of military personnel confronted with evidence that they had lied to Davis's crew; stories of how higher-ranking officers tried to silence subordinates who provided information to CBS; military public relations officers divulging the hardball lobbying tactics they used to win congressional approval of the antiballistic missile system and maintaining that all Pentagon public relations should be outlawed as antidemocratic; and information about how the Navy overestimated Soviet naval strength to win larger appropriations from Congress. On a more mundane level, Davis noted that a member of Assistant Secretary of Defense Henkin's staff tried to proposition a woman on Davis's crew to gain information about *The Selling of the Pentagon* and that an Army major kicked an enlisted man who was describing public relations techniques on his Indiana base to the crew. See "Congressional Pandora," *Nation,* 10 May 1971, 581.

41. John J. O'Connor, "Why Broadcasters Oppose the Fairness Doctrine," *New York Times,* 22 June 1975, 27.

42. The pension critics cited were Senator Hubert Humphrey (D-Minn.), the United Auto Workers, and a retiree, in Richard L. Strout, "Pensions: 'Social Tragedy,'" *Christian Science Monitor,* 22 September 1972, E1.

CHAPTER 5: THE ETHICS OF REPRESENTATION

1. Fred W. Friendly, "Television: The Unselling of *The Selling of the Pentagon,*" *Harper's,* June 1971, 30.

2. House Committee on Interstate and Foreign Commerce, Special Subcommittee on Investigations, *Network News Documentary Practices—CBS "Project Nassau," Hearings,* 91 Cong., 2nd sess., 1970, 151.

3. Joshua Meyrowitz, *No Sense of Place: The Impact of Electronic Media on Social Behavior* (New York: Oxford University Press, 1985), 90.

4. Christopher Sterling and John Kittross, *Stay Tuned: A Concise History of American Broadcasting* (Belmont, Calif.: Wadsworth, 1990), 352.

5. Meyrowitz, *No Sense of Place*, 91.

6. Edward Jay Epstein, *News from Nowhere: Television and the News* (New York: Random House, 1973), 170–72.

7. For this characterization of muckraking magazines, see Thomas C. Leonard, *The Power of the Press: The Birth of American Political Reporting* (New York: Oxford University Press, 1986), 185.

8. Reprinted in *Congressional Record*, 22 March 1961, 4534.

9. Interview with Albert Wasserman, in *The Documentary Conscience: A Casebook in Filmmaking*, ed. Alan Rosenthal (Berkeley: University of California Press, 1980), 93.

10. "Statement by City Manager Joseph McD. Mitchell," *Congressional Record*, 11 September 1962, 19124; Mitchell's complaint was seconded by New York House member Katherine St. George in the *Congressional Record*, 31 January 1962, A747. Boston's political leaders raised similar objections to CBS's 1961 *Biography of a Bookie Joint* (see chapter 6).

11. *Congressional Record*, 31 July 1968, 24432.

12. *Congressional Record*, 5 June 1969, 14984.

13. "An Address by the City Manager of the City of Newburgh, N.Y., Joseph McDowell Mitchell," reprinted in the *Congressional Record*, 11 September 1962, 19120.

14. CBS's 1966 *Sixteen in Webster Groves* also piqued local resentment by examining the materialism, conformity, and racial exclusivity of teenage life in a St. Louis suburb. CBS gave the teens and their parents a rare chance to respond by filming a follow-up documentary, *Webster Groves Revisited*.

15. *Congressional Record*, 23 September 1968, 27811.

16. *Congressional Record*, 31 July 1968, 24432.

17. Sergei Eisenstein, *Film Form: Essays in Film Theory*, ed. and trans. Jay Leyda (New York: Harvest/HBJ, 1949), 82.

18. Friendly, *Good Guys*, 158.

19. Steven J. Simmons, *The Fairness Doctrine and the Media* (Berkeley: University of California Press, 1978), 185, n. 125; *National Broadcasting Company, Inc v. Federal Communications Commission and the United States of America*, 516 F. 2d 1101, 1126–27 (1974). Although it is unlikely that NBC would have voluntarily provided a copy of the film to AIM, there is no indication that the court ever asked for one. The FCC's rationale for deciding whether the fairness doctrine applied to entertainment programming is also revealing in this context. In response to a complaint brought by the National Organization for Women charging that sexist portrayals of women in fictional shows raised the controversial issue of gender relations, the commission stated, "Fairness Doctrine obligations are rooted not in the mere depiction of any role by a women [*sic*], but rather in the discussion—the dialogue—that occurs . . . [The] programming NOW identifies contained no true discussion of the role of women in society" (*American Broadcasting Company*, 52 FCC 98, 115 [1975]). Similarly, the language of section 315 of the 1934 Communications Act, written before the advent of television and not amended by the 1970s, stated that licensees must afford "reason-

able opportunity for the *discussion* of conflicting views on issues of public importance" (emphasis added; 47 USC sec. 315 [a] 4 [1970]).

20. Cited in Lester A. Sobel, *Media Controversies* (New York: Facts on File, 1981), 36.

21. See Richard Campbell, "Word vs. Image: Elitism, Popularity, and TV News," *Television Quarterly* 25 (1991): 73–81.

22. "Mr. Agnew versus CBS versus the DOD," *Washington Post*, 26 March 1971, A26.

23. Richard Salant, "CBS Replies to Editorial on Pentagon Documentary," *Washington Post*, 30 March 1971, A15.

24. "Mr. Salant's Letter," *Washington Post*, 30 March 1971, A14.

25. See "Letters to the Editor: NBC News Chief Reuven Frank and Fred Friendly on Television," *Washington Post*, 2 April 1971, A27.

26. Cited in Small, *Political Power*, 342.

27. "Television—The Art of 'Cut and Paste,'" *Time*, 12 April 1971, 56.

28. That print journalists commonly rearrange, condense, and alter the verbatim wording of quotes is attested to in the many amicus curiae briefs filed by print organizations on behalf of journalist Janet Malcolm in the Supreme Court case of *Masson v. New Yorker Magazine, Inc.*, 111 S. Ct. 2419 (1991). The Court found that altering quotes does not constitute libel as long as journalists do not create a "material change in the meaning conveyed by the statement" in quotation marks—a far less stringent standard than the *Post* applied to *The Selling of the Pentagon*.

29. Since the mid-nineteenth-century advent of the interview in print reporting, there have always been journalistic concerns about the propriety of the technique. Some emerged from positivist fears that interviewers did more to create news than report it. Others stemmed from anxiety about the power of journalists to shape their sources' words against them (print interviews were routinely faked in the late nineteenth century). See Michael Schudson, *The Power of News* (Cambridge, Mass.: Harvard University Press, 1995), 72–93.

30. See House Committee on Interstate and Foreign Commerce, Special Subcommittee on Investigations, *Hearings: Subpoenaed Material Re Certain TV News Documentary Programs*, 92nd Cong., 2nd sess., 1971, 49–52, 97–99, 107–8; *Congressional Record*, 30 March 1971, 8616–18; 31 March 1971, 8840–42, 8936–38; 22 April 1971, 11672–73; 6 May 1971, 13951–53.

31. "F.Y.I.," *Washington Post*, 11 April 1971, C6.

32. Ibid.; "CBS versus Congressman Staggers," *Washington Post*, 29 June 1971, A18.

33. "Television—The Art of 'Cut and Paste,'" 56.

34. Letter from David Buksbaum to *Time* letters to the editor, reprinted in House Committee on Interstate and Foreign Commerce, Special Subcommittee on Investigations, *Hearings: Supoenaed Material*, 350–51.

35. Letter from *Time* letters to the editor to David Buksbaum, reprinted in House Committee on Interstate and Foreign Commerce, Special Subcommittee on Investigations, *Hearings: Supoeanaed Material*, 351.

36. "Mr. Salant's Letter," A14.

37. "Television—The Art of 'Cut and Paste,'" 56.

38. Michael Curtin, "Packaging Reality," *Journalism Monographs* 137 (1993): 1–2.

39. Ibid., 26–27.

40. Interview with Morton Silverstein in Rosenthal, *The Documentary Conscience*, 103.

41. Arthur Barron, "Toward New Goals in Documentary," reprinted in *The Documentary Tradition*, 2nd ed., ed. Lewis Jacobs (New York: W. W. Norton, 1979), 499.

42. See Campbell, *60 Minutes and the News*, 15.

43. Daniel Klugherz, "Documentary—Where's the Wonder?" in *The Documentary Tradition*, 2nd ed., ed. Lewis Jacobs (New York: W. W. Norton, 1979), 452. This essay first appeared in 1967.

44. Frank, *Out of Thin Air*, 406–7.

45. See John Ullman, *Investigative Reporting: Advanced Methods and Techniques* (New York: St. Martin's Press, 1995), 2–3. For additional discussion of the difficulties of defining investigative reporting in exclusive terms, see *IRE Journal*, January–February 1996, 2–3; and Silvio Waisbord, *Watchdog Journalism in South America: News, Accountability, Democracy* (New York: Columbia University Press, 2000), xv–xix.

46. Ullman, *Investigative Reporting*, 2–3.

47. Barry Dornfeld, *Producing Public Television, Producing Public Culture* (Princeton, N.J.: Princeton University Press, 1998), 91.

48. Christine Gledhill, "Genre," in *The Cinema Book*, ed. Pam Cook (London: British Film Institute, 1985), 64.

49. Daniel Chandler, "An Introduction to Genre Theory: The Problem of Definition," http://www.aber.ac.uk/media/Documents/intgenre/intgenre1.html (July 2000).

50. Hugo de Burgh, "Introduction: A Higher Kind of Loyalty?" in *Investigative Journalism: Context and Practice*, ed. Hugo de Burgh (London: Routledge, 2000), 21.

51. Don Shelby, "Investigative Reporting for Television," in *Investigative Reporting*, ed. David Anderson and Peter Benjaminson (Bloomington: University of Indiana Press, 1976), 171.

52. Michael Schudson, *Discovering the News* (New York: Basic Books, 1978), 88–120; David Eason, "Telling Stories and Making Sense," *Journal of Popular Culture* 15 (1981): 125; Campbell, *60 Minutes and the News*, 16–19.

53. Campbell, *60 Minutes and the News*, 16–19.

54. James S. Ettema and Theodore Glasser, *Custodians of Conscience: Investigative Journalism and Public Virtue* (New York: Columbia University Press, 1998), 197–202.

55. See Bill Nichols, *Representing Reality: Issues and Concepts in Documentary* (Bloomington: Indiana University Press, 1991), 34–38, 44–56.

56. Ibid., 35.

57. Interview with Morton Silverstein, *Documentary Conscience*, 108.

58. Schudson, *Discovering the News*, 160, 176–83. The turn to more interpretive print reporting also arose as an economic strategy; in response to television's advantages in covering spot news, print marketed itself as having more "depth" and "opinion."

59. On television reporters' rising claims to cultural and interpretive authority in the 1960s, see Barbie Zelizer, *Covering the Body: The Kennedy Assassination, the Media, and the Shaping of Collective Memory* (Chicago: University of Chicago Press, 1992).

60. "CBS Operating Standards: News and Public Affairs," box MP593, John E. Moss Papers, CSUS.

61. Leonard, *In the Storm*, 126.

62. Davis, phone interview. Many other CBS News employees have made similar comments. See Richard J. Schaefer, "The Development of the CBS News Guidelines during the Salant Years," *Journal of Broadcasting and Electronic Media* 42 (1998): 7.

63. A. William Bluem, *Documentary in American Television: Form, Function, Method* (New York: Hastings House, 1965), 105–6.

64. During the 1960s and early 1970s, CBS producers were immediately overseen by an executive producer responsible for guiding several documentaries at a time. In turn, they reported to the vice president for "soft news," who was responsible for documentaries, news specials, and convention coverage. The president of the news division oversaw all. At NBC, producers and executive producers reported directly to the news president.

65. Leonard, *In the Storm*, 159, 134. Similarly, a study of CBS's Vietnam documentaries concluded that "the effect of executive editing decisions is essentially to curb extreme attitudes, shifting them more toward the center of the opinion spectrum" (Thomas M. McNulty, "Vietnam Specials: Policy and Content," *Journal of Communication* 25 [1975]: 182).

66. Frank, *Out of Thin Air*, 176.

67. House Committee on Interstate and Foreign Commerce, *Proceeding against Frank Stanton*, 107.

68. Arthur Unger, "How Real Are Those 'True Life' Shows?" *Christian Science Monitor*, 17 January 1974, F6.

69. House Committee on Interstate and Foreign Commerce, Special Subcommittee on Investigations, *Network News Documentary Practices—CBS "Project Nassau," Hearings*, 91 Cong., 2nd sess., 1970, 4–5.

70. *Congressional Record*, 27 May 1969, 14100.

71. The 1971 CBS News guidelines stated that payments should not be made to sources in "hard news and hard news-oriented broadcasts." For documentaries and public affairs programs, "nominal sums" were necessary to secure the right to use participants' names and likenesses, "as required by our Law Department." However, payments were not simply for blanket rights but compensated sources differently according to how much of their time they devoted to filming and the presumed market value of their participation ("CBS Operating Standards," 5–6). *Project Nassau* producer Jay McMullen explained that several cash payments to the coup plotters were for film rights although he never asked for written releases from his subjects in exchange for them (House Committee on Interstate and Foreign Commerce, *Network News Documentary Practices*, 177–78).

72. Leonard, *In the Storm*, 126–27.

73. House Committee on Interstate and Foreign Commerce, *Network News Documentary Practices*, 354.

74. Ibid., 146–47.

75. See, for example, the comments of Representative Jamie Whitten in *Congressional Record*, 2 May 1968, 11501–3.

76. Curtin, "Packaging Reality," 21.

77. Frank, *Out of Thin Air*, 196.

78. Cited in Lucas A. Powe Jr., *American Broadcasting and the First Amendment* (Berkeley: University of California Press, 1987), 124.

79. *Congressional Record,* 6 February 1961, 1758.

80. Reuven Frank, letter to the editor, *New York Times,* 20 July 1975, 21.

81. Ibid.

82. Interview with Wasserman, *Documentary Conscience,* 99–100.

83. Nichols, *Representing Reality,* 186.

84. Stanley Fish, *Is There a Text in This Class? The Authority of Interpretive Communities* (Cambridge: Harvard University Press, 1980).

85. Zelizer, *Covering the Body,* 9.

86. Daniel Hallin, "The Passing of the 'High Modernism' of American Journalism," *Journal of Communication* 42 (1992): 14–25. Hallin is arguing for a subtle shift in these power dynamics, not an historical break with them. He recognizes journalists are still too constrained by ideological and institutional ties, and majority sentiment to be considered wholly independent. And, like others, he is deeply critical of the interpretive reporting that has emerged, which restricts itself too often to discussing the techniques of politics and public relations rather than the more substantive issues at stake in public struggles.

87. Bill Nichols, *Blurred Boundaries: Questions of Meaning in Contemporary Culture* (Bloomington: Indiana University Press, 1994), x.

88. "The Selling of a Contempt Citation," *Washington Post,* 11 July 1971, B6.

89. Small, *Political Power,* 360.

CHAPTER 6: THE POLITICS OF REGULATION

1. Presidential commissions and congressional inquiries also addressed live news reporting of crises such as the 1963 assassination of John F. Kennedy, African American urban uprisings, and the 1968 clashes between police and demonstrators at the Democratic National Convention in Chicago. These probes influenced concerns about television news production practices and journalists' role in covering or inspiring crime and civil disobedience but were not the subject of regular attention from the entire regulatory apparatus. In particular, the FCC only addressed itself to the Chicago convention coverage, in a ruling discussed below.

2. 47 U.S.C. § 309 (a) (2000). The discussion of symbolic politics and their application to news distortion cases in this chapter draws on Chad Raphael, "The FCC's Broadcast News Distortion Rules: Regulation by Drooping Eyelid," *Communication Law and Policy* 6 (2001): 485–539.

3. Murray Edelman, *The Symbolic Uses of Politics* (Urbana: University of Illinois Press, 1976), 37.

4. Ibid., 39.

5. Thomas Streeter, *Selling the Air: A Critique of the Policy of Commercial Broadcasting in the United States* (Chicago: University of Chicago Press, 1996), 9, 191–93.

6. For example, the D.C. Circuit Court of Appeals warned the FCC against its "curious neutrality in favor of the licensee" when assigning the burden of proof to complainants and resolving conflicting evidence in favor of the licensee in *Office of Communications of United Church of Christ v. F.C.C.,* 425 F. 2d 543, 547 (D.C. Cir. 1969). Commissioner Nicholas Johnson repeated the phrase in a 1973 dissent involving news distortion charges, deriding the FCC for turning the license renewal process into a wasteful "ritual" in which "the result was preordained a long time ago" (*Chronicle Broadcasting,* 40 FCC 2d 775, 838 [1973]).

7. Streeter, *Selling the Air*, 121, 123.

8. Ford Rowan, *Broadcast Fairness: Doctrine, Practice, Prospects* (New York: Longman, 1984), 71.

9. Radio Act of 1927, section 18. This section was adopted later as section 315 of the Communications Act of 1934.

10. Robert W. McChesney, *Telecommunications, Mass Media, and Democracy: The Battle for the Control of U.S. Broadcasting, 1928–1935* (New York: Oxford University Press, 1993).

11. *Report on Editorializing by Broadcast Licensees*, 13 FCC 1246, 1251 (1949).

12. Hugh Carter Donahue, *The Battle to Control Broadcast News* (Cambridge, Mass.: MIT Press, 1989), 49. The ban was enacted in *Mayflower Broadcasting Company*, 8 FCC 333 (1941).

13. *Letter to the Honorable Oren Harris in Reference to the Fairness Doctrine Implementation*, 40 FCC 582 (1963).

14. Donahue, *Battle to Control*, 74.

15. Ibid., 119–20. Among the most notable of these fairness complaints were those brought against Edward R. Murrow's *See It Now* investigative reports of the 1950s charging that Eisenhower administration farm policies were bankrupting family farmers and exploring plans for Hawaiian and Alaskan statehood.

16. *Cullman Broadcasting Co., Inc.*, 40 FCC 576 (1963).

17. *Office of Communications of the United Church of Christ v. Federal Communications Commission*, 395 F. 2d 994 (D.C. Cir., 1966). The case involved complaints against Jackson, Miss., radio station WLBT, accused, among other things, of carrying racially biased news programming that failed to include the views of its majority black listeners.

18. *Red Lion Broadcasting Co., Inc., et al. v. Federal Communications Commission et al.*, 395 US 390 (1969).

19. Bagdikian, "Pensions," 19.

20. *Report on Editorializing by Broadcast Licensees*, 13 FCC 1246 (1949). See also *KMPC, Station of the Stars, Inc.*, 14 Fed. Reg. 4831 (1949), establishing that a licensee's direction to news personnel to slant the news would raise serious questions about the character qualifications of the licensee.

21. *Report on Editorializing by Broadcast Licensees*, 13 FCC 1246, 1249 (1949).

22. Erwin G. Krasnow and Lawrence D. Longley, *The Politics of Broadcast Regulation*, 2nd ed. (New York: St Martin's Press, 1978).

23. On the modest impact of the 1960s liberal reformers, see Willard D. Rowland Jr., "The Illusion of Fulfillment: The Broadcast Reform Movement." *Journalism Monographs* 59 (1982): 27–28.

24. *Letter to the Honorable John F. Thompson*, 40 FCC 523, 524–25 (1962). Thus, there were regulatory advantages to citing official sources although this probably influenced documentarians' choice of sources less than it did their attorneys' arguments before the commission.

25. *Letter to Mr. Joseph McD. Mitchell*, 40 FCC 526, 527 (1962), 527–28.

26. *Letter to Thompson*, 523–24.

27. Michael Curtin, *Redeeming the Wasteland: Television Documentary and Cold War Politics* (New Brunswick, N.J.: Rutgers University Press, 1995), 250; Jack Gould, "'Newts' for Networks," *New York Times*, 12 August 1962, sec. 2, 13.

28. *Hunger in America*, 20 FCC 2d 143, 151 (1969).

29. *Network Coverage of Democratic National Convention (Letter to ABC et al.)*, 16 FCC 2d 650, 656–57 (1969).

30. House Committee on Interstate and Foreign Commerce, Special Subcommittee on Investigations, *Deceptive Programming Practices. Hearings on Staging of Marihuana Broadcast: Pot Party at a University*, 90th Cong., 2nd sess., 1968, 7–8.

31. *Columbia Broadcasting System, Inc. (WBBM)*, 18 FCC 2d 124 (1969).

32. Ibid.

33. 20 FCC 2d 143, 147.

34. The FCC refused to address two other staging charges. Gonzalez accused CBS of coaching interviewees to portray hunger in more "dramatic" ways than they would have otherwise. A San Antonio doctor claimed that CBS producers pressured him to stop "hedging too much" and to offer "more dramatic statements or more impressive cases" of hunger. The producers said they only asked the physician to speak in less technical terms that the general public could understand and that they declined to use the interview in the final version of *Hunger in America* because it was too technical. The FCC decided it would be inappropriate to hold hearings to resolve this "conflict of evidence." Gonzalez also maintained that CBS had staged a long line outside the San Antonio surplus commodities distribution center by asking employees to close their doors for an hour and forty-five minutes so that the camera crew could set up its equipment. The FCC found conflicting testimony on this issue from commodities distribution workers, and it argued that since CBS used no film of the line in *Hunger in America*, there was no cause for concern.

35. 20 FCC 2d 143, 150–51. See also *Letter to ABC*, 650.

36. 20 FCC 2d 143, 151.

37. William Ray, chief of the FCC's Complaints and Compliance Division, was unconvinced by CBS's protestations of innocence. He later noted that the commission found it "inappropriate" to hold an evidentiary hearing on whether CBS or the nurse was telling the truth "although that is why evidentiary hearings are held" (Ray, *FCC*, 9).

38. 20 FCC 2d 143, 151.

39. Ibid., 151–52. The articles claimed the child's father was a college student, that the parents denied they were malnourished, and that the mother reportedly gave birth prematurely after taking a bad fall. See Kemper Diehl, "Father Disputes TV Hunger Charge," *San Antonio Express-News*, 14 July 1968, reprinted in *Congressional Record*, 22 July 1968, 22738–39.

40. Ray, *FCC*, 9–10.

41. 30 FCC 2d 150, 153.

42. Cited in Mayer, *About Television*, 269.

43. 30 FCC 2d 150, 153.

44. 20 FCC 2d 143, 150.

45. "Broadcast Action: Response to Congressman Staggers on CBS 'Project Nassau,'" public notice, FCC Report No. 10409, 21 January 1972-B, 3. Obtained by the author from the FCC.

46. House Committee on Interstate and Foreign Commerce, Special Subcommittee on Investigations, *Inquiry into Alleged Rigging of Television News Programs: Hearings*, 92nd Cong., 2nd sess., 1972.

47. "No Further Action Warranted on Alleged 'Staging' Incidents by ABC and CBS; Both Networks Warned on Incomplete Inquiries," FCC press release, 27 November 1973. Obtained by the author from the FCC.

48. Salant's memos are in the New Canaan, Conn., public library. Many of them are summarized in Susan and Bill Buzenberg, *Salant, CBS, and the Battle for the Soul of Broadcast Journalism* (Boulder, Colo.: Westview Press, 1999), 187–209. On CBS News' employees' disregard for the guidelines, see Richard J. Schaefer, "The Development of the CBS News Guidelines During the Salant Years," *Journal of Broadcasting and Electronic Media* 42 (1998): 7.

49. On growing executive oversight of documentaries, see the panel discussion of news managers and reporters in Mary Ann Watson, "The Golden Age of American Television Documentary," *Television Quarterly* 23 (1988): 57–75.

50. Ray, *FCC*, 6.

51. See Raphael, "FCC's News Distortion Rules," 517, 528. Although several journalists have tried, none has won an FCC decision for distortion against their employer. In 2000, an investigative reporter relied on the distortion rules to win her case against former employer WTVT-TV under a state whistle-blower law written to protect employees who alerted authorities to violations of federal law or regulation. The court found station managers fired the journalist in retaliation for advising them that she planned to alert the FCC that she was told to falsify a report on food safety, in violation of the news distortion rules. This was the first time that the distortion policy has been used to protect journalists in this way, but the FCC played no role (Sarah Schweitzer, "TV Reporter Wins Lawsuit over Firing from Station," *St. Petersburg Times,* 19 August 2000, 1B). For a fuller account of the case from the journalist's perspective, see Steve Wilson, "BGH Bulletin," http://www.foxbghsuit.com/ (October 2000).

52. WXUR, the radio station that sparked the Supreme Court's *Red Lion* decision upholding the doctrine, lost its license on other grounds. An appeals court upheld the FCC's decision to strip the license because the station knowingly misrepresented its programming plans to the commission. *Brandywine-Main Line Radio, Inc. v. Federal Communications Commission,* 473 F. 2d 16 (1972).

53. Ray, *FCC*, 91.

54. Barry G. Cole and Mal Oettinger, *Reluctant Regulators: The FCC and the Broadcast Audience* (Reading, Mass.: Addison-Wesley, 1978), 123.

55. Rowan, *Broadcast Fairness*, 51.

56. Cole and Oettinger, *Reluctant Regulators*, 123.

57. Steven J. Simmons, *The Fairness Doctrine and the Media* (Berkeley: University of California Press, 1978), 210–11.

58. *RTNDA Communicator,* October 1983, 28.

59. Rowan, *Broadcast Fairness*, 71.

60. Here and below, I summarize arguments found in *Accuracy in Media, Inc.,* 44 FCC 2d 958 (1973); *Accuracy in Media, Inc.,* 44 FCC 2d 1027 (1973); *National Broadcasting Company, Inc v. Federal Communications Commission and the United States of America,* 516 F. 2d 1101 (1974).

61. AIM and the FCC made all of these points except the most important one: the documentary suggested that there were problems that should be reformed that were not addressed in the administration's plan. Therefore, it did not simply cover consensus issues at the time it was broadcast.

62. 44 FCC 2d 1027, 1028 (1973).

63. Ibid., 959. The FCC's 1964 fairness doctrine primer stated that it relied upon "the licensee, in applying the Fairness Doctrine . . . to make reasonable judgments in good faith on the facts of each situation—as to whether a controversial issue of public importance is involved, as to what viewpoints have been or should be presented, as to the format and spokesmen to present the viewpoints, and all the other facets of such programming" (*Applicability of the Fairness Doctrine in the Handling of Controversial Issues of Public Importance,* 40 FCC 598, 599 [1964]).

64. 44 FCC 2d 1027, 1029 (1973).

65. Ibid.

66. 516 F. 2d 1101, 1133 (1974).

67. These are listed in 40 FCC 2d 958, 963–66 (1973).

68. Simmons, *Fairness Doctrine,* 163.

69. In a 1970 decision also involving NBC, the commission stated, "If every statement, or inference from statements or presentations, could be made the subject of a separate and distinct fairness requirement, the Doctrine would be unworkable." The ruling added the caveat that a licensee "could not cover an issue, making two important points in his discussion of that issue; afford time for the contrasting viewpoint on one of these two points; and on the other point, reject fairness requests on the ground that it is a 'subissue'" (*National Broadcasting Co.,* 25 FCC 2d 735, 736–37 [1970]). As Simmons noted, the commission applied its distinction between issues and subissues erratically. What he does not say is that it generally did so to rule in broadcasters' favor (Simmons, *Fairness Doctrine,* 148–50). For example, the commission dismissed, without offering a rationale, a complaint against a report entitled *Hunger in America: A National Disgrace,* finding that it could reasonably be said not to have raised the issue posed by its title (*American Conservative Union,* 23 FCC 2d 33 [1970]).

70. 44 FCC 2d 1027, 1040 (1973).

71. John J. O'Connor, "Why Broadcasters Oppose the Fairness Doctrine," *New York Times,* 22 June 1975, 27.

72. 44 FCC 2d 1027, 1030 (1973).

73. 516 F. 2d 1101, 1123 (1973).

74. Senator William Proxmire (D-Wis.) praised the ruling on the Senate floor, telling his colleagues, "The legal lesson is that the Fairness Doctrine can interfere with journalistic discretion, particularly in investigative reporting" (*Congressional Record,* 3 October 1974, 33819). For other reactions, see Friendly, *Good Guys,* 150; Simmons, *Fairness Doctrine,* 165.

75. 44 FCC 2d 1027, 1042 (1973).

76. Ibid., 1032–33.

77. Cited in *AIM Report,* October 1974, 5.

78. O'Connor, "Why Broadcasters Oppose the Fairness Doctrine," 27.

79. Friendly, *Good Guys,* 229; Simmons, *Fairness Doctrine,* 160–66.

80. Friendly, *Good Guys,* 235.

81. John E. Moss to Rosel Hyde, 11 June 1969, folder 7c, box MP83, John E. Moss Papers, CSUS.

82. House Committee on Interstate and Foreign Commerce, *Network News Documentary Practices,* 151.

83. See the President's Advisory Council on Executive Organization, *A New Regulatory Framework: Report on Selected Independent Regulatory Agencies* (Washington, D.C.: U.S. Government Printing Office, 1971). In addition, the House conducted a

detailed review of the FCC and other regulatory agencies, rating them on many categories including public participation (the FCC got a middle grade for "only recently . . . loosening its close relationship with the broadcasting and telephone industries"), and the Senate Committee on Government Operations reviewed the commission in 1977 and 1978 as part of larger study of federal regulation. See Krasnow and Longley, *Politics of Broadcast Regulation*, 195–206.

84. Marilyn Lashner, *The Chilling Effect in TV News* (New York: Praeger, 1984), 188.

85. *Congressional Record*, 30 March 1971, H 2157–58; 7 April 1971, H 2618; 28 April 1971, H 3198; 29 March 1971, 2373; 27 April 1971, H 3010; 28 April E 3601; 20 May 1971, E 4831.

86. Lashner, *Chilling Effect*, 207; William J. Small, *To Kill a Messenger: Television News and the Real World* (New York: Hastings House, 1974), 278.

87. *Congressional Record*, 25 September 1968, 28109; 5 February 1969, 2862.

88. "Investigations Unit Cut to Five; Role Uncertain," *Broadcasting*, 8 March 1971, 39.

89. David E. Price, "Investigations and Oversight," in *The Commerce Committees*, ed. David E. Price (New York: Grossman, 1975), 314.

90. These organizations filed amicus briefs on NBC's behalf in the *Pensions* case, as did the *New York Times* (44 FCC 2d 1027 [1973]).

91. *WCBS-TV*, 8 FCC 2d 381 (1967).

92. Courts upheld the doctrine's application to cigarette commercials in *Banzhaf v. F.C.C.*, 405 F. 2d 1082 (1968), and to automobile advertising in *Friends of the Earth v. Federal Communications Commission*, 449 F. 2d 1164 (1971).

93. Senate Committee on the Judiciary, Subcommittee on Constitutional Rights, *Hearing: Freedom of the Press*, 92nd Cong., 1st and 2nd sess., 1971–1972, 53–67, 77–106, 557–74. On news freedom as the basis for delicensing in the 1930s, see McChesney, *Telecommunications*, 240–42.

94. The fairness doctrine's way of making strange political bedfellows was in evidence at the court of appeals hearing on *Pensions*, where AIM was joined by liberal reformers including the Office of Communication of the United Church of Christ, the Center for the Public Interest, and the National Citizens Committee for Broadcasting.

95. Friendly, *Good Guys*, 211.

96. Jeremy Tunstall, *Communications Deregulation: The Unleashing of America's Communications Industry* (Oxford: Basil Blackwell, 1986), 208–9.

97. Whitehead to Colson et al., 31 January 1972, Subject Files, Confidential Files, box 67, WHSF, WHCF, Charles Colson, NPM; Colson to Peter Flanigan, 31 January 1971, Subject Files, Confidential Files, box 67, WHSF, WHCF, Charles Colson, NPM; Whitehead to Flanigan, 3 May 1971, Subject Files, Confidential Files, box 54, WHSF, WHCF, Charles Colson, NPM; Flanigan to John Ehrlichman and Colson, 3 May 1971, Subject Files, Confidential Files, box 54, WHSF, WHCF, Charles Colson, NPM.

98. Clarence Petersen, "Journalism Suffering from 'Politicization,'" *Chicago Tribune*, 28 February 1973, 1, 9.

99. According to Colson's notes on a 23 June 1970 meeting, Nixon urged John Swearingen, chairman of the board of Standard Oil of Indiana, to take the lead on raising funds for the American Enterprise Institute (AEI). Nixon characterized AEI as the "ammunition factory" needed to supply speeches and research to Congress and a counterweight to the influence of the Brookings Institute (Colson, "Memorandum

for the President's File," 15 July 1970, box 21, CD, Colson files). The following year, Colson noted of AEI that "we have now more than doubled their operating budget; they are taking on a number of assignments that are very important to us and are fast becoming a very valuable resource" (Colson to Dwight Chapin, 5 April 1971, Chronological Files, April 1971, box 128, CD, Colson files).

100. AIM executive secretary Abraham Kalish claimed that he did not receive complaints about the media from the White House (Daniel Epstein, "The Aims of AIM: A Critical Look at One of the Press Critics," *American Society of Newspaper Editors Bulletin,* March 1974, reprinted in Subcommittee on Domestic Monetary Policy, *Audit of the Federal Reserve,* 94th Cong., 1st sess., 1975, 40). At a congressional hearing in 1975, AIM's Reed Irvine denied that the group was "somehow related to the animosity of Richard Nixon toward the press" (ibid., 99). White House aide Lyndon (Mort) Allin told a reporter in 1973 that AIM had "done some very good stuff . . . but we haven't had any contact with them" (John Pierson, "A Group Keeps Busy Trying to Ensure Accuracy of Media," *Wall Street Journal,* 1 May 1973, 18).

101. Louis Wolf, "Accuracy in Media Rewrites News and History," *Covert Action Information Bulletin* (Spring 1984): 28–29.

102. These complaints were against PBS's *Special Report: The President on Vietnam,* two programs by New York public station WNET featuring antiwar spokespeople, and a segment on drug trafficking by Southeast Asian allies from NBC's *Chronolog,* all aired in 1972.

103. "AIM Maintains Pressure on Fairness Doctrine Complaints," *AIM Report,* March 1973, 4.

104. Colson to the staff secretary, 22 December 1971, Chronological Files, box 130, CD, Colson files.

105. "The New York Times Attacks the Treasury Department—With a Falsehood," *AIM Report,* October 1973, 1.

106. "Scandal Sheet Story Results in Check of Ft. Knox Gold," *AIM Report,* October 1974, 6–7.

107. "AIMing at the Columnists," *AIM Report,* August–September 1973, 7.

108. Charles Colson to Peter Flanigan, 6 January 1971, Chronological Files, box 131, CD, Colson files.

109. Colson to Flanigan, 7 May 1971, Chronological Files, May 1971, box 129, CD, Colson files.

110. Colson to Flanigan, 22 July 1971, Chronological Files, box 129, CD, Colson files.

111. Flanigan to the president, 14 September 1971, President's Handwriting File, box 13, CD, WHSF, POF, NPM.

112. Colson to H. R. Haldeman, 15 May 1972, Chronological Files, box 131, CD, Colson files.

113. Charles Colson to Haldeman, 11 October 1971, Chronological Files, box 130, CD, Colson files.

114. James Keogh, *President Nixon and the Press* (New York: Funk and Wagnalls, 1972); "'Painfully Obvious' Bias," *AIM Report,* September 1972, 5–7. An AIM advisory board member, Rear Admiral William C. Mott, retired, was a former ITT executive.

115. Colson to Haldeman, 2 August 1972, Chronological Files, box 132, CD, Colson files. Another administration aide later reported that one of his subordinates was "working directly with the Accuracy in Media group along with Keogh" by giving Keogh

material for speeches and articles and transmitting examples of media "bias" to AIM through him (Ken Clawson to Haldeman, 29 July 1972, Chronological Files, box 132, CD, Colson files).

116. "Anti-Military Bias: ABC Is Too Much," *AIM Report*, September 1972, 4–5; "ABC Corrects Errors in TV Documentary on National Defense," *AIM Report*, October 1972, 1–2. Peeved by a CBS news item on Vietnam, Colson advised a staff member that it was "worse than the Anthony Lewis episode which I think we very effectively discredited. I suggest you work with Keogh, [AIM executive secretary Abraham] Kalish and Co. and see if we could raise some hell over this" (Colson to Jim Schurz, 21 September 1972, Chronological Files, box 132, CD, Colson files). AIM had run an ad in the *New York Times* three months earlier attacking a article on Vietnam by Lewis, a *Times* columnist ("Review of Recent Activity of Accuracy in Media," *AIM Report*, August 1972, 6).

117. Colson to Schurz, 21 September 1972, Chronological Files, box 132, CD, Colson files.

118. Colson to Clawson, 30 August 1972, Chronological Files, box 132, CD, Colson files; "CBS News Shows Favoritism to McGovern," *AIM Report*, October 1972, 2–5. Colson or his staff mentioned feeding material to AIM in at least five other memos written in 1971 and 1972.

119. Colson to Haldeman, 15 May 1972, Chronological Files, box 131, CD, Colson files.

120. "NBC Distorts the Pension Picture, Giving Assistance to Controversial Legislation," *AIM Report*, January 1973, 1. Commentators on the case have accepted AIM's profession of independence at face value. See Friendly, *Good Guys*, 147; Richard E. Labunski, *The First Amendment Under Siege: The Politics of Broadcast Regulation* (Westport, Conn.: Greenwood Press, 1981), 78.

121. H. R. Haldeman and Joseph DiMona, *The Ends of Power* (New York: Times Books, 1978), 59.

122. Murray Baron, an AIM fundraiser (and later president of the group) was a former Teamsters' official. Baron later persuaded a foundation run by friend and former Teamster official George D. Barasch to give over $500,000 in donations to AIM. Barasch and other union officials were accused in a 1965 House hearing of misappropriating almost $5 million in union pension funds. Barasch suddenly retired from his Teamster job during the House inquiry (Wolf, "Accuracy in Media," 35).

123. In its newsletter, AIM claimed "not to take any position on the proposed [pension] legislation," yet it urged its readers to write not to the FCC directly but to Congress, "asking them to find out what action the FCC intends to take in this case . . . since pending legislation is influenced by the unfair NBC program" ("NBC Distorts the Pension Picture, Giving Assistance to Controversial Legislation," *AIM Report*, January 1973, 5). This was a clever way of generating letters to Congress against pension reform, not simply of bringing pressure to bear on the FCC.

CHAPTER 7: THE PRIVATIZATION OF REGULATION

1. In the 1980s, the FCC forwarded an average of six fairness complaints per year to broadcasters asking for a response and found only one licensee in violation of the doctrine during that time. See *Broadcasters and the Fairness Doctrine: Hearing before the*

Subcommittee on Telecommunications and Finance of the House Committee on Energy and Commerce, 100th Cong. (1987), 12, 63. In 2000, the U.S. Court of Appeals for the District of Columbia struck down the FCC's personal attack rule, which directed stations to notify and offer reply time to the targets of character attacks during discussions of controversial public issues on the air, and the commission's political editorializing rule, which required a licensee to offer response time to legally qualified political candidates when it opposed their candidacies or endorsed their opponents on the air. See *Radio-Television News Directors Association v. FCC,* 229 F. 3d 269 (D.C. Cir., 2000).

2. Raphael, "FCC's Broadcast News Distortion Rules," 487.

3. Jack M. Balkin, "Some Realism about Pluralism: Legal Realist Approaches to the First Amendment," *Duke Law Journal* (1990): 380–81.

4. Onora O'Neill, "Practices of Toleration," in *Democracy and the Mass Media,* ed. Judith Lichtenberg (Cambridge: Cambridge University Press, 1990), 178.

5. Martin M. Shapiro, "Libel Regulatory Analysis," *California Law Review* 74 (1986): 883.

6. Randall P. Bezanson, Gilbert Cranberg, and John Soloski, *Libel Law and the Press: Myth and Reality* (New York: Free Press, 1987), 123, 23. The authors caution that some of the increase in resolved cases was probably attributable to the growth of pretrial involvement and appellate review in the 1970s, which telescoped resolutions into the early 1980s.

7. Harry R. Kaufman et al., "Tort Reform and Libel," *Communications and the Law* 10 (1988): 22–23.

8. Rodney A. Smolla, *Suing the Press: Libel, the Media, and Power* (New York: Oxford University Press, 1986), 73–74, 77, 14.

9. Media Institute, *Media Abuses: Rights and Remedies* (Washington, D.C.: Media Institute, 1983), 58–59.

10. Jerome H. Skolnick, "Foreword: The Sociological Tort of Defamation," *California Law Review* 74 (1986): 686.

11. Connie Bruck, "The Mea Culpa Defense," *American Lawyer,* September 1983, 82; Karen Rothmyer, "Westmoreland v. CBS," *Columbia Journalism Review,* May–June 1985, 25.

12. Thomas A. Mascaro, "Lowering the Voice of Reason: The Decline of Network Television Documentaries in the Reagan Years" (Ph.D. diss, Wayne State University, 1994), 267.

13. Donald M. Gillmor, *Power, Publicity, and the Abuse of Libel Law* (New York: Oxford University Press, 1992), 135–37.

14. Bezanson, Cranberg, and Soloski, *Libel Law and the Press,* 122, 201.

15. *Anderson v. Liberty Lobby,* 477 U.S. 242 (1986).

16. Marianne Lavelle, "Food Abuse: Basis for Suits," *National Law Journal,* 5 May 1997, A1. Although media reports consistently recall the incident as an unfounded "alar scare" perpetrated by an environmental group and *60 Minutes,* ample scientific evidence suggested that the chemical was indeed dangerous (Peter Montague, "How They Lie—The True Story of Alar," *Rachel's Environment and Health Weekly,* 20 January–27 February, 1997).

17. The lower estimate is from Tim Jones, "In Victory, Winfrey May Stand Alone," *Chicago Tribune,* 1 March 1998, 1; the higher estimate is from John Stauber, "Food Fight Comes to America," *Nation,* 27 December 1999, 18.

18. Matthew D. Bunker, Sigman L. Splichal, and Sheree Martin, "Triggering the First Amendment: Newsgathering Torts and Press Freedom," *Communication Law and Policy* 4 (1999): 280–83; Jane E. Kirtley, "Vanity and Vexation: Shifting the Focus to Media Conduct," *William and Mary Bill of Rights Journal* 4 (1996): 1080.

19. An exception is intentional infliction of emotional distress, to which the Supreme Court extended the *Sullivan* fault standard in *Hustler Magazine, Inc. v. Falwell,* 485 U.S. 46 (1988).

20. See, for example, Andrew B. Sims, "Food for the Lions: Excessive Damages for Newsgathering Torts and the Limitations of Current First Amendment Doctrines," *Boston University Law Review* 78 (1998): 507.

21. Michael W. Richards, "Tort Vision for the New Millennium: Strengthening News Industry Standards as a Defense Tool in Law Suits over Newsgathering Techniques," *Fordham Intellectual Property, Media, and Entertainment Law Journal* 10 (2000): 501.

22. *Food Lion, Inc. v. Capital Cities/ABC, Inc.,* 194 F. 3d 505 (4th Cir., 1999).

23. ABC News, "Nightline: Hidden Cameras and Hard Choices," 12 February 1997, Lexis-Nexis, News Library, ABC News Transcripts File.

24. *Food Lion, Inc. v. Capital Cities/ABC, Inc.,* 194 F. 3d 515, 522 (4th Cir., 1999).

25. Susanne A. Roschwalb and Richard A. Stack, introduction to *Litigation Public Relations: Courting Public Opinion,* ed. Susanne A. Roschwalb and Richard A. Stack (Littleton, Colo.: F. B. Rothman, 1995), xi.

26. Mary Gottschall, "The Rise of Litigation Public Relations," in *Litigation Public Relations: Courting Public Opinion,* ed. Susanne A. Roschwalb and Richard A. Stack (Littleton, Colo.: F. B. Rothman, 1995), 33–46.

27. Richard A. Oppel Jr. and Joe Simnacher, "GM Officials Questioned Truck Safety, Memos Show," *Dallas Morning News,* 17 November 1992, 1A.

28. See, for example, Howard Kurtz, "Why the Press Is Always Right: Being a Journalist Means Never Having to Say You're Sorry," *Columbia Journalism Review,* May–June 1993, 33–35; Carleton R. Bryant, "Staging the News: NBC's Bang May Spark Scorn for All Media," *Washington Times,* 10 February 1993, A3; Jim Kenzie, "NBC Truck Fiasco Shows TV Journalism at Worst," *Toronto Star,* 13 February 1993, G3; Pat Widder, "Playing with Fire: Blur of Fact and Fiction Costs NBC," *Chicago Tribune,* 11 February 1993, 1.

29. James C. Goodale, "The Inside Edition of 'GM v. NBC,'" *New York Law Journal,* 2 April 1993, 3.

30. Rather than forcing GM to recall the vehicles, the Department of Transportation quietly permitted GM to pay $51 million into a fund to be used for safety and research programs (Alicia C. Shepard, "Fighting Back," *American Journalism Review,* January–February 1996, 34).

31. This paragraph draws on James C. Goodale, "The Libel Suit That Never Was," *National Law Journal,* 8 March 1993, 17.

32. *Herbert v. Lando,* 441 US 153 (1979).

33. Anthony Lewis, *Make No Law: The Sullivan Case and the First Amendment* (New York: Vintage Books, 1991), 202.

34. Smolla, *Suing the Press,* 73; Kirtley, "Vanity and Vexation," 1083. Despite the presence of shield laws in many states, which protect reporters from having to reveal

confidential sources in court proceedings, these laws are often modified or ruled inapplicable in defamation cases (ibid., 1076).

35. Bezanson, Cranberg, and Soloski, *Libel Law and the Press,* 199.

36. Michael Massing, "The Libel Chill: How Cold Is It Out There?" *Columbia Journalism Review,* May–June 1985, 31.

37. Cited in Richard Labunski, *Libel and the First Amendment* (New Brunswick, N.J.: Transaction Books, 1986), 226.

38. According to network news monitor the *Tyndall Report,* cited in Frank Rich, "Bennett's Moral Filter," *New York Times,* 9 December 1995, 15.

39. Philip J. Hilts, *Smokescreen: The Truth behind the Tobacco Industry Cover-Up* (Reading, Mass.: Addison-Wesley, 1996), 120.

40. "Censored: The Leaked ABC Tape," *Mother Jones,* May–June 1996, 63.

41. Bill Carter, "CBS-TV Station Drops Commercial Critical of Smoking," *New York Times,* 11 November 1995, 39.

42. Sheldon Rampton and John Stauber, "Monsanto and Fox: Partners in Censorship," *PR Watch* 5 (accessed 31 December 1998) http://www.prwatch.org/98–Q2/fox-bgh.html.

43. Susan and Bill Buzenberg, *Salant, CBS, and the Battle for the Soul of Broadcast Journalism: The Memoirs of Richard S. Salant* (Boulder, Colo.: Westview Press, 1999), 66.

44. Phyllis Kaniss, *Making Local News* (Chicago: University of Chicago Press, 1991), 110, 129–30.

45. Raymond L. Carroll, "Factual Television in America: An Analysis of Network Television Documentary Programs, 1948–1975" (Ph.D. diss., University of Wisconsin–Madison, 1978), 404.

46. Committee of Concerned Journalists, "Changing Definitions of News," http://www.journalism.org/ccj/resources/chdefonews.html (April 1998).

47. Neil Hickey, "Where TV Has Teeth," *Columbia Journalism Review,* May–June 2001, http://www.cjr.org/year/01/3/hickey.asp.

48. Tom Rosenstiel et al., "Quality Brings Higher Ratings, But Enterprise Is Disappearing," http://www.journalism.org/publ_research/special_rep.html (1998).

49. Aaron Barnhart, "Lawrence Company Has Its Finger on the Pulse of TV Topics," *Kansas City Star,* 10 January 1998, E4.

50. *Harvest of Shame* producer David Lowe spent a year on the report (Richard J. Schaefer, "Reconsidering *Harvest of Shame:* The Limitations of a Broadcast Journalism Landmark," *Journalism History* 19 [1994]: 124). According to *The Selling of the Pentagon,* CBS spent ten months on the project. The network spent eight months on its *Project Nassau* documentary before abandoning it.

51. Madsen, *60 Minutes,* 50.

52. The lower estimate is from Robert MacNeil, *The People Machine* (New York: Harper and Row, 1968), 75. The higher one is what CBS reported as its costs for *Project Nassau* in House Committee on Interstate and Foreign Commerce, *Network News Documentary Practices,* 64.

53. In 1993, a newsmagazine hour cost about $500,000 (John Brodie, "The Truth Squads," *Mother Jones,* http://www.motherjones.com/mother_jones/SO93/brodie.html [Sept.–Oct. 1993]). Inflation calculations used 1966 as the base year and the Gross Domestic Product Deflator, which is a measure of average prices of all things pro-

duced in the economy, as the inflation index. The calculation was performed using the Economic History Services inflation calculator at http://eh.net/hmit/compare/.

54. On the diversion of news gathering resources to star salaries, see James Fallows, *Breaking the News* (New York: Pantheon Books, 1996), 57–60.

55. William Powers, "Making Sausage," *New Republic,* 20 January 1997, 14.

56. Howard Good, "Epilogue: Muckraking and the Ethic of Caring," in *The Muckrakers: Evangelical Crusaders,* ed. Robert Miraldi (Westport, Conn.: Praeger, 2000), 157.

57. Radio-Television News Directors Association, "RTNDA Code of Ethics," Radio-Television News Directors Association and Foundation (accessed 15 February 2005) http://www.rtnda.org/ethics/coe.shtml. The insights into prepackaged investigative reports in this paragraph are from Michael Stoll, "News from Nowhere," *Grade the News* (accessed 15 February 2005) http://www.stanford.edu/group/gradethenews/pages/nowhere%20news.htm.

58. Brendan O'Neill, "Leaking Self-Doubt," *Spiked* (electronic journal; accessed 15 February 2005) http://www.spiked-online.com/Articles/0000000CA521.htm.

59. Bill Kovach and Tom Rosenstiel, *Warp Speed: America in the Age of Mixed Media* (New York: Century Foundation Press, 1999).

60. Lawrence Soley, "The Power of the Press Has a Price," *Extra!,* July–August 1997, 11.

61. Cited in Carl Jensen, "What Happened to Good, Old-Fashioned Muckraking?" in *Into the Buzzsaw: Leading Journalists Expose the Myth of a Free Press,* ed. Kristina Borjesson (Amherst, N.Y.: Prometheus Books, 2002), 343.

62. House Committee on Energy and Commerce, Subcommittee on Health and the Environment, *Regulation of Tobacco Products: Hearings before the Subcommittee on Health and the Environment of the Committee on Energy and Commerce,* 103rd Cong., 2nd sess. (1995), 4–31.

63. Steve Weinberg, "Smoking Guns: ABC, Philip Morris, and the Infamous Apology," *Columbia Journalism Review,* November–December 1995, 29–37.

64. Clay Calvert, "Stumbling Down Tobacco Road: Media Self-Censorship and Corporate Capitulation in the War on the Cigarette Industry," *Loyola of Los Angeles Law Review* 30 (1996): 142.

65. Shepard, "Fighting Back," 35.

66. Kristina Borjesson, *Into the Buzzsaw: Leading Journalists Expose the Myth of a Free Press* (Amherst, N.Y.: Prometheus Books, 2002).

67. Dan Gillmor, *We the Media: Grassroots Journalism by the People, for the People* (Sebastopol, Calif.: O'Reilly, 2004).

68. My account of the story is based on Dick Thornburgh and Louis D. Boccardi, *Report of the Independent Review Panel on the September 8, 2004 60 Minutes Wednesday Segment "For the Record" Concerning President Bush's Texas Air National Guard Service* (Washington, D.C.: Kirkpatrick and Lockhart Nicholson Graham LLP, 2005); Corey Pein, "Blog-Gate," *Columbia Journalism Review,* January–February 2005, 30–35.

69. Pein, "Blog-Gate," 30.

70. Bill Carter, "Post-Mortem of a Flawed Broadcast," *New York Times,* 11 January 2005, 1.

71. Marc A. Franklin put the figure at 72 percent in "Suing Media for Libel: A Liti-

gation Study," *American Bar Foundation Research Journal* (1981): 807. A later study found 81 percent of plaintiffs were such figures (Bezanson, Cranberg, and Soloski, *Libel Law and the Press*, 243).

72. See Raphael, "FCC's Broadcast News Distortion Rules," 509.

73. Quoted in Stoll, "News from Nowhere."

74. Bernard D. Nossiter, "The FCC's Big Giveaway Show," *Nation*, 26 October 1985, 402.

75. The Supreme Court asserted that commercial speech is less deserving of First Amendment protection than political speech in *Virginia State Board of Pharmacy v. Virginia Citizens Consumer Council, Inc.*, 425 U.S. 748, 770 (1976).

CHAPTER 8: MEDIA, STATE, AND INVESTIGATIVE REPORTING

1. Raymond Lee Carroll, "Factual Television in America: An Analysis of Network Television Documentary Programs, 1948–1975" (Ph.D. diss., University of Wisconsin–Madison, 1978), 475.

2. Robert MacNeil, *The People Machine* (New York: Harper and Row, 1968), 81.

3. *Face to Face: What about Documentaries?* (Memphis: WMC-TV, ca. 1977), Wisconsin Center for Film and Television Research, SHSW.

4. Protess et al., *Journalism of Outrage*, 251.

5. Ibid., 234.

6. Ibid., 237.

7. The same kind of distraction of the media from the subjects of investigative reporting is also shown in a study of reaction to two disputed reports from the 1990s (Chad Raphael, Lori Tokunaga, and Christina Wai, "Who Is the Real Target? Media Response to Controversial Investigative Reporting on Corporations," *Journalism Studies* 5, no. 2 [2004]: 165–78).

8. The original demonstration of this effect is in Maxwell E. McCombs and Donald L. Shaw, "The Agenda-Setting Function of the Mass Media," *Public Opinion Quarterly* 36 (1972): 176–87.

9. Antonio Gramsci, *Selections from the Prison Notebooks* (New York: International Publishers, 1971).

10. David Sallach, "Class Domination and Ideological Hegemony," in *The TV Establishment: Programming for Profit and Power,* ed. Gaye Tuchman (Englewood Cliffs, N.J.: Prentice-Hall, 1974), 166.

11. Gitlin, *The Whole World Is Watching*, 255.

12. Raymond Williams, *Marxism and Literature* (Oxford: Oxford University Press, 1977), 34.

13. T. J. Jackson Lears, "The Concept of Cultural Hegemony: Problems and Possibilities," *American Historical Review* 90 (1984): 569.

14. Cited in ibid., 577.

15. On the composition of the New Right, see Thomas Ferguson and Joel Rogers, *Right Turn: The Decline of the Democrats and the Future of American Politics* (New York: Hill and Wang, 1986).

16. John Fiske, "Moments of Television: Neither the Text Nor the Audience," in *Remote Control,* ed. Ellen Seiter et al. (London: Routledge, 1989), 73.

17. Sallach, "Class Domination," 166. In addition, corporations are often pleased to

cater to cultural difference when doing so shifts focus from the subordinated's common relations to the economic structure, when semiotic fragmentation frustrates the common social meanings and pleasures that might unite diverse groups, and when subcultures provide capital with new products and markets (David Tetzlaff, "Divide and Conquer: Popular Culture and Social Control in Late Capitalism," *Media, Culture, and Society* 13 [1991]: 9–33).

18. On functionalist fallacies in applications of hegemony, see Nancy Fraser, *Unruly Practices: Power, Discourse, and Gender in Contemporary Social Theory* (Minneapolis: University of Minnesota Press, 1989), 156. The analysis in this paragraph draws on Chad Raphael, "Rethinking Media and Movements," *Radical History Review* 78 (2000): 130–37.

19. Gitlin, *The Whole World Is Watching*, 291.

20. Charlotte Ryan, *Prime Time Activism: Media Strategies for Grassroots Organizing* (Boston: South End Press, 1991), 21.

21. William A. Gamson and Gadi Wolfsfeld, "Movements and Media as Interacting Systems," *Annals of the American Academy of Political and Social Science* 528 (1993): 118.

22. Douglas Kellner, *Television and the Crisis of Democracy* (Boulder: Westview Press, 1990), 118.

23. I draw these policy ideas from Robert W. McChesney and John Nichols, "The Making of a Movement," *Nation,* 7 January 2002, 11–17.

INDEX

CHAD RAPHAEL is an associate professor of communication at Santa Clara University. He has published research on broadcast history and regulation, mass media and democratic theory, and environmental communication. Raphael has also contributed research to investigative reports by media organizations such as PBS *Frontline* and the Center for Investigative Reporting in San Francisco, as well as exposés by public interest organizations working on labor, affordable housing, and environmental issues. His dissertation on investigative reporting won awards from the National Communication Association and the American Journalism Historians Association.

The History of Communication

The University of Illinois Press
is a founding member of the
Association of American University Presses.

———————————————————————

Composed in 10/13 New Caledonia
with New Caledonia display
at the University of Illinois Press
Designed by Paula Newcomb
Manufactured by Thomson-Shore, Inc.

University of Illinois Press
1325 South Oak Street
Champaign, IL 61820-6903
www.press.uillinois.edu